SEDUCTION BY CONTRACT

SEDUCTION BY CONTRACT

LAW, ECONOMICS, AND PSYCHOLOGY IN CONSUMER MARKETS

OREN BAR-GILL

OXFORD
UNIVERSITY PRESS

OXFORD
UNIVERSITY PRESS

Great Clarendon Street, Oxford, OX2 6DP,
United Kingdom

Oxford University Press is a department of the University of Oxford.
It furthers the University's objective of excellence in research, scholarship,
and education by publishing worldwide. Oxford is a registered trade mark of
Oxford University Press in the UK and in certain other countries

First Edition published in 2012

Impression: 1

British Library Cataloguing in Publication Data

Data available

Library of Congress Cataloging in Publication Data

Library of Congress Control Number: 2012941355

ISBN 978-0-19-966336-1

Printed in Great Britain
CPI Group (UK) Ltd, Croydon, CR0 4YY

For Sigal, Noam, and Guy
Nechama and Aharon

Acknowledgements

This book is the culmination of several years of research and writing on consumer contracts. This work appeared in several prior publications:

- Credit Card Pricing: The CARD Act and Beyond (with Ryan Bubb), forthcoming in *Cornell Law Review*.

- Pricing Misperceptions: Explaining Pricing Structure in the Cell Phone Service Market (with Rebecca Stone), forthcoming in *Journal of Empirical Legal Studies*.

- Product Use Information and the Limits of Voluntary Disclosure (with Oliver Board), 14 *American Law and Economics Review* 235, (2012).

- Competition and Consumer Protection: A Behavioral-Economics Account, in *Swedish Competition Authority, The Pros and Cons of Consumer Protection*, ch. 2 (2012).

- Informing Consumers about Themselves (with Franco Ferrari), Symposium: Juxtaposing Autonomy and Paternalism in Private Law, 3 *Erasmus Law Review* 93 (2010).

- Mobile Misperceptions (with Rebecca Stone), 23 *Harvard Journal of Law and Technology* 49 (2009).

- The Law, Economics and Psychology of Subprime Mortgage Contracts, 94 *Cornell Law Review* 1073 (2009).

- Making Credit Safer (with Elizabeth Warren), 157 *University of Pennsylvania Law Review* 1 (2008).

- The Behavioral Economics of Consumer Contracts, in Oren Bar-Gill and Richard Epstein, Exchange: Consumer Contracts: Behavioral Economics vs. Neoclassical Economics, 92 *Minnesota Law Review* 749 (2008).

- Bundling and Consumer Misperception, Symposium: Homo Economicus, Homo Myopicus, and the Law and Economics of Consumer Choice, 73 *University of Chicago Law Review* 33 (2006).

- Seduction by Plastic, 98 *Northwestern University Law Review* 1373 (2004).

The analysis in this book builds upon and extends the research in these articles.

My thinking and research on consumer contracts has benefited from the generous comments and suggestions provided by many colleagues and friends—on drafts of this book or on the aforementioned articles. For their comments and suggestions, I would like to thank Barry Adler, Yael Aridor Bar-Ilan, Jennifer Arlen, Adi Ayal, Ian Ayres, Douglas Baird, Jonathan Baker, Lily Batchelder, Vicki Been, Jean-Pier Benoit, Susan Block-Lieb, Gabriella Blum, Jonathan Bolton, Paul Calem, Stephen Choi, Marcus Cole, Robert Cooter, Richard Craswell, Kevin Davis, Rochelle Dreyfus, Einer Elhauge, Lee Anne Fennell, Chaim Fershtman, Harry First, Eleanor Fox, Jesse Fried, Barry Friedman, Mark Geistfeld, Clayton Gillette, David Gilo, Ronald Gilson, Jeffery Gordon, Solomon Greene, Ofer Grosskopf, Michael Grubb, Assaf Hamdani, Sharon Hannes, Alon Harel, Claire Hill, Samuel Issacharoff, Raghuram Iyengar, Christine Jolls, Marcel Kahan, Ehud Kamar, Emir Kamenica, Louis Kaplow, Aron Katz, Avery Katz, Kevin Kordana, Lewis Kornhauser, Russell Korobkin, Adriaan Lanni, Michael Levine, Daryl Levinson, Adam Levitin, Ronald Mann, Yoram Margalioth, Florencia Marotta Wurgler, Martha Minow, Edward Morrison, Anthony Ogus, Eric Orts, Gideon Parchomovski, Nicola Persico, Richard Pildes, Eric Posner, Martin Raphan, Luis Rayo, Elizabeth Renuart, Ariel Rubinstein, Daniel Schwarcz, Alan Schwartz, Steven Shavell, Howard Shelanski, Peter Siegelman, Avi Tabbach, Doron Teichman, Richard Thaler, Diane Thompson, Avishalom Tor, Jing Tsu, Willem van Boom, Philip Weiser, Lauren Willis, and Eyal Zamir. I would also like to thank workshop participants at Bar-Ilan, Berkeley, Chicago, Columbia, Fordham, Haifa, Harvard, IDC Hertzelia, Jerusalem (Hebrew U.), NYU, Penn, Seton Hall, Stanford, Tel-Aviv, Texas, University of Illinois, USC, Virginia and Yale, as well as conference participants at several meetings of the ALEA, EALE, ILEA, at the University of Chicago Law School conference on *Homo Economicus* and *Homo Myopicus*, at the Rotterdam Workshop on Juxtaposing Autonomy and Paternalism in Private Law, and at the Swedish Competition Authority Conference on the Pros and Cons of Consumer Protection.

For excellent research assistance, I thank Efrat Assaf, Michael Biondi, Osnat Dafna, Joseph Eno, Winnie Fung, Paul McLaughlin, Robin Moore, Tal Niv, Margot Pollans, Benjamin Roin, Michael Schachter, Lee Schindler, and James Sullivan. The presentation was substantially improved by James King, Briony Ryles, and the wonderful team at OUP. I owe special thanks to my OUP editor, Alex Flach, for believing in this book from the very beginning.

I gratefully acknowledge the financial support of the Filomen D'Agostino and Max E. Greenberg Research Fund at NYU School of Law, the John M. Olin Center for Law and Economics at Harvard Law School, the William F. Milton Fund of Harvard University, and the Cegla Center for Interdisciplinary Research of the Law in Tel-Aviv University. I thank the Center for Customer Relationship Management at Duke University for letting Rebecca Stone and me use its Telecom Dataset in Chapter 4.

This book was written in one of the most nurturing intellectual environments imaginable—the New York University School of Law. I am immensely grateful to my Dean, Richard Revesz, for creating such an amazing environment and for providing limitless support and encouragement for my academic work. I am also grateful to Tel-Aviv University for its hospitality during my visit there, when part of this book was written.

I owe special thanks to my co-authors, Oliver Board, Ryan Bubb, Franco Ferrari, Rebecca Stone, and Elizabeth Warren. It has been a privilege to work with, and learn from, these amazing colleagues. My thinking, as reflected in this book, builds, in large part, on my co-authored work. I am especially grateful to Rebecca for allowing me to use material from our joint work in Chapter 4.

I am grateful to my "nemesis" Richard Epstein. Debating the theory of consumer contracts with Richard in the Exchange we published in the Minnesota Law Review, and beyond, has been an intellectual treat.

I would like to thank my teacher and friend, Ariel Porat, for two decades' worth of advice and support; and for many great comments on parts of this book.

Last but not least, I am grateful, beyond words, to my mentors and friends, Lucian Bebchuk and Omri Ben-Shahar. They put me on the path of scholarship. With their intellect, integrity, and dedication, they set the example that I have been striving to follow. Their advice and guidance, throughout my career, has been invaluable. Their unforgiving comments have made this book much better than it otherwise would have been. In fact, there would be no book without Lucian. He first conceived the idea of this book and made sure the idea turned into reality.

Contents

List of Figures and Tables

Abbreviations

CHAPTER 4

CDMA   Code Division Multiple Access
CPUC   California Public Utility Commission
EA   Economic Areas
ETF   early termination fee
FCC   Federal Communications Commission
GSM   Global System for Mobile
HHI   Herfindahl–Hirschman Index
HV   High-Variation
LV   Low-Variation
TCO   total-cost-of-ownership
TDMA   time division multiple access

Introduction

We are all consumers. As consumers we routinely enter into contracts with providers of goods and services—from credit cards, mortgages, cell phones, insurance, cable TV, and internet services to household appliances, theater and sports events, health clubs, magazine subscriptions, transportation, and more.

This book is about consumer contracts. It traces design features common among multiple types of consumer contracts and explores and explains the forces responsible for these design features. Why, for example, do sellers design contracts to provide short-term benefits and impose long-term costs? Why are low introductory prices so common? Why are cell phones given away for free, so long as the consumer signs a two-year service contract?

Why are the contracts themselves so complex? What's the rationale behind creating credit card and mortgage contracts featuring numerous fees and interest rates calculated via complex formulas? Why do cellular service contracts use complicated, three-part tariff pricing—a fixed monthly fee, a number of included minutes, and an overage fee for minutes used beyond the plan limit—and then further complicate matters by distinguishing between peak minutes, night and weekend minutes, in-network and out-of-network minutes, minutes used to call a pre-set list of "friends," and minutes used to call everyone else? Separate and equally complex pricing structures are developed and enforced for messaging and data services.

While clearly contributing to a consumer contract's complexity, a contract's "fine print" is not the focus of this book. That no one reads the fine print is old news. That sellers hide one-sided terms in the fine print is not surprising. The goal of *Seduction by Contract* is to explain the design of pricing structures and other contract terms that are often clearly disclosed—"dickered terms" that consumers are aware of and consent to.

Market Forces and Consumer Psychology

A main theme of this book is that the design of consumer contracts can be explained as the result of the interaction between market forces and consumer psychology. We consumers are imperfectly rational, our decisions and choices influenced by bias and misperception. Moreover, the mistakes we make are systematic and predictable. Sellers respond to those mistakes. They design products, contracts, and pricing schemes to maximize not the *true* (net) benefit from their product, but the (net) benefit *as perceived by the imperfectly rational consumer.* Consumers are lured, by contract design, to purchase products and services that appear more attractive than they really are. This *Seduction by Contract* results in a behavioral market failure.

Competition, many believe, works to increase efficiency and protect consumers. But competition does not alleviate the behavioral market failure. It may even exacerbate it. Here's why: In a competitive market, sellers have no choice but to align contract design with the psychology of consumers. A high-road seller who offers what she knows to be the best contract will lose business to the low-road seller who offers what the consumer mistakenly believes to be the best contract. Put bluntly, competition forces sellers to exploit the biases and misperceptions of their customers.

The interaction between market forces and consumer psychology explains many of the complex design features so common in consumer contracts. The temporal ordering of costs and benefits—with benefits accelerated and costs deferred—is linked to consumer myopia and optimism. Complexity responds to bounded rationality, to the challenge of remembering and then aggregating multiple dimensions of costs and benefits. These two features—complexity and cost deferral—serve one ultimate purpose: to maximize the (net) benefit from the product, as perceived by the imperfectly rational consumer.

This behavioral-economics theory is subject to the standard critique that questions the robustness of the underlying biases and misperceptions in a market setting. I take this critique seriously. Therefore, I begin by studying possible rational-choice, efficiency-based explanations for specific contract design features. Only when I conclude that the rational-choice accounts are unconvincing or incomplete do I develop the behavioral economics alternative. The prevalence of contracts and prices that cannot be fully explained within a rational-choice framework proves the robustness of the biases and misperceptions driving the behavioral-economics theory.

A main goal of this book is to explain the design of consumer contracts. But the descriptive story is the beginning, not the end. Understanding consumer contracts as the product of an interaction between market forces and consumer psychology raises a host of normative questions and legal policy challenges. Addressing these questions and challenges is another main ambition of this book.

Social Costs of the Behavioral Market Failure

The behavioral market failure mentioned earlier threatens social welfare at several levels. As contractual complexity increases in response to consumers' imperfect rationality, the cost of comparison shopping also increases, resulting in hindered competition. Recall the complex, multidimensional cell phone contract. Now imagine an imperfectly rational consumer trying to choose among several such complex, multidimensional contracts. The task is a daunting one. Many consumers will simply avoid it. Markets don't work well when consumers do not shop for the best deal. In the absence of effective comparison-shopping, prices rise, hurting consumers. Also, consumers who do not compare offers from different sellers might not be matched with the seller that best fits their needs. This reduces market efficiency.

While hindered competition reduces social welfare, even intense competition would not ameliorate the behavioral market failure. The competitive forces that remain would work to maximize the perceived (net) benefit rather than the actual (net) benefit from the product. Specifically, short-term, salient prices would be reduced while long-term non-salient prices would be increased. Examples of this dynamic are the low credit card teaser-rates accompanied by high back-end fees and rates, or the free cell phones that you get when you "agree" to pay a host of usage fees and penalties for the duration of the two-year lock-in contract.

Prices that are salience-based rather than cost-based produce skewed incentives—for both product choice and product use. And as the perceived total price falls below the actual total price, demand for the product becomes artificially inflated. For example and as we will see later in the book, inflated demand for subprime mortgages, *fueled by contract design*, contributed to the subprime expansion and, later, to the subprime meltdown of 2008.

Finally, complexity and deferred costs raise distributional concerns, since their effects are not evenly distributed across different groups of consumers.

The interaction between market forces and consumer psychology, then, creates a market failure. This behavioral market failure imposes substantial welfare costs. Can legal intervention help? A comprehensive answer is beyond the scope of this book. Instead, the book focuses on a single regulatory technique: disclosure mandates. It develops a new approach to disclosure, one that directly responds to the imperfect rationality problem.

Toward More Effective Disclosure Mandates

While existing disclosure mandates focus largely on product attribute information—*what* the product is and what it does—the analysis and findings described in this book suggest that more attention should be given to the disclosure of product-use information, namely, *how* the product will be used by the consumer. Rational consumers can be expected to predict their future-use patterns fairly accurately or at least know their own use patterns better than the sellers do. Disclosure of product-use information by sellers is, therefore, superfluous in a rational-choice framework.

The same is not true, however, when consumers are imperfectly rational. As we will see, consumers often have a poor sense of their future use patterns. Do you know how much you talk on your cell phone? How many text messages you send and receive? How many megabytes of data you use? Do you how much you will borrow on your credit card? How fast you will pay down your balance? Whether you will ever require a cash advance? How likely are you to miss a payment and incur a late fee? The imperfectly rational consumer can benefit substantially from disclosure of product-use information—information that sellers, like cell phone companies and credit card issuers, make it their business to know.

Moreover, the imperfect rationality of consumers suggests that, to be effective, disclosure regulation must adopt one of the following two strategies:

- First, simple disclosures that target consumers. The idea is to design aggregate, one-dimensional disclosures that facilitate comparison between competing products. For example, cell phone companies could be required to disclose the total annual cost of using a cell phone. The disclosure would combine both product-attribute information and product-use information. The annual cost of cellular service would combine rate information with the consumer's use-pattern information. Such simple, aggregate disclosures would help imperfectly rational consumers make better choices.

- Second, re-conceptualized disclosure aimed not at imperfectly rational consumers, but at sophisticated intermediaries. Accordingly, this disclosure could be more comprehensive and complex. Consider a consumer who is considering switching from her current cell phone company to a competing provider. Consider also an intermediary who wishes to help the consumer identify the best plan for her needs. The intermediary has information on the different plans offered by all cell phone companies. The intermediary, however, has little information on how the specific consumer uses her cell phone. Since different plans can be optimal for different consumers, depending on their use patterns, not having product-use information substantially reduces the ability of the intermediary to offer the most valuable advice. Now, the consumer's current cell phone company has a lot of information on the consumer's use patterns. It could be required to disclose this information in electronic form so that the consumer could forward it to the intermediary. The intermediary could then combine the product-use information with the information it has on different plans and provide the consumer with valuable advice.

★ ★ ★

This book aims to tell a general story about consumer contracts. But each consumer contract or, more accurately, each class of consumer contracts in each particular market has its own story. Accordingly, after fleshing out common themes in Chapter 1, the lion's share of the book is dedicated to three case studies of three important consumer markets—credit cards (Chapter 2), mortgages (Chapter 3), and cell phones (Chapter 4). A detailed market-specific analysis is necessary to fully answer the descriptive question—why do these contracts look the way they do?—the normative question—what's wrong with these contracts?—and the prescriptive question—what can the law do to help?.

I

The Law, Economics, and Psychology of Consumer Contracts

Introduction

Outcomes in consumer markets are the product of interactions between market forces and consumer psychology. Most of this book explores these interactions and their legal policy implications in three consumer markets: credit cards (Chapter 2), mortgages (Chapter 3), and cellular phones (Chapter 4). These three chapters present case studies that expose the unique features of economics–psychology interactions in each market. Indeed, they show that broad generalizations can rarely be drawn, especially when considering if and how the law should intervene in consumer markets.

While each market is unique, a common methodology can be applied to analyze different consumer markets. Such a common methodology—a behavioral-economics methodology—is described in this chapter. The bulk of the analysis is descriptive, examining how market forces interact with consumer psychology to produce observed contract design and pricing structures in the market.[1] In this chapter, the descriptive analysis begins with consumer biases and misperceptions and ends with contracts and

1. See Michael S. Barr, Sendhil Mullainathan, and Eldar Shafir, *Behaviorally Informed Financial Services Regulation* (New America Foundation, 2008) (similarly emphasizing the importance of the interaction between consumer psychology and market forces, but not focusing on the implications of this interaction for contract design). Important contributions in the burgeoning field of Behavioral Industrial Organization consider questions of contract design, albeit with less emphasis on policy implications. For an excellent recent textbook that summarizes and synthesizes this important literature—see Ran Spiegler, *Bounded Rationality and Industrial Organization* (Oxford University Press, 2011). Spiegler's text, and the economic theory literature that it summarizes, is of foundational importance to many of the themes explored in *Seduction by Contract*. Through-

prices. The goal is to highlight predictions of the behavioral-economics theory. By way of contrast, the case studies presented in the following chapters begin with the observed contract designs and pricing schemes, and then seek a theoretical explanation for the observed contracts and prices. Moreover, the case studies first consider possible rational-choice, neoclassical economics explanations for the observed contracts and prices. The behavioral-economics theory enters only after the standard accounts are shown to be unsatisfactory or incomplete. Indeed, the failure of the standard approach provides the impetus for developing an alternative, behavioral-economics theory.

Following the descriptive analysis, the next step is to explore the normative implications of the outcomes produced by the interaction of market forces and consumer psychology. Are these contracts and prices enhancing or diminishing the welfare of the consumer and of society? As noted in the introduction, when sellers design contracts and prices in response to the demand generated by imperfectly rational consumers, the result is a behavioral market failure. Several common welfare costs associated with this market failure are incurred, including efficiency costs and distributional costs. These welfare costs are often mitigated by market solutions; specifically, learning by consumers and education by sellers. Yet these market solutions are imperfect. Welfare is not maximized. And this opens the door for considering legal policy interventions. The range of possible policy responses is broad and it varies from market to market. Here, and in the remainder of the book, the discussion of policy implications focuses on a single regulatory tool: disclosure mandates.

I. The Behavioral Economics of Consumer Contracts

The behavioral-economics theory rests on two tenets:

(1) Consumers' purchasing and use decisions are affected by systematic misperceptions

out the chapter, I often cite Spiegler, rather than the original research papers on which he relies. For an earlier survey of the economics literature—see G. Ellison, "Bounded Rationality in Industrial Organization," in R. Blundell, W. K. Newey, and T. Persson (eds.), *Advances in Economics and Econometrics: Theory and Applications*, Ninth World Congress, Vol. II, ch. 5 (2006).

(2) Sellers design their products, contracts, and prices in response to these misperceptions.

That individual decision-making is affected by a myriad of biases and misperceptions is well documented.[2] An important question is whether these biases and misperceptions persist in a market context and are large enough to influence market outcomes. As we will see in the following chapters, in many cases the answer to this question is "yes."

How does consumer psychology influence contract design and pricing structure? The basic claim is that market forces demand that sellers be attentive to consumer psychology. Sellers who ignore consumer biases and misperceptions will lose business and forfeit revenue and profits. Over time, the sellers who remain in the market, profitably, will be the ones who have adapted their contracts and prices to respond, in the most optimal way, to the psychology of their customers. This general argument is developed in Section A below. In particular, the interaction between consumer psychology and market forces results in two common contract design features: complexity and cost deferral. Section B describes these features and explains why they appear in many consumer contracts.

A. Designing Contracts for Biased Consumers

1. General

It is useful to start by reciting the standard, rational-choice framework. This standard framework will then be adjusted to allow for the introduction of consumer biases and misperceptions. Juxtaposing the standard and behavioral frameworks will help compare market outcomes under the two models.[3]

In the rational-choice framework, a consumer contract provides the consumer with an expected benefit, B, in exchange for an expected price, P. As elaborated below, both the benefit and the price can be multidimensional. The number of units sold, which will be referred to as the demand for a seller's product, D, is increasing in the benefit that the product provides, B, and decreasing in the price that the seller charges, P. Demand is a function

2. See, e.g., Daniel Kahneman, Paul Slovic, and Amos Tversky (eds.), *Judgment under Uncertainty: Heuristics and Biases* (Cambridge University Press, 1982).
3. A more formal treatment of the issues presented in Sections I.A.1 and I.A.2 is offered in the Appendix. For an excellent exposition of the economic theory literature on the topics addressed in Section A—see Spiegler, above note 1. See also M. Armstrong, "Interactions between Competition and Consumer Policy" *Competition Policy International* 4 (2008) 97.

of benefits and prices: $D(B,P)$. The seller's revenue is determined by the number of units sold, namely, the demand for the product multiplied by the price per unit. The seller's profit is equal to revenue minus cost.

When consumers are imperfectly rational, suffering from biases and mis-perceptions, this general framework must be extended as follows: There is a perceived expected benefit, $\hat{B}$, which is potentially different from the actual expected benefit, B. Similarly, there is a perceived expected price, $\hat{P}$, which is potentially different from the actual expected price, P. Demand is now a function of perceived benefits and prices, rather than of actual benefits and prices: $D(\hat{B},\hat{P})$. Revenues—and profits—are a function of perceived benefits and prices, which affect the demand for the product, and of the actual price.

Before proceeding further, the relationship between imperfect information and imperfect rationality should be clarified. Rational-choice theory allows for imperfect information. A divergence between perceived benefits and prices on the one hand and actual benefits and prices on the other is also possible in a rational-choice framework with imperfectly informed consumers. The focus here, however, is on systemic under- and overestimation of benefits and prices. Perfectly rational consumers will not have systemically biased beliefs; imperfectly rational consumers will. The main difference is in how perfectly and imperfectly rational consumers deal with imperfect information. Rational-choice decision-making provides tools for effectively coping with imperfect information. These tools are not used by the imperfectly rational consumer. Instead, he relies on heuristics or cognitive rules-of-thumb, which result in predictable, systemic biases and misperceptions.[4]

Sellers must keep costs down and revenues up to maximize profits. As we have seen, revenues are the product of the number of units sold, or the demand for the product, multiplied by the price per unit. These observations imply two tradeoffs that determine the seller's strategy in a rational-choice framework: First, the seller wants to increase the benefits from the product in order to increase demand, but increased benefits usually entail increased costs. The seller will, therefore, increase the benefits only if the resulting revenue boost more than compensates for the increased costs. The second tradeoff focuses on the price: a lower price increases demand, but

4. Moreover, while the perfectly rational consumer realizes that she is imperfectly informed, the imperfectly rational consumer might be blissfully unaware of the extent of his ignorance.

also decreases the revenue per unit sold. The seller will set prices that optimally balance these two effects.[5]

The tradeoffs that determine a seller's optimal strategy when facing
rational consumers are muted in the behavioral-economics model with
imperfectly rational consumers. When perceived benefit is different from
actual benefit, a seller may be able to increase demand by raising the perceived benefit without incurring the added cost of raising the actual benefit.
Similarly, when the perceived price is different from the actual price, demand
can be increased by lowering the perceived price, while keeping revenue per
unit up with a high actual price. Sellers benefit from the divergence between
perceived and actual benefits and between perceived and actual prices. They
will design their contracts and prices to maximize this divergence.

2. The Objects of Misperception: Product Attributes and Use Patterns
When consumers are imperfectly rational, demand, $D(\hat{B}, \hat{P})$, increases with
perceived benefit and decreases with perceived price. The problem is that
consumers will overestimate the total benefit and underestimate the total
price, resulting in artificially inflated demand.[6] Why would a consumer
overestimate benefits and underestimate prices? To answer this question, we
must identify the factors that determine these benefits and prices. Moreover,
as explained below, identifying the objects of misperception will prove
important to the welfare and policy analysis presented in the latter half of
this chapter.

Benefits and prices are a function of product attributes and use patterns.
Product attributes define what a product is and what it does. They include
product features, contract terms, and prices. For example, the credit limit
(a product feature) and the interest rate (a price term) are attributes of the
credit card product. Product attributes affect the total benefit and total price.
Misperceptions about product attributes lead to misperceptions of the total
benefit and total price.

While product features define what a product is and what it does, use
patterns define how the product is used. A credit card's borrowing feature,

5. In addition, certain price dimensions affect how the consumer will use the product and thus
   the benefit that the consumer derives from the product. These effects also influence the optimal design of products, contracts, and prices, as explained in subsection 2 below.
6. It also possible that consumers will underestimate the total benefit and overestimate the total
   price, resulting in artificially deflated demand. This possibility, however, should be less common,
   since sellers have strong incentives to alleviate misperceptions that drive consumers away.

for example, is used frequently by some consumers and less frequently by others. Some borrow heavily, while others not at all. Product use is clearly affected by the product's attributes. But, as detailed below, use patterns are also affected by other factors. Product use affects the total benefit and total price. Misperceptions about use patterns lead to misperceptions of the total benefit and total price.

Given the importance of use patterns, it is worthwhile to conceptualize the total benefit as a function of the per-use benefit and use level. Similarly, it is helpful to conceptualize the total price as a function of the per-use price and the use level.[7]

The total benefit will be overestimated when a consumer overestimates the per-use benefit or use level. For example, the total benefit of a credit card's borrowing feature will be overestimated if the consumer overestimates the benefit-per-dollar borrowed. The total benefit will also be overestimated if the consumer overestimates how much he will borrow.

In this same way, the total price will be *under*estimated when a consumer underestimates the per-use price or use level. The total amount paid in interest will be underestimated if the consumer underestimates the interest rate, which can be viewed as the per-use price—the price per dollar borrowed. The total amount paid in interest will also be underestimated if the consumer underestimates how much he will borrow.

Benefit misperception, then, is a function of misperceived per-use benefits or misperceived use levels while price misperception is a function of misperceived per-use prices or misperceived use levels.

Let's dig deeper: Why would a consumer misperceive the per-use benefit or per-use price? Why would a consumer misperceive the intensity with which he will use the product, or a product feature?

To understand why the per-use benefit might be misperceived, one must identify the underlying forces affecting the per-use benefit. Misperception of any of these underlying forces will result in misperception of the per-use benefit. Consider a credit card's borrowing feature. The benefit of this feature is a function of the feature itself: Some cards allow for more borrowing, setting a higher credit limit, while others are more restrictive, setting a lower credit limit. The per-use benefit from borrowing drops to

---

7. The benefit per unit of use need not be constant across all use units. Similarly, the price per unit of use need not be constant across all use units. In some cases, use is a simple binary variable—the product or feature is either used or not.

zero when the credit limit is reached. The benefit from borrowing is also a function of the consumer's intertemporal preferences: Some consumers are more willing than others to finance present consumption with debt. Finally, the benefit of borrowing is a function of external forces affecting the consumer's desire or need to borrow, such as present and expected available income and conditions affecting the demand for funds, for example illness or unemployment. The per-use benefit from the credit card's borrowing feature will be misperceived when the consumer misperceives the credit limit, his own preferences, or the strength of external forces that create a desire or need to borrow.

Next, the per-use price. The per-use price is set by the seller. Some prices are simple, one-dimensional prices. For example, suppose a movie ticket costs $12. Such a price will rarely be misperceived. Other prices are complex and multidimensional. Think of an adjustable interest rate, subject to different caps for per-period changes and various rate-increasing triggers. It is not hard to see how a consumer might come to misperceive the per-use price—the interest rate applicable to a dollar borrowed.

Finally, use levels. The decision on how often to use a product or product feature is influenced by the per-use benefit and per-use price. A higher benefit-per-dollar borrowed (as, for example, when the consumer is between jobs) will induce more borrowing. A lower interest rate will similarly result in more borrowing. The use-level choice might also be influenced by imperfect rationality. For example, consider a credit card feature that allows the consumer to pay late—a feature that provides potential liquidity benefits to the rational consumer. This feature will be "used" more often by imperfectly rational consumers who forget to pay on time. Misperception of any of the factors that influence the per-use benefit or the per-use price will result in misperception of the use level. A failure to recognize one's imperfect rationality will also result in misperception of use levels. In our example, a consumer who underestimates his forgetfulness will underestimate the likelihood of "using" the credit card's late payment feature.

The objects of misperception can now be summarized and categorized. The first category includes product attributes. These are product features and per-use prices determined by the seller when designing the product, contract, and pricing scheme. A consumer makes a product-attribute mistake by misperceiving a product feature or a per-use price. As shown above, product-attribute mistakes can result in misperception of both the total benefit and total price.

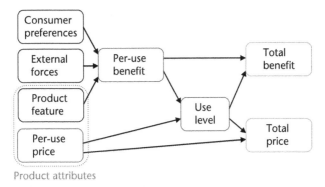

Figure 1.1. Factors affecting the total price and total benefit

The second category of objects of misperception includes use levels. Different product features can be used with different degrees of intensity. Consumers often misperceive these use levels. As explained above, how a product is used is a function of product attributes—product features and per-use prices—and of other factors that influence the per-use benefit (and also other factors that influence the use decision, such as forgetfulness). Product-use mistakes, or use-pattern mistakes, can result in misperception of both the total benefit and total price.

This analysis is presented graphically in Figure 1.1, which shows how product attributes affect total benefit and total price, working through the per-use benefit, the use level, or both. Figure 1.1 also shows the central role of use levels in determining the total benefit and total price. Since the total benefit and total price are a function of product attributes and of use levels, misperceptions of product attributes and use level mistakes result in misperceptions of the total benefit and total price.

The distinction between product attributes and use levels will prove central to the welfare and policy implications discussed in subsequent sections. As we'll see, market forces are less effective in curing product-use mistakes, suggesting that we should be more concerned about such mistakes. Correspondingly, the policy prescriptions outlined in Part IV emphasize the importance of disclosure mandates that incorporate product-use information.

Despite their importance, product-use information and product-use mistakes have received little attention. Moreover, at the policy level, disclosure regulation has focused largely on product-attribute information. The implicit assumption seems to have been that use patterns, being a function of consumer preferences, are known to consumers. But the preceding analysis showed that product use is also a function of product attributes and external forces about which consumers might be imperfectly informed. Moreover, veering away from rational-choice theory, perfect knowledge of one's preferences cannot simply be assumed. The central role of use levels as an object of misperception thus highlights the value of a behavioral-economics approach.

3. A Simple Example
a. Setup

A consumer obtains a credit card. The consumer uses the card for transacting only, intending to pay the full balance each month. This consumer, however, is a bit forgetful. Specifically, he will miss the payment due date exactly one time each year.

The credit card issuer incurs a fixed annual cost of 4, which represents a general account maintenance cost. The issuer also incurs a variable, or per-use, cost of 2 for each late payment. This represents the cost of processing a late payment and the added risk of default implied by a late payment.

The issuer is contemplating a two-dimensional pricing scheme, including an annual fee (p_1) and a late fee (p_2). The total price equals the annual fee plus the late fee: $p_1 + p_2$. More generally, when the number of late payments can vary—some consumers never pay late, some pay late once, some pay late twice, and so on—the total price would equal the annual fee plus the late fee multiplied by the number of late payments. (The late fee is the per-use price of the late payment feature; the number of late payments is the use level.)

b. Misperceptions

A sophisticated, perfectly rational, consumer realizes that he will pay late once a year and incur a late fee. The sophisticated consumer accurately perceives the total price to be $p_1 + p_2$. An imperfectly rational, naive consumer, on the other hand, underestimates his forgetfulness and mistakenly believes that he will never pay late and never incur a late fee. The total price, as perceived by the naive consumer, is p_1. This divergence between the actual and perceived total price will affect the equilibrium pricing scheme.

c. Contract Design

Now let's consider how the issuer will design the credit card contract. How will the magnitudes of the annual fee (p_1) and late fee (p_2) be determined?

The answer depends on consumer psychology and market structure. For ease of exposition and to focus attention on the effect of consumer misperception, assume that the issuer is operating in a competitive market and thus will set prices that just cover the cost of providing the credit card.

Recall that the issuer faces a fixed annual cost of 4 and a variable cost of 2 per incidence of late payment. Accordingly, the efficient contract sets $p_1 = 4$ and $p_2 = 2$. By setting each price equal to the corresponding cost, the (4,2) contract provides optimal incentives and thus maximizes value. The issuer will offer the efficient (4,2) contract to the sophisticated consumer who realizes that there will be one late payment. This contract minimizes the total price paid by the consumer, $4 + 2 = 6$, while still covering the issuer's costs. In fact, in this simple example any set of prices, p_1 and p_2, such that $p_1 + p_2 = 6$, would similarly cover the seller's costs and minimize the total price paid by the consumer. In a more general example, the (4,2) contract would be uniquely efficient.[8]

The efficient (4,2) contract will *not* be offered to a naive consumer—the consumer who mistakenly believes that he will never make a late payment or incur a late fee. For such a consumer, the perceived total price under the (4,2) contract is 4. The efficient (4,2) contract will not be offered in equilibrium, because other contracts appear more attractive to the naive consumer, while still covering the issuer's costs. Consider the (0,6) contract. With this contract, the imperfectly rational, naive consumer perceives a total price of 0, while the actual price is 6. The naive consumer will thus prefer the (0,6) contract over the efficient (4,2) contract.

In this example, the underestimation of forgetfulness results in underestimation of use levels. Contract design amplifies the effect of this product-use mistake on the perceived total price. In other words, contract design is used to minimize the *perceived* total price by amplifying the effect of product-use mistakes. When the perceived likelihood of triggering a certain price dimension—such as a late fee—goes down, the magnitude of the corresponding price—the late fee—goes up. Non-salient prices rise, while

---

8. Such an example is developed in the Appendix. In essence, the efficiency of the (4,2) contract is a result of the general efficiency of marginal cost pricing. A late fee set equal to the issuer's cost from late payment provides optimal incentives for consumers—to pay late only when the benefit to them of late payment exceeds the cost of late payment to the issuer. This advantage of the (4,2) contract assumes that some consumers make a deliberate ex post decision whether to pay late, contrary to the simple example, in the text, where late payment is an inadvertent consequence of forgetfulness.

salient prices are reduced. A price is non-salient, because consumers think it will never be triggered or because the issue (for example, the possibility of paying late) never crosses the consumer's mind.

4. The Limits of Competition

It is widely believed that competition among sellers ensures efficiency and maximizes welfare. This belief is manifested, for example, in antitrust law and its focus on monopolies and cartels. Competition is also supposed to help consumers by keeping prices low.

The behavioral-economics model emphasizes the limits of competition. The example studied in the previous subsection assumed perfect competition. But we saw that, in equilibrium, sellers offered an inefficient contract and consumer welfare was not maximized. The reason is straightforward: Competition forces sellers to maximize the perceived (net) consumer benefit. When consumers accurately perceive their benefits, competition will help consumers. But when consumers are imperfectly rational, competition will maximize the perceived (net) benefit at the expense of the actual (net) benefit.

Focusing on price: When consumers are perfectly rational, sellers compete by offering a lower price. When consumers are imperfectly rational, sellers compete by designing pricing schemes that create an appearance of a lower price. The underlying problem is on the demand side of the market; imperfectly rational consumers generate biased demand. Competition forces sellers to cater to this biased demand. The result: A behavioral market failure.

Modern, neoclassical economics recognizes that even perfectly competitive markets can fail, because of externalities and asymmetric information. Behavioral economics adds a third cause for market failure; misperception and bias. This behavioral market failure is a direct extension of the imperfect information problem. Rational consumers form unbiased estimates of imperfectly known values. Faced with similarly limited information, imperfectly rational consumers form biased estimates. Unbiased estimates can cause market failure; biased estimates can cause market failure.

The preceding analysis, and the failure of competition that it predicts, takes consumers' biases and misperceptions as exogenously given. But perceptions and misperceptions can be endogenous. In particular, sellers can influence consumer perceptions. That's a big part of what marketing is about. What role does competition play in such cases? On the one hand, sellers might try to exacerbate biases that increase the perceived benefit and reduce the perceived price of their products.[9] On the other hand, sellers offering superior, yet underappreciated products and contracts may try to compete by educating consumers and fighting misperception. (See Section III.B below for further discussion.)

5. *Consumer Heterogeneity*

Not all consumers are similarly biased. While some consumers overestimate the net benefit from a product, others might underestimate it. And some consumers accurately perceive benefits and prices. How does this heterogeneity affect the incidence and severity of behavioral market failures?

Contracts are most likely to be designed in response to consumer psychology when many consumers share a common bias. But sellers will design contracts in response to consumer misperception even when different consumers suffer from different misperceptions. In some cases, sellers will be able to identify the different consumer groups and their respective biases and design different contracts for each group. In other cases, sellers will be unable to distinguish between the different groups of consumers ex ante. Still, sellers will be able to offer a menu of contracts. Different contracts in the menu will be attractive to different groups of consumers, according to their specific biases and misperceptions.

B. Common Design Features

The interaction between consumer psychology and market forces influences the design of contracts and pricing schemes. In practice, this influence plays out most often in two common design features: complexity and deferred costs. These design features will figure prominently in the three case studies we'll examine in later chapters. This section defines and illustrates complexity and deferred costs as contract design features and explains why these design features figure prominently in consumer contracts.[10]

---

9. See Edward L. Glaeser, "Psychology and the Market", (2004) 94 *Amer. Econ. Rev. Papers & Proceedings* 408, 409–11 ("Markets do not eliminate (and often exacerbate) irrationality"; "The advertising industry is the most important economic example of these systematic attempts to mislead, where suppliers attempt to convince buyers that their products will yield remarkable benefits." "It is certainly not true that competition ensures that false beliefs will be dissipated. Indeed in many cases competition will work to increase the supply of these falsehoods.")

10. Complexity and deferred costs are also recurring themes in theoretical models of industrial organization with imperfectly rational consumers—see Spiegler above note 1, ch. 12. See also Armstrong, above note 3.

1. Complexity

Most consumer contracts are complex, offering multidimensional benefits and charging multidimensional prices. Complexity and multidimensionality can be both efficient and beneficial to consumers. Compare a simple credit card contract with only an annual fee and a basic interest rate for purchases to a complex credit card contract that, on top of these two price dimensions, adds a default interest rate, a late fee, and a cash-advance fee. The complex card facilitates risk-based pricing and tailoring of optional services to heterogeneous consumer needs. The default interest rate and the late fee allow the issuer to increase the price for riskier consumers. Such efficient risk-based pricing is impossible with the simple card. Instead, the single interest rate implies cross-subsidization of high-risk consumers by low-risk consumers. Similarly, the cash-advance fee allows the issuer to charge separately for cash-advance services, which benefit some consumers but not others. Such tailoring of optional services is impossible with the simple card. Instead, a higher annual fee implies cross-subsidization of consumers who use the cash-advance feature by those who do not.

These efficiency benefits explain some of the complexity and multi-dimensionality found in consumer contracts. But there is another, behavioral explanation. Complexity hides the true cost of the product from the imperfectly rational consumer. A rational consumer navigates complexity with ease, assessing the probability of triggering each rate, fee, and penalty, and then calculating the expected cost associated with each price dimension. The rational consumer may have imperfect information, but will nonetheless form unbiased estimates given the information he or she chooses to collect. Accordingly, each price dimension will be afforded the appropriate weight in the overall evaluation of the product.

The imperfectly rational consumer, on the other hand, is less capable of such an accurate assessment. He is unable to calculate prices that are indirectly specified through complex formulas. Even if he could perform this calculation, he would be unable to simultaneously consider multiple price dimensions. And even if he could recall all the price dimensions, he would be unable to calculate the impact of these prices on the total cost of the product. Bottom line: The imperfectly rational consumer deals with complexity by ignoring it. He simplifies his decision by overlooking non-salient price dimensions.[11] And

---

11. See Richard H. Thaler, "Mental Accounting Matters", *J. Behav. Decision Making*, 12 (1999) 183, 194 (finding that small disaggregated fees are ignored).

he approximates, rather than calculates, the impact of the salient dimensions that cannot be ignored.

In particular, consumers with limited attention and limited memory exclude certain price dimensions from consideration. In addition, limited processing ability prevents consumers from accurately aggregating the different price components into a single, total expected price that would serve as the basis for choosing the optimal product. So while complexity may not faze the rational consumer, it will most likely mislead the imperfectly rational consumer.

As explained above, sellers design contracts in response to systematic biases and misperceptions of imperfectly rational consumers. In particular, they reduce the total price, as perceived by consumers, by decreasing salient prices and increasing non-salient prices. This strategy depends on the existence of non-salient prices. In a simple contract, the one or two price dimensions will generally be salient. Only a complex contract will have both salient and non-salient price dimensions. Complexity thus serves as a tool for reducing the perceived total price.

Moreover, complexity will increase over time as consumers learn to incorporate more price dimensions into their decision. If sellers significantly increase the magnitude of a non-salient price dimension, consumers will eventually learn to focus on this price dimension, making it salient. Sellers then will have to find another non-salient price dimension. When they run out of non-salient prices in the existing contractual design, they may create new ones by adding more interest rates, fees, or penalties.[12]

Another common tactic for increasing complexity is bundling. An example is the bundling of handsets and cellular service, cemented with lock-in contracts and early termination fees. This bundle naturally includes multidimensional pricing; specifically, the price of the handset and the pricing scheme for cellular service (which is itself rather complex). Arguably, one of the main goals of bundling is to create a low perceived total price by

12. A series of recent papers in industrial organization argue that firms introduce spurious complexity into tariff structures and by doing so inhibit competition and reduce welfare. See, e.g., Glenn Ellison, "A Model of Add-On Pricing", Q.J. Econ., 120 (2005), 585; Xavier Gabaix and David Laibson, "Shrouded Attributes, Consumer Myopia, and Information Suppression in Competitive Markets", Q.J. Econ., 121 (2006), 505; Ran Spiegler, "Competition over Agents with Boundedly Rational Expectations", Theoretical Econ., 1 (2006), 207; Glenn Ellison and Sara Fisher Ellison, "Search, Obfuscation, and Price Elasticities on the Internet", Econometrica 77 (2009), 427.

reducing the salient handset price and increasing the non-salient pricing of cellular service. This pricing strategy could not work without bundling: Carriers need the high service prices to compensate for the low, below-cost handset prices. Without bundling, consumers would buy the low-price handset from one seller and get service from a competing carrier, and the practice of offering below-cost handset prices would soon come to an end. There are many other examples of bundling: The credit card bundles transacting and borrowing services. Subprime mortgage contracts bundle secured credit with inspection, appraisal, and insurance services.

In addition to increasing complexity, bundling is used to create deferred-cost contract designs. This occurs when a product or service with short-term benefits and prices is bundled with a product or service with long-term benefits and prices. In the handsets and cellular service example, bundling both increases complexity and facilitates cost deferral.[13]

The focus, thus far, has been on intra-contract complexity. A broader perspective reveals that a consumer's decision process is far more complicated than sorting through the complexity of any single contract. Consumers today must choose from among many complex products offered by competing sellers. At first glance, more choice is better. Consumers are heterogeneous, so more products mean that consumers can find the product that best suits their individual needs. But there's a catch: Searching for the right product among a complex maze of complex products is costly, even for rational consumers. Imperfect rationality exacerbates this cost and may even discourage consumers from searching altogether. *More* choice comes at the expense of *meaningful* choice.

A clarification is in order: In theory, an incomplete understanding of complex contracts is consistent with rational-choice theory. Facing a complex contract, a rational consumer would have to spend time reading the contract and deciphering its meaning. If the cost of attaining perfect information and perfect understanding of the contract is high, the rational borrower would stop short of this theoretical ideal. Imperfect rationality can be viewed as yet another cost of attaining more information and better understanding. When this cost component is added, the total cost of becoming informed goes up, and thus the consumer will end up with less information

---

13. See, generally, Oren Bar-Gill, "Bundling and Consumer Misperception" *U. Chi. L. Rev.* 73 (2006), 33. Clearly, sellers use bundling and tying not only to increase complexity but also to defer costs. Specifically, these tactics can be used for anticompetitive reasons.

and a less complete understanding of the contract. Imperfect rationality, however, is not simply another cost component. Rational consumers who decide not to invest in reading and deciphering certain contractual provisions will not assume that these provisions are favorable; in fact, they will recognize that unread provisions will generally be pro-seller. In contrast, imperfectly rational consumers will completely ignore the unread or forgotten terms or naively assume that they are favorable. Accordingly, a complex, unread term or a hidden fee would lead an imperfectly rational consumer—but not a rational consumer—to underestimate the total cost of the product. As a result, the incentive to increase complexity and hide fees will be stronger in a market with imperfectly rational consumers. The behavioral-economics theory of contract design is an imperfect-rationality theory, not an imperfect-information theory.

2. Deferred Costs

Non-salient price dimensions and prices that impose underestimated costs create opportunities for sellers to reduce the perceived total price of their product. What makes a price non-salient? What leads consumers to underestimate the cost associated with a certain price dimension? While there are no simple answers to these questions, there is one factor that exerts substantial influence on both salience and perception; time.

The basic claim is that, in many cases, non-contingent, short-run costs are accurately perceived, while contingent, long-run costs are underestimated. An annual fee is a non-contingent price that needs to be paid, by a specific date in the near future, regardless of how the consumer uses the card. This cost will figure prominently into the consumer's selection from among competing cards. A late fee, on the other hand, is a contingent price that will be paid in the more distant and unspecified future only if the consumer makes a late payment. This cost, as we have seen, will often be underestimated by the consumer and is, therefore, less likely to affect card choice. If costs in the present are accurately perceived and future costs are underestimated, market forces will produce deferred-cost contracts.

The importance of the temporal dimension of price and cost can often be traced back to two underlying forces; myopia and optimism. Myopic consumers care more about the present and not enough about the future. It is rational to discount future costs and benefits by the probability that they will never materialize. It is also rational to consider the time-value of money; a tax or price deferred is a tax or price saved. It is *not* rational to discount the future simply because it is in the future or because the future seems less real, or harder to picture. Myopia is excessive discounting.

Myopia is common. People are impatient, preferring immediate benefits even at the expense of future costs.[14] Myopia is attributed to the triumph of the affective system, which is driven primarily by short-term payoffs, over the deliberative system, which cares about both short-term and longer-term payoffs. This understanding of myopia, and of intertemporal choice more generally, is consistent with findings from neuroscience.[15]

Future costs are also often underestimated because consumers are optimistic. The prevalence of the optimism bias has been confirmed in multiple studies.[16] Optimistic consumers tend to underestimate the probability of triggering contingent, future costs. They underestimate the likelihood that the contingency will materialize. For example, an optimistic cardholder might underestimate the probability of making a late payment, leading her to underestimate the importance of the late fee.

Similarly, when mortgage contracts set low introductory interest rates coupled with high long-term rates, optimism may cause the consumer to underestimate the importance of the high long-term interest rates. In theory, the high long-term rates can be avoided by exiting the mortgage contract—by selling the house or refinancing the mortgage—before the high rates kick in. In practice, the availability of both the sale and refinancing options decreases when real-estate prices fall. A borrower who is optimistic about real-estate prices will overestimate the likelihood of exiting

---

14. See Ted O'Donoghue and Matthew Rabin, "Doing It Now or Later", *Amer. Econ. Rev.*, 89 (1999), 103 ("[p]eople are impatient—they like to experience rewards soon and delay costs until later."); George F. Loewenstein and Ted O'Donoghue (2004) "Animal Spirits: Affective and Deliberative Processes in Economic Behavior" (May 4), available at SSRN: <http://ssrn .com/abstract=539843> ("people are often powerfully motivated to take myopic actions"— actions that produce immediate benefits at the expense of future costs).

15. See Loewenstein and O'Donoghue, above note 14; Samuel McClure, David Laibson, George Loewenstein, and Jonathan Cohen, "Separate Neural Systems Value Immediate and Delayed Monetary Rewards" (2004) Science, 306, 503–7.

16. See, e.g., Neil D. Weinstein, "Unrealistic Optimism about Future Life Events", *J. Personality & Soc. Psychol.* 39 (1980), 806 (describing two studies revealing that people tend to be unrealistically optimistic about future life events); Ola Svenson, "Are We All Less Risky and More Skillful than Our Fellow Drivers?", *Acta Psychologica* 47 (1981), 143, 143 (describing a study revealing that the majority of people "regard themselves as more skillful and less risky than the average driver"). Like many other cognitive biases, optimism is context specific. Further evidence of optimism in specific consumer markets will be presented in the case-study chapters.

the mortgage contract before the high rates kick in. As a result, such an optimistic borrower will underestimate the importance of the high long-term rates.

Sophisticated sellers facing imperfectly rational consumers will seek to reduce the perceived total price of their products without reducing the actual total price that consumers pay. When consumers are myopic or optimistic, this wedge between perceived and actual prices can be achieved by back-loading costs onto long-term price dimensions. The result: Deferred-cost contracts.

II. Welfare Implications

Complex contracts that defer costs into the future hurt consumers and reduce welfare. They hinder competition and distort the remaining, weakened forces of competition, leading to excessively high prices on more salient price dimensions and excessively low prices on less salient price dimensions. The welfare costs of hindered competition and distorted competition are detailed below. General distributional implications of complexity and deferred costs are also briefly discussed. Other, efficiency and distributive concerns are mar-ket specific and will be addressed in the case studies.[17]

A. Hindered Competition

Excessively complex contracts prevent effective comparison-shopping and thus inhibit competition. Sellers gain market power, increasing profits at the expense of consumers. Limited competition also imposes a welfare cost in the form of inefficient allocation, as consumers are not matched with the most efficient seller.

For competition to work well, consumers must be able to compare the benefits and costs of different products and choose the one that provides the best value, given the consumer's tastes and needs. But as we have seen, gath-ering information on competing products is costly, and complexity—of the product or contract—increases this cost. A rational consumer will collect information until the expected marginal benefit of more information is

---

17. The welfare implications studied in the theoretical literature on industrial organization with imperfectly rational consumers partially overlap with the welfare implications discussed in this Part. See Spiegler, above note 1.

outweighed by the marginal cost of collecting more information. When the cost of collecting information goes up, the rational consumer will collect less information. Less information implies weaker competition.

Imperfect rationality exacerbates this problem. The cost of collecting and processing information is higher for the imperfectly rational consumer. Moreover, the imperfectly rational consumer might not optimally weigh the benefits and costs of additional information. Confronted with a complex array of complex products, the consumer might engage in insufficient collection of information or even avoid comparison-shopping altogether. Competition is not a cure-all, but it does provide important benefits. Complexity stands in the way of effective competition.[18]

B. Distorted Competition

Complexity weakens the forces of competition. But even if sellers vigorously competed for consumers, biases and misperceptions on the demand side of the market distort these competitive efforts, leading to suboptimal outcomes for consumers and reducing social welfare. As explained above, sellers try to maximize the perceived net benefit of their products in the eyes of consumers. When consumer perceptions are biased, the products, contracts, and prices that maximize perceived net benefit are different from those that maximize actual net benefit. The result is distorted contract design, with excessive complexity and deferred costs.

Focusing on price, sellers facing rational consumers will try to minimize the total price of their product. Competition would operate on the total-price level. Imperfectly rational consumers, on the other hand, choose products based on a few salient price dimensions. Competition will thus focus on those salient prices, driving them down, while non-salient prices, free from competitive pressure, increase. And when salience is a function of time—when short-term prices are salient and long-term prices are not—competition will drive short-term prices below cost, with sellers recouping losses through high long-term prices.

These distortions entail two types of efficiency costs. The first pertains to product choice; the second to how the chosen product is used. Let's examine the latter first.

---

18. For a discussion of additional welfare implications of complex contracts—see David Gilo and Ariel Porat, "The Hidden Roles of Boilerplate and Standard-Form Contracts: Strategic Imposition of Transaction Costs, Segmentation of Consumers, and Anticompetitive Effects" *Michigan Law Review*, 104 (2006), 983.

Prices affect product-use decisions. A high late fee deters late payments. A low introductory interest rate induces borrowing during the introductory period. Optimal pricing provides accurate incentives: With an optimal late fee, consumers will pay late if, and only if, the benefit of paying late outweighs the cost of late payment (including the added risk implied by late payment) to the issuer. With an optimal interest rate, consumers will borrow if and only if the benefit from borrowing outweighs the issuer's cost of providing credit. Optimal pricing tracks the seller's cost so that consumers pay the price and use the product only when the benefits to them outweigh the seller's cost. This oversimplified account nonetheless offers a sense of the factors that determine optimal pricing and of the efficiency gains that optimal pricing provides.

When prices are a function of salience rather than cost, efficiency benefits are compromised. Low salient prices will lead to excessive use, high non-salient prices to insufficient use. Consumers will borrow excessively during the introductory period and avoid paying late even when the benefits of paying late exceed the cost to the issuer of a late payment. Distorted competition produces distorted prices, which lead to distorted incentives.

Back to product choice: Sellers reduce salient prices and increase non-salient prices in order to minimize the total price as perceived by the imperfectly rational consumer. Since the perceived total price will be lower than the actual total price, biased consumers may well choose a product that costs more than it is worth to them. The result is inefficient allocation.

This inefficiency exists even with optimal pricing. Here, the non-salient price dimensions will be ignored or underestimated, reducing the perceived total price. Distorted contract design exacerbates the problem by backloading more of the total price onto the non-salient, underestimated dimensions. The gap between actual total price and perceived total price increases—as does the number of consumers who purchase products that reduce their welfare. Bias and misperception result in artificially inflated demand. Distorted contract design adds air to the demand balloon.

C. Distributional Concerns

The distributional implications of complexity and deferred costs are, in large part, market specific. They will be discussed in the case-study chapters. Still, a few general observations can be made here.

Excessive complexity imposes a larger burden on less sophisticated customers and on financially weaker customers who cannot hire advisers to help them navigate the complexity of products and contracts. Thus, complexity has a regressive distributional effect.

The distributional effect of deferred costs is less clear. Distorted pricing—specifically, low salient or short-term prices and high non-salient or long-term prices—shift the burden to the group of consumers who are more likely to pay the high, non-salient prices. In some cases, such as when the non-salient prices are default or penalty prices (late fees and default interest rates, for instance), weaker consumers are more likely to shoulder the burden of the high, non-salient prices. In these cases, the deferred-cost feature will have a regressive distributional effect.

III. Market Solutions and Their Limits

As we have seen, the interaction of consumer psychology and market forces can hurt consumers and reduce welfare. The extent of the harm depends, in large part, on the ability of market forces—specifically, learning by consumers and education by sellers—to address the underlying biases and misperceptions that are responsible for the behavioral market failure. These market solutions, and their limits, are considered below.[19]

A. Learning by Consumers

While bias and misperception can lead to mistakes in product choice and product use, consumers can learn from their own mistakes—intrapersonal learning—and from the mistakes of others—interpersonal learning—to avoid repeating these mistakes.[20] But how quickly will consumers learn? The answer is context-dependent. Context affects the efficacy of both intrapersonal and interpersonal learning.

Starting with intrapersonal learning, the speed with which consumers learn about a latent product risk will depend on how frequently they use the product and on how frequently the risk materializes. Credit cards and

---

19. See also Armstrong, above note 3.
20. See, e.g., Sumit Agarwal, et al., "The Age of Reason: Financial Decisions over the Life-Cycle and Implications for Regulation" (2009) *Brookings Papers on Economic Activity*, Issue 2, 51–117 (showing that consumers learn).

cell phones provide more opportunities for this kind of learning than mortgages do. Even with credit cards and cell phones, certain risks and costs arise more frequently than others. For example, finance charges and overage fees arise more frequently than currency conversion fees and international roaming charges.[21]

When low frequency renders intrapersonal learning less effective, interpersonal learning becomes important. A consumer might take out one or two mortgage loans in a lifetime. It is therefore less likely that a consumer will learn about product risks from personal experience. But if a million consumers take the same type of mortgage loan, it's likely that some of these mortgages will default, thereby exposing the different risky design features in the mortgage contract.

Interpersonal learning, however, is not a panacea and is also context-dependent. Interpersonal learning is effective, for example, when products are standardized; less effective when not. With standardized products, when consumers discover a certain hidden feature of the product, they can share this information with family and friends. Since the information pertains to a standardized product, it is relevant to others. But if the product is not standardized, such interpersonal learning will be less effective. The information obtained by one consumer might not be relevant to another consumer who purchased a different version of the non-standard product.[22]

When the nature of the product is more broadly defined to include the potential uses of the product, the group of standardized products shrinks. The value of a product does not depend only on its intrinsic features, but also on its potential uses. If different consumers use the product differently, then an otherwise standardized product becomes functionally non-standardized. This can inhibit learning: If one consumer uses the product one way and through use discovers information about the product, there is little reason to believe that another consumer who uses the product in a different way will find this information relevant.

21. On the conditions for effective learning and on the limits of learning—see Amos Tversky and Daniel Kahneman, "Rational Choice and the Framing of Decisions," in Robin M. Hogarth and Melvin W. Reder (eds.), *Rational Choice: The Contrast between Economics and Psychology* (University of Chicago Press, 1987) 90–1. On the limits of learning, even by sophisticated decisionmakers in "real world" high-stakes environments—see Cade Massey and Richard H. Thaler, "The Loser's Curse: Overconfidence vs. Market Efficiency in the National Football League Draft" (2010), available at SSRN: <http://ssrn.com/abstract=697121> (documenting persistent bias in NFL draft picks).
22. Even non-standardized products may share standardized features. Interpersonal learning about these features can be effective.

The distinction between product-attribute information and product-use information is also relevant for the efficacy of interpersonal learning. Mistakes about product attributes are more quickly resolved through interpersonal learning. How quickly these mistakes are resolved depends on the number of product units or versions that share the attribute and the extent that the attribute is relevant to different use patterns. For example, consumers will more quickly learn about high currency conversion fees the more common these fees are and the higher the number of consumers who incur the fees while traveling abroad.

Resolving mistakes involving product use is unlikely to happen through interpersonal learning. Consumers might underestimate how often they will make a late payment on a credit card or how often they will exceed the number of allotted minutes on a cell phone calling plan. Even with an otherwise standardized product, because use patterns vary widely among consumers, interpersonal learning becomes much more difficult.

Reputation represents another, different aspect of interpersonal learning. Reputation is most often associated with the seller, rather than a product or contract feature. Therefore, a seller's reputation is not subject to the non-standardization problem. But reputation suffers from a different problem: the information it conveys is less accurate. Sellers with high-quality products and reliable customer service may enjoy sterling reputations even while adopting contract designs that maximize profits at the expense of consumers. Of course, blatant abuses will hurt a seller's reputation, and sellers will be careful to avoid such abuses. The concern is with contractual design features that, while harmful, are unlikely to impose a reputational cost. Reputation is even less effective at the low end of the market. Many consumers seek out sellers with a reputation for offering lower-quality products at lower prices. These consumers might not realize, however, that they are getting harmful contract design along with lower product quality. Having chosen the low-end reputation, sellers will be undeterred (or less deterred) by the threat of a reputational penalty.

While imperfect, reputation is an important force. It helps minimize the adverse effects of the behavioral market failure. Since reputation is learned by consumers and actively nurtured by sellers, it is relevant both to the discussion of learning in this subsection and to the discussion of education in the next subsection.

Another form of learning is based on expert advice. Recognizing their imperfect rationality, consumers take steps to limit the mistakes they make. They do this by seeking advice and consulting with experts before entering the market.[23] These experts include private consultants and advisers, government entities that supply information and guidance, and consumer organizations. Expert advice is clearly useful. But like other forms of learning, it is not without limits.

First, consumers do not seek advice before each and every purchase or use decision. When faced with a major decision, consumers are more likely to take the time and incur the cost of seeking expert advice. They are less likely to do so when faced with a smaller decision. For example, consumers are more likely to seek third-party assistance before taking on a substantial home equity loan. They are less likely to engage in substantial consultations before deciding to buy a pair of sneakers with their credit card. In many markets, consumers make a series of small decisions. In these markets, reliance on expert advice is less prevalent.

Second, expert advice, or good expert advice, is not always available. Certain decisions that consumers face are so complex that even experts make mistakes. For example, in the mortgage market, available expert advice on refinancing ignores the option value of postponing the prepayment decision—an omission that can cost borrowers up to 25 percent of the loan value.[24] Also, advice is useful when the advice-giver has the advice-taker's best interest in mind, which is not always the case. Again, the mortgage market serves as a case in point. Recent legal reform restricted the permissible structure of broker compensation, responding to concerns that mortgage brokers were being rewarded for steering the people who relied on their advice—borrowers—into more expensive loans.[25]

Finally, expert advice is more helpful in curing product-attribute mistakes than in curing product-use mistakes. When the mistake pertains to individual or idiosyncratic use patterns, experts rarely have the information needed to correct the mistake.

Rather than relying solely on experts, consumers sometimes rely on other consumers. Other consumers can facilitate interpersonal learning about risky products and contracts. They can also help drive out risky prod-

23. Richard A. Epstein, "Second-Order Rationality," in Edward J. McCaffery and Joel Slemrod (eds.), *Behavioral Public Finance* (Russell Sage Foundation, 2006) 355, 361–2.
24. Sumit Agarwal, John C. Driscoll, and David Laibson, "Optimal Mortgage Refinancing: A Closed Form Solution" 5–6 (2007) (*Nat'l Bureau of Econ. Research, Working Paper* No. 13487), available at <http://www.nber.org/papers/w13487>.
25. Federal Reserve Board, Press Release, August 16, 2010, <http://www.federalreserve.gov/newsevents/press/bcreg/20100816d.htm>. Similar compensation structures continue to create conflicts of interest in the insurance market.

ucts and contracts, thus eliminating the need to learn about them. This is the "informed minority" argument attributed to Alan Schwartz and Louis Wilde.[26] In theory, even a minority of informed, sophisticated consumers can induce sellers to offer welfare-maximizing products and contracts.

The informed minority argument relies on several assumptions. First, the informed minority must not be too small—there must be a sufficiently large number of informed consumers to affect the design of products and contracts. Second, the preferences of these informed consumers must be aligned with those of the less sophisticated consumers. Third, sellers must not be able to segment the market, offering different contracts to sophisticated and less sophisticated borrowers. When these assumptions fail, the informed minority argument does not apply.[27]

B. Education by Sellers

Learning is an important demand-side market solution to the problem of consumer misperception. A different set of market solutions focus on the supply side: Sellers may invest in correcting consumer misperceptions. Consider the following, common scenario. Seller A offers a product that is better and costs more to produce than the product offered by Seller B. Consumers, however, underestimate the added value from Seller A's product and thus refuse to pay the higher price that Seller A charges. In this scenario, Seller A has a powerful incentive to educate consumers about its product; in other words, to correct their underestimation of the product's value (or total net benefit).

But what if several or more sellers offer identical products or different products that share a certain product risk? Now a collective-action problem interferes with sellers' incentives to educate consumers. To illustrate, let's say Seller A reduces the product risk and then invests in educating consumers about the benefits of its superior product. Seller A will attract a

---

26. See Alan Schwartz and Louis L. Wilde, "Imperfect Information in Markets for Contract Terms: The Examples of Warranties and Security Interests", *Va. L. Rev.*, 69 (1983), 1387; Alan Schwartz and Louis L. Wilde, "Product Quality and Imperfect Information", *Rev. Econ. Stud.*, 52 (1985), 251.

27. See Oren Bar-Gill and Elizabeth Warren, "Making Credit Safer" (2008) 157 *U. Penn. L. Rev.* 1, 22–3. For evidence that the number of informed consumers is too small, at least in certain markets—see Yannis Bakos, Florencia Marotta-Wurgler, and David R. Trossen, "Does Anyone Read the Fine Print? Testing a Law and Economics Approach to Standard Form Contracts," (2009) *NYU Law and Economics Research Paper* No. 09-40, available at SSRN: <http://ssrn.com/abstract=1443256>.

lot of business and make a supra-competitive profit. But this is not an equi-librium. After Seller A invests in consumer education, all the other sellers will free ride on Seller A's efforts. They will reduce the product risk, as Seller A did, and compete away profit that Seller A would have made. Anticipating such a response, Seller A will realize that the investment in consumer education may not be recouped. Seller A may, therefore, choose not to improve the safety of its product; instead, it will continue to offer a higher-risk product. This collective-action problem can lead to continued consumer misperception.[28]

In some markets, the collective-action problem is avoided by a first-mover advantage enjoyed by Seller A. In other words, if it takes time for other sellers to copy Seller A's consumer-friendly product innovation, Seller A may be able to earn sufficient profits during this time to make the initial investment in consumer education worthwhile.

Unfortunately, Seller A is unlikely to enjoy a large first-mover advantage with contract design innovations. To replicate an improvement in a physical product, competitors need to reconfigure assembly lines. This takes time. To replicate a contract-design innovation, however, competitors only need to type and print (or upload on a website) a new contract.

Education by sellers is particularly unreliable when it comes to product-use information. The forces that potentially drive sellers to disclose product-attribute information do not apply to product-use information. Disclosing product-attribute information provides a competitive advantage to the dis-closing seller, until other sellers are able to copy. This information is dis-closed to help buyers appreciate the superiority of the disclosing seller's product, as compared to competitors' products. On the other hand, disclos-ing product-use information might not generate a competitive advantage for the disclosing seller. As long as the disclosed use patterns are common to the entire product category, the now-informed consumer may just as well purchase the product from a non-disclosing seller. Accordingly, sellers have little reason to voluntarily disclose use-pattern information.[29]

---

28. See Howard Beales, Richard Craswell, and Steven Salop, "The Efficient Regulation of Consumer Information", *J. L. & Econ.* 24 (1981), 491, 527 (explaining why sellers might not disclose both positive and negative information). On the limits of advertising as a mistake-correction mechanism—see also Xavier Gabaix and David Laibson, "Shrouded Attributes, Consumer Myopia, and Information Suppression in Competitive Markets", *Q. J. Econ.*, 121 (2006), 505.

29. See Oren Bar-Gill and Oliver Board, "Product Use Information and the Limits of Voluntary Disclosure" *American Law and Economics Review* 14 (2012), 235.

Finally, even apart from the collective-action and product-use information problems, sellers might actually prefer not to correct consumer mistakes. They might even invest in creating misperception. This manipulation of consumer perceptions and preferences is, arguably, one of the main goals of advertising.[30]

IV. Policy Implications: Disclosure Regulation

The interaction between consumer psychology and market forces creates a behavioral market failure. This failure reduces welfare and hurts consumers. Market solutions exist, but their reach is limited. They mitigate the problem but cannot ameliorate it. The persistence of a market failure opens the door for considering the potential role of legal intervention.

The policy discussion here and in the remainder of the book focuses on disclosure regulation. This is not because disclosure always works or because disclosure is always the optimal form of regulatory intervention. Rather, it is because disclosure mandates are the least intrusive form of regulation and, thus, the form of regulation most likely to be adopted. It is also because disclosure mandates, when optimally designed, directly target the mistakes and misperceptions at the core of the behavioral market failure.[31]

The efficacy of disclosure as a regulatory technique for influencing behavior and improving market outcomes has been recently called into

---

30. See Glaeser, above note 9. Additional limits on the efficacy of "education by sellers" as a market solution are discussed in Spiegler, above note 1, ch. 6.
31. Disclosure mandates are a primary example of soft paternalism (or asymmetric paternalism or libertarian paternalism)—helping less sophisticated consumers, while imposing minimal costs on more sophisticated consumers. See Colin Camerer et al., "Regulation for Conservatives: Behavioral Economics and the Case for 'Asymmetric Paternalism'", *U. Penn. L. Rev.*, 151 (2003), 1211; Cass R. Sunstein and Richard H. Thaler, "Libertarian Paternalism Is Not an Oxymoron", *U. Chi. L. Rev.*, 70 (2003), 1159; Richard H. Thaler and Cass R. Sunstein, *Nudge: Improving Decisions about Health, Wealth and Happiness* (Yale University Press, 2008). On the benefits and limits of disclosure mandates—see also Spiegler, above note 1, chs. 10, 12; Armstrong, above note 3. Other policy tools, specifically education/literacy/numeracy programs, are synergetic with disclosure regulation, as they increase consumers' ability to digest disclosed information, and thus allow for effective disclosure of more, and more comprehensive, information.

question by Omri Ben-Shahar and Carl Schneider.[32] In the consumer markets that are the focus of this book, however, evidence suggests that disclosure has been effective to at least some extent. This evidence will be discussed in the case-study chapters that follow. But even if the efficacy of current disclosures is limited, this does not rule out the wisdom of using disclosure as a regulatory strategy. Existing disclosure mandates are poorly designed. One purpose of this section is to provide regulators with guidance on how to better design disclosure mandates for consumer markets.

The goal of this section and of the market-specific treatments of disclosure mandates in the following chapters is not to offer a comprehensive evaluation of existing or proposed regulations. Rather, the goal is to highlight and elucidate a number of key issues pertaining to optimal disclosure regulation. Subsection A highlights the importance of disclosing product-use information. Subsection B discusses optimal design of disclosure mandates. Subsection C concludes the section with a look at some normative concerns raised by disclosure regulation.

Note that the disclosure strategies discussed below, while designed with the imperfectly rational consumer in mind, can also help rational but imperfectly informed consumers.

A. Disclosing Product-Use Information

Section I.A distinguished between product attributes and product use and, correspondingly, between product-attribute mistakes and product-use mistakes. Both types of mistakes interfere with the efficient operation of markets and hurt consumers. Information can cure mistakes. Disclosing product-attribute information can reduce product-attribute mistakes; disclosing product-use information can reduce product-use mistakes.

Consider credit cards. The interest rate on a credit card and the penalty for late payment are attributes of the credit card product. Borrowing patterns and the incidence of late payment indicate how the product is used. The total benefits and costs associated with a product are a function of both product attributes and use patterns. Total interest paid depends on both the interest rate and the

---

32. Omri Ben-Shahar and Carl E. Schneider, *More Than You Wanted To Know: The Failure of Mandated Disclosure* (Princeton University Press, forthcoming).

consumer's evolving balance. Total penalty charges depend on both the late fee and the frequency of late payment. Consumers who underestimate the interest rate and late fee—and those who underestimate how much they will borrow and how often they will pay late—will underestimate the total price of the credit card product. The important role of information disclosure in reducing misperception is widely recognized. To a large degree, however, existing and proposed disclosure mandates focus solely on product-attribute information.[33]

I believe that disclosure mandates should target product-use information as well. As emphasized in Section I, consumers need product-use information to make optimal decisions. But, as documented in the case-study chapters, consumers do not have access to reliable product-use information and, as a result, systemically make mistakes about their future use patterns.

Still, the fact that consumers lack product-use information is insufficient, in and of itself, to justify regulation that mandates disclosure of product-use information. Two preliminary objections must first be considered: First, disclosure only makes sense if sellers have better information than consumers. While sellers presumptively have better information about the attributes of the products that they are offering, the opposite presumption is often applied to use information: consumers are believed to have better information about how *they* are going to use the product. In important consumer markets, however, this presumption is false. The credit card market is such a market. Duncan McDonald, former general counsel of Citigroup's Europe and North America card businesses, noted:

> No other industry in the world knows consumers and their transaction behavior better than the bank card industry. It has turned the analysis of consumers into a science rivaling the studies of DNA. The mathematics of virtually everything consumers do is stored, updated, categorized, churned, scored, tested, valued, and compared from every possible angle in hundreds of the most powerful computers and by among the most creative minds anywhere. In the past 10 years alone, the transactions of 200 million Americans have been reviewed in trillions of different ways to minimize bank card risks.[34]

33. See Oren Bar-Gill and Franco Ferrari, "Informing Consumers about Themselves" *Erasmus Law Review* 3 (2010), 93.

34. Duncan A. MacDonald, "Viewpoint: Card Industry Questions Congress Needs to Ask" *American Banker*, March 23, 2007. See also Charles Duhigg, "What Does Your Credit-Card Company Know about You?" (2009) *New York Times*, May 17 (describing the vast amount of information, especially product-use information, that credit card companies collect, and then analyze using sophisticated algorithms informed by psychology research).

The cellular service market provides another example. A pricing manager at a top US cellular service provider commented that "people absolutely think they know how much they will use [their cell phones] and it's pretty surprising how wrong they are."[35] Presumably, the pricing manager was comparing people's perceived use patterns to a benchmark of actual use patterns, known to the provider and its employees. Even in the mortgage market, lenders often have superior use information on such things as repayment patterns and the likelihood of default. This will often be statistical or average-use information, but lenders also have use information on the specific individual borrower through credit bureaus and information collected over time as the borrower's tenure with the lender lengthens.[36]

Even when sellers have superior use information, disclosure mandates might not be justified because of the second preliminary objection: Why mandate disclosure if sellers can be expected to disclose voluntarily? The answer to this objection is that sellers will not always volunteer the information. This takes us back to the question about market solutions and their limits. As argued above, voluntary disclosure, or education by sellers, cannot always be counted upon. Moreover, product-use information is less likely to be voluntarily disclosed. The prevalence of rules requiring product-attribute disclosure and the relative paucity of mandatory product-use disclosure is, in an important sense, exactly the opposite of what economic theory would recommend.

Product-use disclosures come in two main forms: statistical, average-use disclosures and individual-use disclosures. Individual-use disclosures, based on a consumer's past use patterns, are clearly more effective in supporting optimal decision-making by consumers. Such disclosures, however, will generally be feasible only in service markets, such as the credit card and cell phone markets, where providers have long-term relationships with their customers and collect use information over the course of these relationships. In other markets, product-use disclosures are often limited to statistical information based on the use patterns of the average consumer, or the average consumer within a certain demographic. Heterogeneity among consumers limits the value of such average-use disclosures. Consumer optimism—a "we-are-all-above-average" attitude—also limits the value of average-use disclosures.

---

35. Michael D., Grubb, "Selling to Overconfident Consumers", *Amer. Econ. Rev.* 99 (2009), 1770.
36. Philip, Bond, David K. Musto, and Bilge, Yilmaz, "Predatory Mortgage Lending" (October 10, 2008). *FRB of Philadelphia Working Paper* No. 08-24. Available at SSRN: <http://ssrn.com/abstract=1288094>.

Individual-use disclosures, while more effective, are also subject to certain limits. First, as explained in Section I.A.2, product use is a function of, among other things, product attributes. Accordingly, when consumers switch from one product to another product, their use patterns may change. For example, consider a cell phone user with a 200-minute-per-month plan—a plan with no per-minute charge for the first 200 minutes and with substantial overage fees beyond the 200-minute limit—who switches to a 500-minutes-per-month plan. The consumer may start using the phone more often. Product-use disclosures based on the 200-minute plan may thus be misleading. Second, individual-use disclosure will inevitably be based on past use. Past use is an imperfect predictor of future use. Moreover, optimistic consumers with irresponsible past use—frequent late payments, for example—may think that they'll do better in the future.

While product-use disclosures are not perfect, consumers will often be better off with them than without them. Regulators designing disclosure regimes should consider seriously the potential role of product-use disclosures.

B. Designing Optimal Disclosure Mandates

Disclosure mandates are prevalent but often ill-conceived. Simply providing more information will not always help consumers. Heaps of paper blindly signed at the closing of a mortgage and the impenetrable fine print of a credit card contract are extreme examples of disclosure regulation gone wrong. For sophisticated, rational consumers, the cost of reading and deciphering these complex disclosures often outweighs the benefit. For imperfectly rational consumers, information overload is an even bigger problem.[37]

---

37. See Richard Craswell, "Taking Information Seriously: Misrepresentation and Nondisclosure in Contract Law and Elsewhere", *Va. L. Rev.* 92 (2006), 565 (arguing that provision of additional information dilutes the effectiveness of existing disclosures); Russell Korobkin, "Bounded Rationality, Standard Form Contracts, and Unconscionability", *U. Chi. L. Rev.*, 70 (2003), 1203 (consumers can process only limited amounts of information); Government Accountability Office, "Credit Cards: Increased Complexity in Rates and Fees Heightens Need for More Effective Disclosures to Consumers" (2006), available at <http://www.gao.gov/new.items/d06929.pdf> 46 (finding that credit card disclosures contain too much information); Mark Furletti, "Credit Card Pricing Developments and Their Disclosure" (2003) Federal Reserve Bank of Philadelphia, Payment Cards Center, Discussion Paper, 19 available at <http://www.philadelphiafed.org/pcc/papers/2003/CreditCardPricing_012003.pdf> (concluding that it is not clear that requiring more details in regulatory disclosures would be useful for consumers).

To be effective, disclosure mandates must adopt one of two general approaches. The first approach targets consumers directly, as most current disclosure mandates do. To be effective, however, these disclosures must be kept simple—not exactly a characteristic of most current disclosure mandates. The second approach re-conceptualizes disclosure to target sophisticated intermediaries or sellers rather than consumers directly. These disclosures can be more comprehensive and more complex.[38]

1. Simple Disclosures for Consumers

Designing simple, yet useful disclosures that target imperfectly rational consumers is a difficult task. The challenge is dealing with the inherent tension between providing *more* information and providing *accessible* information. Sellers have a lot of relevant information. A disclosure that is simple enough for consumers to understand will inevitably exclude some relevant information. The goal in designing disclosures, then, should be to maximize what consumers take away from the disclosure. To do that, regulators must identify the most important information and present it in the simplest possible form.

Consumer heterogeneity further complicates matters, since information that is valuable in the eyes of one consumer may not be as valuable to another consumer. Regulators need to mandate disclosure of information that is statistically important; namely important to the majority of consumers. Alternatively, when possible, regulators should mandate disclosure of individualized information—information tailored to the individual consumer. The minimum payment disclosure mandated by the Credit Card Accountability, Responsibility and Disclosure Act of 2009 provides an example. It provides information on the cost of slow repayment, based on the individual consumer's credit card balance.[39]

In many cases, an effective way to provide the most information in the least complex way is by disclosing total-cost-of-ownership (TCO) information. The TCO disclosure is a simple, single-figure disclosure that provides consumers with an estimate of how much they will ultimately pay for

38. The distinction between simple disclosures for consumers and comprehensive disclosures for intermediaries and sellers roughly corresponds to the distinction made by OIRA Administrator, Cass R. Sunstein, between summary disclosure and full disclosure. See Cass R. Sunstein, "Disclosure and Simplification as Regulatory Tools" Memorandum for the Heads of Executive Departments and Agencies (2010), available at <http://www.whitehouse.gov/sites/default/files/omb/assets/inforeg/disclosure_principles.pdf>.

39. For more details—see Chapter 2.

the product over the product's life span. And when the subject of consumer mistakes is likely to be the product's benefits, rather than its cost or price, a total-benefit-of-ownership (TBO) disclosure may be warranted. In some cases, the disclosed total cost or total benefit can be measured over a specified period, typically a year. In these cases, the TCO or TBO disclosures would become annual cost or annual benefit disclosures.[40]

The TCO and annual cost disclosures and the TBO and annual benefit disclosures combine product-attribute information with product-use information. For example, the annual cost of a cell phone plan would combine plan rates with information on use patterns to estimate the annual cost of cellular service. For a new customer, the carrier may have to use average-use information to calculate the annual cost estimate (unless the consumer brings individual-use information from previous experience with another carrier). For existing customers, the carrier should use the individual-use information that it already has. A similar annual cost disclosure can be devised for credit cards, again based on use patterns, which include extent of borrowing, repayment speed, the likelihood of making a late payment, and so forth. And for mortgages the TCO estimate would account for possible interest rate hikes, prepayments, and default.

For consumer credit products, and specifically for mortgages, the Annual Percentage Rate (APR) disclosure was initially envisioned as a type of TCO disclosure. The APR is based on the finance charge which, in theory, encompasses all costs associated with taking the loan. (In practice, many cost dimensions were excluded from the finance charge definition, as explained in Chapter 3.) It then takes this total cost, annualizes it, and presents it as a percentage figure.

These simple, aggregate disclosures, especially the TCO disclosure, are a direct response to the behavioral market failure identified in the first part of this chapter. Sellers facing imperfectly rational consumers will design complex, deferred-cost contracts in order to maximize the wedge between the

---

40. Cf. Sunstein, above note 38, at 5. For an example of a TBO-type disclosure—see the Lifetime Income Disclosure Act (S. 267; HR. 1534), which would require DC retirement plan administrators to disclose the stream of guaranteed lifetime annual benefits that a plan participant could purchase at retirement, given her current retirement savings. Some administrators, e.g. TIAA-CREF and Vanguard, include such projections in their statements voluntarily. See also Gopi Shah Goda, Colleen Flaherty Manchester, and Aaron J. Sojourner, "What's My Account Really Worth? The Effect of Lifetime Income Disclosure on Retirement Savings" (2011) *RAND Working Paper No. WR-873*, available at <http://ssrn.com/abstract=1925064> (showing that these disclosures can be effective).

actual and perceived cost of their products. The TCO disclosure undermines sellers' incentives to design such welfare-reducing contracts. Complexity is used to hide the true cost of the contract by allowing sellers to load costs onto less salient price dimensions. If sellers are required to provide a TCO disclosure that aggregates both salient and non-salient prices, complexity ceases to be a problem for consumers and loses its appeal to sellers.

Similarly, sellers design deferred-cost contracts so that myopic and optimistic consumers will underestimate the cost of the product. A TCO disclosure that aggregates both short-term and long-term costs into a single figure that guides consumer choice would substantially reduce sellers' incentives to defer costs.

TCO and TBO disclosures can help consumers figure out if the benefit from the product exceeds its cost. But the TCO and TBO disclosures have another, perhaps more important role: They facilitate competition by providing a common metric for comparing competing products. This was clearly one of the main goals of the APR disclosure when it was first introduced in the late 1960s as part of the original Truth-in-Lending Act. Congress did not imagine that the average consumer would understand how the APR is calculated. But that didn't matter. All the consumer needed to do was identify the APRs of the two or more financial products under consideration and choose the product with the lowest APR. Of course, if the APR is to guide competition in the right direction, it must correspond to the total cost of the financial product.

The idea of TCO and TBO disclosures as tools for facilitating competition highlights their relationship with other product rating systems. Product ratings on certain consumer websites provide an example. Like the TCO and TBO disclosures, these ratings attempt to aggregate much information in a simple measure. Like the TBO disclosure, product ratings focus on the product's benefits, rather than on its costs. (For many evaluated products, the cost to the consumer is simply the one-dimensional price tag.)[41]

In certain markets, TCO and TBO disclosures are not optimal and a multidimensional disclosure may be needed. This is because a single-figure TCO or TBO disclosure inevitably leaves out relevant information—information that becomes more critical as consumer heterogeneity increases and when this heterogeneity cannot be adequately dealt with by incorporating individ-

41. Sanitation ratings for restaurants provide another example of a rating system. Sanitation ratings, however, focus on one aspect of the consumer experience, and are therefore less closely related to TCO and TBO disclosures.

ual-use information. When designing such disclosures, regulators should be mindful of the tradeoff between *more* information and *accessible* information.

The theory of optimal disclosure design is still not well developed. Most disclosure mandates are issued without any attempt to devise optimal disclosure forms in a scientific manner. In recent years, such regulators as the Federal Trade Commission, the Federal Reserve Board, and the Consumer Financial Protection Bureau have begun to employ consumer-testing methods to identify more effective disclosure forms.[42] These efforts should be extended.

2. Comprehensive Disclosures for Intermediaries and Sellers

The standard disclosure paradigm targets consumers; in other words, the disclosures are supposed to be read and used by consumers. But disclosures can also help consumers even when they are not targeted at consumers directly. Consumers often rely on agents—intermediaries and even sellers—to help them choose among competing products. These agents, however, rarely have enough information to effectively advise consumers. Disclosure regulation can solve this problem.[43]

Consider a consumer who is at the end of a two-year cellular service contract. This consumer needs to decide whether to stay with the current carrier and plan, or switch to a different plan with the same carrier, or switch to another carrier altogether. The consumer must choose among many complex products in the search for the optimal cell phone plan, given his or her particular use patterns. To do that, the consumer could employ the services of an intermediary like BillShrink.com. The intermediary will have information on available plans—product-attribute information. But it will not have information on the consumer's use patterns. Of course, the consumer could provide this information, but as suggested earlier (and as will be demonstrated in Chapter 4), many consumers have a poor sense of their use patterns. This is where disclosure kicks in. The missing information exists in the databases of the consumer's old carrier. Disclosure regulation could require carriers to provide this information, in electronic form, to the consumer. The consumer could forward this data to the intermediary, who will now be in a position to help the consumer choose the product that best fits the consumer's use patterns.

42. For more details—see Chapters 2 and 3. See generally Sunstein, above note 38 at 5 (emphasizing the importance of testing).
43. Cf. Sunstein, above note 38, at 6–7 (discussing full disclosure).

A related model skips the intermediary and relies on competing sellers as agents of consumers. In the scenario above, for example, the consumer's current carrier is at a competitive advantage because it knows the consumer's use patterns. If the current carrier is required to disclose use information in electronic form, the consumer could then forward this information to competing carriers and ask which of their plans best fits his or her use patterns. This type of disclosure would level the playing field between the old carrier and its competitors, to the benefit of the consumer.

This alternative disclosure paradigm avoids the tradeoff between more information and more accessible information. Since the disclosed information is to be used by sophisticated parties—intermediaries or sellers—rather than directly by consumers, the disclosure can be comprehensive and complex. Disclosure that benefits consumers without being targeted directly at consumers has been prominently proposed by Richard Thaler and Cass Sunstein.[44] Sunstein has begun implementing this proposal in his role as Administrator of the Office of Information and Regulatory Affairs (OIRA).[45] The idea is also beginning to percolate in the relevant regulatory agencies. For example, the Federal Communications Commission, in a recent Notice of Inquiry, recognized the potential importance of both electronic disclosure and intermediaries.[46] Finally, the Mydata initiative in the United Kingdom embraces this new disclosure paradigm.[47]

C. Normative Questions

When optimally designed, disclosure can facilitate the efficient operation of market forces and help consumers. This does not mean that disclosure is a silver bullet. It has both limits and costs. A comprehensive cost-benefit anal-

---

44. Thaler and Sunstein, above note 31. See also Bar-Gill and Board, above note 29.
45. See Sunstein, above note 38, at 6–7. See also Cass R. Sunstein, "Informing Consumers through Smart Disclosure" (2011), Memorandum for the Heads of Executive Departments and Agencies, available at <http://www.whitehouse.gov/sites/default/files/omb/inforeg/for-agencies/informing-consumers-through-smart-disclosure.pdf>.
46. Federal Communications Commission, "Notice of Inquiry: Consumer Information and Disclosure", CG Docket No. 09-158, released August 28, 2009.
47. See Department of Business Innovation and Skills and Cabinet Office Behavioural Insights Team, *Better Choices: Better Deals*, April 13, 2011, available at <http://www.cabinetoffice.gov.uk/resource-library/better-choices-better-deals>.

ysis of disclosure mandates is beyond the scope of this book, but a few normative questions should be noted.

As a preliminary matter, it is important to recognize that disclosure is not
without cost. Sellers incur costs of collecting, compiling, and distributing
the information. Some of these costs will be borne by consumers as sellers
increase prices to cover the added cost of the disclosure regulation.[48] These
costs, however, should not be overestimated. In many consumer markets,
sellers collect and compile the relevant information anyway. Therefore, the
disclosure mandate will only add the relatively minor cost of distributing
the information.

This relates to another, indirect cost of disclosure regulation. If sellers are
required to disclose the information they collect, they will have a weaker
incentive to collect information.[49] While this adverse incentive effect is
undeniably true, its magnitude can be expected to be small in many markets
because the business reasons for collecting information will often outweigh
the disclosure disincentive.[50] And, if sharing the information with consumers eliminates its value to sellers, then perhaps the information is collected
only to exploit consumers. In that case, a weaker incentive to collect information should not raise concern. Moreover, if the information is socially
valuable and there is a concern that it will not be voluntarily collected,
regulation can mandate collection of the information. In fact, disclosure
mandates imply an obligation to collect the information to be disclosed.
Of course, when the information would not have been collected absent the
mandate, the cost of collection constitutes a cost of the disclosure regulation—a cost that will be passed on, at least in part, to consumers.

At the end of the day, the cost of disclosure will need to be compared to
the cost of alternative regulatory techniques and to the cost of no regulatory
intervention—the welfare costs of the behavioral market failure.

Another normative question involves disclosure and paternalism. Disclosure regulation is often praised for being minimally paternalistic, helping

---

48. Consumers also incur costs of reading the disclosure and processing the disclosed information.
    These costs can be minimized by optimal disclosure design, as described above.
49. Cf. Anthony. T. Kronman, "Mistake, Disclosure, Information, and the Law of Contracts",
    J. Legal Stud., 7 (1987), 1 (arguing that contract law disclosure obligations might deter the
    acquisition of information).
50. Kronman distinguishes between deliberately acquired information and casually acquired
    information, and argues that casually acquired information can be subject to disclosure man-
    dates. *Id.* In Kronman's terms, much of the information that sellers should disclose is casually
    acquired—it would have been acquired by sellers anyway for business reasons.

consumers make better choices, rather than choosing for them. While disclosure mandates are indeed less paternalistic than most other forms of regulation, they are not completely benign or neutral. With simple disclosures, some information is inevitably lost. Regulators decide what is lost and what is emphasized. In addition, disclosure mandates can affect market outcomes. Requiring sellers to prominently disclose a certain product feature can focus competition on this feature, leading sellers to enhance or improve the disclosed feature, at the expense of other, non-disclosed features.[51] Even with disclosure, some measure of paternalism cannot be avoided.

Comprehensive disclosure targeting intermediaries or sellers avoids many of these issues. But this alternative form of disclosure raises its own set of concerns. The services of intermediaries are costly. Not all consumers will avail themselves of these services. Weaker consumers are especially less likely to seek the help of intermediaries. Disclosure mandates that force sellers to share information—specifically, use information—with competing sellers do not impose a direct cost on consumers. Still, they require the consumer to obtain the electronic disclosure and forward it to the competing seller. Here again, less sophisticated consumers are less likely to take even the relatively simple steps required to benefit from the regulation.

Conclusion

This chapter set out to develop a general approach for analyzing consumer markets and, more specifically, consumer contracts. A behavioral-economics model was used to explain how consumer psychology interacts with market forces to influence the design of consumer contracts. The resulting behavioral market failure entails potentially significant welfare costs, which market solutions can reduce but not eliminate. Optimally designed disclosure mandates, while not a panacea, can enhance efficiency and help consumers.

The goal of this chapter was to outline a general approach and highlight common themes. But as noted at the outset, general theorizing can take us only so far. There are many consumer markets and many more consumer contracts. Each market is embedded in a unique historical, institutional, political, and legal context. Most importantly, the underlying currents of

---

51. See also Sunstein, above note 38, at 4.

consumer psychology and market forces, while following common patterns, manifest in unique ways in different markets. When it comes to considering regulatory intervention, a detailed market analysis is imperative. The remainder of this book will undertake such an analysis in three important consumer markets: the credit card market, the mortgage market, and the cell phone market.

Appendix

The Appendix contains a more formal presentation of the ideas presented in Sections I.A.1 and I.A.2. It also provides a more general example, supplementing and extending the example presented in Section I.A.3.

1. General

In the rational-choice framework, a consumer contract provides the consumer with a set of benefits $(b_1, b_2, \ldots)$ in exchange for a set of prices $(p_1, p_2, \ldots)$, while imposing on the seller a set of costs $(c_1, c_2, \ldots)$. It is useful to think about the total expected benefit $B(b_1, b_2, \ldots)$, the total expected price $P(p_1, p_2, \ldots)$, and the total expected cost $C(c_1, c_2, \ldots)$. The number of units sold, which will be referred to as the demand for a seller's product, D, is increasing in the benefit that the product provides, B, and decreasing in the price that the seller charges, P. The demand function is, therefore, $D(B, P)$, with $\frac{\partial D}{\partial B} > 0$ and $\frac{\partial D}{\partial P} < 0$. The seller's revenue, R, is given by the number of units sold, i.e., the demand for the product, multiplied by the price per unit: $R(B, P) = D(B, P) \cdot P$. And the seller's profit, Π, is equal to revenue minus cost: $\Pi(B, P, C) = R(B, P) - D(B, P) \cdot C = D(B, P) \cdot (P - C)$.

When consumers are imperfectly rational, suffering from biases and misperceptions, this general framework must be extended as follows: In addition to the actual benefits $(b_1, b_2, \ldots)$, there are perceived benefits $(\hat{b}_1, \hat{b}_2, \ldots)$, which are potentially different from the actual benefits. And there is a perceived total expected benefit $\hat{B}(\hat{b}_1, \hat{b}_2, \ldots)$, which is potentially different from the actual total expected benefit $B(b_1, b_2, \ldots)$. Similarly, in addition to the actual prices $(p_1, p_2, \ldots)$, there are perceived prices $(\hat{p}_1, \hat{p}_2, \ldots)$, which are potentially different from the actual prices. And there is a perceived total expected price $\hat{P}(\hat{p}_1, \hat{p}_2, \ldots)$, which is potentially different from the actual total expected price $P(p_1, p_2, \ldots)$. Demand is now a function of perceived benefits and prices, rather than of actual benefits and prices: $D(\hat{B}, \hat{P})$, with $\frac{\partial D}{\partial \hat{B}} > 0$ and $\frac{\partial D}{\partial \hat{P}} < 0$. Revenues are a function both of perceived benefits and prices and of the actual price: $R(\hat{B}, \hat{P}, P) = D(\hat{B}, \hat{P}) \cdot P$. And so are profits: $\Pi(\hat{B}, \hat{P}, P, C) = R(\hat{B}, \hat{P}, P) - D(\hat{B}, \hat{P}) \cdot C = D(\hat{B}, \hat{P}) \cdot (P - C)$.[52]

2. The Objects of Misperception

To better understand the objects of misperception, it is useful to introduce the notion of a product feature, and link the benefits, prices, and costs to different product features. To fix ideas, think of a credit card with n features: $(f_1, f_2, \ldots, f_n)$. Each feature of the product can be used more or less intensely. Each product feature can thus be associated with a use intensity level: $(l_1, l_2, \ldots, l_n)$. These use levels can represent both incidence and intensity (as measured in dollars), e.g., how many times per year the consumer borrows and how much money is being borrowed.[53]

Benefits, prices, and costs are naturally associated with product features and their use levels. Starting with costs, for each product feature, there is a per-use cost; namely, a cost for a single incidence of use (or for a single dollar in each incidence of use), and a total cost, which is a function of the per-use cost and the use level. Feature i has a per-use cost of c_i and a total cost of $C_i(c_i, l_i)$. The seller's costs are not directly relevant to consumers and thus are not an object of (consumer) misperception. The discussion of costs and their relation to product features and use levels is provided for completeness.

Prices *are* objects of consumer misperception. Prices are also commonly associated with specific product features and their use levels. Prices are often quoted per unit of use, such that each product feature is associated with a per-use price and a total price, which is a function of the per-use price and the use level. Feature i has a per-use price of p_i and a total price of $P_i(p_i, l_i)$.

The benefits from a product can also be linked to the product's different features. It is useful to think of a benefit per unit of use and of a total benefit associated with each product feature. Feature i has a per-use benefit of b_i and a total benefit of $B_i(b_i, l_i)$.[54]

---

52. A divergence between perceived benefits and prices and actual benefits and prices is possible also in a rational-choice framework, with imperfectly informed consumers. The focus here, however, is on systemic under- and overestimation of benefits and prices. Perfectly rational consumers will not have systemically biased beliefs.

53. In some cases, it is useful to add a general feature, capturing general benefits from having the product, which is unrelated to any use level. More importantly, this allows for a general price element, which is not a function of use. The example provided in section 3 below includes such a general feature.

54. The benefit per unit of use need not be constant across all use units. For example, the per-use benefit associated with a credit card's late payment feature can be a vector of benefits, including a benefit from the first late payment, a different benefit from the second late payment, etc.

What determines the per-use benefit? As explained in the chapter, there are three factors: the product feature itself, the consumer's own preferences as related to the feature, and external factors that influence the per-use benefit from the feature. And what determines the use level? While the intensity with which a product feature will be used has thus far been taken as given, use levels are endogenously determined as a function of the per-use benefit and the per-use price: $l_i = l_i(b_i, p_i)$. This observation allows for a more subtle characterization of benefits and prices. The total price of feature i becomes $P_i(p_i, l_i(b_i, p_i))$. And the total benefit from feature i becomes $B_i(b_i, l_i(b_i, p_i))$.

With this enriched framework in place, the object of misperception can be more accurately identified. Benefit misperception will be considered first, followed by price misperception. The total benefit from the product will be misperceived when the benefits from one, or more, product features are misperceived. Since the benefit from a product feature is a function of the per-use benefit and the use level, misperception of either element will result in misperception of the benefit from the feature. And since the use level is itself a function of the per-use benefit and the per-use price, the benefit from a product feature will be misperceived when the consumer misperceives either the per-use price or one, or more, of the three factors that influence the per-use benefit—the product feature, consumer preferences, and external forces.

The total price of the product will be misperceived when one or more of the feature prices is misperceived. The total price of a product feature will be misperceived when the per-use price or use level is misperceived. And since the use level is itself a function of the per-use benefit and the per-use price, the price of a product feature will be misperceived when the consumer misperceives either the per-use price or one or more of the three factors that influence the per-use benefit: the product feature, consumer preferences, and external forces.

3. Example

a. Benefits, Costs, and Prices

Consider a credit card contract with two features: (1) a general feature or features that may include the convenience of holding the card, access to customer service, etc., and (2) a late payment feature. A consumer obtains an annual benefit $B_1 = 7$ from the general feature(s). This benefit is enjoyed by any consumer who holds the card, independent of any use level. Alternatively, we could define a degenerate use level $l_1 = 1$ and a per-use benefit $b_1 = 7$, which generate a total benefit $B_1 = l_1 \cdot b_1 = 7$. Occasionally, the consumer is short on cash and finds it difficult to make the minimum monthly payment. The consumer, therefore, benefits from the option to pay late—from the late payment feature. Specifically, there are four instances during the year in which the consumer could benefit from paying late. The benefits from late payment vary from one instance to the other, as detailed in Table 1.1. These are per-use benefits.

Table 1.1. Benefit from paying late

Late payment #	1	2	3	4
Benefit	5	5	3	1

When the consumer sees that paying on time is difficult, the decision becomes whether to make an on-time payment despite this difficulty or to pay late. The consumer will pay late when the benefit from paying late (which corresponds to the difficulty of paying on time), as given in Table 1.1, exceeds the late fee charged by the issuer, as described below. The total benefit to the consumer from late payments, B_2, depends on the per-use benefits and on the use level, i.e., on the number of instances, in which the consumer decides to pay late (l_2); if the consumer pays late once, then $B_2(l_2 = 1) = 5$; if the consumer pays late twice, then $B_2(l_2 = 2) = 5 + 5 = 10$; if the consumer pays late three times, then $B_2(l_2 = 3) = 5 + 5 + 3 = 13$, and if the consumer pays late four times, then $B_2(l_2 = 4) = 5 + 5 + 3 + 1 = 14$. The total benefit from late payments, as a function of the number of late payments, is summarized in Table 1.2.

Table 1.2. Total benefit from late payments

Number of late payments (l_2)	1	2	3	4
Total benefit from late payments (B_2)	5	10	13	14

The total benefit to the consumer from the credit card is: $B(l_2) = B_1 + B_2(l_2) = 7 + B_2(l_2)$, where $B_2(l_2)$ is determined as specified above.

As to costs: The issuer incurs a fixed annual cost of 4—a general account maintenance cost associated with the general feature(s): $C_1 = 4$. The issuer also incurs a variable, or per-use, cost of $c_2 = 2$ per incidence of late payment—the cost of processing a late payment and the added risk of default implied by a late payment. Total costs associated with late payments are: $C_2(c_2, l_2) = l_2 \cdot c_2 = l_2 \cdot 2$. The issuer's total costs are: $C = C_1 + C_2 = 4 + l_2 \cdot c_2 = 4 + l_2 \cdot 2$.

The issuer is contemplating a two-dimensional pricing scheme, including an annual fee (p_1) and a late fee (p_2). The annual fee, which can be interpreted as the price of the general feature(s), is independent of any use level. Or, if we define a degenerate use level $l_1 = 1$, the annual fee is the per-use price and the total price associated with the general feature(s) is: $P_1(p_1, l_1) = l_1 \cdot p_1 = 1 \cdot p_1 = p_1$. The late fee is the per-use price of the late payment feature. The total price of paying late is a function of this per-use price and of the use level—each year the consumer pays p_2 multiplied by the number of late payments per year, l_2: $P_2(p_2, l_2) = l_2 \cdot p_2$. The total amount that a consumer pays per year is: $P(p_1, l_1, p_2, l_2) = P_1(p_1, l_1) + P_2(p_2, l_2) = p_1 + l_2 \cdot p_2$. To simplify notation, the use-level arguments will sometimes be omitted from the total price functions: $P_1(p_1, l_1) = P_1(p_1) = p_1$, $P_2(p_2,l_2) = P_2(p_2) = l_2 \cdot p_2$, and $P(p_1, l_1, p_2, l_2) = P(p_1, p_2) = p_1 + l_2 \cdot p_2$.

b. Misperceptions

A rational consumer will accurately perceive the benefit, $B = B_1 + B_2$, and the price, $P = P_1 + P_2$. An imperfectly rational consumer might not. For the imperfectly rational consumer, there will be a perceived benefit, $\hat{B} = \hat{B}_1 + \hat{B}_2$, and a perceived price $\hat{P} = \hat{P}_1 + \hat{P}_2$. The perceived benefits and prices will generally diverge from the actual benefits and prices. This divergence will affect the equilibrium pricing scheme.

To see this, the form of consumer (mis)perception needs to be specified. Suppose the consumer accurately perceives the general benefit from card use, i.e., $\hat{B}_1=B_1=7$ and the amount to be paid in annual fees, i.e., $\hat{P}_1=P_1=p_1$. Misperception concerns the benefits and costs of paying late. There are two cases:

> Case (1): The consumer mistakenly thinks that there will never be cash flow problems or late payments. (Alternatively, the possibility of paying late might never cross the consumer's mind.) The misperceived benefits from late payments are listed in Table 1.1a(1) below.

> Case (2): The consumer realizes that there will be cash flow problems and thus benefit from paying late, but underestimates this benefit. Specifically, assume that the consumer underestimates the benefit from paying late in the second and third instances, as described in Table 1.1a(2) below.

Case (1) and Case (2) are both examples of misperception of per-use benefit(s) that will result in product-use mistakes.[55]

Table 1.1a(1). Perceived benefit from paying late—Case (1)

Late payment #	1	2	3	4
Benefit	5	5	3	1
Perceived benefit	0	0	0	0

Table 1.1a(2). Perceived benefit from paying late—Case (2)

Late payment #	1	2	3	4
Benefit	5	5	3	1
Perceived benefit	5	1	1	1

55. In this example, the consumer makes a deliberate, and rational, ex post decision whether to pay late; the imperfect rationality concerns the ex ante misperception about the decision that will be made ex post. A different example would assume both ex post and ex ante imperfect rationality: Ex post consumers inadvertently miss the deadline and end up paying late, and ex ante consumers underestimate the likelihood that they will inadvertently pay late and, consequently, underestimate the total amount they will pay in late fees.

c. Contract Design

How will the issuer design the credit card contract? How will the magnitudes of the annual fee (p_1) and late fee (p_2) be determined? The answers depend on consumer psychology and market structure. For ease of exposition and to focus attention on the effect of consumer misperception, assume that the issuer is operating in a competitive market and thus will set prices that will just cover the cost of providing the credit card.

Recall that the issuer faces a fixed annual cost of 4 and a variable cost of 2 per incidence of late payment. Facing a rational consumer, the issuer will set $p_1 = 4$ and $p_2 = 2$. The (4,2) contract guarantees that the issuer's costs are covered. And it maximizes the net benefit enjoyed by the consumer. With a late fee of 2, the consumer will make three late payments for a benefit of 13 (see Table 1.2). The total benefit from the card will be $7 + 13 = 20$. The total price will be $4 + 3 \cdot 2 = 10$. And the net benefit will be 10 ($= 20 - 10$). Any alternative contract will be less efficient.[56]

For example, a lower late fee, say 0.5, would induce the consumer to make four late payments for a total benefit of 14, rather than 13 under the (4,2) contract. But the resulting increase in the annual fee won't be worth the extra unit of benefit. With four late payments, the issuer's total cost would be $4 + 4 \cdot 2 = 12$. Since revenues from late fees will be only $4 \cdot 0.5 = 2$, the issuer will have to charge an annual fee of 10 to break even. With the alternative (10,0.5) contract, the consumer will thus face a total price of $10 + 4 \cdot 0.5 = 12$ and a net benefit of $7 + 14 - 12 = 9$—lower than the net benefit of 10 under the (4,2) contract.

A higher late fee of, say, 4, would also reduce efficiency. With $p_2 = 4$, the consumer will make two late payments for a total benefit of 10. The issuer's total cost would be $4 + 2 \cdot 2 = 8$. Since revenues from late fees, $2 \cdot 4 = 8$, cover all costs, the issuer, operating in a competitive market, will set a zero annual fee. With the alternative (0,4) contract, the consumer will thus face a total price of $0 + 2 \cdot 4 = 8$ and a net benefit of $7 + 10 - 8 = 9$—lower than the net benefit of 10 under the (4,2) contract.

The efficiency of the (4,2) contract is a result of the general efficiency of marginal cost pricing. A late fee set equal to the issuer's cost from late payment provides optimal incentives for consumers—to pay late only when the benefit to them of late payment exceeds the cost of late payment to the issuer.

The efficient (4,2) contract will *not* be offered to an imperfectly rational consumer. Starting with Case (1), the consumer mistakenly believes that there will never be a benefit realized by paying late and thus that he will never make a late payment and never incur a late fee. For such a consumer, the perceived benefit from the credit

56. In this example, because of the discrete nature of the benefit function, there are other contracts that are as efficient as the (4,2) contract. In a more general framework, the (4,2) contract will be strictly more efficient than any other contract.

card is $\hat{B} = \hat{B}_1 + \hat{B}_2 = 7 + 0 = 7$, the perceived total price is $\hat{P}(4, 2) = \hat{P}_1(4) + \hat{P}_2(2)$ $= 4 + 0 = 4$, and the perceived net benefit is 3 (= 7 − 4). The efficient (4, 2) contract will not be offered in equilibrium, because other contracts appear more attractive to the biased consumer, while still covering the issuer's costs. Consider the (0,4) contract, which, as explained above, induces two late payments and just covers the issuer's costs given these two late payments. (While ex ante biased consumers believe that they will never pay late, ex post they will pay late when the benefit exceeds the late fee.) With this contract, the biased consumer perceives a total benefit of $\hat{B} = \hat{B}_1$ $+ \hat{B}_2 = 7 + 0 = 7$, a total price of $\hat{P}(0, 4) = \hat{P}_1(0) + \hat{P}_2(4) = 0 + 0 = 0$, and a net benefit of 7 (= 7 − 0). The biased consumer will thus prefer the (0,4) contract over the efficient (4,2) contract, even though the latter contract provides more value.

Similar results obtain in Case (2), where the consumer recognizes the potential benefits from paying late, but underestimates these benefits. Specifically, as described in Table 1.1a(2), the consumer mistakenly thinks that the benefits from the second and third late payment are 1 each, while in fact they are 5 and 3, respectively. The efficient (4,2) contract sets a late fee $p_2 = 2$, which means that the consumer will pay late whenever the benefit of paying late is larger than 2. Therefore, the consumer will pay late three times, gaining a benefit of 13 (= 5 + 5 + 3) from these late payments, but the consumer mistakenly believes that there will only be one late payment for a benefit of 5. For this consumer, the perceived benefit from the credit card is $\hat{B} = \hat{B}_1 + \hat{B}_2 = 7 + 5 = 12$, the perceived total price is $\hat{P}(4, 2) = \hat{P}_1(4) + \hat{P}_2(2) = 4 + 1 \cdot 2 = 6$, and the perceived net benefit is 6 (= 12 − 6). As in Case (1), the efficient(4,2) contract will not be offered in equilibrium, because other contracts appear more attractive to the biased consumer, while still covering the issuer's costs. Consider the (0,4) contract, which, as in Case (1), induces two late payments and just covers the issuer's costs given these two late payments. With this contract, the biased consumer perceives a total benefit of $\hat{B} = \hat{B}_1 + \hat{B}_2 = 7 + 5 = 12$, a total price of $\hat{P}(0, 4) = \hat{P}_1(0) + \hat{P}_2(4)$ $= 0 + 1 \cdot 4 = 4$, and a net benefit of 8 (= 12 − 4). The biased consumer will thus prefer the (0, 4) contract over the efficient (4, 2) contract, even though the latter contract provides more value.

In both cases, while the initial bias pertains to underestimation of benefits, contract design is used to maximize the underestimation of price, in order to produce the maximal perceived net benefit. Use patterns provide the link between perceived benefit and perceived price. Underestimated benefits result in underestimated use. Contract design amplifies the effect of the product-use mistake on the perceived total price.

This feature of the example appears in many real-world scenarios. Contract design is used to minimize the perceived total price, by amplifying the effect of product-use mistakes. When the perceived likelihood of triggering a certain price dimension goes down, the magnitude of the corresponding price goes up. Non-salient prices rise, while salient prices are reduced. A price is non-salient, because consumers think it will never be triggered, or because the issue (for example, the possibility of paying late) never crosses the consumer's mind.

2

Credit Cards

Introduction

Credit cards are a significant socio-economic phenomenon. In 2008, consumers used almost 1.5 billion credit cards—more than 12 cards per household—to purchase over $2 trillion of goods and services. The average household spent $18,000 in credit card transactions, which is more than 35 percent of median household income in the U.S. Credit cards are also the largest source of non-secured credit. Credit card debt amounted to $976 billion in 2008.[1]

Credit cards have been the subject of heated political debate for many years.[2] Recently, in the wake of the financial crisis, Congress passed the Credit Card Accountability, Responsibility, and Disclosure (CARD) Act of 2009, which imposes substantial constraints on credit card issuers. The Dodd–Frank Wall Street Reform and Consumer Protection Act of 2010 established a new Consumer Financial Protection Bureau charged with more closely overseeing consumer credit markets, including the credit card market.

1. See Bureau of the Census, *Statistical Abstract of the United States: 2011*, tbls. 689, 1187 (hereinafter "2011 Statistical Abstract") (tbl. 689 lists the number of households: 117,181,000, and median household income: $50,303; tbl. 1187 lists the total number of credit cards, the total credit card purchase volume, and the total amount of credit card debt). See also Thomas A. Durkin, "Consumers and Credit Disclosures: Credit Cards and Credit Insurance" (2002) *Fed. Reserve Bull.*, April, at 202 ("Much of the growth of consumer credit in recent years has been in the form of revolving credit, of which credit card credit is the largest component."); Teresa A. Sullivan, Elizabeth Warren, and Jay Lawrence Westbrook, *The Fragile Middle Class: Americans in Debt* (Yale University Press, 2000) 129 ("As the fastest growing proportion of consumer debt, credit card debt has led the way to bankruptcy for an increasing number of Americans. . . . ").
2. In particular, Congress repeatedly debated whether to reinstate usury ceilings. See, e.g., H.R. 78, 100th Cong. (1987), S. 242, 100th Cong. (1987), S. 647, 100th Cong. (1987), H.R. 3769, 102nd Cong. (1991), H.R. 3860, 102nd Cong. (1991), S.AMDTs 1333–34 to S. 543, 102nd Cong. (1991), H.R. 4132, 103rd Cong. (1994). The many proposed usury bills did not mature into law. Rather, Congress opted for a mandatory disclosure policy, as part of the Truth-in-Lending Act, 15 U.S.C. §§ 1601 et seq.

This chapter focuses on the credit card contract. It identifies two features common to most credit card contracts; complexity and deferred costs. In the pages that follow, I'll present a behavioral-economics theory of credit card contracts, and then argue that complexity and deferred costs represent a strategic response by sophisticated issuers to imperfectly rational cardholders. There is a behavior market failure in the credit card industry that reduces efficiency and hurts cardholders. Regulatory intervention can help minimize the adverse effects of this market failure.

A. Contract Design

The common credit card contract is highly complex. The fees and interest rates are staggering in both number and complexity. There are annual fees, cash-advance fees, balance-transfer fees, foreign currency-conversion fees, expedited-payment fees, no-activity fees, late fees, over-limit fees, and returned-check fees. As for interest rates, in addition to the primary, long-term interest rate, there are introductory (teaser) rates, rates on balances transferred from other cards, rates on cash advances, and default interest rates. That's not all: Most of these fees and interest rates are variable and multidimensional, triggered by complex sets of conditions.

Credit card contracts also feature deferred costs and accelerated benefits. The multiple price dimensions of the credit card do not always track the issuer's underlying cost structure. Rather, issuers set lower prices for salient, usually short-term dimensions and higher prices for non-salient, usually long-term dimensions. Consider, for example, the prevalence of low, even zero, introductory interest rates alongside much higher long-term interest rates—not to mention the even higher default interest rates. Similarly, we often see no per-transaction fees, and even negative per-transaction fees positioned as benefits provided by loyalty programs—alongside high currency-conversion fees, late fees, and over-limit fees.

B. Contract Design Explained

Why do credit card contracts couple a high level of complexity with cost deferral? To find out, let's first explore a series of standard, rational-choice theories. These theories do a better, though not completely satisfactory, job of explaining the complexity dimension.

Multiple price dimensions are needed for efficient risk-based pricing and optimal tailoring of the credit card product to the needs of heterogeneous cardholders. Deferred costs are more difficult to explain within a rational-choice, efficiency-based model. Therefore, the design of credit card contracts, especially the deferred-cost feature, cannot be fully explained within a traditional, rational-choice framework. What's needed is an alternative, behavioral-economic theory of the credit card contract.

Complexity plays into the imperfect rationality of cardholders. As we saw in the previous chapter, the imperfectly rational cardholder deals with complexity by ignoring it. Decision problems are simplified by ignoring non-salient price dimensions and "guesstimating," rather than calculating, the impact of the salient dimensions that cannot be ignored. In particular, the imperfectly rational cardholder's limited attention and limited memory might result in the exclusion of certain price dimensions from consideration. And limited processing ability might prevent cardholders from accurately aggregating the different price components into a single, total expected price that would serve as the basis for choosing the optimal card.

Increased complexity may be attractive to issuers, as it allows them to hide the true cost of the credit card in a multidimensional pricing maze. An issuer who understands the imperfectly rational response to complexity can leverage complexity to create an appearance of a lower total price without actually lowering the price. For example, if the currency-conversion fee and the cash-advance fee are not salient to cardholders, issuers will raise the magnitude of these price dimensions. Increasing these non-salient prices will not hurt demand. On the contrary, it will enable the issuer to attract cardholders by reducing more salient price dimensions or by increasing more salient benefit dimensions, such as reward points and frequent-flyer miles. As discussed in the previous chapter, this strategy depends on the existence of non-salient price dimensions. When the number of price dimensions goes up, the number of non-salient price dimensions can also be expected to go up. Issuers thus have a strong incentive to increase complexity and multidimensionality.

The behavioral-economics explanation for deferred costs is based on evidence that future costs are often underestimated. When future costs are underestimated, contracts with deferred-cost features become more attractive to cardholders and thus to issuers. Underestimation of future costs can be traced back, in large part, to two underlying cognitive biases: myopia and optimism. Myopic cardholders focus on short-term benefits and pay

insufficient attention to long-term costs. Optimistic cardholders underestimate their future borrowing and, as a result, underestimate the significance
of the many credit card price dimensions that are contingent upon borrowing. There are two main reasons why cardholders might underestimate their
future borrowing: (a) they might underestimate their self-control problems,
and (b) they might underestimate the likelihood of contingencies bearing
economic hardship. Optimism about one's self-control and about one's
future financial condition drive the underestimation bias.

When non-salient, long-term dimensions are underestimated or ignored
by cardholders, issuers may raise prices on these dimensions of the credit
card contract. In a competitive market, the high prices on these long-term
dimensions will pay for low prices on the salient, short-term dimensions
that drive demand for the credit card product. This interaction between
consumer psychology and market forces produces contracts with deferred
costs and accelerated benefits.

So far, the credit card contract has been portrayed as a tool designed to
exploit consumer biases. Interestingly, to the extent that the credit card market is competitive, issuers *must* exploit consumers' imperfect rationality in
order to survive in this market. Issuers that do not take advantage of consumer biases and, instead, offer lower long-term prices with reduced short-
term perks would not succeed in the marketplace. Consumers would fail to
appreciate the value of reduced long-term prices and would take their business elsewhere. On the other hand, competition could have a positive effect
by creating incentives for issuers to educate consumers and reduce the biases
and misperceptions that give rise to excessive complexity and cost deferral.

C. Welfare Implications

The imperfect rationality of cardholders and the contractual design that
responds to this imperfect rationality impose several welfare costs. First, the
complexity of credit card contracts makes it difficult for consumers to comparison-shop effectively, thus hindering competition in the credit card market. Second, since credit card pricing is, in many cases, salience-based rather
than cost-based, these prices provide inefficient incentives for credit card use.
Zero annual and per-transaction fees, coupled with benefits programs, result
in the creation of too many credit cards and excessive use of these cards.
Teaser rates lead to excessive pre-distress borrowing, which renders the
consumer more vulnerable to financial hardships. Moreover, salience-based

pricing creates an appearance of a cheaper product without actually offering a cheaper product, resulting in artificially inflated demand for credit cards.

Efficiency isn't the only thing threatened by the distorted pricing in the credit card market. Since the high borrowing-related costs are paid by financially weaker cardholders, the behavioral market failure also raises distributional concerns.

D. Policy Implications

The welfare costs cited above provide a *prima facie* case for legal intervention. Cardholder misperceptions that underlie the identified welfare costs also qualify the no-intervention presumption of the freedom-of-contract paradigm. If a contracting party misconceives the future consequences of the contract, then the normative power of contractual consent is significantly weakened.

This chapter focuses on one, common regulatory technique; disclosure mandates. The behavioral-economics model challenges the conventional disclosure approach, which focuses almost exclusively on disclosure of product-attribute information such as interest rates and fees. Issuers should also be required to disclose product-use information. If a consumer mistakenly believes that he or she will never make a late payment, disclosing the magnitude of the late fee will not affect the consumer's credit card choice. Because issuers know more about a consumer's card-related use patterns than the consumers themselves do, they should be required to share this information. Issuers should tell consumers how likely they are to pay late.

Legislators and regulators are beginning to recognize the importance of product-use disclosures. The Dodd–Frank Wall Street Reform and Consumer Protection Act of 2010 imposes a general duty, subject to rules prescribed by the new Consumer Financial Protection Bureau, to disclose information, including usage data, in markets for consumer financial products.[3] And Federal Reserve Board regulations, which took effect along with the CARD Act implementing rules, require that issuers disclose, on the monthly statement, monthly and year-to-date totals of interest charges and fees—a disclosure that combines product-attribute and product-use information.[4] These are important first steps.

---

3. Pub. L. 111–203, Title X, Sec. 1033.
4. CFPB, CARD Act Factsheet <http://www.consumerfinance.gov/credit-cards/credit-card-act/feb2011-factsheet/>.

I conclude this chapter with guidelines for additional steps. At a general level, the benefits of more information should be balanced against the risk that information overload will prevent the imperfectly rational consumer from reading and understanding the disclosed information. There are two solutions to this problem. The first solution relies on simple, total-cost disclosures that combine product-attribute and product-use information. Consumers, choosing among different credit card offers, would then face a straightforward task; choose the card with the lowest total cost. The second solution relies on intermediaries that would digest the information for consumers. Such intermediaries already exist, but they need help from regulators, who could require, for example, that product-use information be available in electronic form.

The remainder of this chapter is organized as follows:

- Part I provides background on the credit card market.
- Part II describes the common credit card contract, focusing on the two identified design features: complexity and cost deferral.
- Part III evaluates possible rational-choice, efficiency-based explanations for the identified design features.
- Part IV develops an alternative, behavioral-economics theory of contract design in the credit card market.
- Part V identifies the welfare costs of cardholder misperception and of contracts designed in response to these misperceptions.
- Part VI discusses market solutions, specifically consumer-friendly credit cards and debit cards.
- Part VII explores legal policy responses, focusing on disclosure regulation.

I. The Credit Card Market

A. Two Functions

What is a credit card? It is a flat, $3\frac{3}{8}$" by $2\frac{1}{8}$" piece of plastic engraved with a name and an account number. This "plastic," as it's commonly known, allows its holder to perform two distinct tasks; to transact quickly and efficiently, and to borrow—to finance a purchase, business, or way of life. Though offered through the same piece of plastic, transacting and financing functions constitute two distinct services provided by the credit card issuer.

Of course, the credit card holder is not required to make use of both functions. Some transact but do not borrow, using the credit card only as a method of payment. While the number of people who use a credit card in this way is not insignificant, most cardholders use both the transacting and financing services provided by their cards.[5]

B. A Brief History

The term "credit card" was coined back in 1887 by Edward Bellamy in his utopian socialist novel, *Looking Backward*. Bellamy provided a futuristic account of the year 2000, when credit cards had entirely supplanted cash. He was not off by much. In 2008, payment cards (credit cards, charge cards, and debit cards) accounted for more than 50 percent of transaction volume in the U.S.[6]

The history of consumer credit in the more modern world began in the early twentieth century, when Sears Roebuck and Company started lending money to its customers so that they could buy the Sears products. Thus, the merchant card (or retail card) was born. Back then, however, the merchant card was only accepted by the merchant that provided the specific card.[7]

The path to the contemporary credit card wound its way through the so-called Travel & Entertainment (T&E) cards, which were special-purpose charge cards that, in time, evolved into all-purpose cards. The Diner's Club card led the way in 1949, followed by American Express and Carte

---

5. See Brian K. Bucks et al., "Changes in U.S. Family Finances from 2004 to 2007: Evidence from the Survey of Consumer Finances", *Fed. Reserve Bull.,* vol. 95 (February 2009), A1-A55 (based on the 2007 Survey of Consumer Finances, 73 percent of families had at least one credit card, and among those families 60.3 percent carried a balance); David S. Evans and Richard Schmalensee, *Paying with Plastic* (MIT Press, 1999) 211 (transactors "comprise roughly a third of cardholders but account for about half of charge volume").

6. For Bellamy's account—see Lawrence M. Ausubel, "The Credit Card Industry: A History, by Lewis Mandell" *J. Econ. Lit.* 30 (1992) 1517, 1518 (book review). For actual payment card transaction volume—see 2011 Statistical Abstract, above note 1, tbls. 683, 1186, 1187 (tbl. 683 lists the number of consumer units: 120,770,000, and the average annual total expenditure per consumer unit: $50,486, the product of which is the total annual expenditure: approximately $6.10 trillion; tbl. 1187 lists the total debit card purchase volume: 1,347 billion; tbl. 1187 lists the total credit card purchase volume: 2,153 billion; the combined—debit card and credit card—purchase volume is $3.5 trillion). See also Ronald Mann, "Adopting, Using, and Discarding Paper and Electronic Payment Instruments: Variation by Age and Race" (2011). *FRB of Boston Public Policy Discussion Paper No. 11-2.* Available at SSRN: <http://ssrn.com/abstract=186216>.

7. Sullivan, Warren, and Westbrook, above note 1, at 109 ("Sears, and then other retailers, gave consumers the credit that banks would not give them."). The company's first application form asked, "How long at your present address?" and "How many cows do you milk?" *Id.*

Blanche, which entered the market in 1958. The T&E cards, while gradually evolving into all-purpose cards, remained charge cards, rather than credit cards, meaning that the balance on these cards was due in full at the end of each month.[8]

In the mid-1960s, with the advent of the Visa and MasterCard systems, the modern credit card was born, combining the all-purpose feature of the evolved T&E cards with the credit feature of the merchant cards. The Visa and MasterCard bankcards grew rapidly as they added more and more bank issuers and merchants to their networks. In 1985, Sears Roebuck and Company introduced its own all-purpose credit card, the Discover card. American Express joined the credit card scene with its Optima card in the late 1980s. As Sullivan, Warren, and Westbrook put it: "By the 1990s the all-purpose card gained dominance over traditional store cards, making it possible for millions of card holders to charge anything from their dental fillings to their parking tickets."[9]

For credit card issuers, the initial steps on the road to success were shaky. With strict usury laws in place that mandated caps on interest rates, issuers initially lost money on their credit card business. The banking industry eventually overcame the strict interest-rate ceilings in an ingenious way. Instead of lobbying each state legislature for more lenient usury laws, the industry targeted, in the Federal courts, the jurisdictional issue of the "exportation" of interest rates, the question being "which state's usury ceiling constrains the interest rate if a bank located in one state issues a credit card to a consumer in a different state."[10]

In 1978, the exportation question reached the United States Supreme Court. The Court, in *Marquette National Bank v. First of Omaha Service Corporation*, ruled that the applicable usury ceiling was the one set by the state in which the issuing bank was located. In effect, the Supreme Court

---

8. *Id.* See also Lewis Mandell, *The Credit Card Industry: A History* (Twayne Publishers, 1990) 1–3 (an historical account of the conception of the Diner's card); Evans and Schmalensee, above note 5, at 10–11 (describing the entry of the American Express and Carte Blanche cards).

9. Sullivan, Warren, and Westbrook, above note 1, at 109; Evans and Schmalensee, above note 5, at 10–11.

10. On the shaky initial steps—see Evans and Schmalensee, above note 5, at 68–9, 73; Lawrence M. Ausubel, "Credit Card Defaults, Credit Card Profits, and Bankruptcy" *Am. Bankr. L.J.* 71 (1997) 249, 260–1 ("Before 1982, credit card interest rates were subject to usury ceilings in most states. These ceilings on interest rates limited credit card profitability during periods, such as 1974–1975 and 1980–1981, when market interest rates on Treasury bills and corporate bonds spiked upward. This led to a sharply-reduced or negative return on assets for credit card activity during such years.") On the interest rate "exportation" solution—see Ausubel, *id.*

"gave banks the option of shifting their credit card operations to wholly owned subsidiaries situated in states without usury laws." The *Marquette* decision fired the opening shot in the inter-state race to attract credit card issuers. To win this race, or to, at minimum, prevent an exodus of banks, many states substantially increased their interest caps or revoked their usury laws altogether. Thus, the *Marquette* decision produced a functionally deregulated credit card market. Moreover, the decision enabled credit card issuers to operate on a national level and thus to enjoy economies of scale.[11]

The sky-high inflation of the late 1970s and early 1980s lifted the final barrier to the profitability of the credit card industry. With the effective abolition of usury laws, credit card interest rates rose to match the high inflation rates. In fact, the causation probably worked in both directions; the high inflation rates were likely instrumental in bringing about the legal rulings (specifically the *Marquette* decision) that triggered the abolition of usury ceilings. Whatever the sequence, credit card interest rates rose with inflation.[12]

As high inflation justified raising interest rates in the late 1970s and early 1980s, the subsequent decline in the inflation rate starting in 1982–83 might have been expected to bring about a reduction in those rates. This reduction, however, never came or, more accurately, was very late to arrive (see below).[13]

The early history of the credit card industry was marked by declining costs and "sticky" interest rates. The high interest rates, which stubbornly failed to keep pace with the declining cost of funds, allowed credit card issuers to offer more credit and to target less credit-worthy consumers.[14]

---

11. The Supreme Court's decision is at 439 U.S. 299 (1978) (henceforth "the *Marquette* decision"). In *Marquette* the Court interpreted 12 U.S.C. § 85. For the implications of the *Marquette* decision—see Lawrence M. Ausubel, "The Failure of Competition in the Credit Card Market" *Amer. Econ. Rev.* 81 (1991) 50, 52; Sullivan, Warren, and Westbrook, above note 1, at 248–9; Evans and Schmalensee, above note 5, at 6, 71–2.

12. See Sullivan, Warren, and Westbrook, above note 1, at 248–9 ("All that changed with the sky-high inflation of the late 1970s and early 1980s. With inflation in double digits, Congress and the Supreme Court effectively legalized what had been usury, overriding the restrictive state laws.").

13. Sullivan, Warren, and Westbrook, above note 1, at 255 ("[T]he single biggest cost for a credit card issuer is the cost of funds for the money it lends to borrowers who repay over time. Between 1980 and 1992, the rate at which banks borrow money fell from 13.4 percent to 3.5 percent. During the same time, the average credit card interest rate rose from 17.3 percent to 17.8 percent. Thus during the period that the credit card issuers' largest cost was plummeting, they were raising the price of credit to their consumers."). See also *id.* at 18–19, 248–9; Ausubel, above note 11, at 53–5.

14. Alternatively, the declining cost of funds led issuers to extend credit to less credit-worthy consumers, and the increased risk prevented the decline in interest rates.

The result: An explosion of consumer credit, which led to a dramatic expansion of consumer debt and also to an increase in consumer bankruptcy rates.[15]

The more recent history of the credit card industry, starting in the early 1990s, has been marked by the technological advances that made risk-based pricing possible. The ability to match interest rates (and other price dimensions) to borrower risk allowed issuers to serve less creditworthy borrowers, thus fueling the continuing expansion of credit cards. Risk-based pricing implies lower interest rates for low-risk consumers and high rates for high-risk consumers. It does not, however, imply a reduction in average rates. But such a reduction did finally occur, starting in the early 1990s, as competition focused on the interest rate, which became more salient to consumers.[16]

C. Economic Significance

Credit cards are a major method of payment, and their prevalence and importance is only growing. By 1995, credit cards had already surpassed cash as a method of payment. In 2008, consumers used almost 1.5 billion credit cards (more than 12 cards per household) to purchase over $2 trillion of goods and services. The average household completed $18,000 of credit card transactions, over 35 percent of the median household income.[17]

The credit card industry has experienced a significant growth rate by any measure, be it transaction volume, number of cards in circulation, or outstanding balances. While in 1970 only 16 percent of households had credit

---

15. Diane Ellis, "The Effect of Consumer Interest Rate Deregulation on Credit Card Volumes, Charge-Offs and the Personal Bankruptcy Rate" (1998) 98–05 Bank Trends (identifying the link between the repeal of usury rates, the increase in consumer credit, and the rise in bankruptcy filing rates). The historical link between the rise of the credit card and the explosion of consumer debt is quite significant. See James Medoff and Andrew Harless, *The Indebted Society: Anatomy of An Ongoing Disaster* (Little Brown & Co., 1996) 9 ("Since the introduction of credit cards, the debt level of the typical American has risen far out of proportion to his or her income.").

16. On the development and implications of risk-based pricing—see Mark Furletti (2003) "Credit Card Pricing Developments and Their Disclosure" (January 2003) (*Fed. Res. Bank of Philadelphia, Payment Cards Center, Discussion Paper,* available at <http://www.phil.frb.org/pcc/papers/2003/CreditCardPricing_012003.pdf>. For the eventual reduction in interest rates—see below, II.B.2.

17. On cards vs. cash—see Sullivan, Warren, and Westbrook, above note 1, at 108; Evans and Schmalensee, above note 5, at 25–6. For the 2008 figures—see 2011 Statistical Abstract, above note 1 (tbl. 689 lists the number of households: 117,181,000, and median household income: $50,303; tbl. 1187 lists the total number of credit cards and the total credit card purchase volume).

cards, 73 percent of households had at least one credit card in 2007. The average monthly household charge was over $1,500 in 2008, as compared to only $165 (in current dollars) in 1970. And the ratio of charges-to-income grew from just under 4 percent in 1970 to about 35 percent in 2008. Credit cards' piece of the total consumer spending pie has increased substantially. A growing body of evidence suggests that they have also contributed to the increase in the size of the consumer spending pie.[18]

Not only do credit cards encourage spending, they encourage borrowing as well. As noted by Sullivan, Warren, and Westbrook:

> Credit card debt has become as much a part of American life as has the credit
> card itself.... Of the three-quarters of all households that have at least one
> credit card, three out of four of them also carry credit card debt from month
> to month.... Increasingly, ... [Americans] do not pay [with their credit cards]—
> they finance. Quietly, without much fanfare, Americans have taken to buying
> school shoes and pizza with debt—and paying for those items over months or
> even years.[19]

18. On the growth of the credit card industry—see generally Evans and Schmalensee, above note 5, at 235–6 ("Between 1971 and 1997, the number of cards in circulation increased by more than 900 percent, while the number of households increased by only 54 percent. The total dollar value of credit card transactions increased by 2,630 percent in that same period while personal consumption expenditures increased by 125 percent. Finally, outstanding balances increased by 2,700 percent while total consumer credit outstanding increased by 140 per-cent.... Payment cards have grown at the expense of other means of payment and other sources of credit.") For the 1970 figures—see Evans and Schmalensee, above note 5, at 85–7, 240 (for 1970, Evans and Schmalensee report an average household charge of $125 in 1998 dollars, which is equivalent to $165 using the CPI). For the 2007 figure—see Bucks et al., above note 5, at A1–A55 (based on the 2007 Survey of Consumer Finances). For the 2008 figures—see 2011 Statistical Abstract, above note 1, tbls. 689, 1187 (for 2008 figures) (the aver-age monthly household charge was calculated by dividing annual credit card purchase volume—$2,153 bil., from tbl. 1157—by the number of households—117,181,000, from tbl. 689—and then by 12, to get monthly figures; the charges to income ratio was calculated by dividing the average household charge by the median household income—$50,303, from tbl. 689). On credit cards and consumer spending—see Lloyd Klein, *It's In The Cards: Consumer Credit and the American Experience* (Praeger, 1999) ("Credit cards facilitated the rise of consumer spending for consumer products or services."); Elizabeth C. Hirschman, "Differences in Con-sumer Purchase Behavior by Credit Card Payment System", *J. Consumer Res.*, 6 (1979), 58 (people who own more credit cards make larger purchases per department store visit); Richard A. Feinberg, "Credit Cards as Spending Facilitating Stimuli: A Conditioning Interpretation", *J. Consumer Res.*, 12 (1986), 384 (restaurant tips are larger when payment is by credit card); Drazen Prelec and Duncan Simester, "Always Leave Home Without It: A Further Investiga-tion of the Credit-Card Effect on Willingness to Pay", *Marketing Letters*, 12 (2001), 5 (respond-ents offered significantly higher prices for Celtics and Red Sox tickets when paying by credit card). These studies preclude a liquidity constraints explanation for the credit card effect. See, e.g., *id.* at 10.

19. Sullivan, Warren, and Westbrook, above note 1, at 110–11. See also David B. Gross and Nicho-las S. Souleles, "Do Liquidity Constraints and Interest Rates Matter for Consumer Behavior?

Credit cards are now the leading source of unsecured consumer credit/debt. And consumers aren't the only ones who use credit card financing; many self-employed owners of small businesses turn to high-interest credit card debt to finance their businesses.[20]

Total credit card borrowing in 2008 amounted to $976 billion. The average credit card debt per household in the U.S. was over $8,300 in 2008. If we focus on the 73 percent of households with credit cards, average debt per household rises to over $11,400. The average debt among the 60 percent of households that carry credit card debt was over $19,000 in 2008. The median credit card debt-to-income ratio was 16.5 percent across all households, 22.7 percent for households with credit cards, and 37.8 percent for households that carry credit card debt. Clearly, credit card debt imposes a substantial burden on many households.[21]

It is not surprising, then, that credit card debt plays a notoriously important role in consumer bankruptcy. Credit card defaults are highly correlated with personal bankruptcies. Based on their empirical investigation of consumer bankruptcy filings, Sullivan, Warren, and Westbrook conclude that "[a]s the fastest growing proportion of consumer debt, credit card debt has led the way to bankruptcy for an increasing number of Americans.... " Three independent statistical studies, by Ronald Mann, by Atif Mian and Amir

Evidence from Credit Card Data", Q. J. Econ., 117 (2002), 149, 151 (Of all households with at least one bankcard "at least 56 percent—a remarkably large fraction—are borrowing on their bankcards, that is, paying interest, not just transacting." These figures, which are based on SCF data, significantly understate the percentage of households with credit card debt, since SCF households substantially underreport their credit card debt.); Klein, above note 18, at 29 ("[t]he 'me generation,' actualized through credit card utilization, was transformed into a debt carrying 'greed generation' wanting and buying everything in sight.")

20. See Sullivan, Warren, and Westbrook, above note 1, at 115–17; Evans and Schmalensee, above note 5, at 34, 103–7.

21. For total and average per-household credit card debt—see 2011 Statistical Abstract, above note 1, tbl. 689, 1187 (average per-household debt was calculated by dividing total credit card borrowing by the number of households—117,181,000, from tbl. 689). For the percentage of households with credit cards and for the share of those households that carry debt—see Bucks et al., above note 5, at A1–A55 (based on the 2007 Survey of Consumer Finances, 73 percent of families had at least one credit card, and among those families 60.3 percent carried a balance). The debt-to-income ratios were calculated by dividing the average debt figures above by the median household income—$50,303. See 2011 Statistical Abstract, above note 1, tbl. 689. The debt-to-income ratio has been growing. See Sullivan, Warren, and Westbrook, above note 1, at 18 ("[R]eal consumer debt has risen dramatically over a long period during which real incomes for many people have stayed the same or declined.") See generally Durkin, above note 1, at 202 ("Much of the growth of consumer credit in recent years has been in the form of revolving credit, of which credit card credit is the largest component."); Sullivan, Warren, and Westbrook, above note 1, at 129 ("As the

Sufi, and by Michelle White, suggest a causal relationship between credit card debt and consumer bankruptcy filings.[22]

D. Market Structure

1. Participants

The credit card market is divided among the major credit card brands: Visa, MasterCard, American Express, and Discover. The bankcard brands, Visa and MasterCard, share a common and more complex structure. Until recently, they were joint ventures of banks, comprising thousands of distinct issuers. In 2006, MasterCard registered as a private-share corporation, owned by its member banks. Visa followed suit in 2008. While many of these bank issuers operate only at the local level, a significant number of others participate at the regional and national levels. In the 1990s, a new group of players entered the credit card scene; non-bank issuers, such as AT&T. While technically these non-bank issuers are necessarily affiliated with a Visa or MasterCard issuing bank and the issued credit card is actually a co-brand card, as in the case of AT&T and MasterCard, the major strategic decisions are undertaken by the non-bank issuer.[23]

Regarding the bankcard brands, it is interesting to note that the Visa and MasterCard associations are quite decentralized. Lawrence Ausubel observed

---

fastest growing proportion of consumer debt, credit card debt has led the way to bankruptcy for an increasing number of Americans...").

22. For the bankruptcy filings study—see Sullivan, Warren, and Westbrook, above note 1, at 129. See also Sullivan, Warren, and Westbrook, above note 1, at 119–20; Evans and Schmalensee, above note 5, at 5. For the three statistical studies—see Ronald J. Mann, *Charging Ahead: The Growth and Regulation of Payment Card Markets around the World* (Cambridge University Press, 2006); Atif R. Mian and Amir Sufi, "Household Leverage and the Recession of 2007–09", *IMF*, 58 (2010), 74–117 ("Overall, the statistical model shows that household leverage growth and dependence on credit card borrowing as of 2006 explain a large fraction of the overall consumer default, house price, unemployment, residential investment, and durable consumption patterns during the recession."); Michelle J. White, "Bankruptcy Reform and Credit Cards" (2007) *J. Econ. Persp.*, 21 no. 4 (2007) ("From 1980 to 2004, the number of personal bankruptcy filings in the United States increased more than five-fold, from 288,000 to 1.5 million per year....I argue that the main explanation is the rapid growth in credit card debt, which rose from 3.2 percent of U.S. median family income in 1980 to 12.5 percent in 2004."). But see Board of Governors of the Federal Reserve System, Report to the Congress on Practices of the Consumer Credit Industry in Soliciting and Extending Credit and their Effects on Consumer Debt and Insolvency, June 2006, 3, 26 ("Though the percentage of families holding credit cards has steadily risen, the household debt service burden has only modestly increased and the majority of households pay their revolving debt on time."; and noting that most bankruptcies in the United States are actually triggered by life crises such as divorce, job loss, and uninsured illness.); Todd J. Zywicki, "The Economics of Credit Cards", *Chap. L. Rev.*, 3 (2003), 79, 82 (doubting the link between credit cards and bankruptcy rates).

23. See Evans and Schmalensee, above note 5, at 4, 48–9, 75–7. See also Ausubel, above note 11, at 51 (there are more than 4,000 card-issuing banks).

that "most relevant business decisions are made at the level of the issuing bank [rather than at the Visa or MasterCard organizations level]. Individual banks own their cardholders' accounts and determine the interest rate, annual fee, grace period, credit limit, and other terms of the account."[24]

Even so, the Visa and MasterCard organizations play an important role. They set the interchange fee for the transfer from the merchant's bank to the card-issuing bank. They promote the company's brand name through advertising. And they lead the competition with the other bankcard brand as well as with the non-bankcard brands.[25]

2. Competition

There are two intertwined levels of competition within the credit card industry; brand-level competition and issuing-level competition.

At the upper level, the major credit card brands—especially Visa, Master-Card, American Express, and Discover—compete among themselves. Visa is the industry leader in terms of both charge volume and credit extended, with MasterCard following closely behind. American Express and Discover occupy the more distant third and fourth places, respectively.[26] The evidence regarding the intensity of competition at this level is mixed. While the four brands clearly compete against each other, the series of antitrust challenges against Visa and MasterCard suggests that the leading brands have taken steps to limit competition at the network level.[27]

Competition at the issuing level is more robust, although there is evidence that competition even at this level is less than perfect. While it may appear that thousands of banks, along with American Express and Discover (as issuers), compete for consumers, the fact is that a relatively small number of large banks control most of the market. There is also mixed evidence about the competitive effect of switching costs. While the economic transaction costs

---

24. Ausubel, above note 11, at 51.
25. *Id*. See also Evans and Schmalensee, above note 5, at 199.
26. See Nilson Report, February 2010. In 2009, the U.S. credit card market was divided among these issuers as follows: Visa—43.4 percent with $764.2 billion in purchase volume; MasterCard—27.1 percent with $476.9 billion in purchase volume; American Express—23.8 percent with $419.8 billion in purchase volume; and Discover—5.7 percent with $100.4 billion in purchase volume. Focusing on credit extended by the four major brands, the 2009 market shares were: Visa—47.4 percent with $366.05 billion of outstanding credit; Master-Card—34.7 percent with $267.57 billion of outstanding credit; American Express—11.1 percent with $86.06 billion of outstanding credit; and Discover—6.8 percent with $52.51 billion of outstanding credit.
27. For a summary of the different antitrust challenges faced by Visa and MasterCard over the years—see Evans and Schmalensee, above note 5, ch. 11.

of obtaining a new card are fairly insignificant for many borrowers, which would lead one to think that consumers would switch cards frequently, there is evidence that psychological switching costs and simple inertia restrict switching rates. One study estimated total switching costs at $150. Moreover, issuers purposefully increase switching costs with loyalty programs.[28]

Competition is also affected by the availability of information and by borrowers' ability to process the information needed to comparison-shop. At first glance, it appears that there's quite a bit of information available, especially through the internet. But it's not clear how many consumers are actually able to find and process this information. As will be explained in the pages that follow, the credit card product is multidimensional and complex. Comparison shopping between several multidimensional, complex products is a daunting task for many consumers. Finally, the profitability of credit card issuers consistently exceeds the average profitability in the banking industry, leading some commentators to conclude that competition in the credit card market is imperfect. And, allegations of coordinated action have been made against the major issuers.[29]

In what follows, I largely sidestep the unresolved question about the level of competition among credit card issuers. I show that the central failure in the credit card market—the behavioral market failure—leads to inefficiencies that cannot be cured by even perfect competition. This justifies placing the credit card industry under scrutiny, even if it is subject to intense competition that dissipates any supra-competitive rents.

II. The Credit Card Contract

Credit card pricing patterns are indicative of a behavioral market failure. In this section, we'll take a look at the relevant features of credit card

28. The Second Circuit noted that "competition…is robust at the issuing level." See *United States v. Visa U.S.A., Inc.*, 344 F.3d 229, 240 (2nd Cir. 2003). Yet the nine largest issuers control approximately 90 percent of the market. See CFPB, CARD Act Factsheet, above note 4. On switching costs—see Evans and Schmalensee, above note 5, at 234–5 (low economic switching costs); Haiyan Shui and Lawrence M. Ausubel "Time Inconsistency in the Credit Card Market" (2004) *Working Paper*, <http://ssrn.com/abstract=586622> (high psychological switching costs).

29. On profitability—see Federal Reserve Board, Report to the Congress on the Profitability of Credit Card Operations of Depository Institutions, June 2009 ("Although profitability for the large credit card banks has risen and fallen over the years, credit card earnings have been consistently higher than returns on all commercial bank activities."). On allegations of coordination—see *In re Currency Conversion Fee Antitrust Litigation* (MDL No. 1409) (class settlement approved); *Ross et al. v. Bank of America, N.A.* (USA), No. 05-cv-7116, MDL No. 1409 (S.D.N.Y.) (settlement reached with a subgroup of the defendants).

pricing.[30] Then we'll explore competing rational-choice and behavioral-economics explanations for these pricing schemes.

A. Complexity

The common credit card contract is complex and multidimensional, with numerous fees and interest rates. Credit card fees can be divided into service fees and penalty fees. The service fees include application fees, set-up fees, annual fees, membership fees, participation fees, cash-advance fees, balance-transfer fees, foreign-currency-conversion fees, credit-limit-increase fees, expedited-payment or phone-payment fees, no-activity fees, fees for stop payment requests, fees for statement copies, fees for replacement cards, and wire-transfer fees. And then there are penalty fees, including late fees, over-limit fees, and returned-check (NSF—No Sufficient Funds) fees. According to one industry source, "an average of 9 cardholder fees and costs [are] found in cardholder fee disclosures."[31]

Now let's look at interest rates. In addition to the main, long-term interest rate for purchases, there are introductory (teaser) rates, rates on balances transferred from other cards, rates on cash advances, and default interest rates.[32]

Most of these fees and interest rates are themselves variable and multidimensional. For example, interest rates are often variable rates that change over time, tracking the movements of a certain index. Introductory rates last for specified time periods, as do default interest rates. Late fees depend (sometimes) on the magnitude of the balance. Etc.[33]

30. I focus on pricing on the consumer side of the credit card market. It should be noted, however, that the credit card market—being a two-sided network market—exhibits interesting pricing patterns also on the merchant side of the market and between the two sides of the market (namely, the interchange fee that acquirers pay to issuers). For a survey of the literature that studies these other aspects of credit card pricing—see Sujit Chakravorti, "Theory of Credit Card Networks: A Survey of the Literature" *Rev. Network Econ.* 2 (2003), 50.
31. CardFlash, "Penalty Fees," January 20, 2009. See also Furletti, above note 16, at 5, 10–13; Federal Reserve Board, "Credit Cards—Fees", <http://www.federalreserve.gov/creditcard/fees.html> (last visited June 24, 2011); Elizabeth Renuart and Diane E. Thompson, "The Truth, The Whole Truth, and Nothing but the Truth: Fulfilling the Promise of Truth in Lending", *Yale J. Reg.*, 25 (2008), 181, 192–4.
32. See Furletti, above note 16, at 14 ("the number of APRs that can be applied to the balances on an account has increased dramatically over the past 10 years (e.g., purchase APR, promotional APR, cash APR, balance transfer APR))"; Federal Reserve Board, "Credit Cards—Interest Rates", <http://www.federalreserve.gov/creditcard/rates.html> (last visited June 24, 2011).
33. See Federal Reserve Board, "Credit Cards—Fees", <http://www.federalreserve.gov/creditcard/fees.html> (last visited June 24, 2011); Federal Reserve Board, "Credit Cards—Interest Rates", <http://www.federalreserve.gov/creditcard/rates.html> (last visited June 24, 2011).

In addition, the amount a consumer pays in interest depends on the balance that she carries, and these balances are calculated using complex formulas. In the late 1990s, issuers moved from monthly to daily compounding of interest, adding finance charges to the balance each day. This change had the effect of increasing the effective APR by as much as 10 to 20 basis points. Moreover, before the practice was banned by the CARD Act of 2009, issuers used another complex calculation called double-cycle billing. Double-cycle billing effectively eliminated the grace period (the interest-free period that consumers who pay their bill in full receive from the time they make a purchase until the date their payment is due) for consumers who made partial payments the month after making a full payment or who made a partial payment the month following a zero-balance.[34]

When a cardholder has multiple balances with the same issuer (for example, one for transferred balances, one for cash advanced, and one for regular purchases), the credit card contract specifies how payments will be allocated among the different balances. This payment-allocation method affects total interest payments. Before the practice was banned by the CARD Act of 2009, many issuers allocated payments to low-interest balances first, thus maximizing the finance charges.[35] The minimum payment requirement also affects total interest payments, since slower repayment results in more interest paid overall. A cardholder who wants to predict his or her total interest payments faces a daunting task.

With respect to contingent penalty fees and rates, the contingency that triggers the fee or rate needs to be specified. For example, when is a payment considered late—when it arrives on the due date or when it arrives

---

34. See Furletti, above note 16, at 15–16 (describing the balance calculation methods); Federal Reserve Board, "What You Need to Know: New Credit Card Rules Effective February 22", <http://www.federalreserve.gov/consumerinfo/wyntk_creditcardrules.htm> (last visited June 24, 2011) (hereinafter FRB, "Credit Card Rules, February 22") (describing the new CARD Act rules).

35. Furletti, above note 16, at 14–15 (describing the payment allocation methods used before they were banned by the CARD Act); PEW Report, Safe Credit Card Standards 1 (2009), available at <http://www.pewtrusts.org/our_work_detail.aspx?id=616>. (A study covering 400 cards offered online by the top 12 issuers, which control more than 88 percent of outstanding credit card debt, found that 100 percent of cards in the study allowed the issuer to apply payments in a manner which, according to the Federal Reserve, is likely to cause substantial monetary injury to consumers.) Furletti concludes that these balance calculation and payment allocation methods have a material effect on issuer revenues, increasing effective yields without affecting the disclosed nominal APRs (Furletti, above note 16, at 14–16). FRB, "Credit Card Rules, February 22," above note 34 (describing the new CARD Act rules).

before a certain hour on the due date? What if the due date falls on a week-end or holiday?

When is a default interest rate triggered? In the not so distant past, many credit card contracts included "universal default" clauses, triggering penalty rates based on a host of factors, such as a change in the cardholder's credit score or a failure to pay a utility bill on time. The CARD Act, while not explicitly banning "universal default," restricts issuers' ability to increase rates.[36]

Many cards also provide a long list of ancillary benefits, including loyalty rewards programs (frequent-flyer miles, cash-back, and the like), rental car insurance, and more. These programs and benefits are themselves quite complex. For example, the program rules detail how miles or points are accumulated, how they can be redeemed, and when they expire if not used. Finally, protection against fraud is of paramount importance to many cardholders. Different issuers offer different mechanisms for protecting their cardholders—another complex benefit.

All these complex details affect the costs and benefits of the credit card product.

B. Deferred Costs

The complex and multidimensional credit card contract provides benefits to consumers while imposing costs on them. These benefits and costs are not randomly distributed across the many dimensions of the contract. Instead, benefits are provided through short-term, more salient dimensions while costs are imposed through long-term, less salient dimensions. With pricing terms, for example, long-term contingent price elements are over-priced while short-term, non-contingent price elements are under-priced. In other words, benefits are accelerated, costs are deferred.

1. Short-Term Benefits
a. No Annual or Per-Transaction Fees
For an issuer, the most straightforward way to cover the fixed costs associated with establishing and maintaining a credit card account would be to

---

36. See Furletti, above note 16, at 8–9 (quoting the language of a common "universal default clause" from a credit card contract); FRB, "Credit Card Rules, February 22," above note 34 (describing the new CARD Act rules).

charge an annual fee—which is, in fact, what they used to do. Nowadays, however, it is common for issuers to charge no annual fee.[37]

Similarly, issuers incur the costs of handling the transactions that consumers charge to their credit cards. Yet most credit card pricing does not include any per-transaction fee. In fact, when considering the benefits or rewards programs associated with many credit cards, issuers are setting *negative* per-transaction fees. The proliferation of membership-rewards programs, frequent-flyer miles, car rental and luggage insurance, discounts on future purchases, and cash-back grants all point to the fact that competitive forces are at play on this dimension of the credit card contract.

Even though they incur positive costs in maintaining credit card accounts and processing transactions, issuers commonly set a zero—or even a negative—price for these services. These observations suggest that issuers are charging below-margin-cost prices on the annual fee and per-transaction fee dimensions of the credit card contract.

But the story is more complex. The preceding account, like the rest of this chapter, focuses on the issuer-consumer contract. This contract sets a low, even negative, price on the per-transaction dimension. A broader analysis would consider also revenue that issuers obtain from merchants, via the interchange fee. (The interchange fee is the percentage—usually 2 percent—that is transferred from the merchant to the issuer on each credit card purchase.) The point is that issuers choose not to charge consumers for the transacting service that the credit card provides. Moreover, while merchants may raise prices to compensate for the "tax" that they pay to issuers, cardholders share the burden of these higher prices with customers using other payment methods.[38]

b. Teaser Rates

Teaser rates are the low, introductory rates that many credit card issuers offer, typically for a period of six months. After that, a higher long-term interest rate kicks in. Some cards even offer a zero-interest rate

---

37. See Furletti, above note 16, at 9–10. (In the mid-1990s issuers eliminated annual fees "in prime portfolios not associated with a rewards program.") See also Evans and Schmalensee, above note 5, at 159.
38. This would not have been true if merchants charged higher prices for credit card purchases. In fact, such a price differential would constitute a de facto per-transaction fee for credit card transactions. Charging different prices as a function of the payment method is, however, quite rare (and, until recently, either illegal or effectively prevented by card networks' no-discrimination rules). See, e.g., Chakravorti, above note 30, at 55–6.

during the introductory period. A zero-interest rate on balance transfers is also common.[39]

Enjoying a low (or no) interest rate is clearly a benefit to consumers, even if this low rate expires after a certain period. Teaser rates also hold the prospect of even greater benefit if consumers transfer their balance to a new card offering a low teaser rate as soon as the introductory period on the current card expires and the post-introductory rate kicks in. The result would be free credit for an indefinite period. While balance transfers—from a card with an expiring teaser rate to a new card with a new teaser rate—do occur, available evidence suggests that they are not as prevalent as one might expect. Rather, substantial borrowing is done at the post-introductory rates. In fact, *most* borrowing is done at the high post-promotion rates, rather than at the low teaser rates.[40]

Teaser rates highlight the disparity between credit card interest rates and the underlying cost of funds. Clearly, the cost of funds is greater than zero, yet zero-percent teaser rates are not uncommon. Teaser rates also imply a sharp discontinuous increase at the end of the introductory period. It is difficult to argue that such a rate increase corresponds to changes in the issuer's cost of funds.

2. Long-Term Costs
a. Long-Term Interest Rates

A central element of credit card pricing is the interest rate charged on credit card debt—the long-term interest rate on purchases that kicks in after the short-term or introductory/teaser interest rate period has expired. (It's important to note that these interest rates on purchases can be different from the long-term interest rates on transferred balances or cash advances.)

Credit card contracts set high interest rates. The average credit card interest rate was 13.30 percent in 2007 and 12.08 percent in 2008.[41] These high

---

39. See CardFlash, "Dec Card Offers," December 23, 2008. ("Zero percent teaser rates for 12 month periods returned in force in Dec. 2008.") See also Stefano DellaVigna and Ulrike Malmendier, "Contract Design and Self-Control: Theory and Evidence", *Q. J. Econ.*, 119 (2004), 353, 377–8; Ausubel, above note 10, at 262.

40. See Gross and Souleles, above note 19, at 171, 179. See also Ausubel, above note 10, at 263 ("a substantial portion of credit card borrowing still occurs at postintroductory interest rates"; "finance charges paid to credit card issuers have not dropped as much as the introductory offers might suggest"); David I. Laibson et al., "A Debt Puzzle," in Philippe Aghion et al. (eds.), *Knowledge, Information, and Expectations in Modern Macroeconomics: In Honor of Edmund, S. Phelps* 228–9 (Princeton University Press, 2003) (finding that consumers pay high effective interest rates "[d]espite the rise of teaser interest rates").

41. See Federal Reserve Statistical Release, "Consumer Credit" (Sep. 8, 2010).

interest rates are not surprising. It is natural for unsecured debt, like credit card debt, to carry higher interest rates than secured debt, such as mortgages, home equity lines of credit, and car loans.

In the 1980s and early 1990s, real concern surfaced about the magnitude of credit card interest rates. This concern was based, in large part, on the "stickiness" of these rates—the evidence that credit card interest rates did not track changes in the underlying cost of funds. David Evans and Richard Schmalensee, both Visa consultants, note: "Not only are credit card interest rates high, they do not always move as quickly as other interest rates in response to changes in the cost of the funds that banks raise to support their lending activities."[42]

The concern about credit card interest rates has dissipated. Since the late 1990s, competition had begun to focus on the interest rate dimension, driving interest rates down and forcing a stronger correlation with the underlying cost of funds.[43]

But while the interest rates themselves are becoming more competitive, there is still concern about interest payments. As explained above, interest payments are not only a function of interest rates; they also depend on how balances are calculated, how payments are allocated to different balances, and on the amount of the minimum payment.

Until the CARD Act banned this practice, most issuers calculated balances using the double-cycle billing method. While the main concern with this method is its complexity and opacity, it also generates elevated interest payments in certain circumstances. Similarly, until banned by the CARD Act, issuers commonly allocated cardholders' payments to the balance bearing the lowest interest rate first. The result was increased overall interest payments.[44]

---

42. Evans and Schmalensee, above note 5, at 248. See also Ausubel, above note 10, at 261 ("throughout the remainder of the 1980s, credit card interest rates displayed a profound unresponsiveness to changes in the cost of funds").

43. See Furletti, above note 16, at 2, 3, 29 ("from 1992 to 2001, however, the average interest rate that issuers charged revolving customers fell 320 basis points, from 17.4 percent to 14.2 percent. Issuer markup, a metric that normalizes for funding costs by subtracting the six-month Treasury bill rate from the average APR, decreased 330 basis points during the same period"; "an overall decrease in the average APR, coupled with an increase in the number of lower income credit users, suggests that the average rate decrease for many cardholders was even more pronounced than the average APR indicates"); Figure 3: Average Credit Card Markup (Average Credit Card APR minus 6m Treasury Bill Rate)—declining since 1992).

44. See Section A above.

The minimum required payment also has a large effect on the overall interest paid by cardholders. Credit card issuers often require only a very small minimum monthly payment, even for large outstanding balances. As long as cardholders do not default, lower monthly payments "increase total revenues by increasing the time it takes to repay the loans and hence the total interest eventually repaid."[45]

b. Penalty Fees and Default Interest Rates

Credit card issuers typically collect sizeable fees from consumers who either run late on their monthly payments or exceed the credit limit. Importantly, the magnitude of these penalties is often measured in fixed-dollar amounts— typically around $35—regardless of the degree of deviation from the credit line or tardiness in making the payment.[46] Thus, for example, a cardholder might pay a $35 penalty if she misses the due date on a $10 balance by a few days. Hard-pressed to justify such a fee structure, some issuers have begun to offer gradation of late fees, such that smaller fees are imposed for tardiness in paying off a smaller balance.

Paying late or exceeding the credit limit is not a fringe phenomenon. According to a Government Accountability Office study of the six largest issuers 35 percent of accounts were assessed late fees and 13 percent of accounts were assessed over-limit fees. Late fees and over-limit fees are a major source of revenue for credit card issuers, reaching almost $20 billion or approximately 10 percent of total card revenues in 2008. Issuers have also been shortening grace periods to further enhance revenues from penalty fees.[47]

---

45. Sullivan, Warren, and Westbrook, above note 1, at 247–8. See also FRB, "Credit Card Lending: Account Management and Loss Allowance Guidance," SR Letter 03–1, 3–4, January 8, 2003, available at <http://www.federalreserve.gov/boarddocs/srletters/2003/sr0301.htm>. ("Competitive pressures and a desire to preserve outstanding balances have led to a general easing of minimum payment requirements in recent years" and "In many cases, reduced minimum payment requirements in combination with continued charging of fees and finance charges have extended repayment periods well beyond reasonable time frames."); Tamara Draut and Javier Silva, *Borrowing to Make Ends Meet: The Growth of Credit Card Debt in the '90s*, p. 37 (Dēmos, 2003) (hereinafter "Dēmos").
46. See CardFlash, "Fee Factor 08," January 14, 2009. (Between 1994 and 2008, average late payment fees increased from $12.52 to $35.36, and average over-limit fees increased from $12.74 to $35.91 (<http://www.carddata.com>)). See also *Pfennig v. Household Credit Services, Inc.*, No. 00–4213 (6th Cir., July 2, 2002) ($29 over-limit charge for every month the balance remained over the credit limit, regardless of the degree of deviation from the credit limit); Sullivan, Warren, and Westbrook, above note 1, at 23 ("penalty fees added on at $50 a pop").
47. On the number of cardholders paying late fees—see U.S. Government Accountability Office, Credit Cards: Increased Complexity in Rates and Fees Heightens Need for More Effective Disclosures to Consumers, 5 (2006) (hereinafter "GAO Complexity Report"). See also Furletti, above note 16, at 11 (Cardweb estimated that half of cardholders had made a late

It's hard to justify, based on the extra costs of extending the loan period or raising the loan limit, the high fees that issuers charge for late payments and for exceeding the credit limit—even accounting for the potentially heightened risk of accommodating a consumer who fails to pay on time or to remain within the specified credit line. This disparity between price and cost is especially striking when the late and over-limit fees are set at fixed-dollar amounts, regardless of the tardiness of the payment or the magnitude of the deviation from the credit limit.[48]

It should be noted that the CARD Act now requires that penalty fees be "reasonable and proportional" to the violation of the account terms in question. These restrictions have led to a substantial reduction in the magnitude of assessed fees. The CARD Act also prohibits issuers from automatically enrolling cardholders in over-the-limit programs, where cardholders can exceed their credit limit but are then charged an over-limit fee. Issuers must now obtain express consent from cardholders who wish to enroll in such programs. This switch, from an opt-out to an opt-in regime, has led many issuers to drop the over-limit fee.[49]

---

payment in 2001). On revenues from late fees—see CardFlash, "Fee Income," January 11, 2010 (total penalty fee income in 2008 amounted to $19 billion; while late fees and over-limit fees account for the lion's share of the $19 billion figure, the $19 billion includes also returned-check (NSF) fees, and currency conversion fees); CardFlash, "Fee Factor 08," January 14, 2009 (total revenues in 2008 were $169 billion; the percentage of total revenues figure was calculated by dividing total penalty fee income by total revenues). See also "National Consumer Law Center, Truth in Lending" 27 (2002 Cumulative Supplement). ("Over-limit fees are a major source of revenue for many credit card issuers.") Penalty fees have been growing rapidly since 1996 when the Supreme Court extended the *Marquette* rule to include late and over-limit fees. See *Smiley v. Citibank*, 517 U.S. 735 (1996). See also CardFlash, "Fee Factor 08," January 14, 2009 ("The rise in fees for a late payment, being over-limit, making a cash advance/balance transfer or an expedited payment were triggered in the wake of the 1996 *Smiley* decision by the U.S. Supreme Court which exempted national card issuers from state restrictions on card fees."); Dēmos, above note 45, at 35 (late fees are the fastest growing source of revenues for issuers). On the shortening of grace periods—see Office of Comptroller of Currency, Advisory Letter: Credit Card Practices, 3, September 14, 2004, available at <http://www.occ.treas.gov/Advlst04.htm> (describing issuer practices: "Credit card issuers may take other actions that also effectively increase the cost of credit for some consumers, such as shortening the due date for receipt of payment.").

48. See Nadia Ziad Massoud, Anthony Saunders, and Barry Scholnick, "The Cost of Being Late: The Case of Credit Card Penalty Fees" (2006) *AFA 2007 Chicago Meetings Paper* available at <http://ssrn.com/abstract=890826> (penalty fees are correlated with risk factors, but also with market share—consistent with the rent extraction theory).

49. See FRB, "Credit Card Rules, February 22," above note 34 (describing the new CARD Act rules); CFPB, CARD Act Fact Sheet, above note 4 (describing the new CARD Act rules and their effects, specifically the reduction in late fees and the "virtual disappearance" of over-limit fees).

Like penalty fees, default interest rates are also a major source of revenue for issuers. These default rates, which exceed 20 percent and sometimes even 30 percent, are easily triggered by such contingencies as a late payment or a charge that exceeds the credit limit. The rates were even more easily triggered before universal default was substantially curtailed by the CARD Act. The Center for Responsible Lending estimated that almost 11 percent of all outstanding credit card balances carried penalty pricing in 2008. And a 2008 study by the PEW Charitable Trusts' Safe Credit Cards Project found that imposing the typical penalty rate costs nearly $500 for the typical, re-priced account. Aggregated across U.S. cardholders, this amounts to over $7 billion a year.[50]

c. Other Fees

The last category of long-term costs comprises a number of non-penalty fees, such as the currency conversion, cash advance, balance transfer, no activity, and convenience or telephone payment fees. These fees bring in substantial revenue for issuers: approximately $10 billion annually. Two of them—the no-activity fee and the convenience fee—have been recently banned by the CARD Act. Another—the currency-conversion fee—was the subject of a $336 million class action settlement. Other terms in the credit card contract, while not direct fees, impose long-term, contingent costs on cardholders. Mandatory arbitration clauses, the subject of recent legal and public scrutiny, are a prime example.[51]

---

50. On the magnitude of default interest rates—see PEW Report, above note 35, at 1 (in a recent study covering 400 cards offered online by the top 12 issuers, which control more than 88 percent of outstanding credit card debt, the median allowable penalty interest rate was 27.99 percent per year); William Weeks, "An Analysis and Critique of Retroactive Penalty Interest in the Credit Card Market" (2007) mimeo (documenting penalty rates of 20 percent to 30 percent and above). For the number of accounts carrying penalty pricing—see Center for Responsible Lending, "Priceless or Just Expensive? The Use of Penalty Rates in the Credit Card Industry," (2008). For the cost of penalty rates to consumers—see PEW Charitable Trusts, "Safe Credit Cards Project: Curing Credit Card Penalties" (2009) 1, available at <http://www.pewtrusts.org/our_work_detail . aspx?id=616>.

51. On fee revenues—see CardFlash, "Fee Income," January 11, 2010 (income from cash advance fees alone amounted to $8 billion in 2009); Furletti, above note 16, at 12 (Convenience and service fees "are generally priced to provide attractive profit margins."). The so-called fee-harvester cards should also be mentioned. See Report, *Fee-Harvesters: Low-Credit, High-Cost Cards Bleed Consumers* (National Consumer Law Center, 2007). For new CARD Act restrictions—see FRB, "What You Need to Know: New Credit Card Rules Effective August 22", <http://www.federalreserve.gov/consumerinfo/wyntk_ creditcardrules.htm> (last visited June 24, 2011) (describing the new CARD Act rules, including a ban on inactivity fees); Credit Card Accountability, Responsibility and Disclosure Act of 2009, Pub. Law 111–24, Sec. 102 (May 22, 2009) (restricting convenience fees). On the

III. Rational-Choice Theories and Their Limits

Why does the common credit card contract look the way it does? What explains its complexity and deferred-cost features? We'll explore these questions by first examining rational-choice, efficiency-based accounts. As we'll see, rational-choice theories explain certain contract design features in certain circumstances, but leave an explanatory gap. We'll fill that gap in Part IV with a behavioral-economics theory.

A. Complexity

1. Interest Rates

The common credit card contract specifies different interest rates, from the basic interest rate for purchases to an interest rate for balance transfers to an interest rate for cash advances. In a rational-choice model, separating the different balances and matching different interest rates to each balance would be efficient if the different balances were associated with different risk levels. Forcing a single, common interest rate would prevent efficient risk-based pricing and lead to cross-subsidization between different groups of cardholders.

Balance calculation and payment-allocation methods also affect interest payments and add to the complexity of the credit card contract. Identifying a rational-choice, efficiency-based explanation for the complex-balance calculation and payment-allocation methods is a difficult task. It is not clear how double-cycle billing enhances efficiency. Similarly, while allocating payments to low-interest balances first increases issuers' revenues, it is not clear how it increases overall efficiency.

currency conversion fee class action—see *In re Currency Conversion Fee Antitrust Litigation* (MDL 1409) (Class Action Complaint and Preliminary Approval of Settlement documents are available at <http://www.ccfsettlement.com/>; on November 8, 2006 the U.S. District Court for the Southern District of New York approved a class action settlement, by which Visa and MasterCard agreed to pay $336 million to credit card and debit card holders for allegedly unlawful currency conversion practices (Visa and MasterCard deny any wrongdoing). The class action suit claimed, among other things, that issuers charged currency conversion fees that were not appropriately disclosed, violating the provisions of TILA and EFTA.) On mandatory arbitration clauses—see Dodd–Frank Act, Sec. 1028 (giving the CFPB authority to ban pre-dispute consumer arbitration); "The Arbitration Trap: How Credit Cards Companies Ensnare Consumers", <http://www.citizen.org/publications/release.cfm?ID=7545>.

2. Fees

The common credit card contract includes a long list of penalty and non-penalty fees. Non-penalty fees include cash advance, balance transfer, foreign currency conversion, and expedited-payment fees. These fees apply to optional services used by some, but certainly not all, cardholders. In the absence of such fees, issuers would have to cover the cost of these optional services by raising a basic non-contingent price term—the annual fee, for example. Setting separate fees or prices for each optional service avoids the cross-subsidization that a single high annual fee entails and allows for more efficient tailoring of the product to the needs and preferences of different borrowers.[52]

Next, consider the penalty fees and rates: the late fee, the over-limit fee, and the default interest rate. In a rational-choice model, these price terms reflect efficient risk-based pricing. The assumption is that paying late, exceeding the credit limit, or engaging in a host of other behaviors that can trigger a default rate is correlated with an increased risk of non-payment. If this increased risk is not priced ex post through the penalty fees and rates, then it would have to be priced ex ante through non-contingent price terms, such as the general interest rate or the annual fee. The penalty fees and rates facilitate a better match of risk and price. They also avoid ineffi-cient cross-subsidization.[53]

3. A Complex Array of Complex Products

A single credit card contract is complex. And consumers face more than one contract. When shopping for the credit card that best suits them, consumers need to read, understand, and compare multiple contracts—a daunting task.

The standard efficiency explanation for the large variety of products available in many markets is consumer heterogeneity. In the credit card mar-ket, different borrowers have different preferences and face different con-straints. A credit card contract that is ideal for one cardholder could be

---

52. Furletti, above note 16, at 10 ("In lieu of charging all of their customers an annual fee that subsidized the costs associated with the behaviors of a few, [issuers] began to assess fees directly on those customers whose card usage behaviors drove costs higher. As issuers started unbun-dling costs and creating behavior-based fees, fees rebounded and have again become an important component of issuer revenues (Figure 6).").

53. Furletti, while noting the benefits of behavior-based and risk-based pricing, acknowledges that "[a] pricing structure that better allocates issuer's risk and servicing expenses has likely come at a cost in the form of a complex and customized product whose pricing is difficult to summarize." Furletti, above note 16, at 18.

wrong for another. With more products to choose from, each cardholder, in theory, is able to choose the credit card and associated credit card contract that is best for him or her. This explanation, however, assumes that informed choice is possible, despite the high level of complexity of the choice problem.

B. Deferred Costs

We've seen how the common credit card contract defers costs and accelerates benefits. Can this pricing pattern be explained within a rational-choice model? Several rational-choice, efficiency-based explanations have been offered for the relatively high interest rates that issuers charge. As noted above, the concern about high interest rates has, in large part, dissipated. More importantly, focusing solely on the interest rate dimension ignores a large part of the overall picture.

Dagobert Brito and Peter Hartley have argued that high credit card interest rates can be explained by the transaction costs involved in obtaining credit from alternative, lower interest rate sources, specifically bank loans.[54] Transaction costs may well play an important role, but they cannot account for the observed pricing patterns in the credit card market. One reason is that, given current technology, it is no longer clear why the cost of providing a closed-end loan would be higher than the cost of maintaining a credit card account. Also, while the transaction-costs model may explain why credit card issuers set a higher overall price, it does not explain why issuers systematically choose to use interest rates rather than annual or per-transaction fees to achieve this higher price.

Similarly, it has been argued that high credit card interest rates are needed to cover other cost elements, such as the cost of building a viable credit card portfolio, operating expenses (such as rent and salaries), and the cost of services beyond lending that the card provides.[55] But while these fixed costs—or, at least, costs that are fixed with respect to lending—can explain above-marginal cost pricing, they cannot explain why, of all possible dimensions of the credit card price, issuers choose to use high interest rates to

54. Dagobert L. Brito and Peter R. Hartley, "Consumer Rationality and Credit Cards" (1995) 103 J. Pol. Econ'y. 103 (1995), 4000. See also Zywicki, above note 22, at 100.
55. See Evans and Schmalensee, above note 5, at 249–50, 254–5. See also Zywicki, above note 22, at 120 (operating costs, rather than the cost of funds, are the main component of issuers' costs).

cover their fixed costs. Why not use annual fees or per-transaction fees? Other rational-choice models similarly focus on the interest rate dimension and thus cannot account for the multidimensional pricing patterns identified in this chapter.[56]

An alternative explanation that is not confined to the interest rate dimension relies on the notion of rational ignorance. According to this theory, consumers do not read their credit card contracts and, therefore, are unaware of or indifferent to variations in different provisions of this contract. But consumers are extremely sensitive to some components of the credit card contract; specifically, the short-term components. In other words, rational-choice models allow for imperfect information. Their failure is in explaining why consumers are informed about certain dimensions of the credit card contract but not others.

C. Summary

Credit card contracts are complex. They defer costs and accelerate benefits. The rational-choice theory leaves an explanatory gap, as it explains some—but not all—of these design features. The behavioral-economics theory, which we'll take a look at next, attempts to fill this gap.

IV. A Behavioral-Economics Theory

As explained in Chapter 1, the design of credit card contracts can be explained as the product of an interaction between consumer psychology and market forces. The behavioral-economic account is developed below. I begin with the complexity feature, in Section A. The theory behind the deferred-cost feature is presented in Section B. Section C introduces the concept of salience, which is intimately linked to both the complexity and cost-deferral features. Salience provides a useful conduit between the imperfect rationality of cardholders and the contract terms that are designed for them. Finally, in Section D, I briefly explore to what extent

---

56. For instance, Loretta Mester, using a screening model with collateralized loans and unsecured credit card loans, explains why credit card interest rates are not sensitive to reductions in the bank's cost of funds. See Loretta J. Mester, "Why Are Credit Card Rates Sticky?", *Econ. Th.*, 4 (1994), 505. Mester, however, does not explain why credit card interest rates exceed the risk-adjusted cost of funds, nor does she explain the other pricing patterns identified in this chapter.

the behavioral-economics theory is consistent with the market's reaction to the CARD Act of 2009.

This Part develops a behavioral-economics theory of credit cards. It also provides empirical evidence in support of this theory. This evidence takes two forms. First, observed contract design features that cannot be explained within the rational-choice framework provide strong, indirect evidence in support of the behavioral-economics theory. Second, direct evidence—both survey evidence and evidence of mistakes in product choice and product use—shows that many cardholders are imperfectly rational. This evidence lends further support to the behavioral-economics theory. Moreover, the direct evidence of imperfect rationality proves the importance of the behavioral account also for design features that can be explained within a rational-choice framework. Even if a certain design feature can be explained while maintaining the assumption that cardholders are perfectly rational, this explanation would be unsatisfactory if most cardholders are shown to fall short of the perfect rationality ideal.

A. Complexity

The typical credit card contract is complex. It specifies numerous interest rates, fees, and penalties, the magnitude and applicability of which may be contingent on unknown future events. As explained in Chapter 1, imperfectly rational cardholders would find it very difficult to deal with such complexity. They would ignore certain price dimensions, miscalculate others, and, as a result, fail to appreciate the total cost of the credit card product.

Evidence confirms that many cardholders fall far short of the perfect rationality ideal. A study conducted by the Center for Responsible Lending found that the majority of borrowers being charged penalty rates do not realize it. Consumer testing commissioned by the Federal Reserve Board (FRB) revealed that (1) many credit card fees go unnoticed, (2) even consumers who are aware of the different credit card rates and fees do not understand how those rates and fees would be applied, and (3) consumers do not notice the cumulative effect of paying small amounts of fees every month. A study by Sumit Agarwal, John Driscoll, Xavier Gabaix, and David Laibson found that consumers also do not understand the workings of balance-transfer offers. Another study by the Center for Responsible Lending found that only 3 percent of borrowers have the knowledge and capacity to evaluate credit card companies' payment-allocation policies.[57]

On a more general level, a survey conducted by the Center for American Progress found that 38 percent of consumers believe that "[m]ost financial products, such as mortgage loans and credit cards, are too complicated and lengthy for [them] to fully understand." A report commissioned by the FRB noted that a significant number of consumers "lack fundamental under-standing of how credit card accounts work." And the General Accounting Office, in a report to Congress, concluded that credit card contracts are too complex for consumers to understand.[58]

Increased complexity may be attractive to issuers, as it allows them to hide the true cost of the credit card in a multidimensional pricing maze. An issuer who understands the imperfectly rational response to complex-ity can use complexity to its advantage by creating an appearance of a lower total price without actually lowering the price. For example, if the currency-conversion fee and the cash-advance fee are not salient to card-holders, issuers will raise the magnitude of these price dimensions.[59] Increasing these prices will not hurt demand. On the contrary, it will enable the issuer to attract cardholders by reducing more salient price dimensions or by increasing more salient benefit dimensions (like reward points and frequent-flyer miles). This strategy depends on the existence of non-salient price dimensions. When the number of price dimensions goes up, the number of non-salient price dimensions can also be expected to go up. Issuers thus have a strong incentive to increase complexity and multidimensionality.

---

57. See Center for Responsible Lending, "Priceless or Just Expensive? The Use of Penalty Rates in the Credit Card Industry," December 16, 2008; Macro International, "Design and Testing of Effective Truth in Lending Disclosures" (2007) at vii, 9, 26, available at <http://www .federalreserve.gov/dcca/regulationz/20070523/Execsummary.pdf>; Ann Kjos, "Proposed Changes to Regulation Z: Highlighting Behaviors that Affect Credit Costs" (2008) *FRB of Philadelphia, Payment Cards Center Discussion Paper No. 08–02*, available at SSRN: <http:// ssrn.com/abstract=1160257>; Sumit Agarwal, John Driscoll, Xavier Gabaix, and David Laib-son, "The Age of Reason: Financial Decisions over the Life-Cycle and Implications for Reg-ulation" (2009) *Brookings Papers on Economic Activity. Issue 2,* 51–117; Center for Responsible Lending, "What's Draining Your Wallet? The Real Cost of Credit Card Cash Advances," December 16, 2008.
58. Ctr. for Am. Progress et al., Frequency Questionnaire (2006), <http://www .americanprogress.org/kf/debt_survey_frequency_questionnaire.pdf>; Macro International, above, at 91; GAO Complexity Report, above note 47, at 49.
59. See Furletti, above note 16, at 12 (noting that service fees, which are likely non-salient, "are generally priced to provide attractive profit margins.").

Indeed, there is evidence that the high level of complexity was a deliberate design feature of the credit card contract. Shailesh Mehta, former CEO
of Providian, acknowledged that credit card pricing was designed so that it
would require "some kind of degree" to understand.[60]

Complexity can be expected to increase as cardholders learn to effectively incorporate more price dimensions into their decision-making. If issuers significantly increase the magnitude of a non-salient price dimension,
cardholders will eventually learn to focus on this price dimension and it will
become salient. Issuers will have to find another non-salient price dimension. When they run out of non-salient prices in the existing contractual
design, they can create new ones by adding more interest rates, fees, or
penalties.

B. Deferred Costs

1. General

The behavioral-economics explanation for deferred-cost contracts is based
on evidence that future costs are often underestimated. When future costs
are underestimated, contracts with deferred-cost features become more
attractive to cardholders and thus to issuers. Consider a simplified credit
card contract with two price dimensions: a short-term price, P_{ST}, such as an
introductory interest rate, and a long-term price, P_{LT}, such as a long-term
interest rate. Assume that the optimal credit card contract sets $P_{ST} = 0.1$ and
$P_{LT} = 0.1$, as these prices provide optimal incentives and minimize total
costs. If cardholders are rational, issuers will offer this optimal contract.

Now assume that cardholders underestimate future costs. For example,
assume that cardholders underestimate the likelihood of borrowing on their
credit card after the introductory period: while they will borrow an amount
of $100 both during and after the introductory period, when they obtained
the credit card they predicted that they would borrow $100 during the
introductory period but only $50 after the introductory period ends.

As a result of such misperception, issuers will no longer offer the optimal
contract. To see this, compare the optimal contract, the (0.1,0.1) contract,
with an inefficient, deferred-cost contract setting $P_{ST} = 0.05$ and $P_{LT} = 0.16$,
the (0.05,0.16) contract. Assume that under both contracts, the issuer just
covers the total cost of offering the credit card product; under the optimal

60. See Interview in Frontline, "The Credit Card Game," November 24, 2009.

(0.1,0.1) contract, total interest payments are: $P(0.1,0.1) = 0.1 \cdot 100 + 0.1 \cdot 100 = 20$ (assuming, for clarity of exposition, that the introductory period and the post-introductory period are one year each and that interest is assessed at the end of the period; time-discounting is also ignored for simplicity). Under the inefficient (0.05,0.16) contract, total interest payments are: $P(0.05,0.16) = 0.05 \cdot 100 + 0.16 \cdot 100 = 21$. The total-cost and total interest payments are higher under the inefficient, deferred-cost contract.

Now consider the cost of the credit card as perceived by the imperfectly rational cardholder. Perceived total interest payments under the optimal (0.1,0.1) contract are: $\hat{P}(0.1,0.1) = 0.1 \cdot 100 + 0.1 \cdot 50 = 15$. Perceived total interest payments under the inefficient (0.05,0.16) contract are: $\hat{P}(0.05,0.16) = 0.05 \cdot 100 + 0.16 \cdot 50 = 13$. Cardholders would prefer, and thus lenders will offer, the inefficient, deferred-cost contract.

We've seen that if future costs are underestimated, issuers will offer deferred-cost contracts. Let's now consider the idea that cardholders underestimate future costs. Two underlying biases are responsible for this underestimation; myopia and optimism. A myopic cardholder focuses on short-term benefits and ignores or discounts long-term costs. An optimistic cardholder underestimates self-control problems with using the card and the likelihood of unexpected developments that may bring economic hardship. This optimism results in underestimation of future borrowing.[61] Since many long-term price dimensions in the credit card contract are contingent upon borrowing, the underestimation of future borrowing leads to an underestimation of future costs.

The effect of myopia on the underestimation of future costs is obvious. The effect of optimism is more subtle. As noted above, in the credit card market, optimism operates on perceptions of the extent of self-control and of the likelihood of contingencies bearing economic hardship. These manifestations of the optimism bias are considered in subsections 2 and 3 below. The cost of credit card debt depends not only on how much is borrowed, but also on how fast the debt is paid off. Optimism also inflicts predictions about repayment speed, as explained in subsection 4. Other misperceptions are discussed in subsection 5.

---

61. See Ausubel, above note 11, at 70–1 ("[T]here are consumers who do not intend to borrow but continuously do so"); Lawrence M. Ausubel, "Adverse Selection in the Credit Card Market" (1999) 20 (unpublished manuscript) (empirically testing and confirming the "underestimation hypothesis").

2. *Optimism Take 1: Underestimating Self-Control Problems*

Imperfect self-control provides one major explanation for consumers' underestimation of their future borrowing. Many consumers overestimate their ability to resist the temptation to finance consumption by borrowing; consequently, they underestimate future borrowing.[62]

When obtaining a credit card, the consumer may intend to use the card for transacting only or to limit borrowing to a certain amount. But this limit is not specified in the credit card contract, and therefore is not binding on the consumer's "future self," the self that will make the borrowing decision. And with imperfect self-control, this future self may well exceed the intended limit.

a. Hyperbolic Discounting

Why would consumers end up borrowing more than they initially anticipated? What is the source of such weakness of the will? The answer can be traced to a concept called "hyperbolic discounting." Neoclassical economics assumes that individuals discount the future at a constant rate, an assumption captured by an exponential discount function. In contrast, consumers are said to be a hyperbolic discounters if their short-run discount rate is larger than their long-run discount rate. In other words, at a given point in time, t, a hyperbolic discounter heavily discounts costs and benefits that will materialize in the near future, at $t + 1$, but assigns only a smaller *additional* discount for costs and benefits that will materialize in the more distant future, at $t + 2$. This systematic disparity between people's short-term and long-term discount rates has been consistently demonstrated both in the laboratory and in the real world. When hyperbolic discounters are naive about the nature of their time preferences, they will optimistically overestimate their willpower, and consequently underestimate their future borrowing.[63]

---

62. See Evans and Schmalensee, above note 5, at 109 ("[R]eal people have trouble keeping track of [card] balances during the month and resisting the ever-present temptation to use future income to enjoy life a bit more today."); Thomas H. Jackson, *The Logic and Limits of Bankruptcy Law* (Harvard University Press, 1986) 234, 238–99 (hereinafter *Logic and Limits*) (arguing that individuals underestimate "the risks that their current consumption imposes on their future well-being," and invoking the "human tendency to lack impulse control"—that is, a tendency "to choose current over postponed gratification, even if it is known that the latter holds in store a greater measure of benefits").

63. On exponential discounting in neoclassical economics—see Paul Samuelson, "A Note on Measurement of Utility", *Rev. Econ. Stud.*, 4 (1937), 155; Tjalling C. Koopmans, "Stationary Ordinal Utility and Impatience", *Econometrica*, 28 (1960), 287. For experimental evidence supporting the hyperbolic discounting model—see, e.g., Richard H. Thaler, "Some Empirical Evidence on Dynamic Inconsistency", *Econ. Letters*, 8 (1981), 201, 202 (one of the first experiments); Shane Frederick et al., "Time Discounting and Time Preference: A Critical

Consider a consumer who decides to obtain a credit card at T = 0. From the T = 0 perspective, this consumer considers the likelihood of borrowing on the credit card at T = 1. The consumer weighs the future benefit of a credit card purchase at T = 1 against the more distant T = 2 cost of debt repayment, including payment of interest charges. Recall that from the T = 0 perspective, the discount between T = 1 and T = 2 is relatively small. Hence, given the substantial costs of credit card borrowing, even though the costs of borrowing lie in the more distant future, at T = 0 the consumer would prefer *not* to borrow at T = 1. And assuming the consumer thinks that this ex ante preference will be followed, at T = 0, the consumer believes that no borrowing will take place at T = 1.

To examine the validity of this belief, let's move down the timeline to T = 1, when the actual borrowing decision takes place. At this point, T = 1 is the present and T = 2 is the near future. As explained above, hyperbolic discounting implies that from the T = 1 perspective the T = 2 costs will be heavily discounted. Therefore, even if the future (T = 2) cost of borrowing is substantially higher than the present (T = 1) benefits, the consumer, at T = 1, may decide to borrow on his or her credit card.

This preference reversal—a T = 0 preference *not* to borrow evolving into a preference and a decision to borrow at T = 1—is an immediate implication of hyperbolic discounting. Figure 2.1 illustrates the reversal of preferences with respect to credit card borrowing.

Review", *J. Econ. Lit.*, 40 (2002), 351, 360 (a recent survey). Outside the laboratory, hyperbolic discounting is evident in consumption decisions;—see Richard H. Thaler, "*The Winner's Curse: Paradoxes and Anomalies of Economic Life*" (Princeton University Press, 1992) 94, 105; insufficient saving for retirement—see Brigitte C. Madrian and Dennis Shea, "The Power of Suggestion: Inertia in 401(k) Participation and Savings Behavior", *Q. J. Econ.*, 116 (2001), 1149, 1150; David Laibson et al., "Self-Control and Saving for Retirement" (1998) 1 *Brookings Papers on Economic Activity* 91; Ted O'Donoghue and Matthew Rabin, "Procrastination in Preparing for Retirement," in Henry Aaron (ed.), *Behavioral Dimensions of Retirement Economics* (Brookings Institute Press, 1999) 125; addiction, whether to cigarettes, alcohol, or more serious drugs—see George Ainslie, "Derivation of 'Rational' Economic Behavior from Hyperbolic Discount Curves" *Amer. Econ. Rev.* 81 (1991) 334; Jonathan Gruber and Botond Koszegi, "Is Addiction 'Rational'? Theory and Evidence" (2000) *NBER Working Paper No. 7507*; dieting—see Thaler, *The Winner's Curse*, id., at 98; and health club attendance—see Stefano DellaVigna and Ulrike Malmendier, "Paying Not to Go to the Gym", *Amer. Econ. Rev.*, 96 (2006), 694. In a recent study, Laibson et al. show that allowing for hyperbolic discounting helps explain the large fraction of households that borrow on their credit cards. See Laibson et al., above note 40, at 229–30. See also George-Marios Angeletos et al., "The Hyperbolic Consumption Model: Calibration, Simulation, and Empirical Evaluation" *J. Econ. Perspect.* 15 (2001) 47 ("[H]ouseholds with hyperbolic discount functions are very likely to borrow on their credit cards to fund instant gratification. Thus households with hyperbolic discount functions are likely to have a high level of revolving debt, despite the high cost of credit card borrowing.").

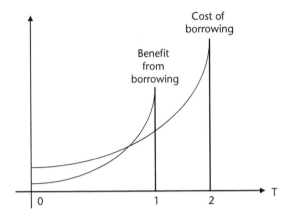

Figure 2.1. Preference reversal in credit card borrowing

The vertical line at T = 1 represents the T = 1 value of the benefits from borrowing. The curved line descending from this vertical line (to the left) represents the discounted value of these benefits at any point in time prior to T = 1, and especially at T = 0. Similarly, the vertical line at T = 2 represents the T = 2 value of the costs associated with credit card borrowing. And the curved line descending from this vertical line (to the left) represents the discounted value of these costs at any point in time prior to T = 2, and especially at T = 1 and at T = 0. As illustrated in Figure 2.1, the two curved lines start with a steep descent, which then levels off as the temporal distance from the curve's point of origin increases. This varying slope of the discounted present value curves captures the hyperbolic discounting phenomenon.

In Figure 2.1 we see that at T = 0, the curve representing the discounted present value of the *costs* of borrowing lies above the curve representing the discounted present value of the *benefits* from borrowing. Hence, at T = 0, the consumer would prefer not to borrow (at T = 1). However, between T = 0 and T = 1 the relative position of the two curves switches, and at T = 1 the benefits curve lies above the costs curve, implying that the consumer will, in fact, choose to borrow at T = 1.

Figure 2.1 illustrates the temporal inconsistency resulting from hyperbolic discounting. At T = 0, the consumer does not wish to borrow, but ends up doing so anyway at T = 1. Note, however, that temporally inconsistent preferences do not necessarily entail inaccurate ex ante beliefs. Sophisticated consumers, aware of their hyperbolic discounting, would anticipate the preference reversal. At T = 0, such consumers, while preferring not to borrow at T = 1, would nevertheless know that they will end up borrowing at T = 1. Unfortunately, not many consumers are that sophisticated with respect to their intertemporal preferences. Many consumers are at least a little naive, at T = 0, about their ability to effectuate, at T = 1, their T = 0 preferences. Specifically, they might fail to take into account the T = 1 preference reversal when making the T = 0 decision.[64] Naive hyperbolic discounters thus believe ex ante that they will not borrow, but actually do borrow on their credit card ex post. In other words, the hyperbolic discounter optimistically underestimates future borrowing.

Note how credit cards, as an open-end credit vehicle, give rise to imperfect self-control and to the underestimation of future borrowing. When a consumer takes on a closed-end loan, all the parameters of the loan contract, including the amount of the loan, are determined up-front. No discretion is reserved for a later period; thus, self-control is not an issue. The credit card, on the other hand, separates the decision to obtain a card—and the decision which card to obtain—from the actual borrowing decision (or decisions). The amount of the loan is left open. And an open-end loan inevitably opens the door to self-control problems. In other words, a closed-end loan serves as a commitment device, enabling the consumer to constrain his or her future self by committing to a maximum amount of debt. The credit card does not provide such a commitment device.[65]

A recent study by Stephan Meier and Charles Sprenger directly tests, and confirms, the behavioral-economics account. Meier and Sprenger compare time-preference data from a field experiment with a "targeted group of low-to-moderate income consumers," with credit report data on these consumers. The authors find that consumers who exhibit hyperbolic discounting and dynamically inconsistent intertemporal choices borrow more, and specifically borrow more on their credit cards. This result suggests that

---

64. See, e.g., Madrian and Shea, above note 63 (evidence from 401(k) investments); DellaVigna and Malmendier, above note 63 (evidence from health club attendance).

65. Many accounts of credit card borrowing mention consumers' weakness of will, or imperfect self-control. The notion is that consumers do not intend to borrow, but end up doing so anyway. See, e.g., Ausubel, above note 10, at 262. The credit card borrower is sometimes compared to an alcoholic, who is aware of the dangers inherent in her drinking problem, yet cannot avoid purchasing another bottle. Another common analogy compares the credit card borrower to a failed dieter. The dieter wants to lose weight, but when that chocolate cake presents itself, he cannot resist the temptation. The alcoholism and dieting analogies highlight the self-control problem. See Sullivan, Warren, and Westbrook, above note 1, at 120, 247, 250.

"individuals borrow more...than they actually would prefer to borrow given their long-term objectives."[66]

b. Borrowing a Little at a Time

Imperfect self-control leading to the underestimation of future borrowing has been traced back to the temporal separation between the decision to obtain a credit card and the decision to borrow on the credit card. The fact is, however, that there are many borrowing decisions, not just one. Each time consumers swipe their card, they take on a new loan. This piecemeal borrowing phenomenon, or "a-little-at-a-time borrowing," exacerbates the self-control problem.[67]

A 2008 Dēmos survey found that smaller purchases of non-essential goods and services, such as meals at restaurants, movies, and DVDs, were the most frequently cited expense category contributing to credit card debt (cited by 48 percent of respondents). Sullivan, Warren, and Westbrook observe that "[d]ebtors who never dream of seeking a $5,000 bank loan might run up $5,000 in charges of $50 at a time." The distinction between the traditional discrete loan and the gradually accumulating credit card debt should not be underestimated: "One need not have a deep understanding of human nature to appreciate the risks of incremental foolishness. There are many mistakes we would not make all at once that we will make a little at a time...."[68]

As fallible decision-makers, we inevitably make mistakes. But we will try harder to avoid such mistakes—wisely so—when the stakes are higher (or appear to be higher). This general observation is applicable to decisions about incurring additional debt: "The debt itself is incurred a little bit at a time, so that even large amounts of debt do not involve a single, sober decision to take on $25,000 or even $2,500 of debt."[69]

Credit cards opened the door to "the seductiveness of incremental irresponsibility," as manifested in a-little-at-a-time borrowing. The outcome of such borrowing behavior is usually detrimental to consumers. Sullivan,

---

66. Stephan Meier, and Charles Sprenger. "Present-Biased Preferences and Credit Card Borrowing", *Amer. Econ. J.*, 2 (2010), 193.
67. See Sullivan, Warren, and Westbrook, above note 1, at 130 ("[C]redit cards make it far easier to incur consumer debt by encouraging a-little-at-a-time borrowing and too-little-at-a-time repayment.").
68. See Dēmos, "The Plastic Safety Net: How Households Are Coping in a Fragile Economy" (2009) 6; Teresa A. Sullivan, Elizabeth Warren, and Lay Lawrence Westbrook, *As We Forgive Our Debtors: Bankruptcy and Consumer Credit in America* (Oxford Universtiy Press, 1989) 178; Sullivan, Warren, and Westbrook, above note 1, at 247.
69. Sullivan, Warren, and Westbrook, above note 1, at 245-6.

Warren, and Westbrook describe a category of debtors, whom they call "sliders": "[m]any people slide into debt, falling a little farther behind on their cards every month until bankruptcy is the only way out." Optimism prevents cardholders from fully appreciating the risks of a-little-at-a-time borrowing, resulting in the underestimation of future borrowing and of deferred costs associated with borrowing.[70]

   3. Optimism Take 2: Underestimating the Risk of Economic Hardship
Evidence shows that a substantial amount of credit card borrowing is triggered by adverse contingencies, especially job loss and medical problems, which decrease income and increase expenses, respectively.[71] Underestimation of future borrowing may stem from an optimism bias that leads consumers to underestimate the likelihood of adverse events that might generate a need to borrow. Optimistic individuals tend to underestimate the probability that they or a loved one will have an accident or illness that requires costly treatment (not covered, or not entirely covered, by insurance). Individuals also tend to underestimate the likelihood that they will lose their job, or underestimate the length of time it will take to find a new job.[72] These and other manifestations of the optimism bias will lead consumers to underestimate the likelihood that they will be forced to resort to credit card borrowing.

   The underestimation of future borrowing has been traced back to two manifestations of the optimism bias—a consumer's overestimation of will-power and underestimation of the likelihood of encountering adverse contingencies. The two problems may reinforce one another. Imperfect will-power might push the consumer into a fragile financial condition, increasing vulnerability to adverse events, such as an accident, illness, or job loss.[73]

---

70. See Sullivan, Warren, and Westbrook, above note 68, at 179; Sullivan, Warren, and Westbrook, above note 1, at 111.

71. See Dēmos, "The Plastic Safety Net: The Reality behind Debt in America" (2005) 7–12, available at <http://www.accessproject.org/adobe/the_plastic_safety_net.pdf>; Dēmos, above note 68, at 8 ("[M]ore than one-half of indebted low- and middle-income households cited medical expenses as contributing to their credit card debt. In fact, compared to all other expenses inquired about in the survey, out-of-pocket medical expenses was the most frequently reported expense that contributed to credit card debt. On average, these households reported that $2,194 in credit card debt was attributable to medical expenses.").

72. Sullivan, Warren, and Westbrook, above note 1, at 25, 114 ("The recently unemployed, hopeful that they will be back at work in a matter of days or weeks, may not be prepared to tell the children there will be no new soccer shoes this season or no back-to-school clothes.").

73. See Sullivan, Warren, and Westbrook, above note 1, at 113–15 (Many consumers reach a state of indebtedness that renders them vulnerable to unexpected costs). See also Bruce A. Markell,

4. *Optimism Take 3: Underestimating the Cost of Slow Repayment*

The amount to be borrowed is clearly a major factor affecting the cost of borrowing. But it is not the only factor. The cost of borrowing also depends on the speed of repayment. Many borrowers underestimate the period it will take them to repay their credit card debt. The hyperbolic discounting phenomenon, which accounts for the underestimation of future borrowing, also explains consumers' underestimation of the repayment period. Naive hyperbolic discounters often anticipate a quick repayment schedule, but when actual payments need to be made revert to the minimum payment. According to one account: "Each month the debtor might make the small minimum payment with a vow to start paying off the balance the next month." Again, optimism about self-control problems results in the underestimation of the costs associated with credit card debt.[74]

Optimistic underestimation of the risk of economic hardship can similarly lead borrowers to overestimate the speed of repayment and thus underestimate the costs associated with credit card debt. Optimistic cardholders often overestimate their ability to repay quickly because they underestimate the likelihood of adverse contingencies that would render quick repayment difficult. Evidence of low repayment rates is consistent with this behavioral explanation. In 2008, the monthly payment rate—the amount that cardholders pay on their credit card debt—hovered around 18 percent.[75] The same factors that lead consumers to underestimate future borrowing will lead them to also overestimate their ability to repay quickly.

Because issuers profit from slow repayment, they often set low minimum payments. They even design the credit card bill such that the minimum payment figure is more salient than the total balance figure. They do this to "persuade" consumers to pay only the minimum payment. For instance, the "minimum payment" box is often closer to the "actual payment" box and highlighted with a distinct color or font size, while the "total balance" box

---

"Sorting and Sifting Fact from Fiction: Empirical Research and the Face of Bankruptcy: The Fragile Middle Class: Americans in Debt By Teresa A. Sullivan, Elizabeth Warren and Jay Lawrence Westbrook" (2001) 75 Am. Bankr. L.J. 149 (book review) ("Americans who file bankruptcy generally have incurred debt beyond a rational ability to repay, and are thus vulnerable to economic events that challenge their fragile condition.").

74. See Sullivan, Warren, and Westbrook, above note 68, at 178; Paul Heidhues and Botond Koszegi, "Exploiting Naiveté about Self-Control in the Credit Market", *Amer. Econ. Rev.* 100 (2010), 2279.

75. CardFlash, "Payment Rates Hit a Four-Year Low in July," August 27, 2008; CardFlash, "Monthly Payment Rates Edge Up Slightly," March 18, 2009.

is further away and less conspicuous. Sometimes the minimum payment figure is the only figure appearing on the payment stub itself.[76]

5. Other Misperceptions

Deferred-cost contracts are a response to the underestimation of future costs. We've seen how imperfect rationality can lead cardholders to underestimate future costs by underestimating future borrowing or overestimating the speed of repayment. But future costs can also be underestimated without regard to the extent of borrowing or the speed of repayment.

For instance, the common credit card contract sets high penalty fees for late payments and for exceeding the credit limit. These design features can be linked to the misperceptions discussed above; optimism about the strength of self-control or about the risk of financial hardship. Imperfect self-control may result in higher-than-expected borrowing, perhaps even above the consumer's credit limit, triggering over-limit fees. High debt levels imply higher minimum payments and thus might lead to late payment, triggering late fees. Also, consumers may be forced to exceed their credit line or to defer payment beyond the due date as a result of an accident, an illness, or unemployment, thus linking over-limit fees and late fees to the underestimation of adverse contingencies.

But consumers might also miss the due date simply through forgetfulness. Similarly, they might exceed their credit line simply because they lost track of the total balance. Since forgetfulness is a common trigger of the penalty clauses in the credit card contract, optimism regarding the extent of such forgetfulness is important in explaining these features of credit card pricing.[77]

---

76. See Scott D. Schuh and Joanna Stavins, "Summary of the Workshop on Consumer Behavior and Payment Choice" (2008) *FRB of Boston Public Policy Discussion Paper No. 08–5*, 9, available at SSRN: <http://ssrn.com/abstract=1310350> ("monthly credit card statements emphasize the minimum payment due—often denoted in bold font—but not the total amount of debt.") See also CardFlash, "Minimum Payments," December 17, 2008. (A 2008 study by Neil Stewart found that the average monthly payment on a credit card account increased by 70 percent when the minimum monthly payment amount was not included on the statement. The study suggests that consumers are encouraged to pay less on their balances when credit card companies present the minimum monthly payment option amount on credit card statements.)

77. Consistent with the forgetfulness explanation, Satngo and Zinman find that many consumers could have easily avoided paying late fees and over-limit fees by either paying a bill using available checking balances, or by using a different card with sufficient available credit. See Victor Stango and Jonathan Zinman, "What Do Consumers Really Pay on Their Checking and Credit Card Accounts? Explicit, Implicit, and Avoidable Costs", *Amer. Econ. Rev.* 99 (2009), 424–9.

Other features of the credit card contract may be linked to different biases and misperceptions. A consumer shopping for a credit card may underestimate the need to use the credit card abroad, and thus underestimate the likelihood of paying a currency-conversion fee. The cardholder may also underestimate the benefit of paying the credit card bill over the phone and thus underestimate the likelihood of incurring a "convenience" fee.

The underlying source of these underestimation biases is not always clear. Perhaps the temporal dimension is once again playing a role: individuals excessively discount the likelihood of future events, such as traveling abroad or the number of times when paying by telephone may be especially convenient. When the future is difficult to imagine, the probability of future events even taking place will be discounted.

Consumers might pay insufficient attention to certain terms, such as a currency-conversion or convenience fee, because they underestimate the probability of triggering these fees. They may also pay insufficient attention to these fees simply because such fees never cross their minds. The significance of a contract term can be underestimated because the probability of triggering the term is perceived to be small. But a term can also be ignored for reasons that are more difficult to identify and articulate.

C. Salience

Faced with the complex, multidimensional credit card contract, imperfectly rational consumers will not be able to focus equally on all terms. Only a handful of terms will be salient. Salience is, therefore, inexorably linked to the complexity feature. The preceding analysis has shown that salience has an important temporal dimension. Short-term prices are generally more salient than long-term prices. This explains the deferred-cost feature. But while salience has an important temporal dimension, timing is not the only factor affecting the salience of a price or other contractual dimension. For example, advertising by issuers or government-mandated disclosures can make a long-term price salient to consumers.

In any event, an issuer operating in a competitive market will quickly discover which features are salient and which are not. Salient features will be made attractive by lowering prices on those features and increasing the benefits that they provide. Non-salient features, on the other hand, will constitute the revenue centers. They will be designed to cover the issuer's costs and pay for the salient benefits.

1. Salience and the Design of Credit Card Contracts

The behavioral-economics theory explains the design considerations behind many of the features of the common credit card contract. Many long-term price dimensions are less salient to cardholders. These include late fees, over-limit fees, cash-advance fees, and currency-conversion fees. These fees are set at a relatively high level. Many short-term dimensions are more salient to cardholders. These include annual fees and introductory interest rates. Both are set at very low levels, with a zero annual fee and a zero teaser rate being quite common.[78]

The notion that short-term dimensions are more salient than long-term dimensions has a strong empirical basis. Evans and Schmalensee, in their book, cite evidence that a zero annual fee is the prime selection criterion in credit card choice for 15 percent of consumers. Similarly, Lawrence Ausubel notes: "the experience of credit card marketers is that consumers are much more sensitive to increases in the annual fee than to commensurate increases in the interest rate."[79]

Regarding teaser rates, despite the fact that most borrowing is done at high post-promotion rates, consumers appear to be extremely sensitive to teaser rates. Ausubel found that "consumers are at least three times as responsive to changes in the introductory interest rate as compared to dollar-equivalent changes in the post-introductory interest rate."[80] Survey evidence suggests that more than a third of all consumers consider an attractive introductory interest rate to be the prime selection criterion in credit card choice.[81]

Scrutinizing consumers' choices among competing teaser-rate offers lends further support to the behavioral-economics model: Shui and Ausubel found that when faced with otherwise identical credit card offers, consumers prefer a credit card with a 4.9 percent teaser rate lasting for an introductory period of six months over a credit card with a 7.9 percent teaser rate lasting for an introductory period of twelve months. Consumers in this study carried an average balance of $2,500 over a one-year period. Those who accepted the six-month introductory offer paid a post-introductory rate of 16 percent during the latter half of the year. These results indicate

---

78. The theory behind teaser rates is a bit more subtle. See Appendix.
79. See Evans and Schmalensee, above note 5, at 225; Ausubel, above note 11, at 72.
80. See Ausubel, above note 61, at 21. Moreover, "consumers are two to three times as responsive to changes in the introductory interest rate as compared to dollar-equivalent changes in the duration of the introductory offer." Id. at 22.
81. See Ausubel, above note 61, at 21; Evans and Schmalensee, above note 5, at 225.

that at least some consumers were making a significant mistake, opting for the lower-rate, shorter-duration card even though they paid $50 more in interest on this card than they would have with the longer-duration alternative. One possible explanation: Consumers systematically underestimate the amount that they will borrow, or at least the amount they will borrow on a specific card, in the post-introductory period.[82]

As noted above, the correlation between temporal distance and salience is not perfect. Transacting, like borrowing, occurs in the future, relative to the time period in which the cardholder chooses a credit card and a credit card contract. Yet, there are no per-transaction fees; in fact, once the benefits or rewards commonly attached to credit card purchases are taken into account, many cardholders enjoy a negative per-transaction fee.[83]

Of course, transacting and borrowing are very different. The optimism-related biases explaining the underestimation of future borrowing do not apply to transacting. Consumers applying for a credit card, while hoping that they will not need to borrow on their card, surely expect to use the card for transacting purposes. Accordingly, transacting and transacting-related pricing are salient. Many cardholders rank loyalty programs among the top features they look for when choosing a credit card.[84] As previously noted, the interchange fee, to the extent that it translates into higher purchase prices, can be viewed as a per-transaction fee. But this only reinforces the behavioral-economics theory because when charging a per-transaction fee, issuers make sure to do so in an indirect way that reduces its salience to consumers.

Similarly, the basic (not introductory) interest rate on purchases is a long-term price dimension, which is nonetheless quite salient to cardholders and thus the subject of competition among issuers. It is noteworthy that this was not always the case. As explained above, until fairly recently the basic interest rate was not salient to cardholders, and thus the interest rate was quite high. But salience is a dynamic concept. Over time, consumers learned to appreciate the importance of the interest-rate dimension, arguably with some assistance from legislators and regulators. When interest rates became salient

82. See Shui and Ausubel, above note 28, at 8–9.
83. There is some evidence that rewards come with higher long-term rates, consistent with the behavioral-economics theory. See CardFlash, "Reward Card Review," June 2, 2008 (according to Consumer Reports, cash-back, gas, and grocery rewards credit cards can offer some relief for costly essential items, but often carry higher rates than traditional credit cards).
84. Evans and Schmalensee cite survey evidence suggesting that 20 percent of consumers consider rewards and rebates to be the prime selection criterion in their credit card choice. See Evans and Schmalensee, above note 5, at 225.

to consumers, competition focused on this price dimension, as the behavioral-economics theory predicts.

Perhaps the most convincing evidence supporting the behavioral-economics theory comes from "admissions" by the credit card industry: David Evans and Richard Schmalensee, the Visa consultants, acknowledge that "[s]ervice fees (such as late fees, over-limit fees, and finance charges on cash advances) provide revenues to issuers but are likely to be largely invisible to most consumers trying to choose between different credit card plans." Evans and Schmalensee also acknowledge that issuers reduce salient fees while increasing non-salient fees: "It is certainly possible, in theory, that issuers who reduce their annual fees may raise other fees less visible to consumers. Available data on annual and service fees [e.g. late fees, over-limit fees] strongly suggest that, over time, issuers in the aggregate have done just this."[85]

Similarly, in *Beasley v. Wells Fargo Bank*, the bank's "Credit Card Task Force" proposed increasing "late" and "over-limit" fees as a "good source of revenue." Penalty fees are considered a "good source of revenue," because the industry perceives—in line with the behavioral-economics theory developed here—that "[t]here (are) very few cardholders that switch cards because the late fee is too high." As explained by Shailesh Mehta, former CEO of Providian, issuers increased late fees, because people do not think they will be late. If people do not think they will be late, they will not switch cards because the late fee is too high.[86]

Industry sources also confirm the behavioral-economics prediction that issuers will aggressively compete on salient price dimensions and recoup losses through non-salient price dimensions. Andrew Kahr, a financial services consultant who is credited with inventing the zero-percent teaser rate (among other consumer-lending strategies), argued that issuers use penalty fees and rates to recoup losses on teaser rates.[87]

2. Dynamics of Salience

The behavioral-economics theory predicts low prices on salient price dimensions and high prices on non-salient price dimensions. Salience thus

---

85. See Evans and Schmalensee, above note 5, at 211, 260.
86. See *Beasley v. Wells Fargo Bank*, 235 Cal. App. 3d 1383, 1389 (1991); "Credit Card Fees Soar Again," *CNNMoney*, August 18, 1998 (quoting Peter Davidson, Executive VP at Speer and Associates in Atlanta, on the industry's belief that high late fees will not drive cardholders away); Frontline, "The Credit Card Game," November 24, 2009 (interview with Shailesh Mehta).
87. See Patrick McGeehan, "Soaring Interest Compounds Credit Card Pain for Millions," *New York* Times, November 21, 2004 (quoting Mr. Kahr).

becomes critical to the analysis of market outcomes. As explained earlier, salience has a strong temporal dimension, which explains the cost-deferral feature in many credit card contracts. But salience has other non-temporal dimensions as well. Moreover, salience is fluid, evolving over time. A non-salient price or term can eventually become salient.

For example, before the early 1990s, the annual fee was salient to consumers and issuers competed by lowering or waiving the annual fee. At the time, the interest rate—the basic interest rate for purchases—was not salient to consumers. Accordingly, issuers did not compete on interest rates. This changed in the early 1990s: Consumer awareness of the purchase Annual Percentage Rate (APR) increased and interest rates decreased. The increased salience of the APR is probably responsible, at least in part, for the teaser rate innovation as well.[88] (Other forces contributing to the success of teaser rates include consumer myopia and optimism about the extent of borrowing beyond the introductory period and the ability to switch to another card with a new teaser rate.)

As competition focused on interest rates, interest revenues declined, and issuers set out to find, or create, new non-salient price dimensions. Starting in the late 1990s, issuers shifted focus to behavior-based fees, such as risk-based fees and convenience fees. Late fees, over-limit fees, and cash-advance fees increased significantly and new fees—such as returned-check (NSF) fees, balance-transfer fees, foreign currency exchange surcharges, and expedited-payment fees—were introduced. According to one industry source, over-limit fees did not exist in the 1980s and late fees averaged about $10, reflecting the cost of making a reminder phone call or sending a reminder letter. In the late 1990s, fees stopped being "cost-based" and became "profit-driven."[89]

---

88. See FRB, Profitability of Credit Card Operations of Depository Institutions, 5 (2009), available at <http://www.federalreserve.gov/Pubs/reports_other.htm> ("Prior to the early 1990s, card issuers competed primarily by waiving annual fees and providing credit card program enhancements such as airline mileage programs." Since the early 1990s "interest-rate competition has played a much more prominent role....Many issuers have attempted to gain or maintain market share by offering very low, temporary rates on balances rolled over from competing firms or to select current customers and by offering a wide variety of enhancements."); Furletti, above note 16, at 3, 7 ("Consumer awareness of annual percentage rate as a key cost measure, combined with the ability to easily find new card offers and switch issuers, inevitably affected price competition and rate stickiness."; "Ultimately, a card's nominal APR became a competitive focal point and drove widespread adoption of risk-based pricing.").

89. On the rise of fees—see Furletti, above note 16, at 11; CardFlash, "Fee Factor 08," January 14, 2009. See also Furletti, above note 16, at 33, Figure 7 (showing how the "average late fee being assessed" has increased since 1994). On the move from cost-based to profit-driven fees—see CardFlash, "Fees and Recession," December 19, 2008.

Philadelphia Federal Reserve Bank economist, Mark Furletti, who examined credit card contracts in the late 1990s and early 2000s, concluded that "risk-based fees have become an important source of revenue for card issuers and have replaced a significant portion of the revenues lost from the elimination of annual fees and lowered APRs." And the same is true for convenience and service fees. Furletti found that these fees were priced "to provide attractive profit margins." By 2008, total revenues from cardholder fees reached $28.9 billion.[90]

D. Recent Events: The CARD Act

The Credit Card Accountability, Responsibility and Disclosure Act of 2009 affected a major change in the regulation of the credit card market. The behavioral-economics theory offers predictions about market responses to the new rules.

The CARD Act imposed restrictions on late and over-limit fees and on interest rate hikes. This led to a reduction in back-end profits. In response, issuers would be expected to raise front-end fees and other salient prices, such as annual fees and purchase APRs. Issuers would also be expected to cut back on front-end, salient benefits, such as rewards programs, simply because the back-end funding for these front-end perks is drying up. In

---

90. On risk-based fees—see Furletti, above note 16, at 11–12. See also Furletti, above note 16, at 10–11 ("With average interest rates on the decline and annual fees becoming unpopular among their customers, issuers developed more targeted fee structures to replace lost revenues."); Frontline, "The Credit Card Game," November 24, 2009 (interview with Shailesh Mehta, former CEO of Providian: Competition eliminated annual fees, and issuers compensated with penalty pricing). On convenience and service fees—see Furletti, above note 16, at 12. The total revenue from cardholder fees—$28.9 billion—was calculated by subtracting revenue from interchange fees: $39.1 billion (CardFlash, "Merchant Fees," January 13, 2009) from total fee income: $68 billion (CardFlash, "Fee Factor 08," January 14, 2009). See also Furletti, above note 16, at 32, Figure 6 (showing a sharp increase in "fee income as a percentage of total revenue" since 1996); Improving Federal Consumer Protection in Financial Services: Hearing Before the H. Comm. on Financial Services, 110th Cong. app. 94–95 (2007) (statement of Sheila C. Bair, Chairman, Federal Deposit Insurance Corporation) (noting that net non-interest income for insured institutions has been growing faster than total net operating revenue); CardFlash, "Fee Factor 08," January 14, 2009 (Fee income increased from 17.3 percent of total revenues in 1994 to 40 percent of total revenues, or $68 billion, in 2008. While these figures include both merchant and cardholder fees, the increase in fee income has been driven by the rise in late payment fees, over-limit fees, and cash advance fees, coupled with newer fees such as balance transfer fees, foreign currency exchange surcharges, and expedited payment fees.) The shift to fees was made possible by the Supreme Court's 1996 "Smiley" decision which exempted national card issuers from state restrictions on card fees. CardFlash, "Fee Factor 08," January 14, 2009.

addition, issuers would be expected to respond by finding alternative back-end revenue sources—either by increasing back-end, non-salient fees that are not covered by the CARD Act or by introducing new, or redesigned, non-salient terms.[91]

Existing evidence on the effects of the CARD Act is inconclusive. It may be too soon to empirically assess the Act's effect on credit card pricing. Nevertheless, it is worth noting that industry sources suggest that issuers are expected to respond—or have already responded—to the Act by increasing annual fees and purchase APRs. And there is some evidence that issuers are searching for alternative back-end revenue sources by expanding the use of non-salient fees and terms not covered by the CARD Act and by introducing new, non-salient fees and terms.[92]

V. Welfare Implications

What are the costs of the identified contractual designs, especially when understood as a response to cardholders' imperfect rationality? First, complex, multidimensional contracts hinder competition in the credit card market. Second, complex and deferred-cost contracts distort the remaining, weakened forces of competition, leading to excessively high prices on less salient price dimensions and excessively low prices on more salient price dimensions. Third, these contractual design features increase the cost of

---

91. It should be noted that some of these predicted responses are also consistent with a rational-choice theory of credit card pricing—see Oren Bar-Gill and Ryan Bubb, "Credit Card Pricing: The CARD Act and Beyond" forthcoming in Cornell L. Rev.

92. On the limits of existing evidence on the effects of the CARD Act—see Bar-Gill and Bubb, *id*. For industry sources suggesting increases in annual fees and purchase APRs—see Andrew Martin, "Credit Card Industry Aims to Profit from Sterling Payers," *New York Times*, May 19, 2009 ("Banks are expected to look at reviving annual fees…, according to bank officials and trade groups"); CardFlash, "BofA Changes," August 18, 2009 (Bank of America expects an increase in the average APR and a decrease in the variance of APRs); CardFlash, "BofA Basic," September 17, 2009 ("The impact of the new credit card rules became clear today as Bank of America announced plans to launch a new credit card next month with a core interest rate of prime + 14 percent, compared to the prime + 9.9 percent APR that dominated the market for the past decade"); CardFlash, "CARD Act Impact," November 10, 2009 (according to the Fed's "Senior Loan Officer Opinion Survey on Bank Lending Practices" from October 2009, about 40 percent of banks expected to raise annual fees for prime borrowers and about 45 percent of banks expected to raise annual fees for nonprime borrowers). For evidence that issuers are looking for alternative back-end revenue sources—see Joshua M. Frank, "Dodging Reform: As Some Credit Card Abuses Are Outlawed, New Ones Proliferate," Center for Responsible Lending, 2009, <http://www.responsiblelending.org/credit-cards/research-analysis/CRL-Dodging-Reform-Report-12-10-09.pdf>.

financial distress. Fourth, the identified contractual designs raise distributional concerns, as they impose disproportionate burdens on weaker cardholders. Let's take a closer look at each one of these costs.

A. Hindered Competition

Perhaps the largest cost associated with excessively complex contracts comes
from the inhibited competition that they foster. As described previously,
complexity prevents the effective comparison-shopping that is necessary for
vigorous competition. The market power gained by issuers clearly helps
issuers at the expense of cardholders. But the limited competition also
imposes a welfare cost in the form of inefficient allocation: Cardholders are
not matched with the most efficient issuers.

Complexity harms consumers in yet another way. The imperfectly
rational consumer, and even the rational consumer who declines to invest
the necessary time and money needed to fully understand these complex
contracts, may well end up with a product that is not best for them—
another instance of allocative inefficiency.

B. Distorted Competition

Competition in the credit card market focuses on salient dimensions of the
credit card contract. There is much less competition on the non-salient
dimensions. The result is salient provisions that are favorable to cardholders
and non-salient provisions that are unfavorable to cardholders. Is this outcome
necessarily bad for cardholders? The answer is yes. The up-front benefits do
not fully compensate for the back-end costs. Distorted competition in the
credit card market leads to inefficient contracts. Inefficient contracts reduce
both the total surplus created by the issuer–cardholder relationship and the
cardholder's share of this surplus. (See the example in Section IV.B.1.)

Contracts with up-front benefits and back-end costs are inefficient
because they provide incentives to use the credit card in welfare-
reducing ways. The different dimensions—specifically, the different price
dimensions—of the credit card contract affect a cardholder's use of the
product. For example, a lower introductory interest rate leads to more short-
term borrowing; a high currency-conversion fee leads to less use of the
credit card outside the United States. A welfare-increasing contract sets
prices efficiently; in other words, to provide incentives for optimal use of

the credit card across the different dimensions. An inefficient contract, in which prices are set according to their salience instead of the underlying cost structure, provides the wrong incentives. Using the preceding example, if short-term credit entails a positive cost to the issuer, but the short-term interest rate is set at zero, because this dimension is salient to cardholders, then cardholders will engage in excessive short-term borrowing. If the currency-conversion fee is set above the cost to the issuer of processing foreign transactions, because this dimension is non-salient, then cardholders will engage in suboptimal use of their cards while abroad.

More fundamentally, distorted competition, with the resulting distorted contracts, can be expected to artificially inflate the demand for credit cards. Recall that the reason issuers reduce salient prices and increase non-salient prices is to create the appearance of a cheaper product without actually offering a cheaper product. When misperception leads cardholders to underestimate the total cost of the credit card (or overestimate the net benefit from the card), then demand for credit cards will be too high. Add to that the low, even negative, per-transaction fee, and we get too many credit cards used too often (for transacting).[93]

C. Financial Distress

There are two distinct arguments about the relationship between credit cards and financial distress.

The first argument is that credit cards cause financial distress. There is empirical evidence from three independent studies conducted by Ronald Mann, Michelle White, and Atif Mian and Amir Sufi, suggesting a causal link between credit card debt and consumer bankruptcies.[94] To the extent that credit cards and inefficient credit card contracts increase the risk of financial distress, they impose a cost on cardholders and on society.

The second argument is that, while not causing financial distress, credit cards, with their distorted contractual design, exacerbate the cost, to cardholders, from financial distress. Deferred-cost contracts often defer the costs to periods when the cardholder is in financial distress. The financially distressed cardholder is more likely to incur a late payment fee, pay an

---

93. See Sujit Chakravorti and William R. Emmons, "Who Pays for Credit Cards?" (2001) *Fed. Reserve Bank of Chi. Emerging Payments Occasional Paper Series, No. 1*, at 1 (it may well be that credit cards are "overused").
94. See above Section I.C.

over-limit fee, and trigger a default interest rate. Economic theory suggests that paying these high prices when in financial distress is especially painful, because of the decreasing marginal utility from money.

The abstract principle of decreasing marginal utility from money reflects the very concrete real-world experience of credit card holders. When a consumer is employed in a well-paid job, saving money on annual fees, per-transaction fees, and short-term interest rates is a nice but insignificant perk. But when the consumer is between jobs, struggling to make ends meet, or facing the financial burden of unexpected and mounting medical bills, paying this same amount of money (realistically, much more) in penalty fees and rates would likely be quite painful.

D. Distributional Concerns

Typically, consumers who benefit from rewards programs and frequent-flyer miles are not the same consumers who pay penalty fees and default interest rates. As we have seen, long-term prices finance short-term perks. We have not yet addressed the question of whether the same group of consumers pay the long-term prices and enjoy the short-term perks. There is reason to believe that there is only a partial overlap between the paying group and the benefiting group. There is also reason to believe that socio-economic status is not randomly divided across the two groups. The distorted pricing in the credit card market leads to regressive cross-subsidization between the different consumer groups.[95]

The cross-subsidization argument assumes that short-term perks for the rich are funded by the high, long-term prices that the poor pay. This argument needs to be qualified. The analysis in this chapter focuses on the issuer–cardholder relationship, sidestepping the important role of the merchant who accepts the card and transfers a percentage of the transaction amount (the interchange fee) to the issuer. It is possible that short-term perks for the rich are funded by the interchange revenues from the high-volume transactions of these rich cardholders. But this raises a different

95. See Federal Reserve Bank of Boston, "Consumer Behavior and Payment Choice: 2006 Conference Summary" (2007) *Public Policy Discussion Paper 07–4, 49*, available at <http://www.bos.frb.org/economic/ppdp/2007/ppdp0704.htm> (hereinafter "FRB Boston Conference Proceedings") (summarizing the proceedings of the second Consumer Behavior and Payment Choice conference, held at the Federal Reserve Bank of Boston on July 25–27, 2006, where participants noted "that non-revolving credit card users who have rewards programs are subsidized by revolving users without rewards programs").

distributional concern: If merchants increase retail prices to compensate for the interchange tax that they transfer to issuers, then *all* customers—including poorer cash customers—end up funding those short-term perks for the rich.[96] In any event, the weaker cardholders will still pay more of the high long-term prices and enjoy less of the short-term perks, even if the short-term perks are not funded by revenues from the long-term prices.

VI. Market Solutions

The welfare costs of credit cards designed in response to consumer biases can be large. Legal policy intervention may be needed to curb these welfare costs. But before considering legal intervention, we should explore the ability of the market to overcome the behavioral market failure on its own. Such market solutions exist. Some issuers offer credit card products that do not exhibit the distorted contract design described above. Perhaps most importantly, the rise of debit cards can be seen as a market solution to the problems with credit cards. Many of the misperceptions that are prevalent in the credit card market are borrowing-related. By removing the borrowing service, debit cards avoid triggering these misperceptions.[97]

Ultimately, however, these market solutions are imperfect because they cater to only a limited slice of the credit card market; namely, the more sophisticated consumers. The underlying problem is that markets respond to consumer demand. If imperfectly rational consumers demand distorted products, issuers will meet this demand. The solution, then, must focus on the demand problem. Consumers can (and often do) overcome their mistakes and biases, but learning is slow and not everyone learns.[98] Also, issuers have insufficient incentives to educate consumers and help them overcome their imperfect rationality. Consequently, less sophisticated consumers will continue to purchase the distorted products. Only the more sophisticated,

96. It is not clear that merchants will in fact increase retail prices to compensate for the interchange tax. See, e.g., Steven Semeraro, "The Reverse-Robin-Hood-Cross-Subsidy Hypothesis: Do Credit Card Systems Effectively Tax the Poor and Reward the Rich?", *Rutgers L.J.*, 40 (2009), 419.
97. Prepaid cards should also be mentioned as a potential market solution.
98. See Sumit Agarwal, John C. Driscoll, Xavier Gabaix, and David I. Laibson, "Learning in the Credit Card Market", February 8, 2008, available at SSRN: <http://ssrn.com/abstract=1091623> (Borrowers learn to avoid fees, but learning is imperfect and borrowers gradually forget what they have learned.)

rational consumers (and those who are aware of their imperfect rationality) will be attracted to the non-distorted products, to the market solutions.[99]

A. Consumer-Friendly Credit Cards

The credit card market is a large, diverse market. The preceding analysis focused on design features of the common credit card contract. But not all cards are created equal, nor do all cards exhibit all of the problematic design features highlighted in previous sections. Some issuers, in fact, offer consumer-friendly cards.

There are, for example, credit cards with a less complex, more transparent contract design than has been described previously. For example, in 2009, Bank of America introduced its "BankAmericard Basic," which has one rate for all transactions and no over-limit fees. In 2011, Citi introduced the "Simplicity Card," featuring a single rate across all purchases, balance transfers, and cash advances—with no late fees or penalty rate.[100]

Not all cards defer costs to the same extent. A recent study by Ryan Bubb and Alex Kaufman found that credit cards offered by credit unions exhibit less cost deferral than credit cards offered by investor-owned issuers. Bubb and Kaufman explain that credit unions have less incentive to make a profit at the expense of their members. The credit union's ownership structure serves as a commitment to spare the consumer the high prices affixed to non-salient dimensions. Bubb and Kaufman argue that more sophisticated consumers, who are aware of their biases, are attracted to credit unions. While clearly an optimistic finding, this optimism is tempered by the limited market share of credit unions, which stands at less than 5 percent.[101]

---

99. This problem restricts the impact of another market solution—third-party intermediaries, like creditcards.com and creditkarma.com, that provide easy comparison among card offers. Efficient comparisons will not help, if the consumer is comparing the wrong product dimensions or not placing proper weights on the different product dimensions. See section V.B. (Distorted Competition).

100. On Bank of America offerings—see CardFlash, "BofA Clarity," November 30, 2009. Bank of America also made a "Credit Card Clarity Commitment," as part of its campaign to simplify loan information for consumers, and mailed out a one-page summary of customers' rates, fees, and payment information to 40 million current cardholders. Id. On Citi's offerings—see CardFlash, "Citi Offers Credit with Single APR and No Late Fees," July 26, 2011.

101. See Ryan Bubb and Alex Kaufman, "Consumer Biases and Firm Ownership," (2009) Working Paper. The market share of credit unions—less than 5 percent—is based on 2006 data from the 2007 Card Industry Directory (by SourceMedia, Inc.).

Good behavior among credit card issuers is not limited to credit unions. For example, before the practice was banned by the CARD Act, Chase voluntarily eliminated double-cycle billing. Several issuers offer online financial education and specialized tools to help consumers manage their credit. For example, in 2010, Discover Financial Services launched its "Straight Talk" consumer website, designed to help consumers more easily understand how credit cards work. Discover also offers a variety of tools and resources to help consumers manage their credit, including "The Spend Analyzer," "The Paydown Planner," and "The Purchase Planner." Other issuers offer similar tools. Some also offer an automatic payment service, which can eliminate the risk of late payment.[102]

B. Debit Cards

Perhaps the solution to the problems inflicting the credit card market lies in a sister product: the debit card. Debit cards have enjoyed substantial growth in recent years. This growth has come, at least in part, at the expense of credit cards.[103] As noted earlier, debit cards are used only for transacting and thus offer a more consumer-friendly product when biases are borrowing-related.

To understand the rise of the debit card and to assess whether debit cards can reduce the welfare costs in the credit card market, we need to understand the drivers of the demand for debit cards. At first blush, the growth in debit card use is puzzling, at least to the extent that this growth is fueled by consumers who have, or can get, a credit card. After all, the credit card is a better product. It does everything that a debit card does and more. A consumer who wants a convenient, secure payment method can use a credit card and pay her balance in full each month. The credit card *allows* you to

102. See CardFlash, "Chase Pricing," November 20, 2007; CardFlash, "Straight Talk," February 23, 2010; CapitalOne, Credit Card Payment Calculator, <http://www.capitalone.com/calculator/>; American Express, A Notice About Your Account Alerts, email message received by Oren Bar-Gill, July 29, 2009 (introducing the Spend Tracking Alert and Balance Tracking Alert).
103. See CardFlash, "Visa Debit," May 5, 2009. (In 2002, U.S. Visa debit transactions surpassed credit transactions for the first time. In the fourth quarter of 2008, 70 percent of U.S. Visa transactions were debit transactions. Also, the fourth quarter of 2008 was the first period when debit cards surpassed credit cards in U.S. Visa payment volume: Debit payments volume was $206 billion, compared with credit payments volume of $203 billion.) A large part of debit card growth came at the expense of cash and checks. See FRB Boston Conference Proceedings, above note 95. But debit cards are also replacing credit cards. See Jonathan Zinman, "Debit or Credit?" (2006) *Dartmouth College Economics Department Working Paper* 3–4.

borrow; it doesn't force you to do so. In fact, credit cards are a better choice than debit cards for consumers who wish to transact but not to borrow, as they offer superior fraud-protection.[104]

Credit cards are also better than debit cards for non-borrowers, as they provide more lucrative rewards programs and other perks, like extended warranties and car rental insurance.[105] The behavioral-economics theory provides one explanation for the added benefits that credit cards offer to non-borrowers: The back-end revenues that credit card issuers obtain from borrowers on the non-salient, borrowing-related terms help finance the greater front-end benefits and perks offered to non-borrowers. These advantages of credit cards may explain the substantial delay in the introduction of debit cards in the United States.[106]

Still, the number and transacting volume of debit cards are growing fast. Why? One explanation is that consumers are becoming more sophisticated and less optimistic about their willpower, their ability to avoid financial hardship, and the probability of inadvertently triggering hidden fees. These consumers, armed with their newfound awareness, want to make a "pre-commitment" to stay away from the seduction of credit card borrowing and

104. See Mann, above note 22 (debit cards offer fewer legal protections); Privacy Rights Clearinghouse/UCAN, "Paper or Plastic? What Have You Got to Lose" March 2011, available at <http://www.privacyrights.org/fs/fs32-paperplastic.htm>.

105. Rewards on debit cards, while growing, are not as prevalent or as generous as credit card rewards. See FRB Boston Conference Proceedings, above note 95, at 22–3 (Debit card reward programs, while still relatively rare, are increasing rapidly); Andrew Ching, and Fumiko, Hayashi, "Payment Card Rewards Programs and Consumer Payment Choice" (May 13, 2008), available at SSRN: <http://ssrn.com/abstract=1114247>; CardFlash, "Debit Cards," August 18, 2008 (the "2008 Debit Issuer Study," conducted by Oliver Wyman for PULSE and covering more than 74 million debit cards issued by 62 financial institutions—including large banks, community banks, and credit unions—revealed that 51 percent of respondents now offer cards with rewards programs, compared to 37 percent in 2006); CardFlash, "Debit Rewards," August 28, 2009 (based on First Data's "Customer Loyalty Study"—in 2009, membership in debit card reward programs increased to 45 percent compared to 34 percent in 2008, but only 23 percent of respondents indicated that the benefits available through the reward program was "very influential" in their choice of financial institution).

106. See Evans and Schmalensee, above note 5, at 55, 76–7 and ch. 12 ("[D]ebit cards languished [in the United States] until the mid-1990s."). Debit cards have their own back-end costs, specifically overdraft fees. See CardFlash, Debit Overdraft, July 12, 2007 (a Center for Responsible Lending study found that debit card overdrafts are now the single largest source of overdraft fees. The study also found that consumers paid about $17.5 billion in fees for $15.8 billion in abusive overdraft loans.) Revenues from these overdraft fees may have helped fund the debit card reward programs, at least until they were limited by regulation that requires banks to obtain explicit consent before enrolling a consumer in an overdraft protection plan. See FRB, "What You Need to Know: New Overdraft Rules for Debit and ATM Cards, <http://www.federalreserve.gov/consumerinfo/wyntk_overdraft.htm>.

the costs it entails. Sophisticated consumers wish to tie their own hands. Debit cards provide the rope.

There are two problems, however, with debit cards as a market solution. The first is that the debit card solution is limited in scope. Only sophisticated consumers who understand the risks of credit cards will choose debit cards instead. Using back-end revenue to finance lucrative front-end perks, credit card issuers will be able to prevent the less sophisticated consumers from switching to debit cards. The second problem is that the shift to debit cards, to the extent that it occurs, is a second-best solution. Debit cards can be better than bad credit cards—those designed in response to consumer misperception. But they are not necessarily better than good credit cards. Credit cards can provide low-cost, convenient access to credit, which can be beneficial to many consumers.

The goal should not be to abolish credit cards, but to reshape the credit card product. Policymakers can play an important role in pushing the market in the right direction.

VII. Policy Implications: Rethinking Disclosure

A. Focusing on Disclosure

The welfare costs detailed above and the limits of market solutions provide the basis for considering legal intervention in the credit card market. The proposed behavioral-economics theory provides guidance for the design of potential policy responses. Here, I focus on one regulatory technique; disclosure mandates.

Any discussion of credit card regulation must note the important reforms put in place by the CARD Act of 2009. The CARD Act, and its implementing regulations, enhanced the mandatory disclosure regime governing credit cards, as we will see shortly. But unlike most previous legal interventions in the credit card market, the CARD Act did not stop at disclosure. It imposed substantive restrictions, banning practices and limiting prices. Some of these restrictions are clearly welfare-enhancing, such as the prohibition on allocating payments to low-interest balances first. Others, like the restrictions on risk-based pricing, are more controversial. These debates are beyond the scope of this Part, which, as noted earlier, focuses on disclosure.

Any treatment of disclosure as a regulatory technique should begin with the question of efficacy: Are disclosure mandates able to affect behavior and improve market outcomes? In the credit card market, evidence suggests that disclosure has been effective, at least to some extent. A series of studies by Federal Reserve economists have found that Truth-in-Lending disclosures have raised consumer awareness of the APR as a key determinant of the cost of credit. Moreover, these studies found that the increased salience of the APR has led to competition on this price dimension.[107]

There is also evidence that the enhanced disclosures mandated by the CARD Act have been effective. Specifically, a *Consumer Reports* survey found that 23 percent of respondents were motivated by the new Minimum Payment Warning on their bills to pay off their credit cards faster.[108] But even if the efficacy of current disclosures is limited, this still would not condemn disclosure as a regulatory strategy, because existing disclosure mandates are not optimally designed. In this Part, we'll look at ways regulators can design better disclosure mandates for the credit card market.

B. Disclosing Product-Use Information

The preceding analysis suggests that consumer misperception is responsible for the distorted design of the credit card contract. The problem, in essence, is that when shopping for a credit card, consumers are not armed with a sufficiently accurate assessment of how they will use the credit card product. Legal policy can address this problem. If consumers misperceive their use patterns, legislators and regulators should require issuers to provide product-use information to consumers.

While disclosure mandates are perhaps the main regulatory technique used in the credit card market, existing mandates focus almost exclusively on the disclosure of product-attribute information. Consider the Truth-in-Lending Act (TILA) and Regulation Z, which require specific disclosures in credit card applications and solicitations. These rules mandate disclosure of product-attribute information, specifically interest rates and fees.[109]

Disclosure regulation should go beyond the current scope of TILA. The goal is not only to educate consumers about credit terms, but also to

---

107. See Furletti, above note 16, at 9; Thomas A. Durkin, "Credit Cards: Use and Consumer Attitudes, 1970–2," *Fed. Reserve Bull.*, September 2, 623–34; Jinkook Lee and Jeanne M. Hogarth, "The Price of Money: Consumers' Understanding of APRs and Contract Interest Rates", *J. of Pub. Pol'y and Marketing*, 18 (1999), 66.
108. See CardFlash, "Consumer Reports," October 20, 2010.
109. 15 U.S.C. § 1637(c); 12 C.F.R. §§ 226.18, 226.5a.

educate them about their own preferences and cognitive biases. Knowledge of credit terms is meaningless if the consumer mistakenly precludes the possibility of a future need to borrow. Similarly, knowing the magnitude of a late fee is not helpful if the consumer mistakenly believes that he or she will never pay late.[110]

The declared purpose of TILA is "to assure a meaningful disclosure of credit terms...and to protect the consumer against inaccurate and unfair billing and credit card practices." The Interpretive Notes and Decisions accompanying TILA's opening section elaborate that the purpose of TILA is "to help correct what Congress perceived as widespread consumer confusion about the nature and cost of credit obligations."[111] Confusion about the cost of credit can persist, even when consumers know all relevant product attributes. "[M]eaningful disclosure" should include product-use information.

C. Designing Product-Use Disclosures

Designing disclosures that incorporate product-use information is not a trivial task. Product-use information can be disclosed at different levels. Issuers can be required to disclose—

• average-use information, where use patterns are averaged out across the entire population of consumers or, preferably, across some demographic or socio-economic subgroup of consumers; or
• individual-use information, based on historic use-pattern information collected on the individual consumer.

Individual-use information, when available, is preferable to statistical, average-use information. Existing evidence suggests that disclosure of statistical evidence is not always convincing. In particular, if the disclosed average level of borrowing or average number of late payments per year is taken across a large group of consumers, any individual consumer may believe that she is among the few who will not borrow and never pay late. Individual-use information is immune against such "I am better than

110. See Furletti, above note 16, at 5 ("Recent changes in how issuers price credit cards, however, have resulted in new levels of pricing complexity and created a structure of credit costs that can impact some customers very differently than others. That is, the cost that a consumer faces greatly depends on the way he or she uses the credit card."); CardFlash, "Reward Card Analysis," June 2, 2008 (consumers must know their use patterns in order to choose the optimal rewards card for themselves).
111. See 15 U.S.C. § 1601(a) and the accompanying Interpretive Notes and Decisions.

average" reasoning. When confronted with disclosures about their own levels of borrowing and the number of late payments that they made, consumers are not able to dismiss the information as an abstract, irrelevant statistic. Still, even individual-use information may not be entirely convincing, as the consumer could believe that past borrowing is not indicative of future choices.[112]

Importantly, issuers have a lot of individual-use information, which they collect and use to maximize profits. Duncan McDonald, former general counsel of Citigroup's Europe and North America card businesses, noted:

> "No other industry in the world knows consumers and their transaction behavior better than the bank card industry. It has turned the analysis of consumers into a science rivaling the studies of DNA. The mathematics of virtually everything consumers do is stored, updated, categorized, churned, scored, tested, valued, and compared from every possible angle in hundreds of the most powerful computers and by among the most creative minds anywhere. In the past 10 years alone, the transactions of 200 million Americans have been reviewed in trillions of different ways to minimize bank card risks."[113]

Issuers should be required to share this information with their customers.

Optimal disclosure design should also consider the advantages of combining product-use information with product-attribute information. For example, providing information on the number of late payments made during the past year is helpful. Providing information on the total amount of money paid in late fees during the past year is even more helpful. This

---

112. On the limits of average-use disclosures—see Christine Jolls et al., "A Behavioral Approach to Law and Economics", *Stan. L. Rev.*, 50 (1998), 1471, 1542 (people tend to underestimate their future risks even if they actually understand average risks); and compare: Svenson (fn 15, Chapter 1, this volume) 117 (a vast majority of drivers believe that their driving skills are above average). On the advantages of individualized disclosure—see generally Cass Sunstein and Richard Thaler, *Nudge* (describing their RECAP proposal) (fn 31, Chapter 1, this volume). See also Barry Nalebuff and Ian Ayres, *Why Not?* (Harvard Business School Press, 2003) 181 (arguing that issuers should be required to disclose to consumers the likelihood that they will incur late and over-limit fees, preferably based on individual data that the issuer collects on the specific consumer).

113. Duncan MacDonald, "Viewpoint: Card Industry Questions Congress Needs to Ask," *American Banker*, March 23, 2007. See also FRB, "Report to the Congress on Practices of the Consumer Credit Industry in Soliciting and Extending Credit and their Effects on Consumer Debt and Insolvency," 19 (June, 2006), available at <http://www.federalreserve .gov/boarddocs/rptcongress/bankruptcy/bankruptcybillstudy200606.pdf> (detailing the huge amounts of information that issuers have and use); Charles Duhigg, "What Does Your Credit-Card Company Know about You?" *New York Times*, May 17, 2009 (describing the vast amount of information, especially product-use information, that credit card companies collect, and then analyze using sophisticated algorithms informed by psychology research).

disclosure combines product-use information (the number of late payments) with product-attribute information (the magnitude of the late fee).

Timing is another important dimension in designing disclosure mandates, specifically when use information is concerned. When should the information be disclosed? Perhaps the easiest way to provide use information is on the monthly statement. As the consumer uses the card, the issuer collects and discloses use information. Recent reforms have substantially improved disclosures on the monthly statement, including disclosures that combine attribute and use information. Under FRB regulations, which took effect along with the CARD Act implementing rules, issuers must disclose, on the monthly statement, both monthly and year-to-date totals of interest charges and fees, separately.[114]

But disclosures on the monthly statement are not enough. To ensure competition and positive market outcomes, the consumer should be able to compare a current credit card to others being offered. Disclosures on the monthly statement, when it incorporates use information, tells consumers how much they are paying on their current card. In addition, consumers need to know how much they would pay if they decide to switch to a different card. This takes us from monthly statement disclosures to disclosures in advertisements and solicitations. Under existing law, these disclosures do not contain any use information, the idea being that the new issuer does not have any use information to disclose.[115]

Product-use information can be included in advertisements and solicitations. One option is to provide statistical use information or combine statistical use information with attribute information.[116] Another, more promising, option is to utilize individual-use information from the consumer's previous experiences, if any, in the credit card market. Under this option, the current issuer would be required to provide its customers with an electronic file containing all the use information that it collected. This might take the form of an Excel spreadsheet, for instance, with the consumer's individual-

114. See CFPB, CARD Act Factsheet, above note 4.
115. See Elizabeth Renuart and Diane E. Thompson, "The Truth, The Whole Truth, and Nothing but the Truth: Fulfilling the Promise of Truth in Lending", *Yale J. Reg.*, 25 (2008), 181, 188 ("Fees are presumed to be unknown").
116. Compare: Renuart and Thompson, *id.*, at 189 (describing a proposal by the National Consumer Law Center to require disclosure of a "typical" APR, calculated as an average of effective APRs paid by borrowers—these effective APRs include fees, such as late fees and over-limit fees, that are not included in the APR disclosed on advertisements, solicitations, and at account opening).

use data from the past three years. Consumers could take this file to the new issuer and get a total price quote, based on their use patterns. Such electronic disclosure can also facilitate the work of intermediaries. Companies like BillShrink can combine the use information with attribute information and recommend the card that best fits the consumer's needs.

Disclosures in advertisements and solicitations and on the monthly statement provide two options for the timing of disclosure. A third option, real-time disclosure, is particularly promising with respect to product-use information. In certain cases, disclosure can be more effective if the information is provided before the end of the billing cycle. According to a proposal by Ronald Mann, issuers would be required to provide point-of-sale information. For instance, if by charging a current purchase to a certain credit card the consumer would exceed the credit limit on that card and incur a fee, this information would be provided to the consumer, allowing him or her to use a different card or an alternative payment system.[117]

Finally, optimal disclosure design must address concerns about information overload. This is a general concern that applies to both product-attribute and product-use disclosures. There are two responses to this concern. One is to design simple disclosures. The year-to-date total interest paid is an example of such a simple disclosure. The idea is to provide highly aggregated information that can be understood and applied by the imperfectly rational consumer. The second approach is to provide much more information—raw, disaggregated information—but not to consumers. Recall the Excel file with detailed use information. The consumer wouldn't be expected to read and analyze the information in that file. Rather he or she would take the file to a competing issuer or to an intermediary for processing.

D. Steps in the Right Direction

Legislators and regulators are starting to understand the importance of product-use disclosures. The Dodd–Frank Wall Street Reform and Consumer Protection Act of 2010 imposes a general duty, subject to rules prescribed by the new Consumer Financial Protection Bureau, to disclose information, including usage data, in markets for consumer financial products.[118]

---

117. See Mann, above note 22.
118. Pub. L. 111–203, Title X, Sec. 1033.

Focusing on more concrete steps, the CARD Act requires that issuers disclose a Minimum Payment Warning on the monthly bill that includes information on the amount of time it will take to pay off the balance and the aggregate total payment if only the minimum amount is paid each month. The CARD Act also requires that issuers calculate and disclose the monthly payment that would pay off the cardholder's balance in three years, as well as the savings—in total payments—from this faster repayment schedule.[119] The minimum payment disclosures address the slow repayment problem identified earlier. They combine product-attribute information with certain use patterns specified by the Act and implementing regulations—comparing slow repayment (making only the minimum payment) to faster repayment (paying off the balance in three years).

Recent regulations also mandate that issuers disclose, on the monthly statement, monthly and year-to-date totals of interest charges and fees, separately.[120] As mentioned above, this is an example of a disclosure that combines individual-use information and product-attribute information. While promising, this disclosure can and should be improved. First, disclosing a single total cost figure can be more effective than disclosing two separate figures—one for interest and one for fees. Second, year-to-date figures make sense for monthly statement disclosures but contain limited use information. Issuers could be required to provide a year-end summary with total annual cost figures that are based on a longer history of use patterns—three years, perhaps. Finally, to facilitate competition, use-based information needs to be disclosed also by new issuers. For this purpose, regulators should require existing issuers to provide, in electronic form, detailed use information that could be then transferred to new issuers or to intermediaries.

Disclosing use-based, total-cost information, by both existing and new issuers, can potentially eliminate the complexity and cost-deferral problems. Consumers should not care about complexity if issuers are required to disclose the bottom-line, aggregate costs. Moreover, issuers will have no incentive to artificially increase complexity, only to disguise the true cost of credit,

---

119. See FRB, "Credit Card Rules, February 22", above note 34 (describing the new CARD Act rules).
120. See CFPB, CARD Act Factsheet, above note 4. It is important that all fees be included. Otherwise, issuers will have an incentive to increase excluded fees. Cf. Renuart and Thompson, above note 115, at 185, 203 (explaining the adverse effects of an APR disclosure that excludes certain fees, Renuart and Thompson note: "The excluded fees can contribute mightily, yet invisibly, to the cost of credit. As a result, lenders are motivated to structure their credit transactions to take advantage of these exclusions.").

since they must—by law—disclose the total cost of credit anyway.[121] A total cost disclosure can also address the deferred-costs problem. The total cost measure would take into consideration the temporal dimension of credit card pricing, combining short-term and long-term costs. Accordingly, consumers who shop for credit based on the total-cost figure will not underestimate long-term costs. And, as a result, issuers will have no incentive to defer costs.

Conclusion

Credit card contracts are complex and multidimensional. Credit card pricing is, in many cases, salience-based rather than cost-based. This contract design is the product of a behavioral market failure, a result of the interaction between consumer psychology and market forces. The market failure stifles competition by increasing the costs of comparison shopping. It distorts competition because, to attract imperfectly rational cardholders, issuers compete by reducing the perceived total price rather than the actual total price. The costs of financial distress are increased, and distributional concerns are raised.

The identification of a market failure—the behavioral market failure—opens the door for legal intervention. Recent reforms, specifically the CARD Act and the Dodd–Frank Act, take important steps in the right direction. Focusing on the design of optimal disclosure mandates, this chapter provided guidance to lawmakers, including those entrusted with the implementation of the CARD Act and the Dodd–Frank Act, on how to most effectively address the behavioral market failure.

---

121. Board of Governors of the Federal Reserve System and the Department of Housing and Urban Development, "Joint Report to the Congress Concerning Reform to the Truth and Lending Act and the Real Estate Settlement Procedures Act" 9 (1998), available at <http://www.federalreserve.gov/boarddocs/press/general/1998/19980717/default.htm> (discussing the benefits of the APR as a total cost of credit measure, the Report notes: "The APR concept deters hidden or 'junk' fees to the extent that the fees must be included in the APR calculation.").

Appendix: Teaser Rates

Why are teaser rates so effective? The answer is that a consumer with a current financing need will take the teaser-rate "bait." For such consumers, who have already decided to incur debt on the new credit card, the interest rate on this debt will be important. Moreover, if the new card permits balance transfers from old cards, the switch may present a current benefit. On the other hand, if consumers incorrectly believe that they will not borrow beyond the introductory period, they will not mind the steep jump in the interest rate from the low teaser rate to the high post-introductory level.[122]

To better understand the operation of teaser rates, let us return to the hyperbolic discounting model. Consider two pairs of points on a timeline starting at $T = 0$, such that the temporal distance between the two points in the first pair is equal to the temporal distance between the two points in the second pair, and the first pair is closer to $T = 0$ relative to the second pair. Hyperbolic discounting implies that the discounting, from the $T = 0$ perspective, between the two points in the first pair will be greater than the discounting between the two points in the second pair. Consequently, the likelihood of a preference reversal is greater for the temporally distant pair. Returning to teaser rates, this implies that the likelihood of unanticipated borrowing is increasing in the temporal distance between $T = 0$ and the point in time when the actual borrowing decision will be made. This means that consumers are less likely to underestimate their short-run level of borrowing, which would make them more sensitive to short-term interest rates.

Figure 2.2 offers a graphic illustration of short-run borrowing ($T = 1,2$), as compared to long-run borrowing ($T = 3,4$). While a preference reversal is obtained with respect to long-run borrowing, leading to underestimation of future borrowing, there is no preference reversal with respect to short-run borrowing. The consumer believes at $T = 0$ that he or she will borrow, and indeed borrows at $T = 1$. Since there is no underestimation of short-run borrowing, this consumer would be more sensitive to short-run interest rates. This explains the competition between credit card issuers on the teaser-rate dimension.

Another related explanation for the prevalence of teaser rates is based on the concept of switching costs. In its simple form, the argument is that the costs of switching from one credit card to another prevent such switching, at least to a certain degree. Therefore, issuers can lure consumers with low introductory interest rates, counting on switching costs to prevent at least some consumers from switching

---

122. See Ausubel, above note 10, at 262–3.

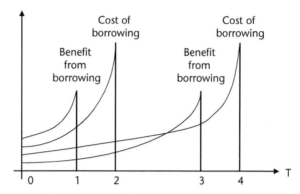

Figure 2.2. Borrowing in the near versus the more distant future

to another card once the introductory period is over.[123] The problem with this simple version of the switching-cost argument is that rational consumers anticipate the lock-in effect. Recognizing that they would not switch to a new card, consumers would weigh also the high, post-introductory interest rates when choosing among competing credit card products.

The behavioral-economics theory suggests a more persuasive version of the switching-cost story. Even if consumers anticipate lock-in, they still underestimate the cost of lock-in, since they do not expect to borrow (or to borrow as much) in the future. Hyperbolic discounting reinforces this revised version of the switching-cost argument. Naive hyperbolic discounters may wrongly anticipate that they would switch to a new card, but in fact will not switch when the introductory period ends. From an ex ante perspective, when both the switching costs and the benefits of switching lie in the future, a naive hyperbolic discounter might believe that she will switch to a new card at the end of the introductory period offered by

123. See Ausubel, above note 10, at 263 ("[E]conomic theory suggests that firms in a market with substantial search/switch costs will find advantage in utilizing introductory offers or sign-up bonuses to lure new customers."). In the credit card market there may be non-trivial switching costs. Shui and Ausubel estimated the cost of switching, including psychological costs, at $150. See Shui and Ausubel, above note 28. See also National Consumer Law Center, *Truth in Lending* (4th edn., 1999) 262. Rewards programs based on the accumulation of points or frequent-flyer miles generate additional switching costs. Also, switching becomes extremely difficult as the size of a borrower's outstanding balance increases. See Ronald J. Mann, "'Contracting' for Credit", *Mich. L. Rev.*, 104 (2006), 899, 925; Paul S. Calem et al., "Switching Costs and Adverse Selection in the Market for Credit Cards: New Evidence" *J. Banking and Fin.*, 30 (2006), 1653, 1655; Victor Stango, "Pricing with Consumer Switching Costs: Evidence from the Credit Card Market", *J. Indus. Econ.*, 50 (2002), 475, 477, 479–80; Ronald J. Mann, "Bankruptcy Reform and the 'Sweat Box' of Credit Card Debt", *U. Ill. L. Rev.*, [vol. no] (2007), 375, 389. Interestingly, while the teaser rate strategy surely relies on switching costs to limit defection at the end of the introductory period, one of the main purposes of teaser rates is to induce switching.

the old card. However, when the introductory period offered by the old card ends, the switching costs are imminent while the benefits from switching still lie in the future. Thus, applying the high short-term discount rate, the consumer may decide not to switch. This more sophisticated version of the switching-cost argument helps explain consumers' heightened sensitivity to teaser rates and the resulting prevalence of teaser rates in credit card offers.[124]

124. See DellaVigna and Malmendier, above note 39, at 26–7 (naive agents underestimate the probability that they will "renew the contract," i.e. continue to borrow after the introductory period); Ran Spiegler, *Bounded Rationality and Industrial Organization* (Oxford University Press, 2011), ch. 2 (describing teaser rates as a contract design response to demand generated by naive consumers).

3

Mortgages

Introduction

Almost 3 million subprime loans were originated in 2006, bringing the total value of outstanding subprime loans to over a trillion dollars.[1] A few months later, the subprime crisis began. Foreclosure rates soared. Hundreds of billions—perhaps trillions—of dollars were lost by borrowers, lenders, neighborhoods, and cities, not to mention broader effects on the U.S. and world economies.[2]

In this chapter, we'll examine the subprime mortgage contract and its central design features. As we will see, for many borrowers these contractual design features were not welfare maximizing. In fact, to the extent that the design of subprime mortgage contracts contributed to the subprime crisis, this welfare loss to borrowers—substantial in itself—is compounded by much broader social costs. A better understanding of the market failure that

---

1. See Yuliya Demyanyk and Otto Van Hemert, "Understanding the Subprime Mortgage Crisis" *Rev. Fin. Stud.*, 24 (2011), 1848, 1853, 1854 (tbl. 1) (analyzing data covering approximately 85 percent of securitized subprime loans. In 2006, 75 percent of subprime loans were securitized, and the authors' data set included 1,772,000 subprime loans originated in 2006, implying a total of 1,772,000/(0.85 * 0.75) = 2,779,608); State of the U.S. Economy and Implications for the Federal Budget: Hearing before the H. Comm. on the Budget, 110th Cong. 10 (2007) (hereinafter "Hearing") (prepared statement of Peter Orszag, Director, Congressional Budget Office) ("By the end of 2006, the outstanding value of subprime mortgages totaled more than $1 trillion and accounted for about 13 percent of all home mortgages."); Center for Responsible Lending, "A Snapshot of the Subprime Market" <http://www.responsiblelending.org/issues/mortgage/quick-references/a-snapshot-of-the-subprime.html> (estimating that as of November 27, 2007, there were 7.2 million outstanding subprime loans with an estimated total value of $1.3 trillion).
2. See Cong. Budget Office, *The Budget and Economic Outlook: Fiscal Years 2008 to 2018* (2008) 23 (hereinafter "CBO Outlook"), available at <http://www.cbo.gov/ftpdoc.cfm?index=8917andtype=1> (noting estimates of between $200 billion and $500 billion for total subprime-related losses and noting the additional—and potentially substantial—indirect adverse effects of the subprime crisis on the economy).

produced these inefficient contracts should inform the ongoing efforts to reform the regulations governing the subprime market.

A. Contract Design

During the five years preceding the crisis, the subprime market experienced staggering growth as riskier loans were made to riskier borrowers.[3] Not surprisingly, these riskier loans came at the price of higher interest rates to compensate lenders for the increased risk that they undertook. But high prices themselves are not the central problem. The root cause of the problem is that lenders hid these high prices and borrowers underappreciated them. In the prime market, the traditional loan is a standardized, thirty-year fixed-rate mortgage (FRM). Lenders could have covered the increased risk of subprime loans by simply raising the interest rate on the traditional FRM. They chose not to do this for a number of reasons. To uncover some of those reasons, let's look at the features of the common subprime mortgage contract.

The subprime market boasted a broad variety of complex loans with multidimensional pricing structures. Hybrid loans (which combine fixed and variable rates), interest-only loans, and option-payment adjustable-rate mortgages (ARMs)—each product type with its own multidimensional design—were all common in the expanding subprime market. It should be noted that many of these contractual designs were known in the prime market since the early 1980s. But it was in the subprime market where they first took center stage.[4]

Common subprime mortgage contracts exhibited the two design features highlighted throughout this book; complexity and cost deferral. Let's consider cost deferral first. Again, an important note: All loan contracts, of course, involve deferred costs. The loans we're examining feature deferral of costs beyond that which is necessarily implied by the nature of a loan.

---

3. See Demyanyk and Van Hemert, above note 1, at 1852, 1854 (tbl. 1); Center for Responsible Lending, "Mortgage Lending Overview," <http://www.responsiblelending.org/issues/mortgage/>.

4. A note on terminology: The residential mortgage market is divided into the prime segment and the nonprime segment. The nonprime segment is further divided into subprime (higher risk) and Alt-A (lower risk), although the line between subprime and Alt-A is not always clear. See below Part I.A. Many of the contractual design features studied in this chapter were common in both the subprime and Alt-A segments. For expositional convenience, I will sometimes refer to these two segments together as "subprime".

The traditional prime mortgage required a 20 percent down-payment, which implies a loan-to-value (LTV) ratio of no more than 80 percent. In the subprime market, in 2006, more than 40 percent of loans had LTVs exceeding 90 percent. Focusing on purchase-money loans, in 2005, 2006, and the first half of 2007, the median subprime borrower put no money down, borrowing 100 percent of the purchase price of the house.

The schedule of payments on the loan itself exhibits the same deferred-cost characteristic. Under the standard prime FRM, the borrower pays the same dollar amount each month—a flat payment schedule. Under a conventional ARM, where the monthly payment is calculated by adding a fixed number of percentage points to a fluctuating index, the dollar amount paid varies from month to month but without any systemic trajectory. By way of contrast, the majority of subprime loans exhibited an increasing payment schedule. They set a low interest rate for an introductory period—typically two years—and a higher interest rate for the remaining term of the loan. Other subprime loans exhibited an even steeper payment schedule. Interest-only loans and payment-option ARMs allowed for zero or negative amortization during the introductory period, further increasing the step-up in the monthly payment after the introductory period ended. A direct impact of an escalating-payments contract is often "payment shock," which occurs when a rate-reset leads to a significant increase in the monthly payment—sometimes as much as 100 percent.

The second contractual design feature, common to most subprime mortgages, is complexity. While the traditional FRM sets a single, constant interest rate, the typical subprime mortgage includes multiple interest rates, some of which are implicitly defined by nontrivial formulas that adjust rates from one period to the next. The typical subprime loan also features a host of fees, some applicable at different time periods during the loan term, some contingent on various exogenous changes or on borrower behavior. The numerous fees associated with a subprime loan fall under two categories:

(1) Origination fees, including a credit check fee, an appraisal fee, a flood certification fee, a tax certification fee, an escrow analysis fee, an underwriting analysis fee, a document preparation fee, and separate fees for sending emails, faxes, and courier mail; and

(2) Post-origination fees, including late fees, foreclosure fees, prepayment penalties, and dispute-resolution or arbitration fees.

These fees can add up to thousands of dollars or up to 20 percent of the loan amount. The prepayment option, of special importance in the subprime market, further complicates the valuation of these contracts, as does the (implicit) default option.

Because a borrower must choose among many different, complex products, each with a different set of multidimensional prices and features, the complexity of the borrower's decision is exponentially greater than the already high level of complexity of a single contract.[5]

B. Contract Design Explained

What explains these contractual design features? To find out, let's explore possible rational-choice explanations, starting with the cost-deferral feature. A common explanation for deferred-cost contracts is based on the affordability argument. Many subprime borrowers, at the time they take out their loans, are liquidity constrained: They can afford only a small down payment and a small monthly payment. The catch, of course, is that a small down payment and a small initial monthly payment eventually convert to higher monthly payments when the initial rate resets to the post-introductory level. Accordingly, the rationality of the affordability argument depends on the borrower's ability to either make the high future payment or to avoid it. In this way, the argument then splits into two sub-arguments: the "make" argument and the "avoid" argument.

The "make" argument holds that the borrowers will anticipate being able to make the higher payment if they expect their income to increase substantially by the end of the introductory period. Some subprime borrowers rationally expected such a substantial increase in income; many others did not.

The "avoid" argument posits that borrowers will be able to avoid the higher payment if they expect to prepay the mortgage before the introductory period ends. The prepayment option depends on the availability of refinance loans with attractive terms. Attractive refinancing options will be

5. "Truth in Lending," 73 Fed. Reg. 44,522, 44,524–25 (July 30, 2008) (codified at 12 C.F.R. pt. 226) ("[P]roducts in the subprime market tend to be complex, both relative to the prime market and in absolute terms. . . .").

available if the borrower's credit score improves, market interest rates fall, or house prices increase. Some borrowers during the subprime mortgage boom rationally expected that such positive realizations would enable them to refinance their deferred-cost mortgage and avoid the high long-term costs. For many other borrowers, these expectations were overly optimistic.

An alternative, rational-choice explanation portrays the deferred-cost mortgage as an investment vehicle designed to facilitate speculation on real-estate prices. According to this explanation, if house prices rise, the speculator will be able to sell the house (or refinance) and pocket the difference between the lower buy price and the higher sell price without ever paying the high long-term cost of the deferred-cost loan. If house prices fall, the explanation continues, the speculator will default on the mortgage—again avoiding the high long-term cost. Of course, default is not a cost-free proposition, but as long as the probability of a price increase is high enough, the upside benefit will offset the downside risk. Some subprime borrowers were surely speculators and benefited from this strategy. Many others, however, were not—and did not.

Let's turn to the second design feature; complexity and multidimensionality. We'll start with the multiple, indirectly defined interest rates.[6] The index-driven rate adjustments of an ARM—further complicated by maximum adjustment caps—can be explained as a means to efficiently allocate the risk of fluctuating interest rates between lenders and borrowers. This explanation, however, was more powerful when interest-rate risk was shared by the lender and borrower. During the subprime expansion, when securitization was prevalent, this risk could have been—and sometimes was—passed on to diversified investors.

Next, consider the proliferation of fees common in subprime mortgage contracts. A rational-choice model can explain at least some of these fees. Charging separate fees for separate services allows each borrower to pick and choose from the offered services according to individual preferences. But this applies only to optional services, not to the many non-optional yet separately priced services, such as the credit check and document preparation. Another explanation holds that the proliferation of fees reflects efficient risk-based pricing. For example, delinquency imposes a cost on lenders. Late fees and foreclosure fees allocate this cost to the delinquent borrowers. Absent such fees,

6. To the extent that interest-rate complexity is an artifact of the deferred-cost features, the preceding discussion applies here as well.

lenders would raise interest rates to compensate for the forgone fees, and non-delinquent borrowers would bear a large share of the costs imposed by delinquent borrowers. Again, this explanation is plausible only for certain fees.

Rational-choice theories, then, explain some of the observed contractual designs in some contexts. They do not provide a complete account. A rational-choice model does not fully explain the prevalence of cost deferral and the exceedingly high level of complexity. To fill this explanatory gap, we'll consider a behavioral-economics theory of the subprime mortgage contract, applying the general framework of Chapter 1 to the mortgage world. We'll see that the design of subprime mortgage contracts can be explained as a rational market response to the imperfect rationality of borrowers.

The cost-deferral feature can be traced back to borrowers' myopia and optimism bias. Myopic borrowers focus on the short-term dimensions of the loan contract and pay insufficient attention to the long-term dimensions. Optimistic borrowers underestimate the future cost of the deferred-cost contract. They overestimate their future income and expect unrealistically attractive refinance options. Or they overestimate the expected value of a bet placed on the real-estate market, perhaps because they irrationally expect that a 10 percent price increase last year will be replicated next year. If myopic and optimistic borrowers focus on the short term and discount the long term, lenders will offer deferred-cost contracts with low short-term prices and high long-term prices.[7]

A similar argument explains the complexity of subprime mortgage contracts. Imperfectly rational borrowers will not be able to effectively aggregate multiple price and non-price dimensions and discern from them the true total cost of the mortgage product. Inevitably, these borrowers will focus on a few salient dimensions. If borrowers cannot process complex, multidimensional contracts and thus ignore less salient price dimensions, lenders will offer complex, multidimensional contracts, shifting much of the loan's cost to the less salient dimensions.[8]

---

7. See Ben S. Bernanke, Chairman, Bd. of Governors of the Fed. Reserve Sys., Speech at the Women in Housing and Finance and Exchequer Club Joint Luncheon, Washington, D.C.: "Financial Markets, the Economic Outlook, and Monetary Policy" (January 10, 2008), available at <http://www.federalreserve.gov/newsevents/speech/bernanke20080110a.htm> (suggesting that the ARM design responds to optimism about house prices).

8. See Edmund L. Andrews, "Fed and Regulators Shrugged as the Subprime Crisis Spread: Analysis Finds Trail of Warnings on Loans," *New York Times*, December 18, 2007, at A1 (quoting Edward M. Gramlich, the former Federal Reserve governor, asking: "Why are the most risky loan products sold to the least sophisticated borrowers... The question answers itself—the least sophisticated borrowers are probably duped into taking these products.").

While focusing on only one part of the subprime picture—the design of subprime loan contracts—this chapter develops an alternative account of the dynamics that led to the subprime crisis. One common account focuses on unscrupulous lenders who pushed risky credit onto borrowers who were incapable of repaying. Another common account focuses on irresponsible borrowers who took out loans they could not repay. Both accounts capture some of what was going on during the subprime boom, but both accounts are incomplete. In many cases, borrowers were not reckless; they were imperfectly rational. And in many cases lenders were not evil; they were simply responding to a demand for financing driven by borrowers' imperfect rationality.

This chapter highlights a demand-side market failure; imperfectly rational borrowers "demanded" complex, deferred-cost loan contracts and lenders met this demand. But the failures in the subprime mortgage market were not limited to the demand side. A supply-side market failure explains why lenders willingly catered to borrowers' imperfectly rational demand—even when the demanded product designs increased the default risk borne by lenders.[9]

The main culprit in this supply-side failure was securitization—the process of issuing securities backed by large pools of mortgage obligations. Securitization created a host of agency problems as a series of agents—intermediaries responsible for originating loans, pooling and packaging them into mortgage-backed securities, and assessing the risk associated with the different securities—stood between the principals (the investors who ultimately funded the mortgage loans) and the borrowers. The compensation of these agents/intermediaries was not designed to align their interests with those of the principals/investors. Instead, their fees were based on the quantity, not quality, of processed loans. Consequently, the agents/intermediaries had strong incentives to increase the volume of originations—even low-quality, high-risk ones—by promoting mortgage products that, through high levels of complexity and cost deferral, created the appearance of affordability.[10]

---

9. An immediate response is that lenders priced the increased risk. But this response is misleading. The evidence shows that subprime risks were not accurately priced.
10. See HUD, Report to Congress on the Root Causes of the Foreclosure Crisis, 31–2 (2010) (hereinafter "HUD Report").

Another factor: It is likely that even sophisticated investors and financial intermediaries got caught up in the frenzy of the real-estate boom and underestimated the risks associated with the mortgage products that they were peddling.[11] The multibillion dollar losses incurred by these sophisticated players provide (at least suggestive) evidence that imperfect rationality was not confined to the demand side of the subprime market.[12] And there is more direct evidence. For example, in an email message uncovered by an SEC investigation, Angelo R. Mozilo, Countrywide's CEO, wrote: "We have no way, with any reasonable certainty, to assess the real risk of holding these loans [Payment Option ARMS] on our balance sheet....The bottom line is that we are flying blind on how these loans will perform in a stressed environment of higher unemployment, reduced values and slowing home sales."[13]

C. Welfare Implications

Back to the demand-side failure, which is the focus of this chapter: The proposed behavioral-economics theory offers a more complete account of sub-

---

11. See HUD Report, above note 10, at 37 (concluding that investors overestimated the ability of innovations in financial market instruments (e.g., CDOs and CDSs) to shield them from risk). Much of this underestimation of risk harkens back to optimism about house prices. See, e.g., Kristopher S. Gerardi et al., *Making Sense of the Subprime Crisis* (2008) (*Fed. Reserve Bank of Boston, Public Policy Discussion Paper No. 09–1*), 1, available at <http://www.bos.frb.org/economic/ppdp/2009/ppdp0901.htm> (finding that analysts in 2005 understood the risks of a steep decline in house prices but believed that the probability of such a decline was very low); Julio Rotemberg, *Subprime Meltdown: American Housing and Global Financial Turmoil* (Harvard Business School, 2008) 1 (quoting a letter that Fannie Mae CEO Franklin Raines sent to shareholders in 2001: "Housing is a safe, leveraged investment—the only leveraged investment available to most families—and it is one of the best returning investments to make...Homes will continue to appreciate in value. Home values are expected to rise even faster in this decade than in the 1990s.").
12. See Jennifer E. Bethel, Allen Ferrell, and Gang Hu, "Legal and Economic Issues in Litigation Arising from the 2007–2008 Credit Crisis" 21, 81 tbl. 2 (2008) (*Harvard Law and Econ. Discussion Paper* No. 212), available at <http://ssrn.com/abstract=1096582> (summarizing the tens of billions of dollars worth of subprime-related write-offs by banks; citing an estimate of $150 billion in writedowns as of February 2008 and a forecast that this amount will more than double); Press Release, Standard and Poor's, "Subprime Write-Downs Could Reach $285 Billion, but Are Likely Past the Halfway Mark" (March 13, 2008), available at <http://www2.standardandpoors.com/portal/site/sp/en/us/page.article/4,5,5,1,1204834027864.html> (discussing Standard and Poor's increased estimate of writedowns at $285 billion, up from $265 billion earlier in the year). These losses do not provide conclusive evidence that sophisticated players made mistakes; they could be the realization of the large (!) downside risk in an (ex ante) rational bet.
13. See Gretchen Morgenson, "S.E.C. Accuses Countrywide's Ex-Chief of Fraud," *New York Times*, June 4, 2009 (quoting from Mozilo's email).

prime market dynamics and of how these dynamics shaped the design of subprime loan contracts. These contractual design features have significant welfare implications, especially when understood as a market response to the imperfect rationality of borrowers. First, excessive complexity prevents effective comparison-shopping and thus hinders competition. Second, deferred-cost features are correlated with increased levels of delinquency and foreclosure, which impose significant costs not only on borrowers but also on surrounding communities, lenders, loan purchasers, and the economy at large. Third, excessively complex deferred-cost contracts have adverse distributive consequences, disproportionally burdening financially weaker—often minority—borrowers. Finally, loading a loan's cost onto less salient or underappreciated price dimensions artificially inflates the demand for mortgage financing and, indirectly, for residential real estate. The proposed theory thus establishes a causal link between contractual design and the subprime expansion and real-estate boom. Accordingly, the subprime meltdown that followed this expansion can also be attributed, at least in part, to the identified contractual design features.[14]

Importantly, the identified contractual design features and the welfare costs associated with them are not necessarily the result of less-than-vigorous competition in the subprime market. Enhanced competition could even make these design features more pervasive. If borrowers focus on the short term and discount the long term, competition might force lenders to offer deferred-cost contracts. And if borrowers faced with complex, multidimensional contracts ignore less salient price dimensions, competition might force lenders to offer complex, multidimensional contracts and to shift much of the loan's cost to the less salient price dimensions.

On the other hand, competition may create incentives for lenders to educate consumers and reduce the biases and misperceptions that give rise to excessive complexity and cost deferral. Measures designed to ensure robust competition in the subprime mortgage market, while desirable, should not be relied upon to solve the behavioral market failure.

---

14. See Section V.B. below. While contractual design contributed to the subprime expansion, there are other factors that likely played a more central role in generating the subprime expansion, including (1) the advent of new technology that enabled efficient risk-based pricing, and (2) the increase in the supply (or availability) of funds brought about by securitization and the global saving glut.

D. Policy Implications

The subprime crisis has spurred a plethora of reforms and reform proposals.[15] In this chapter, we'll focus on disclosure regulation—specifically, the Annual Percentage Rate (APR) disclosure, the traditional centerpiece of the mortgage disclosure regime.

The importance of the APR, and of total-cost-of-credit measures more generally, has been reaffirmed by the new laws and regulations. The Mortgage Reform and Anti-Predatory Lending Act, enacted as Title XIV of the Dodd–Frank Wall Street Reform and Consumer Protection Act of 2010, requires disclosure of total-cost information. And the new disclosure forms being developed by the Consumer Financial Protection Bureau (CFPB), the result of a direct Congressional mandate in the Dodd–Frank Act, secure an important place for the APR.[16] The APR disclosure has the potential to undo the adverse effects of imperfect rationality, including the identified contractual design features and the welfare costs they impose.

The APR disclosure was the most important innovation of the Truth in Lending Act (TILA) of 1968.[17] A normalized total-cost-of-credit measure, the APR was designed to assist borrowers in comparing different loan products. In theory, the APR should solve—or at least mitigate—both the complexity and cost-deferral problems. Complexity and multidimensionality pose a problem if they hide the true cost of the loan. The APR responds to this concern by folding the multiple price dimensions into a single measure. The APR should similarly help short-sighted borrowers grasp the full cost of deferred-cost loans, as the APR calculation assigns proper weight to the long-term price dimensions. Moreover, since the APR—in theory—strips away any competitive advantage of excessive complexity and cost deferral, lenders will have no reason to offer loan contracts with these design features.

15. Major new laws and regulations include (1) the Mortgage Reform and Anti-Predatory Lending Act, enacted as Title XIV of the Dodd–Frank Wall Street Reform and Consumer Protection Act of 2010, Pub. L. 111–203 (hereinafter "Dodd–Frank Act'), and (2) the new set of regulations governing mortgage lending issued by the Federal Reserve Board (FRB) in July 2008–"Truth in Lending," 73 Fed. Reg. 44,522, 44,524–25 (July 30, 2008) (codified at 12 C.F.R. pt. 226).
16. See Dodd–Frank Act, Sec. 1419 (requiring disclosure of total cost information) and Sec. 1032(f) (directing the CFPB to develop a new disclosure form). See also CFPB, "Know Before You Owe Initiative," <http://www.consumerfinance.gov/knowbeforeyouowe/>.
17. Truth in Lending Act, Pub. L. No. 90–321, § 107, 82 Stat. 146, 149 (1968) (codified as amended at 15 U.S.C. § 1606 (2006)) (defining the APR); Truth in Lending Act, Pub. L. No. 90–321, §§ 121–31, 82 Stat. 146, 152–7 (1968) (codified as amended at 15 U.S.C. §§ 1631–49 (2006)) (requiring disclosure of the APR).

The APR can solve these problems, but only if it lives up to the expecta-tions of the Congress that enacted it, namely, if it provides a timely, true measure of the total cost of credit and borrowers rely on it in choosing among different loan products. In the run-up to the subprime crisis, the APR disclosure did not live up to these expectations. Why? Three reasons. First, the APR disclosure often came too late to be useful for comparison-shopping. Second, the APR did not, and still does not, measure the total cost of credit. This is because numerous fees paid by mortgage borrowers are excluded from the regulatory definition of a "finance charge" and are thus ignored in the APR calculation.

Third, the APR calculation assumed, and still assumes, that the borrower will hold the loan for the nominal loan period, typically 30 years. The actual duration of a mortgage loan is, however, closer to five years on average in the subprime market. Most borrowers refinance and prepay (or default) long before the thirty-year mark. By ignoring the possibility of prepayment (and default) the APR disclosure fails to reflect the true total cost of the loan. This distortion was especially pronounced during the recent subprime expansion, when for many loans the prepayment option constituted a substantial value component. When a borrower expects to prepay a deferred-cost loan by the end of the low-rate introductory period, it makes little sense for this bor-rower to rely on an APR that presumes continued payments at the high post-introductory rate. Since the APR disclosure often came too late and did not reflect the true cost of credit, borrowers stopped relying on the APR as the main tool for comparison shopping among loan products. This dimin-ished its power as an effective antidote to imperfect rationality.

Recent reforms and existing reform proposals address some of the short-comings of the APR disclosure. The timing-of-disclosure problem was addressed and partially solved by the Federal Reserve Board's (FRB's) new mortgage regulations and by the recently enacted Housing and Economic Recovery Act.[18] These reforms are commendable, but more should be done. In the most recent and most comprehensive proposal to create a more inclusive APR, Elizabeth Renuart and Diane Thompson are advocating a broader definition of a "finance charge," one that would cover all, or most,

---

18. See Truth in Lending, 73 Fed. Reg. at 44,524 ("The final rule requires creditors to provide transaction-specific mortgage loan disclosures such as the APR and payment schedule for all home-secured, closed-end loans no later than three business days after application, and before the consumer pays any fee except a reasonable fee for the review of the consumer's credit history."); Housing and Economic Recovery Act of 2008 § 2502(a).

of the costs paid by borrowers.[19] The analysis in this chapter supports the spirit of the Renuart–Thompson proposal while also recognizing that a comprehensive cost-benefit analysis may justify keeping certain price dimensions outside the scope of the "finance charge" definition.

Recent reforms and existing reform proposals do not address the exclusion of the prepayment option (nor the default option) from the APR definition. We'll explore ways the APR calculation would have to be adjusted to incorporate the prepayment option. There are costs involved, of course, and policymakers will need to carefully weigh these costs against the potentially substantial benefits of an APR that accounts for the prepayment option. But if borrowers ignored the traditional APR figure because it excluded the prepayment option, they should embrace an APR that incorporates that option. And as the APR reclaims its rightful position at the forefront of the mortgage disclosure regime, borrowers—and society—will again benefit from the APR's unique ability to undo the adverse effects of imperfect rationality.

While this chapter focuses on the subprime mortgage market, much of the analysis applies to the other segments of the residential mortgage market—the Alt-A segment and even to the prime segment. There, too, highly complex, deferred-cost contracts began to appear in increasing numbers, alongside the traditional FRM. In fact, the most extreme forms of cost deferral—the interest-only and payment-option mortgages—were more common in the Alt-A and prime segments than in the subprime segment. Moreover, it was in the Alt-A and prime segments where introductory rates were substantially below the fully indexed market rate. While the crisis began with subprime, it did not end there. Defaults and foreclosures have appeared in substantial numbers in the Alt-A and even prime markets.[20]

19. See Elizabeth Renuart and Diane E. Thompson, "The Truth, the Whole Truth, and Nothing but the Truth: Fulfilling the Promise of Truth in Lending" *Yale J. Reg.* 25 (2008), 181. Renuart and Thompson, however, are not the first to recognize that the APR is not sufficiently inclusive, nor are they the first to propose a more inclusive APR. See U.S. Dep't of Hous. and Urban Dev. and U.S. Dep't of the Treasury, *Curbing Predatory Home Mortgage Lending* (2000) 69, available at <http://www.huduser.org/publications/hsgfin/curbing.html> (hereinafter "HUD-Treasury Report") (proposing that the law be amended "to require that the full costs of credit be included in the APR"); William N. Eskridge, Jr., "One Hundred Years of Ineptitude: The Need for Mortgage Rules Consonant with the Economic and Psychological Dynamics of the Home Sale and Loan Transaction", *Va. L. Rev.,* 70 (1984), 1083, 1166 (proposing, over twenty years ago, a more inclusive APR).

20. On cost deferral in the Alt-A market—see Christopher L. Cagan, First Am. CoreLogic, Inc., *Mortgage Payment Reset: The Issue and the Impact* (2007) 2. On defaults and foreclosures in the Alt-A and Prime markets—see Stan J. Liebowitz, "Anatomy of a Train Wreck: Causes of the

This chapter proceeds as follows:

*   Part I provides some background on the subprime mortgage market.
*   Part II describes the central design features of subprime mortgage contracts.
*   Part III evaluates the rational-choice explanations for the identified contractual design features, emphasizing the limits of these rational-choice theories.
*   Part IV develops an alternative, behavioral-economics theory that fills the explanatory gap left by the rational-choice accounts.
*   Part V describes the welfare costs of the identified contractual design features.
*   Part VI considers policy implications.

I. The Subprime Mortgage Market

A. Defining Subprime

Subprime mortgage loans are generally sold to riskier borrowers. These high-risk loans come at a high price (a high interest rate), as compared to the less-risky prime loans that come at a lower price (a lower interest rate). But this definition and the difference between prime and subprime lending establishes a misleading dichotomy. The risks and, accordingly, loan prices vary along a continuum. Still, because the mortgage industry itself follows this rough categorization, as do policymakers, it is helpful to focus on a subset of high-risk, high-price loans even if the line that divides this category of loans from the lower-risk, lower-price category is arbitrary and blurry.

While the boundaries of the subprime segment may be fuzzy, the industry, researchers, and regulators all use the same parameters to classify a loan as subprime. According to one rough division, borrowers with FICO scores—a common measure of creditworthiness—lower than 620 are considered subprime borrowers. Of course, a borrower's FICO score is only

Mortgage Meltdown," in Holcombe, R.G., and Powell, B. (eds.), *Housing America: Building Out of a Crisis* (The Independent Institute, 2009) (explaining that ARM defaults and foreclosures are as prevalent in the prime market as in the subprime market).

one of several factors determining risk level. Thus, industry participants consider additional risk factors, such as the LTV ratio, when classifying a loan as subprime.[21] Moving from risk factors to price, a common subprime threshold is a loan APR that is three or more points above the treasury rate for a security of the same maturity. The three-point threshold defines "higher-priced loans" under the Home Mortgage Disclosure Act (HMDA). In its new subprime mortgage regulations, the FRB adopted a slightly different definition of "higher-priced mortgage loans," setting the threshold APR at 1.5 points above the "average prime offer rate."[22]

B. Subprime Mortgage Loans: The Numbers

The subprime mortgage market grew substantially from the early 2000s to 2006. In 2001, approximately 985,000 first-lien subprime loans were originated, while in 2006 that number was approximately 2,780,000 and represented over 20 percent of total loan-origination volume. According to the Congressional Budget Office (CBO), subprime mortgages at the end of 2006 accounted for 13 percent of all outstanding home mortgage loans. The Alt-A market—encompassing "medium risk" loans between subprime and prime—also experienced significant growth, expanding from 2 percent of total originations in 2003 to 13 percent of originations in 2006.[23]

---

21. Credit Suisse, *Mortgage Liquidity du Jour: Underestimated No More* (2007) 13, 21 (hereinafter "Credit Suisse Report"); Kristopher Gerardi, Adam Hale Shapiro, and Paul S. Willen, "Subprime Outcomes: Risky Mortgages, Homeownership Experiences, and Foreclosures" (2007) 5–7 (*Fed. Reserve Bank of Boston, Working Paper No. 07-15*), available at <http://www.bos.frb.org/economic/wp/wp2007/wp0715.htm>.

22. For the older HMDA definition—see Michael LaCour-Little, "Economic Factors Affecting Home Mortgage Disclosure Act Reporting", *J. Real Est. Res.*, 29 (2007), 479, 506 n.3. For the new definition—see Truth in Lending, 73 Fed. Reg. 44,522, 44,531–32 (codified at 12 C.F.R. pt. 226) (stating that "[t]he definition of 'higher-priced mortgage loans' appears in § 226.35(a)" and that the average prime offer rate is derived from the Freddie Mac Primary Mortgage Market Survey®).

23. See Demyanyk and Van Hemert, above note 1, at 1853, 1854 (tbl. 1). (The authors' data include 452,000 loans in 2001 and 1,772,000 loans in 2006. These data cover approximately 85 percent of securitized subprime loans. In 2001, 54 percent of subprime loans were securitized, implying a total of 452,000/(0.85 * 0.54) = 984,749. In 2006, 75 percent of subprime loans were securitized, implying a total of 1,772,000/(0.85 * 0.75) = 2,779,608.); CBO Outlook, above note 2, at 23–4 (reporting the 20 percent and 13 percent figures); Christopher J. Mayer, Karen M. Pence, and Shane M. Sherlund, "The Rise in Mortgage Defaults" 3 (2008) (*Bd. of Governors of the Fed. Reserve Sys., Fin. and Econ. Discussion Series Paper No. 2008–59*) (recording LP data showing a rise in subprime originations from 1.1 million in 2003 to 1.9 million in 2005). On the Alt-A market—see Truth in Lending, 73 Fed. Reg. at 44,533; see also Mayer et al., *id.*, at 3 (explaining that "Alt-A originations grew . . . from 304,000 in 2003 to 1.1 million in 2005").

The average size of a subprime loan has also increased. In 2006, the average size of a first-lien subprime loan was $212,000, up from $126,000 in 2001. In terms of loan purpose, in 2006, 42.4 percent of first-lien subprime loans were purchase loans; 57.6 percent were refinance loans. The average subprime borrower had a debt-to-income ratio of approximately 40 percent and a FICO score of 618.1. The median subprime borrower had a FICO score of 620. The median Alt-A borrower had a FICO score of 705.[24]

C. Market Structure

1. Participants

Traditionally, a single entity, commonly the neighborhood bank, was the only party involved in the mortgage transaction (other than the borrower, of course). The bank would originate the loan, provide the funds for the loan, and service the loan. In the modern mortgage market, however, these various roles—origination, financing, and servicing—are often performed by different entities.[25] Let's focus on the parties involved in origination and financing, since they exert the most influence on the design of the mortgage contract.

In the subprime and Alt-A markets, mortgages were originated primarily by depository institutions (banks or bank subsidiaries and affiliates) and by mortgage companies, with the bulk of loan volume originated by mortgage companies. Another important group of participants in the mortgage origination process, brokers, accounted for 58 percent of total origination activity in 2006.[26]

24. See Demyanyk and Van Hemert, above note 1, at 1854 (tbl. 1); Mayer et al., above note 23, at 6; Michael Fratantoni et al., Mortgage Bankers Ass'n, *The Residential Mortgage Market and Its Economic Context in 2007* (MBA Research Monograph Series, 2007) at 24.
25. See Henry M. Paulson, Jr., U.S. Sec'y of the Treasury, "Remarks on Current Housing and Mortgage Market Developments at the Georgetown University Law Center" (October 16, 2007), available at <http://www.treasury.gov/press/releases/hp612.htm> ("A mortgage loan is likely to be originated, serviced, and owned by three different entities. Originators often sell mortgages to securitizers who package them into mortgage-backed securities, which are then divided and sold again to a global network of investors.").
26. U.S. Gov't Accountability Office, Report to the Chairman, Subcommittee on Housing and Transportation, Committee on Banking, Housing, and Urban Affairs, U.S. Senate, GAO-06–1021, *Alternative Mortgage Products: Impact on Defaults Remains Unclear, but Disclosure of Risks to Borrowers Could Be Improved* (2006) 7 (hereinafter "GAO AMP Report"); Robert B. Avery, Kenneth P. Brevoort, and Glenn B. Canner, "Opportunities and Issues in Using HMDA Data", *J. Real Est. Res.* 29 (2007), 351, 353; Press Release, Access Mortgage Research and Consulting, Inc., "New Broker Research Published" (August 17, 2007), available at <http://accessmtgresearch.com/?p=40>.

Traditionally, depository institutions originated loans and funded them with the deposits they held. During the subprime expansion, origination volume shifted to mortgage companies that had no independent means to fund the originated loans. These mortgage companies, and increasingly also depository institutions, sold the loans that they originated to Wall Street investment banks. The banks pooled the loans, carved up the expected cash flows, and converted these cash flows into bonds that were secured by the mortgages. At the peak of the subprime expansion, most mortgages were financed through this process of securitization. As a result, the "owners" of the loans were the investors who purchased shares in these Mortgage (or Asset) Backed Securities (MBSs or ABSs).[27]

Loan originators have direct control over the design of the mortgage contract. Investment banks and their clients also influence the design of mortgage contracts because the demand for MBSs—and thus the price that investment banks are willing to pay the originators for the loans—depends on the contractual design.

2. Competition

Competition in a market can also affect the design of the products and con-tracts sold in this market. In the years before the subprime crisis, the loan origination market appeared to be fairly competitive. In 2006, the top fif-teen subprime lenders accounted for 80.5 percent of the market, with no lender holding more than a 13-percent share. The Department of Housing and Urban Development's (HUD) list of lenders that specialize in subprime lending named 210 lenders (although not all of these lenders offer loans nationally). Barriers to entry in this industry were substantially lowered with the growth in securitization, which enables entry by new, small lend-ers. The internet enhanced competition by reducing shopping costs. For these reasons, the FRB characterized this market as competitive.[28]

---

27. See, e.g., Kathleen C. Engel and Patricia A. McCoy, "Turning a Blind Eye: Wall Street Finance of Predatory Lending", *Fordham L. Rev.* 75 (2007), 2039, 2045. On securitization rates—see Credit Suisse Report, above note 21, at 11 (finding 75 percent securitization rate); Demyanyk and Van Hemert, above note 1, at 1853 (n. 6) (reporting securitization rates of 76 percent and 75 percent in 2005 and 2006, respectively).

28. On market shares—see Credit Suisse Report, above note 21, at 22. See also *2 Market Share Reporter: An Annual Compilation of Reported Market Share Data on Companies, Products, and Services: 2008* (Robert S. Lazich, ed., 2008) at 704–5 (reporting that the top ten lenders commanded less than 58.8 percent of the market with no single lender controlling more than 8.3 percent of the market,

Nevertheless, because many consumers engage in limited shopping, several observers have expressed concerns about the level of competition in the subprime market. As will be explained in Section V.1, the increasing complexity of mortgage products renders comparison shopping more difficult and limits the efficacy of the shopping that does take place. This limited shopping may be a rational response to its reduced efficacy. The result: imperfect information and imperfect competition.

HUD's amendments to its Real Estate Settlement Procedures Act (RESPA) regulations were intended to enhance competition in the mortgage market. Two studies—one by the Government Accountability Office (GAO), the other by the Federal Trade Commission (FTC) and the Department of Justice (DOJ)—expressed concern about the level of competition in the real estate brokerage industry, which, as explained above, plays an important role in the loan origination process.[29]

based on a conservative combination of the two sources cited in Market Share Reporter). On HMDA's list of 210 subprime lenders—see Randall M. Scheessele, "HUD Subprime and Manufactured Home Lender List," HUD User, March 16, 2007, <http://www.huduser .org/datasets/manu.html> (describing the 2005 list). Many other lenders, while not specializing in subprime lending, also offer subprime loans. See Avery et al., above note 41, at 353 (noting that there were 8,850 Home Mortgage Disclosure Act (HMDA) reporting institutions in 2005). On the role of securitization in reducing barriers to entry—see Engel and McCoy, above note 27, at 204. For an indication of the role played by the internet in enhancing competition—see, e.g., LendingTree.com, Lender Ratings, <http://www .lendingtree.com/stm3/lenders/scorecard.asp>. For the FRB's assessment—see Truth in Lending, 73 Fed. Reg. 1672, 1674 (proposed January 9, 2008) (codified at 12 C.F.R. pt. 226) ("Underwriting standards loosened in large parts of the mortgage market in recent years as lenders—particularly nondepository institutions, many of which have since ceased to exist—competed more aggressively for market share.").

29. On the concern of commentators about limited shopping—see Eskridge, above note 19; Marsha J. Courchane, Brian J. Surette, and Peter M. Zorn, "Subprime Borrowers: Mortgage Transitions and Outcomes", J. Real Est. Fin. and Econ. 29 (2004), 365, 371–2; Lauren E. Willis, "Decisionmaking and the Limits of Disclosure: The Problem of Predatory Lending: Price", Md. L. Rev. 65 (2006), 707, 749. The limits of advertising in the subprime market further increase the cost of comparison shopping. See Truth in Lending, 73 Fed. Reg. 44,522, 44,524 (July 30, 2008) (codified at 12 C.F.R. pt. 226) ("[P]rice information for the subprime market is not widely and readily available to consumers. A consumer reading a newspaper, telephoning brokers or lenders, or searching the Internet can easily obtain current prime interest-rate quotes for free. In contrast, subprime rates, which can vary significantly based on the individual borrower's risk profile, are not broadly advertised and are usually obtainable only after application and paying a fee."). On HUD's RESPA Amendments and the motivation for these amendments—see "Real Estate Settlement Procedures Act (RESPA): Rule to Simplify and Improve the Process of Obtaining Mortgages and Reduce Consumer Settlement Costs," 73 Fed. Reg. 68,204, 68,207 (November 17, 2008) (codified at 24 C.F.R. pts. 203, 3500) (describing "important changes that should increase consumer understanding and competition in the mortgage marketplace"). On the limited competition among brokers—see U.S. Gov't Accountability Office, Report to the Committee on Financial Services, House of Representatives, "Real Estate Brokerage: Factors That May Affect Price Competition" GAO-05-947 (2005); U.S. Dep't of Justice and Fed. Trade Comm'n, "Competi-

As already noted, contractual design is not determined solely by the loan originator. Thus, competition (or lack thereof) in other markets may have influenced the design of mortgage contracts. In particular, securitization enhanced competition in the loan-origination market but simultaneously transferred some control over contractual design away from the originators and into the hands of securitizers. The securitization market appears to have been relatively competitive. In 2007, the top 10 securitizers—Lehman Brothers, Bear Stearns, Morgan Stanley, JP Morgan, Credit Suisse, Bank of America Securities, Deutsche Bank, Royal Bank of Scotland Group, Merrill Lynch, and Goldman Sachs—controlled 73.4 percent of the market, with no single bank controlling more than 10.8 percent of the market.[30]

D. Regulatory Scheme

Before the financial crisis, regulatory authority over mortgage lending was divided between the federal and state levels and among several regulators at the federal level. Federal banking agencies—the FRB, the Office of the Comptroller of the Currency (OCC), the Office of Thrift Supervision (OTS), the Federal Deposit Insurance Corporation (FDIC), and the National Credit Union Administration (NCUA)—regulated depository institutions. The Federal Trade Commission Improvements Act of 1980 authorized the Federal Reserve to identify unfair or deceptive acts or practices by banks and to issue regulations prohibiting them. Moreover, the federal banking agencies could use Section 8 of the Federal Deposit Insurance Act to prevent unfair or deceptive acts or practices under Section 5 of the Federal Trade Commission Act, regardless of whether there was an FRB regulation defining the particular act or practice as unfair or deceptive. Focusing on high-priced mortgage loans, the Home Ownership and Equity Protection Act (HOEPA) granted the FRB broad powers to police unfair or deceptive lending practices. The FRB also promulgated disclosure regulations under TILA. Non-depository institutions—that is, nonbanks, including mortgage companies, brokers, and advertisers—fell under the jurisdiction of the FTC. The FTC enforced TILA, HOEPA and § 5 of the Federal Trade Commission Act.[31]

tion in the Real Estate Brokerage Industry: A Report by the Federal Trade Commission and the U.S. Department of Justice" (2007), available at <http://www.ftc.gov/reports/realestate/V050015.pdf>.

30. See Bethel et al., above note 12, at 81 tbl. 2.

31. On the regulation of unfair or deceptive acts or practices by the banking agencies—see 15 U.S.C. §§ 57b-1 to -4 (2006) (FRB authority to issue regulations); Comptroller of the Currency, Administrator of National Banks, "Guidance on Unfair or Deceptive Acts or Practices," Advisory Letter No. AL 2002–3 (March 22, 2002), available at <http://www.occ.treas

At the state level, mini–FTC statutes prohibited unfair and deceptive acts and practices. Likewise, mini–HOEPA statutes, as well as other statutes, banned or restricted specific practices, such as prepayment penalties and balloon clauses. There was, however, substantial variation in the scope and enforcement of state-level laws. Because some states clearly went further than federal regulators in their attempts to protect borrowers, heated preemption battles erupted, especially with the OCC and OTS. These battles were often won by the federal regulators.[32]

This regulatory landscape was substantially altered by the Dodd–Frank Wall Street Reform and Consumer Protection Act of 2010. Congress recognized that when authority and responsibility for protecting borrowers is divided between multiple federal agencies, coordination problems and regulatory competition gone awry leave borrowers inadequately protected. Moreover, the old regulatory scheme exhibited a fundamental mismatch: banking agencies that care more about the safety and soundness of financial institutions and less about consumer protection were given the authority to protect consumers, while the FTC—the one federal agency with a primary consumer protection mission—was denied authority over depository institutions.[33]

.gov/ftp/advisory/2002-3.doc> (banking agencies' enforcement authority); Truth in Lending, 73 Fed. Reg. 44,522, 44,527 (July 30, 2008) (codified at 12 C.F.R. pt. 226) (FRB authority with respect to high-priced loans). On disclosure regulation—see 12 C.F.R., Part 226, Subpart C (Regulation Z). Additional disclosure regulations were promulgated by HUD under RESPA, which governs the loan-closing process. See 24 C.F.R. pts. 203, 3500. On the FTC's authority with respect to non-depository institutions—see Letter from Donald S. Clark, Sec'y, U.S. Fed. Trade Comm'n, to Jennifer L. Johnson, Sec'y, Bd. of Governors of the Fed. Reserve Sys. 1 (September 14, 2006), available at <http://www.federalreserve.gov/SECRS/2006/November/20061121/OP-1253/OP-1253_53_1.pdf> (hereinafter "FTC Comment").

32. On state-level regulation—see Raphael W. Bostic et al., "State and Local Anti-Predatory Lending Laws: The Effect of Legal Enforcement Mechanisms", *J. Econ. and Bus.* 60 (2008), 47; Anthony Pennington-Cross and Giang Ho, "The Termination of Subprime Hybrid and Fixed Rate Mortgages" (2006) (*Fed. Reserve Bank of St. Louis, Research Div., Working Paper No. 2006-042A*) 8–9, available at <http://research.stlouisfed.org/wp/2006/2006-042.pdf> Ctr. for Responsible Lending, CRL State Legislative Scorecard: Predatory Mortgage Lending, <http://www.responsiblelending.org/issues/mortgage/statelaws.html>. On the tension between state-level and federal-level regulation and the preemption battles—see Oren Bar-Gill and Elizabeth Warren, "Making Credit Safer" *U. Penn. L. Rev.* 157, (2008) 1, 79–83; Kurt Eggert, "Limiting Abuse and Opportunism by Mortgage Servicers", *Housing Pol'y Debate*, 15 (2007) 753, 774–5; Julia Patterson Forrester, "Still Mortgaging the American Dream: Predatory Lending, Preemption, and Federally Supported Lenders", *U. Cin. L. Rev.*, 74 (2006), 1303; Christopher L. Peterson, "Preemption, Agency Cost Theory, and Predatory Lending by Banking Agents: Are Federal Regulators Biting Off More Than They Can Chew?", *Am. U. L. Rev.*, 56 (2007), 515 (2007).

33. See Bar-Gill and Warren, above note 32.

In response to these systemic failures, the Dodd–Frank Act created the Consumer Financial Protection Bureau (CFPB) and entrusted it with broad authority over providers of consumer credit. In essence, Congress took the consumer protection powers that were dispersed across multiple agencies and gave them to the CFPB, along with some new powers. Congress also sought to restore some of the power taken from the states in the preemption battles.[34]

E. Summary

The subprime mortgage market experienced significant growth between 2000 and 2006. This rapid growth slowed dramatically in 2006, and when the subprime crisis erupted in 2007, the market basically shut down.[35] Still, the analysis that follows is more than a historical account of a market that no longer exists. While few new subprime loans are being originated, many subprime loans are still outstanding. The goal of this chapter is to contribute to a fuller assessment of the welfare costs that have been—and continue to be—generated by these loans. The analysis will also point to policy reforms that can prevent a second subprime crisis when subprime lending resumes. Also, the results of our analysis will be relevant beyond subprime, as loan contracts in other segments of the mortgage market share certain design features with subprime contracts. Finally, an analysis of the subprime market holds important lessons on the interaction between market forces and borrower psychology—lessons applicable to other consumer credit markets and even to noncredit markets.

II. The Subprime Mortgage Contract

The traditional, prime mortgage contract is a relatively simple, fixed-rate, thirty-year loan for 80 percent or less of the home price (that is, requiring a down payment of at least 20 percent). The typical subprime mortgage contract was very different from this traditional benchmark. In this Part, we'll look at the two main design features that distinguish the common

---

34. See Dodd–Frank Act, Title X.
35. See, e.g., Ben S. Bernanke, Chairman, Bd. of Governors of the Fed. Reserve Sys., Testimony before the Committee on the Budget, U.S. House of Representatives: The Economic Outlook (January 17, 2008), available at <http://www.federalreserve.gov/newsevents/testimony/bernanke20080117a.htm> (noting the "virtual shutdown of the subprime mortgage market").

subprime mortgage contract from the traditional prime FRM: deferred costs and a high level of complexity.

A. Deferred Costs

The common subprime loan defers costs via three contractual design features: small down payments and high LTVs, escalating payments, and prepayment penalties.

1. Small Down Payments and High LTVs

The down payment, while not a component of the loan contract, is a component of the payment stream that home buyers face. This payment stream consists of a "time zero" payment, the down payment, and the payment schedule specified in the loan contract. This broader, payment-stream perspective is helpful for two reasons. First, from the buyer's perspective, it makes little difference if a payment is made to the seller or to the lender. Second, in many cases, a close (formal or informal) relationship between the seller and the lender allows payment shifting between these two parties.[36]

One way to defer the costs associated with a home purchase is to reduce the down payment. Indeed, the amount of the average down payment declined during the subprime expansion. Traditionally, a home buyer was required to make a down payment equal to at least 20 percent of the purchase price. In 2005 and 2006, the median subprime home buyer put no money down, borrowing 100 percent of the purchase price of the house. Down payments were a bit higher in the Alt-A market, with a median value of 5 percent in 2006.[37]

---

36. See Eskridge, above note 19, at 1124–7.
37. On traditional down payment requirements—see FTC Comment, above note 31, at 5. On down payment requirements in 2005–06 in the subprime market—see Mayer et al., above note 23, at 33 tbl. 2B; see also FTC Comment, above note 31, at 10 n. 45 (indicating that, in the few years prior to 2005, over 40 percent of first-time home buyers did not make any down payment at all); Gerardi et al., above note 21, at 44 tbl. 2 (finding—using the HUD-list definition of "subprime" and Massachusetts data—that the average LTV of an initial-purchase subprime loan rose from 0.76 in 1988 to 0.84 in 2007 and that the median LTV rose from 0.80 in 1988 to 0.90 in 2007); Amy Hoak, "100 Percent More Difficult: First-Time Home Buyers Struggle to Find Down-Payment Money," *MarketWatch*, March 9, 2008, <http://www.marketwatch.com/news/story/first-time-home-buyers-struggle-find/story.aspx?guid=%7B4BF19BC0-C4EE-4107-ACFC-F6524E878D5A%7D)> (stating that for the period between July 2006 and June 2007, the National Association of Realtors estimated that 45 percent of first-time home buyers opted for 100 percent financing). On down payment requirements in 2006 in the Alt-A market—see Mayer et al., above note 23, at 33 tbl. 2B.

The flip side of the down payment is the LTV ratio. In a purchase loan, a 10 percent down payment is equivalent to a 90 percent LTV. For the borrower, higher LTV means lower cost in the present but higher cost in the future. While the traditional mortgage has an LTV ratio of (at most) 80 percent, over 40 percent of subprime loans originated in 2006 had combined LTVs exceeding 90 percent. LTVs were somewhat lower in the Alt-A market.[38]

2. Escalating Payments

The traditional FRM features a constant payment stream throughout the loan period. In contrast, the typical subprime and Alt-A loans stipulated monthly payments that increase over the loan period. In 2006, only 19.9 percent of first-lien subprime loans were FRMs.[39] The vast majority of loans were ARMs or hybrid mortgages that featured an initial fixed-rate period followed by an adjustable-rate period. According to the FRB, approximately three-fourths of originations in securitized subprime "pools" from 2003 to 2007 were ARMs or hybrids with two- or three-year "teaser" rates, followed by substantial increases in the rate and payment (so-called "2–28" and "3–27" mortgages).[40] In 2006, the average initial rate was 8.4 percent, while the average long-term rate, calculated as the sum of the relevant index (usually the 6-month LIBOR) and the contractually specified margin, was 11.4 percent.[41] The expected increase in the monthly payment at the end of the low-rate introductory period

38. For subprime LTVs—see Ben S. Bernanke, Chairman, Bd. of Governors of the Fed. Reserve Sys., Speech at the Independent Community Bankers of America Annual Convention, Orlando, Florida: "Reducing Preventable Mortgage Foreclosures" (March 4, 2008), available at <http://www.federalreserve.gov/newsevents/speech/bernanke20080304a.htm> (hereinafter "Bernanke March 2008 Speech") (basing this figure on information about loans in securitized pools from First American LoanPerformance). For Alt-A LTVs—see Mayer et al., above note 23, at 33 tbl. 2B. The relevant measure is the combined LTV, which includes both the first- and second-lien mortgages. The first-lien mortgage often has an LTV of 80 percent, but the borrower then takes a second-lien mortgage—a piggyback loan—that further increases the combined LTV.

39. See Demyanyk and Van Hemert, above note 1, at 1854 (tbl. 1) (counting only non-I/O, non-balloon FRMs); see also Pennington-Cross and Ho, above note 32, at 1 (finding that, between 2003 and 2005, "the ARM market share for securitized subprime loans has ranged from just approximately 60 percent to over 80 percent").

40. See Truth in Lending, 73 Fed. Reg. 44,522, 44,540 (July 30, 2008) (codified at 12 C.F.R. pt. 226).

41. See Demyanyk and Van Hemert, above note 1, at 1854 (tbl. 1) (reporting the average initial rate, 8.4 percent, and the average margin, 6.1 percent). The average long-term rate is the sum of the margin and the index. The average value of the most popular index, the 6-month LIBOR, was 5.3 percent in 2006. See ARM Index Values—2006 Fannie Mae LIBOR, <http://www.efanniemae.com/sf/refmaterials/libor/index.jsp>; see also Mayer et al., above note 23, at 11 (in 2006 and early 2007, the fully indexed rate was closer to 300 basis points above the initial rate).

was substantial.[42] Monthly payments escalated even more steeply in Alt-A (and some prime) mortgages, where teaser rates were set further below the market rate. These contracts stipulated an increase of up to 100 percent, or $1,500 on average, in the monthly payment at the end of the introductory period.[43] According to one estimate, rate resets have increased borrowers' annual mortgage payments by about $42 billion.[44]

The escalating-payments feature was most pronounced in interest-only (I/O) mortgages and payment-option (or simply, option) mortgages. Under an I/O mortgage, the borrower pays interest only during the introductory period, generally one to ten years, paying the principal only after the introductory period ends. The most popular I/O mortgages were hybrid loans, where the introductory interest rate is fixed and the post-introductory interest rate is variable. In 2006, approximately 20 percent of subprime originations and over 40 percent of Alt-A originations were I/O mortgages.[45]

An even more extreme escalating-payments contract is the option ARM. As described by the FTC,

[o]ption ARMs generally offer borrowers four choices about how much they will pay each month during the loan's introductory period. Borrowers may pay: (1) a minimum payment amount that is smaller than the amount of interest accruing on the principal; (2) the amount of interest accruing on the loan

42. The actual payment shock experienced on 2005 and 2006 2–28 mortgages turned out to be less severe, thanks to relatively low market interest rates and correspondingly low index values in 2007 and 2008, when the interest rates on these loans reset. Still, the average monthly payment increased by more than 10 percent at reset. See Bernanke March 2008 Speech, above note 38 (stating that even with the currently low LIBOR, a typical reset would raise the monthly payment by more than 10 percent); Paul Willen, "Would More Disclosure of Loan Terms Have Helped?" (presentation at FTC Mortgage Conference, May 29, 2008) 10, available at <http://www.ftc.gov/be/workshops/mortgage/presentations/willen_paul.pdf> (finding that payment shock for a typical subprime borrower in 2007 was 15 percent). In any event, contractual design is determined by the ex ante expected payment shock at origination, not by the ex post actual payment shock realized two years later.

43. For Alt-A reset figures—see Cagan, above note 20, at 13 tbl. 4, 44 (showing "red" nonsubprime loans with steeper resets than the "orange" subprime loans; estimating a 97 percent, or $1500, increase in the monthly payment).

44. See Cagan, id. The $42 billion figure covers the entire residential mortgage market, not only the subprime and Alt-A segments, but ARMs and resets were common mainly in these two segments.

45. See FTC Comment, above note 31, at 6–7 (describing I/O loans and noting the popularity of hybrid-rate I/O loans). On the market shares of I/O loans—see Credit Suisse Report, above note 21, at 28 (showing that I/O loans constituted $171 billion of the $824 billion in subprime loans); see also Mayer et al., above note 23, at 7 ("Forty percent of Alt-A mortgages involved only interest payments without any scheduled principal repayment (only about 10 percent of subprime mortgages have such an interest-only feature).").

principal; (3) the amount of principal and interest due to fully amortize the loan on a 15-year payment schedule; or (4) the amount of principal and interest due to fully amortize the loan on a 30-year payment schedule.

Option ARMs vary in the length of the introductory periods they offer. Some, especially in the subprime market, have introductory periods of only one year, six months, or even one month. When the loan's introductory term expires, the loan is recast, amortizing to repay principal and the variable interest rate over the remaining term of the loan.[46]

While I/O mortgages are zero-amortization loans, option ARMs imply negative amortization by allowing below-interest monthly payments. Accordingly, at the end of the introductory period, or even earlier, a borrower might end up owing more than the value of the home. This might happen even when home prices are steady or rising, but, of course, it is more likely to happen when home prices are falling.[47] Option ARMs were rare in the subprime market but quite popular in the Alt-A market. By 2006 and 2007, more than 25 percent of Alt-A loans were option ARMs.[48]

Overall, in the Alt-A market in 2006, a large majority of originations were nontraditional mortgage products, allowing borrowers to defer principal or both principal and interest. These deferrals led to substantial increases—exceeding 100 percent in some cases—in the monthly payment at the end of the introductory period.[49]

3. Prepayment Penalties

Another deferred-cost component, common in subprime and Alt-A contracts, is the prepayment penalty—a penalty imposed on a borrower who repays the loan before the maturity date. Approximately 70 percent of subprime loans and 40 percent of Alt-A loans included a prepayment penalty.

---

46. FTC Comment, above note 31, at 7.
47. See Cagan, above note 20, at 56 tbl. 30 (finding that, as of December 2006, 22.4 percent of subprime ARMs originated between 2004 and 2006 had zero or negative equity). Another 5 percent drop in house prices, as happened after December 2006, increases the 22.4 percent figure to 36 percent.
48. See Mayer et al., above note 23, at 13–14; see also Credit Suisse Report, above note 21, at 26, 28 (finding, based on nonagency MBS data, that in 2006, option ARMs comprised approximately 0.5 percent of the subprime market and 30 percent of the Alt-A market).
49. See Truth in Lending, 73 Fed. Reg. 44,522, 44,541 (July 30, 2008) (codified at 12 C.F.R. pt. 226) (stating that, according to one estimate, 78 percent of Alt-A originations in 2006 were either I/O or option mortgages); GAO AMP Report, above note 26, at 14 (describing an example with a 128 percent increase in the monthly payment at the end of the 5-year payment option period); FTC Comment, above note 31, at 9 (referring to "payment shock").

The penalty amount is usually expressed as a percentage of the outstanding balance on the loan, up to 5 percent, or as the sum of a specified number of monthly interest payments, usually six. This adds up to a significant amount. For example, a 3-percent penalty on a $200,000 balance amounts to $6,000.[50] The economic importance of prepayment penalties to lenders is undeniable. They generate substantial revenues. For example, Countrywide's revenues from prepayment penalties amounted to $268 million in 2006.[51]

Prepayment penalties can be viewed as a necessary supplement to the escalating-payments feature: If borrowers prepay before the end of the low-rate introductory period and thus avoid the high post-reset rates, then the escalating-payments feature becomes moot. Prepayment penalties make it more difficult for borrowers to avoid the escalating payments. It stands to reason, then, that prepayment penalties played a supporting role in some escalating-payments contracts. But in many other escalating-payments contracts, this prepayment-deterrence role was less pronounced. Prepayment penalties are generally limited to certain time periods; in other words, the prepaying borrower will pay a penalty only if the prepayment is made during a specified period. In many loan contracts, signed during the subprime expansion, the prepayment-penalty period expired before the end of the low-rate introductory period.[52]

Prepayment penalties are also an independent deferred-cost component of a mortgage, regardless of their role in supporting the escalating-payments

50. On the prevalence of prepayment penalties—see Mayer et al., above note 23, at 7; see also Demyanyk and Van Hemert, above note 1, at 1854 (tbl. 1) (showing that in 2006, 71 percent of first-lien subprime loans included a prepayment penalty). Prepayment penalties are most common in hybrid loans: 70 percent of hybrids have prepayment penalties, as compared to FRMs, only 40 percent of which have prepayment penalties. See Pennington-Cross and Ho, above note 32, at 11–12. On the size of prepayment penalties—see Michael D. Larson, "Mortgage Lenders Want a Commitment—and They're Willing to Pay You for It," Bankrate.com, August 26, 1999, <http://www.bankrate.com/brm/news/mtg/19990826.asp> (describing one contractual design that specifies a penalty of 3 percent of the outstanding balance for prepayment in the first year, a 2 percent penalty for prepayment in the second year, and a 1 percent penalty for prepayment in the third year).
51. Gretchen Morgenson, "Inside the Countrywide Lending Spree", New York Times, August 26, 2007, § 3, at 1; see also Eric Stein, Coal. for Responsible Lending, "Quantifying the Economic Costs of Predatory Lending" (2001) 7–9, available at <http://www.responsiblelending.org/pdfs/Quant10-01.pdf> (estimating prepayment penalty revenues at $2.3 billion each year).
52. See Michael LaCour-Little and Cynthia Holmes, "Prepayment Penalties in Residential Mortgage Contracts: A Cost-Benefit Analysis", Housing Pol'y Debate, 19 (2008), 631, 635 (prepayment penalties are generally limited in time); Mayer et al., above note 23, at 12 ("[P]repayment penalties were scheduled to be in effect after the end of the teaser period for only 7 percent of the subprime short-term hybrids originated from 2003 to 2007, and over these years the share originated with such a provision dropped from 10 to 2 percent.").

feature. To the extent that it fails to deter prepayment, the prepayment penalty becomes a significant cost that is deferred until the time of prepayment. This long-term cost is linked to a reduction in the short-term cost of the loan. Loans with prepayment penalties have lower interest rates and thus lower monthly payments.[53] Prepayment penalties thus produce the temporal-shift characteristic of deferred-cost contracts; pay less now, pay more later.

The use of prepayment penalties has been substantially curtailed by the Dodd–Frank Wall Street Reform and Consumer Protection Act of 2010. The Act restricts prepayment penalties to a subset of prime, fixed-rate mortgages. Moreover, when allowed, prepayment penalties are restricted in amount and duration: The prepayment penalty may not exceed 3 percent of the prepaid amount during the first year after consummation, 2 percent during the second year after consummation, and 1 percent during the third year after consummation. There can be no prepayment penalty after the end of the third year after consummation.[54]

B. Complexity

In addition to a variety of features that defer costs, subprime and Alt-A mortgages during the mortgage boom were also characterized by a high level of complexity. The complexity was the product of a proliferation of fees and other price dimensions combined with elaborate rules governing the application of these multiple prices.[55] Beyond multidimensional pricing, the prepayment option and the (implied) default option increased the com-

---

53. See Gregory Elliehausen, Michael E. Staten, and Jevgenijs Steinbuks, "The Effect of Prepayment Penalties on the Pricing of Subprime Mortgages", *J. Econ. and Bus.*, 60 (2008), 33, 34; LaCour-Little and Holmes, above note 52, at 642; Christopher Mayer, Tomasz Piskorski, and Alexei Tchistyi, "The Inefficiency of Refinancing: Why Prepayment Penalties Are Good for Risky Borrowers" (2011) *Columbia Business School Working Paper*. But see Engel and McCoy, above note 44, at 2060. (Other studies found a positive, not negative, correlation between prepayment penalty and ex ante interest rates.)
54. Pub. L. 111–203, Sec. 1414.
55. See U.S. Gen. Accounting Office, Report to the Chairman and Ranking Minority Member, Special Committee on Aging, U.S. Senate, "Consumer Protection: Federal and State Agencies Face Challenges in Combating Predatory Lending" Gao-04-280 (2004) 6, 21 (emphasizing "the complexity of mortgage transactions" and the "greater variety and complexity of risks" associated with subprime loans as compared to prime loans); Renuart and Thompson, above note 19, at 196 ("The lender-created complexity of mortgage loans now exceeds what most consumers, even highly educated consumers, are capable of comprehending."); Todd J. Zywicki and Joseph D. Adamson, "The Law and Economics of Subprime Lending" *U. Colo. L. Rev.* 80 (2009), 1, 55–6 (explaining that subprime loans are more complex than prime loans, and that it is more likely that a subprime borrower will misunderstand her loan terms).

plexity involved in valuing these mortgage products. In addition, since complexity should be measured at the market level—not at the contract level—the existence of numerous complex products increased—exponentially—the complexity of the decision that a borrower faced.

1. Interest Rates

The traditional FRM has a single interest rate that implies a constant monthly payment. The typical subprime mortgage during the subprime boom, the 2–28 hybrid, had an initial rate that applied for the first two years of the loan. After the two-year introductory period expired, the loan became an ARM with an interest rate calculated as the sum of a specified index and a preset margin—a calculation that is repeated at the end of each adjustment period. To make things even more complex, the loan contract commonly specified caps that could limit the magnitude of both the periodic and total rate adjustment.[56]

Other products were even more complex. As detailed above, option ARMs commonly specified four different options for each monthly payment. These payment options were not predetermined sums; nontrivial calculations were necessary to figure out what the options were. Moreover, these contracts, while allowing negative amortization, typically capped the level of permissible negative amortization, recasting the loan—even before the end of the introductory period—if this cap was reached.

2. Fees

Beyond the multiple interest rates, the typical subprime and Alt-A loan boasted a long list of fees. These fees can be divided into two categories: origination fees and post-origination fees. Origination fees are paid at closing—that is, at the consummation of the credit transaction. Before closing a loan contract, the lender performs credit checks and obtains appraisals to assess the risk that it is about to undertake. The lender also commissions various inspections, examinations, and certifications, such as pest inspection, title examination, flood certification, and tax certification regarding the borrower's outstanding tax obligations.[57] During the subprime boom, many

56. See Joe Peek, "A Call to ARMs: Adjustable Rate Mortgages in the 1980s", *New Eng. Econ. Rev.*, March–April, (1990), 53.
57. See Elizabeth Renuart, "An Overview of the Predatory Mortgage Lending Process", *Housing Pol'y Debate*, 15 (2004), 467, 493.

lenders charged the borrower separate fees for each of these information-acquisition services. For example, LandSafe, Countrywide's closing-services subsidiary, charged a $36 fee for the credit check, a $26 fee for flood certification, and a $60 fee for the tax certification. In 2006, Countrywide's appraisal fee revenues totaled $137 million, and its credit report fee revenues totaled $74 million.[58]

Separate fees were also charged for analyzing the acquired information. These included escrow analysis fees to cover the cost of determining the appropriate balance for the escrow account and the borrower's monthly escrow payments, and underwriting analysis fees to cover the costs of analyzing a borrower's creditworthiness. Still more fees were charged in the forms of premiums for credit insurance, title insurance, and private mortgage insurance (PMI).[59]

Also at the closing for many of these subprime loans, the lender charged fees for administrative services associated with the loan-origination process, such as preparing documents, notarizing documents, and sending e-mails, faxes, and courier mail. For example, some Countrywide loans included fees of $45 to ship documents overnight and $100 to e-mail documents. And then there were the general fees for such things as loan origination, loan processing, signing documents, and closing.[60] Some subprime lenders charged up to fifteen different origination fees, which added up to thousands of dollars or as much as 20 percent of the loan amount.[61] The fees were often financed into the loan amount and formed the basis for additional interest charges.

---

58. Morgenson, above note 51.

59. See Renuart, above note 57, at 493; Willis, above note 29, at 725. According to one—now dated—estimate, financed credit insurance costs borrowers $2.1 billion each year. See Stein, above note 51, at 5–7.

60. Renuart, above note 57, at 493; Morgenson, above note 51.

61. See Willis, above note 29, at 786; see also HUD-Treasury Report, above note 19, at 21 (noting origination fees of up to 10 percent of the loan amount, "far exceed[ing] what would be expected or justified based on economic grounds"). According to HUD, borrowers are paying excess fees averaging $700 per mortgage. See News Release, U.S. Dep't of Hous. and Urban Dev., "HUD Proposes Mortgage Reform to Help Consumers Better Understand Their Loan, Shop for Lower Costs" (March 14, 2008), available at <http://www.hud.gov/news/release .cfm?content=pr08-033.cfm.> According to Michael Kratzer, founder of FeeDisclosure.com, a website intended to help consumers reduce fees on mortgages, of the estimated $50 billion in transaction fees paid by mortgage borrowers (not only in the subprime and Alt-A markets), $17 billion consist of junk fees, like $100 e-mail charges, $75 document preparation fees, and $25 FedEx charges. See Gretchen Morgenson, "Clicking the Way to Mortgage Savings," *New York Times*, December 23, 2007, § 3, at 1. Kratzer estimates that "junk fees" have risen 50 percent in recent years. See Gretchen Morgenson, "Given a Shovel, Digging Deeper into Debt," *New York Times*, July 20, 2008, at A1.

In addition to the multiple fees charged at closing, the loan contract specified a series of future, contingent fees, including late fees, foreclosure fees, prepayment penalties, and dispute-resolution or arbitration fees. Again, these fees were substantial. Prepayment penalties and foreclosure fees amounted to thousands of dollars. Late fees could amount to 5 percent of the monthly payment.[62]

3. Prepayment and Default

Most mortgage contracts in the United States allow the borrower to prepay the loan before it matures. The prepayment option may seem straightforward, but it actually adds a substantial dose of complexity to the mortgage contract. To accurately value the contract, the borrower must estimate the likelihood and timing of prepayment, which depend on a host of future market conditions and personal circumstances—not to mention any existing prepayment penalty. Calculating the optimal timing for prepayment is an example of how complex the decision can become. A common rule of thumb for borrowers is to prepay when the expected savings from refinancing to a lower-interest loan exceeds the transaction costs associated with terminating one loan and originating another (including the prepayment penalty). But this rule of thumb turns out to be a very poor approximation of the optimal prepayment decision. The reason is that the rule ignores the option value of rejecting the current refinancing offer, even when expected benefits exceed transaction costs, and waiting for even better refinancing opportunities in the future.

Accounting for this option value complicates the optimal prepayment decision. In fact, the optimal prepayment problem is so complex that it can be solved only by high-powered computers implementing sophisticated numeric algorithms. A closed-form approximation exists, but it, too, is far from simple.[63] In addition to the explicit prepayment option, every mortgage contract includes an implicit default option. The borrower can always walk away from the mortgage, albeit at a price—that will usually include

---

62. See Willis, above note 29, at 725. On the magnitude of prepayment penalties—see above Part II.A.3. On the magnitude of late fees—see Freddie Mac, Glossary of Finance and Economic Terms, <http://www.freddiemac.com/smm/g_m.htm#L>; see also Morgenson, above note 51 (noting that, in 2006, Countrywide's revenues from late charges amounted to $285 million).

63. See Sumit Agarwal, John C. Driscoll, and David Laibson, "Optimal Mortgage Refinancing: A Closed Form Solution" 5–6 (2007) (*Nat'l Bureau of Econ. Research, Working Paper* No. 13487), available at <http://www.nber.org/papers/w13487>.

lost equity, a damaged credit rating, and the risk of losing other assets (if the loan is not a no-recourse loan). As with the prepayment option, valuing the default option is a complex task.

4. A Complex Array of Complex Products

The typical subprime or Alt-A contract, during the mortgage boom, was multidimensional and complex. Complexity, however, should not be evaluated at the single-contract level. From a functional perspective, it is more informative to evaluate the complexity of the decision that a borrower faces.

Borrowers must choose from among numerous mortgage products. To make an informed choice, a borrower must read and understand numerous complex contracts. This process would be challenging even if the competing contracts shared the same dimensions and varied only with respect to the values assigned to each dimension. But in the subprime and Alt-A markets, the borrower had to compare different complex contracts, each with its own set of multidimensional prices and its own rules for determining when the different prices apply. Consider a borrower facing a 2–28 hybrid and an option ARM: The 2–28 has an introductory period and an initial rate. The option ARM has a different introductory period, during which four different payment options are available. The 2–28 specifies an index and a margin for the post-introductory period with certain caps on rate adjustments. The option ARM specifies a different index, margin, and adjustment caps. The complexity of this choice is evident. In reality, the borrower had to choose between more than two products.[64]

C. Summary

In this Part, we examined several common contractual design features of subprime and Alt-A mortgages. It should be noted that these design features were not an innovation of the subprime expansion. For example, relatively complex ARMs with a deferred-cost structure, created by lower initial rates and higher long-term rates, have been offered in the

---

64. See William C. Apgar, Jr. and Christopher E. Herbert, U.S. Dep't of Hous. and Urban Dev., "Subprime Lending and Alternative Financial Service Providers: A Literature Review and Empirical Analysis" § 2.2.3 (2006) (describing "the bewildering array of mortgage products available").

prime market since the early 1980s.[65] While cost deferral and high levels of complexity are not unique to subprime loans, these design features have been enhanced in subprime and Alt-A contracts. Since complex deferred-cost loans have been around for a while, they cannot be the only cause of the subprime expansion and the ensuing subprime crisis. They are probably not even the main cause. But, as we'll see in the following Parts, these complex, deferred-cost loans did play an important role in the rise and fall of the subprime market.

III. Rational-Choice Theories and Their Limits

Why were subprime mortgage contracts designed to defer costs? Why was the total cost of the loan divided into so many different interest rates and fees? In this Part, we'll evaluate the standard rational-choice explanations for these contractual design features. The rational-choice theories explain some of the observed practices in the subprime market, but there is much that they cannot explain. This explanatory gap will be filled in Part IV by a behavioral-economics theory.

A. Deferred Costs

1. Affordability

Perhaps the most common justification for deferred-cost contracts is affordability. If borrowers cannot afford to make a substantial down payment, then they will take a mortgage with a high LTV. If they currently cannot afford to make high monthly payments, then they will take a mortgage with low initial monthly payments. Deferred-cost contracts create short-term affordability.[66] Indeed, by most accounts, deferred-cost contracts were designed to

---

65. See Peek, above note 56, at 50, 54; see also Zywicki and Adamson, above note 55, at 5–7 (explaining how legal reform in the early 1980s—specifically the Alternative Mortgage Transaction Parity Act of 1982—lifted severe restrictions on the design of mortgage contracts). Moreover, deferred-cost loans are common in other countries (interest-only mortgages are standard in the United Kingdom) and in other sectors (corporate bonds are designed as interest-only loans).

66. See GAO AMP Report, above note 26, at Abstract ("Federally and state-regulated banks and independent mortgage lenders and brokers market AMPs [mostly I/O and payment-option loans], which have been used for years as a financial management tool by wealthy and financially sophisticated borrowers. In recent years, however, AMPs have been marketed as an

secure short-term affordability. But short-term affordability is not a rational-choice explanation. For affordability to be a rational-choice explanation for cost deferral, long-term affordability must be the key consideration. In other words, the borrower must be able to service the loan both now and in the future. While deferred-cost contracts clearly enhance short-term affordability, it is by no means clear that they enhance long-term affordability. Paying less now means paying more later. Smaller down payments (higher LTVs) and lower initial payments are followed by higher monthly payments in the future. Affordability in the long term can rationally explain deferred-cost contracts only if the borrower's available income is expected to increase as fast as (or faster than) the escalating mortgage payments.[67]

In this spirit, the FRB advises borrowers that "[d]espite the risks of these loans, an I-O mortgage payment or a payment-option ARM might be right for you if...you have modest current income but are reasonably certain that your income will go up in the future (for example, if you're finishing your degree or training program)...."[68] But how many borrowers fit this description? Notice that the FRB is not talking about standard, gradual pay raises. Those would not match the substantial increase in the monthly mortgage payment at the end of the introductory period that many subprime and Alt-A contracts stipulated. The FRB is referring to students and train-

'affordability' product to allow borrowers to purchase homes they otherwise might not be able to afford with a conventional fixed-rate mortgage."); Mayer et al., above note 23, at 7 ("[S]ubprime borrowers may have turned to these products in an attempt to obtain more affordable monthly payments."). Affordability concerns were especially acute in areas where rapidly rising home prices forced borrowers to take larger loans.

67. The failure to adopt this long-term affordability perspective has been the subject of criticism. In particular, lenders have been criticized for qualifying borrowers who can make the low short-term payments but not the high long-term payments. See Hearing, above note 1, at 11 ("Some subprime lenders...established borrowers qualification for mortgages on the basis of initially low teaser rates."). This concern was addressed by the ability-to-repay requirement in Sec. 1402 of the Dodd—Frank Act. See also Truth in Lending, 73 Fed. Reg. 44,522, 44,539 (July 30, 2008) (codified at 12 C.F.R. pt. 226). The effect of these regulations, had they come sooner, could have been substantial. In a presentation to investors, Countrywide Financial acknowledged that it would have refused 89 percent of its 2006 borrowers and 83 percent of its 2005 borrowers, representing $138 billion in mortgage loans, had it followed the long-term affordability standards adopted in the FRB's regulations. See Binyamin Appelbaum and Ellen Nakashima, "Banking Regulator Played Advocate over Enforcer: Agency Let Lenders Grow out of Control, Then Fail," *Wash. Post*, November 23, 2008, at A1.

68. See Bd. of Governors of the Fed. Reserve Sys. et al., "Interest-Only Mortgage Payments and Payment-Option ARMs—Are They for You?" (2006) 7, available at <http://www.federalreserve .gov/pubs/mortgage_interestonly/mortgage_interestonly.pdf> (hereinafter FRB, Interest Only); see also FTC Comment, above note 31, at 8 (noting the advantage of alternative mortgage products for "upwardly mobile" borrowers).

ees. Indeed, 2–28 hybrids, and even I/O and option mortgages, may be beneficial for a second-year law student who anticipates a sharp increase in income after graduation. These students and trainees are good candidates for escalating-payments contracts, yet there are too few of them to explain a significant fraction of the approximately two million hybrid loans originated per year at the height of the subprime market.[69]

While borrowers with rising incomes are the natural candidates for escalating-payments contracts, borrowers with variable incomes may also find some of these contractual designs beneficial. The FRB advises that a borrower with volatile income who can afford to make only small monthly payments in low-income periods may rationally prefer a loan contract that requires lower monthly payments.[70] But the typical loan does not offer the low-payment option for more than two years. Accordingly, the income of the target borrower should be volatile only temporarily. Moreover, rational borrowers with volatile income should have no problem making fixed-amount mortgage payments—all they need to do is save some of their earnings from the high-income periods. As with rising-income borrowers, the number of variable-income borrowers who would benefit from deferred-cost loans seems small relative to the number of loans with these design features.

The long-term affordability explanation covers a small fraction of deferred-cost originations. This assessment is consistent with the evidence of especially high foreclosure rates on homes financed by deferred-cost loans.[71] If deferred-cost loans were designed to address short-term liquidity problems, then defaults and foreclosures would be rare. But perhaps there is another, more plausible version of the affordability explanation. Thus far, long-term affordability has been assumed to imply an ability to make the high future payments from rising income. A less literal interpretation of affordability may include an expectation to avoid, rather than actually make,

---

69. The two million estimate is based on the 2,780,000 first-lien subprime loans originated in 2006, see above Part I.B, multiplied by the 75 percent of hybrid ARMs among subprime loans. See above Part II.A.2.
70. See FRB, Interest Only, above note 68 (advising borrowers that I/O loans and option ARMs may be suitable for them if they "have irregular income (such as commissions or seasonal earnings) and want the flexibility of making I-O or option-ARM minimum payments during low-income periods and larger payments during higher-income periods"); see also FTC Comment, above note 31, at 8 (noting the advantage of alternative mortgage products for borrowers with variable income).
71. See Paulson, above note 25.

the high future payments by refinancing the loan before the low-rate introductory period ends.[72]

There are three circumstances under which a borrower could expect to obtain a new mortgage with lower monthly payments:

(1) The borrower's credit score improves by regularly making the low payments during the introductory period.[73]

(2) The market interest rate falls.

(3) House prices increase, resulting in a lower LTV for the new mortgage.

The question then is how many borrowers rationally expected that such positive developments would enable them to refinance their deferred-cost mortgage and avoid the high long-term costs. From an ex post perspective, it is clear that the subprime crisis and the ensuing tightening of credit eliminated the refinancing option for many borrowers. The FRB infers that even from an ex ante perspective, which is the relevant perspective for judging the affordability explanation, many borrowers could not have rationally expected to have the opportunity to benefit from attractive refinancing options:

> [E]vidence from recent events is consistent with a conclusion that a widespread practice of making subprime loans with built-in payment shock after a relatively short period on the basis of assuming consumers will accumulate sufficient equity and improve their credit scores enough to refinance before the shock sets in can cause consumers more injury than benefit.[74]

---

72. See Truth in Lending, 73 Fed. Reg. 1672, 1687 (January 9, 2008) (codified at 12 C.F.R. pt. 226) ("Consumers may also benefit from loans with payments that could increase after an initial period of reduced payments if they have a realistic chance of refinancing, before the payment burden increases substantially, into lower-rate loans that were more affordable on a longer-term basis. This benefit is, however, quite uncertain, and it is accompanied by substantial risk...."); FTC Comment, above note 31, at 8 ("[B]orrowers who are confident they will sell or refinance their homes for an equal or increased value before the introductory period of the loan expires may benefit from alternative loan options."). Prepayment to avoid high post-reset rates was common before the subprime crisis hit and the credit crunch set in. See Pennington-Cross and Ho, above note 32, at 10 (finding, based on LP data, that hybrid mortgages tend to prepay quickly around the first mortgage reset date); Shane M. Sherlund, "The Past, Present, and Future of Subprime Mortgages" (2008) 10 (*Bd. of Governors of the Fed. Reserve Sys. Fin. and Econ. Discussion Series Paper No. 2008–63*) (finding that "prepayments jump during reset periods").

73. See Mayer et al., above note 23, at 11 ("Industry participants claim that teaser mortgages were never designed as long-term mortgage products. Instead, they argue that the two- or three-year teaser period was designed for consumers with tarnished credit to improve their credit scores by making regular payments....").

74. Truth in Lending, 73 Fed. Reg. at 1688.

The possibility of refinancing and prepayment, together with short-term affordability concerns, can also explain the prevalence of another deferred-price dimension: prepayment penalties. The prepayment option benefits borrowers. But borrowers must pay for this benefit. One way they pay is through a higher initial interest rate. Short-term affordability concerns render this ex ante payment unattractive. The alternative is to pay for the prepayment option ex post with a prepayment penalty. In other words, the penalty reduces the value of the prepayment option to the borrower but also reduces the cost that this option imposes on the lender. This explains the lower interest rates on loans with prepayment penalties.[75] While this explanation for the prevalence of prepayment penalties is persuasive, it is incomplete, because it implies that prepayment penalties replace higher interest rates. There is evidence, however, that the amounts paid in penalties ex post exceed the foregone interest payments that were not paid ex ante.[76]

2. Speculation

An alternative rational-choice explanation portrays the deferred-cost mortgage as an investment vehicle designed to facilitate speculation on real-estate prices.[77] This explanation applies to the substantial portion—10 percent in the subprime market and 25 percent in the Alt-A market—of loans that were originated on investment properties.[78] It may also apply to loans originated on owner-occupied properties. The speculator purchases a house with a deferred-cost mortgage and begins making the initial, low monthly payments. If real-estate prices go up, the speculator will either sell the house and pocket the difference between the lower buy price and the higher sell price or refinance the loan using the increased equity to obtain lower long-term rates. If real-estate prices go down, the speculator will simply default on the

75. See above Part II.A.3.
76. See LaCour-Little and Holmes, above note 52, at 662 (comparing 2–28 ARMs with lower initial rates and prepayment penalties to 2–28 ARMs with higher initial rates and without prepayment penalties, and finding that the total interest-rate savings is significantly less than the amount of the expected prepayment penalty). And according to some studies there is even no negative correlation between prepayment penalties and ex ante interest rates. See above Part II.A.3.
77. I focus on the effects of home-price trends and expectations about home-price trends. A similar argument can be made about market interest rates and expectations about market interest rates.
78. Mayer et al., above note 23, at 19 (reporting the shares of loans originated on investment properties in the subprime and Alt-A markets).

mortgage. The speculator enjoys the upside benefit, while the lender bears the downside cost. This attractive arrangement is purchased at the bargain price of the low, initial payments on a deferred-cost mortgage. The high, long-term costs are avoided.[79]

Speculation with the help of deferred-cost loans, however, is not really a risk-free prospect. The speculator does not *simply* default on the mortgage. Default is costly. First, in jurisdictions where the lender has recourse to the borrower's assets, default places these assets at risk. It is important to note, however, that a large number of states, including subprime hot spots like California, Colorado, Nevada, and Arizona, have no-recourse laws. And even in states without no-recourse laws, filing an action for deficiency is often not cost-effective for the lender, and thus the loan becomes a de facto no-recourse loan.

A second cost of default is foregone equity, although this cost is also often small due to high initial LTVs and even higher LTVs at the time of default (recall that default is triggered by falling house prices). A third cost of default is the damage to the borrower's credit rating and the increased future cost of credit that a damaged credit rating implies. Finally, default entails foreclosure and relocation—both costly prospects. While there is no consensus estimate for the cost of default and foreclosure, for many borrowers this cost will amount to tens of thousands of dollars. These costs may explain why strategic default (when house prices fall below the outstanding loan amount) is relatively rare.[80]

Despite the cost of default, however, the downside risk is still outweighed by the upside benefit as long as the probability of a positive result is sufficiently high. In other words, if house prices are expected to rise high enough

79. Adopting the "heads—borrower wins, tails—lender loses" strategy is rational for borrowers but not for lenders. The speculation explanation is incomplete absent an account of lenders' incentives. Why did lenders play along? Agency problems—within lending institutions and among the different parties in the securitization process—provide one set of answers. See above note 10 and accompanying text.

80. On the issue of recourse—see Michael T. Madison, Jeffry R. Dwyer, and Steven W. Bender, The Law of Real Estate Financing vol. 2 § 12:69 (Thomson Reuters/West, rev. edn. 2008); Zywicki and Adamson, above note 55, at 29 n.134 (estimating that about fifteen to twenty states, including many larger states, have no-recourse laws); Zywicki and Adamson, *id.* at 30 (on de facto no-recourse). On the cost of a damaged credit rating—see Kenneth P. Brevoort, and Cheryl R. Cooper, Foreclosure's Wake: The Credit Experiences of Individuals Following Foreclosure (October 12, 2010), available at <http://ssrn.com/abstract=1696103>. On the relatively low frequency of strategic default—see Luigi Guiso, Paola Sapienza, and Luigi Zingales, "Moral and Social Constraints to Strategic Default on Mortgages" (2009) *NBER Working Paper No. 15145.*

and fast enough, then speculation is rational even if the costs incurred in the unlikely event of default are substantial.[81]

The question, therefore, is whether such borrower expectations of a continuing, rapid increase in house prices were rational. An initial observation is that during the subprime expansion, home prices were high relative to underlying fundamentals. As noted by Peter Orszag, the CBO director, "for a time, the expectation of higher prices became a self-fulfilling prophecy that bore little relation to the underlying determinants of demand, such as demographic forces, construction costs, and the growth of household income."[82] But expectations that deviate from long-term fundamentals are not necessarily irrational. For example, a rational borrower may recognize that home prices must fall eventually but expect to exit the market before the correction. This expectation, while it proved to be erroneous for many subprime and Alt-A borrowers ex post, may well have been rational ex ante.

There were surely rational speculators in the subprime and Alt-A markets who rode the real estate bubble armed with accurate ex ante estimates (that turned out to be false ex post) about the timing of the bubble's inevitable end. But there were also other borrowers/speculators with optimistic expectations of future house prices that were not rationally formed. Specifically, the irrational borrowers extrapolated from past price trends: If home prices increased by 10 percent over the past year, these borrowers expected that home prices would also increase by 10 percent over the next year. Indeed, in an influential study, Karl Case and Robert Shiller found that many home buyers overestimate the correlation between past trends and future price movements. In other words, backward-looking tendencies drive expectations of future price growth (beyond what could plausibly be justified in a rational-expectations model).[83] The subprime and Alt-A markets

81. The upside benefit is also not as straightforward as implied in the initial description. Sale and refinancing involve transaction costs and, in many cases, also prepayment penalties. Moreover, even with increasing house prices, a borrower may be left with low or negative equity, the result of high initial LTVs and slow—zero or even negative—amortization, severely reducing sale and refinancing options. But, again, this only means that a rational speculator must have expected a substantial increase in house prices—an increase sufficient to outweigh the costs and difficulties of sale and refinancing.

82. Hearing, above note 1, at 10. See also Robert J. Shiller, "Understanding Recent Trends in House Prices and Home Ownership" (2007) 4–5 (*Yale Univ. Econ. Dep't, Working Paper No. 28*), available at <http://www.econ.yale.edu/ddp/ddp25/ddp0028.pdf>.

83. See Karl E. Case and Robert J. Shiller, "The Behavior of Home Buyers in Boom and Post-Boom Markets", *New. Eng. Econ. Rev.*, (November–December 1988) 29; see also Karl E. Case and Robert J. Shiller, "Is There a Bubble in the Housing Market?" (2003) *Brookings Papers on Econ. Activity*, No. 2, at 299; Robert J. Shiller, "Speculative Prices and Popular

experienced both rational and irrational speculation.[84] The relative proportion of these two species of speculators remains an open question.

B. Complexity

1. Interest Rates

Mortgage loans, like any other long-term credit product, are subject to interest-rate risk—the risk that market interest rates will change over the life of the loan, departing, often substantially, from the interest rates that prevailed at the time of origination. In a rational-choice framework, ARMs, with their complex formulas for setting interest rates, are designed to optimally allocate interest-rate risk between the lender and the borrower. While an FRM allocates all interest-rate risk to the lender, a pure ARM, with an interest rate that closely tracks a market index, provides the polar opposite allocation, imposing all the interest-rate risk on the borrower. The more complex and common ARMs, with caps that limit interest rate adjustments, enable a range of risk allocations between these two extremes.

Models", *J. Econ. Persp.*, Spring (1990), at 55, 58–61. Moreover, Case and Shiller found that many home buyers believe that home prices cannot decline. *Id.*, at 59. Case and Shiller repeated their study for the recent housing bubble, obtaining similar results. See Karl E. Case and Robert J. Shiller, "Home Buyer Survey Results 1988–2006" (unpublished paper, Yale University, 2006); see also Shiller, above note 82, at 11. These survey results are also supported by evidence of borrower behavior. In particular, home buyers extend themselves more—via higher LTVs and higher payment-to-income ratios—when buying a home in markets with high historical appreciation rates. See Christopher Mayer and Todd Sinai, "Housing and Behavioral Finance" (2007) (unpublished manuscript), available at <http://real.wharton.upenn.edu/~sinai/papers/Housing-Behavioral-Boston-Fed -v9.pdf>. Mayer and Karen Pence found that "[a] one standard deviation increase in house price appreciation in [2004] is associated with a 39 percent increase in subprime loans [in 2005]." Christopher J. Mayer and Karen Pence, "Subprime Mortgages: What, Where, and to Whom?" (2008) (*Nat'l Bureau of Econ. Research, Working Paper No. 14083*), available at <http://ssrn.com/abstract=1149330>. Since it is a lagged appreciation variable that is correlated with the increase in subprime originations, this finding is consistent with a behavioral story that demand for subprime loans was driven by expectations of future house-price appreciation based on extrapolation from past trends.

84. This is consistent with a leading economic theory of bubbles, which posits the existence of both rational and irrational traders. See J. Bradford De Long et al., "Noise Trader Risk in Financial Markets", *J. Pol. Econ.'y* 98 (1990), 703, 705; J. Bradford De Long et al., "Positive Feedback Investment Strategies and Destabilizing Rational Speculation", *J. Fin.*, 45 (1990), 379, 380; Andrei Shleifer and Lawrence H. Summers, "The Noise Trader Approach to Finance", *J. Econ. Persp.*, Spring (1990), at 19, 28–9; see also Robert J. Shiller, *Irrational Exuberance* (Princeton University Press, 2000) 60–4 (developing a market-psychological theory of bubbles).

ARMs were initially developed in the early 1980s to protect lenders from the interest-rate risk that they bore under the traditional FRM.[85] In a time when loan originators held mortgages on their own balance sheets, shifting the risk to the borrower was an important means of minimizing the risk. This explanation for ARMs is less powerful, however, in the era of securitization. Originators no longer bear much, if any, of the interest-rate risk. The securitizers spread this risk among multiple investors, who are usually better situated to bear this risk than the typical borrower.

2. Fees

As explained in Part II, many different services and costs are associated with the mortgage transaction. In the past, most of these costs were folded into the loan's interest rate. During the subprime expansion, lenders and their affiliates—mortgage settlement/closing companies and servicers—charged separate fees for each service rendered or cost incurred. There are two rational-choice, efficiency-based explanations for the proliferation of fees.

First, to the extent that some services are optional, setting separate prices for these services allows for more efficient tailoring of the product to the needs and preferences of different borrowers. This explanation is plausible for some services and fees but not for others. Specifically, it is not plausible for the many non-optional services that all borrowers purchase, such as credit checks, document preparation, and appraisals. Moreover, evidence of "[w]ild variation" in fees charged for largely standardized services is inconsistent with a claim that borrowers paid the cost of optional services that they requested.[86]

The second rational-choice explanation describes the proliferation of fees in subprime mortgage contracts as reflecting a desirable shift to risk-based pricing. For example, if the costs of delinquency and foreclosure proceedings are folded into the interest rate, then non-defaulting borrowers will pay for the delinquency and foreclosures of defaulting borrowers. Separate late fees and foreclosure fees eliminate this cross-subsidization. Again, this explanation is plausible for certain fees, but not for others.

---

85. See Peek, above note 56, at 48.

86. See Mark D. Shroder, "The Value of the Sunshine Cure: The Efficacy of the Real Estate Settlement Procedures Act Disclosure Strategy", *Cityscape: J. Pol'y Dev. and Res.*, No. 1, (2007) at 73, 84 (noting, for example, that the cost of obtaining a credit report, "a standard national, largely automated, service" is typically about $50, yet credit report fees range from $25 to $100).

3. Prepayment and Default

The implied default option is an inevitable component of any loan product. So let's focus on the prepayment option that, while ubiquitous in mortgage contracts in the United States, is much more limited in most other countries.[87] The prepayment option serves two main goals. First, by allowing borrowers who improve their credit ratings to refinance into lower-rate loans, the prepayment option allows individuals to achieve home ownership earlier. Second, the prepayment option protects borrowers from the risk of paying a mortgage interest rate that is substantially above the current market rate. These benefits, however, should be weighed against the difficulty of valuing a mortgage with a prepayment option.

4. A Complex Array of Complex Products

The decision problem faced by a potential borrower was made difficult by the complexity of the typical subprime or Alt-A mortgage and even more difficult by the need to choose among multiple complex mortgage products. The standard efficiency explanation for the large variety of products available in many markets is consumer heterogeneity. In the mortgage market, different borrowers have different preferences and face different constraints. A mortgage design that is ideal for one borrower could be terrible for another. With more products to choose from, each borrower, in theory, can choose the mortgage that is best for her. This explanation, however, assumes that informed choice is possible, despite the high level of complexity of the choice problem.[88]

C. Summary

Efficiency-based rational-choice theories can explain many, though not all, of the contractual design features observed in the subprime and Alt-A markets. Moreover, even for the design features that can be explained within a rational-choice framework, the rational-choice theories have limited reach. Rational-choice theories explain the demand structure of rational borrow-

---

87. Richard K. Green and Susan M. Wachter, "The American Mortgage in Historical and International Context", *J. Econ. Persp.*, Fall (2005) 93, 101.

88. The rational-choice account recognizes that complexity—of a single product and of the array of offered products—increases the cost of shopping. When shopping costs more, the rational borrower will shop less. Since shopping creates a positive externality, there is a risk that the market will produce an inefficiently high level of complexity.

ers and the contractual-design response to this demand. As we will see in Section IV.C., however, not all borrowers, and especially not all subprime and Alt-A borrowers, were financially sophisticated, rational borrowers. Rational-choice theories leave an explanatory gap. Let's look at how to fill this gap.

IV. A Behavioral-Economics Theory

The subprime mortgage contract is a product of the interaction between the forces of supply and demand in the subprime mortgage market. When lenders respond to a demand for financing that is influenced by borrower psychology, the resulting loan contract will feature deferred costs and a high level of complexity. The recent history of the subprime market thus serves as an example of the general theory proposed in Chapter 1.

A. Deferred Costs

As we have seen in previous chapters, the behavioral-economics explanation for deferred-cost contracts is based on evidence that future costs are often underestimated. When future costs are underestimated, contracts with deferred-cost features become more attractive to borrowers and thus to lenders. Consider a simplified loan contract with two price dimensions: a short-term price, P_{ST}, and a long-term price, P_{LT}. Assume that the optimal mortgage contract sets $P_{ST} = 5$ and $P_{LT} = 5$, as these prices provide optimal incentives and minimize total costs. If borrowers are rational, lenders will offer this optimal contract.

Now assume that borrowers underestimate future costs. Assume that borrowers perceive the long-term payments to be one-half of the actual long-term payments: $\hat{P}_{LT} = \frac{1}{2} \cdot P_{LT}$. As a result of such misperception, lenders will no longer offer the optimal contract. To see this, compare the optimal (5,5) contract, with an inefficient, deferred-cost contract setting $P_{ST} = 3$ and $P_{LT} = 8$, the (3,8) contract. Assume that under both contracts, the lender just covers the total cost of making the loan. (The total cost is higher under the inefficient, deferred-cost contract: $8 + 3 > 5 + 5$.) Total payments under the optimal contract, as perceived by the imperfectly rational borrowers, would be $\hat{P}(5,5) = 5 + \frac{1}{2} \cdot 5 = 7.5$. (Time discounting is ignored for simplicity.) Perceived total payments under the inefficient, deferred-cost contract would be $\hat{P}(3,8) = 3 + \frac{1}{2} \cdot 8 = 7$. Borrowers would prefer, and thus lenders will offer, the inefficient, deferred-cost contract.[89]

There are several reasons to expect systematic underestimation of future costs. Myopia is one such reason. High LTV contracts are attractive to myopic borrowers, who place excessive weight on the short-term benefits of a low down payment (or a large cash-out in a refinance loan) and insufficient weight on the long-term consequences of a high LTV, such as higher interest payments and greater difficulty to refinance. Escalating-payments contracts are similarly attractive to myopic borrowers, who are attracted to the initial low payments while failing to consider the future high payments. Myopia will also lead borrowers to discount the costs associated with a prepayment penalty—either the penalty itself or the cost of delayed prepayment.

Another bias responsible for the underestimation of future costs is optimism. Borrowers might be optimistic about their future income. They might also optimistically underestimate the probability of an adverse contingency, such as job loss, accident, or illness, causing them financial hardship. As a result, borrowers might overestimate their ability to service a loan with high, deferred costs. In addition, borrowers might overestimate their ability to refinance the loan at an attractive rate and to avoid the high, long-term costs associated with a deferred-cost loan by doing so. Such overestimation may result from optimism about future home prices, future interest rates, and the borrower's future credit score.

During the subprime boom, some borrowers were both myopic and optimistic. Moreover, some lenders and brokers reinforced borrowers' myopia

---

89. As noted by the Federal Reserve Board when revising its Truth in Lending regulations:

A consumer may focus on loan attributes that have the most obvious and immediate consequence such as loan amount, down payment, initial monthly payment, initial interest rate, and up-front fees (though up-front fees may be more obscure when added to the loan amount, and "discount points" in particular may be difficult for consumers to understand). These consumers, therefore, may not focus on terms that may seem less immediately important to them such as future increases in payment amounts or interest rates, prepayment penalties, and negative amortization. . . . Consumers who do not fully understand such terms and features, however, are less able to appreciate their risks, which can be significant. For example, the payment may increase sharply and a prepayment penalty may hinder the consumer from refinancing to avoid the payment increase. Thus, consumers may unwittingly accept loans that they will have difficulty repaying.

Truth in Lending, 73 Fed. Reg. at 44,525–26. See also David Miles, "The U.K. Mortgage Market: Taking a Longer-TermView, Interim Report: Information, Incentives and Pricing" (2003) 3, available at <http://www.hm-treasury.gov.uk/consult_miles_index.htm> (noting that borrowers tend to focus disproportionately on the initial, rather than the long-term, cost of a loan).

and optimism.[90] These biases provide an alternative, behavioral explanation for the prevalence of cost deferral. Myopia and optimism explain why short-term affordability, rather than rational, long-term affordability, took center stage in the subprime and Alt-A markets. These biases—especially optimism about future house prices—also add an important dose of reality to the speculation explanation.

B. Complexity

The typical subprime and Alt-A mortgage contract during the boom years was complex. It specified numerous interest rates, fees, and penalties, the magnitude and applicability of which were often contingent on unknown future events. Rational borrowers could navigate this complexity with ease. They could accurately assess the probability of triggering each rate, fee, and penalty, and then accurately calculate the expected magnitude of each rate, fee, and penalty. Accordingly, each price dimension would have been afforded the appropriate weight in the overall evaluation of the mortgage product.

Imperfectly rational borrowers, however, were incapable of such accurate assessments. They were unable to calculate prices that were not directly specified. Even if they could have performed this calculation, it is unlikely that they would have been able to simultaneously consider 10 or 15 (or even more) price dimensions. And even if they could have remembered all the price dimensions, they probably would have been unable to calculate the impact of these prices on the total cost of the loan. While the rational

90. See Truth in Lending, 73 Fed. Reg. 44,522, 44,542 (July 30, 2008) (codified at 12 C.F.R. pt. 226) ("In addition, originators may sometimes encourage borrowers to be excessively optimistic about their ability to refinance should they be unable to sustain repayment. For example, they sometimes offer reassurances that interest rates will remain low and house prices will increase; borrowers may be swayed by such reassurances because they believe the sources are experts."); see also Complaint, *People v. Countrywide Fin. Corp.*, (Cal. Super. Ct. June 24, 2008) (claiming that Countrywide encouraged borrowers to take complex hybrid and option ARMs by emphasizing low teaser rates and misrepresenting long-term costs) (the complaint, the California settlement, signed by the California Attorney General on October 6, 2008, and the Multistate Settlement Term Sheet, signed by the Attorneys General of Arizona, Connecticut, Florida, Illinois, Iowa, Michigan, Nevada, North Carolina, Ohio, and Texas, can be found at <http://www.consumerlaw.org/unreported>); Gretchen Morgenson, "Countrywide Subpoenaed by Illinois," *New York Times*, December 13, 2007, at C1 (stating that the Illinois Attorney General sued a Chicago mortgage broker and is investigating Countrywide Financial, the broker's primary lender, for abusive lending practices, specifically pushing borrowers into payment-option ARMs by emphasizing the low short-term payments and deemphasizing the high long-term costs).

borrower was unfazed by complexity, the imperfectly rational borrower might have been misled by complexity.

As we have seen, imperfectly rational borrowers often deal with complexity by ignoring it. They simplify the decision problem by ignoring non-salient price dimensions and approximating, rather than calculating, the impact of the salient dimensions that cannot be ignored. In particular, limited attention and limited memory might result in the exclusion of certain price dimensions from consideration. And limited processing ability might prevent borrowers from accurately aggregating the different price components into a single, total expected price that would serve as the basis for choosing the optimal loan.[91]

Increased complexity may be attractive to lenders because it allows them to hide the true cost of the loan in a multidimensional pricing maze. A lender who understands the imperfectly rational response to complexity can use complexity to its advantage—to create an appearance of a lower total price without actually lowering the price. For example, if the tax certification fee and the late-payment fee are not salient to borrowers, lenders will raise the magnitude of these price dimensions. Increasing these prices will not hurt demand. On the contrary, it will enable the lender to attract borrowers by reducing the magnitude of more salient price dimensions. This strategy depends on the existence of non-salient price dimensions. When the number of price dimensions goes up, the number of non-salient price dimensions can also be expected to go up. Lenders thus have a strong incentive to increase complexity and multidimensionality.

Lenders also have a strong incentive to increase the complexity of salient price dimensions, like the options in an option ARM and the adjusting interest rate in a 2–28 hybrid with adjustment caps. The borrower who is unable to calculate these prices will try to approximate them. This makes complexity attractive to lenders because the borrower's approximation is usually an underestimation.

91. See GAO AMP Report, above note 26, at Abstract ("Regulators and others are concerned that borrowers may not be well-informed about the risks of AMPs, due to their complexity and because promotional materials by some lenders and brokers do not provide balanced information on AMPs benefits and risks."); FTC Comment, above note 31, at 14 ("[F]or loans with more complexity—such as nontraditional mortgages—consumers face further challenges in understanding all significant terms and costs."); Hearing, above note 1, at 13 (the CBO suggested that "[t]he rise in defaults of subprime mortgages may also reflect the fact that some borrowers lacked a complete understanding of the complex terms of their mortgages and assumed mortgages that they would have trouble repaying.").

Finally, complexity can be expected to increase as borrowers learn to effectively incorporate more price dimensions into their decision. If lenders significantly increase the magnitude of a non-salient price dimension, borrowers will eventually learn to focus on that price dimension and, eventually, it will become salient. Lenders will have to find another non-salient price dimension. When they run out of non-salient prices in the existing contractual design, they may create new ones by adding more interest rates, fees, or penalties. Similarly, borrowers will eventually learn to accurately estimate those prices that, while salient, are indirectly defined using complex formulae and whose impact depends on a host of unknown future realizations. When this happens, lenders will have an incentive to increase even further the complexity of these or other prices.

C. Heterogeneity in Cognitive Ability

The limits of the rational-choice theories, explored in Part III, open the door to the consideration of an alternative, behavioral-economics theory. By integrating psychology and economics, this theory can better explain the contractual design features observed in the subprime and Alt-A mortgage markets. But the two theoretical approaches—the neoclassical, rational-choice approach and the behavioral approach—are not mutually exclusive. The rational-choice theories explain the behavior of the more sophisticated borrowers and the market's response—specifically the contractual-design response—to the demand generated by these borrowers. Meanwhile, the behavioral-economics theory explains the demand generated by less sophisticated borrowers and how lenders designed their contracts in response to this demand.[92]

The relative domain of the two competing theoretical approaches can be indirectly assessed using evidence on the cognitive abilities of borrowers. Available evidence suggests that imperfect rationality is pervasive in the residential mortgage market and especially in the subprime market. A recent study, by Sumit Agarwal, Gene Amromin, Itzhak Ben-David, Souphala Chomsisengphet, and Douglas D. Evanoff, found that mandated financial

---

92. Cf. Allie Schwartz, "Who Takes Out Adjustable Rate Mortgages?" (2009) *Harvard University Working Paper* (2009) (cited in Daniel Bergstresser and John Beshears, "Who Selected Adjustable-Rate Mortgages?: Evidence from the 1989–2007 Surveys of Consumer Finances", (2010) *HBS Working Paper* 10-083, 5) (showing that the ARM market is split into two very different submarkets—a high-income, wealthy segment and a low-income, credit-constrained segment).

counseling is correlated with less risky ARM contracts, specifically with higher short-term teaser rates and lower long-term rates.[93] These counseling sessions likely address both an information and a cognitive deficit among borrowers.

Survey studies and consumer testing conducted by the FRB and the FTC found that borrowers simply do not understand mortgage terms. Also, in testing the efficacy of proposed disclosures, the FTC identified substantial framing effects; different disclosure forms containing the same information led to different choices—a result that would not be expected if borrowers were perfectly rational.[94] A recent survey study, by Annamaria Lusardi, concludes that many individuals are not well informed and knowledgeable about their terms of borrowing and that a sizeable group does not know the terms of their mortgages. Lusardi also found that "the majority of Americans lack basic numeracy and knowledge of fundamental economic principles, such as the workings of inflation, risk diversification, and the relationship between asset prices and interest rates."[95]

93. Sumit Agarwal et al., "Can Mandated Financial Counseling Improve Mortgage Decision-Making?: Evidence from a Natural Experiment" (2009) (*Fisher Coll. of Bus., Working Paper* No. 2008-03-019) 27, available at <http://ssrn.com/abstract=1285603>. In a related study, the same authors found that financial education reduces mortgage delinquency rates, and attributed the improved performance to, among other things, the type of mortgage contract extended to the graduates. See Sumit Agarwal et al., "Learning to Cope: Voluntary Financial Education Programs and Loan Performance During a Housing Crisis" (2009) *Charles A. Dice Center Working Paper No. 2009-23*, available at SSRN: <http://ssrn.com/abstract=1529060>. See also Annamaria Lusardi, "Household Saving Behavior: The Role of Financial Literacy, Information, and Financial Education Programs" (2008) (*Nat'l Bureau of Econ. Research, Working Paper No. 13824*) 2, available at <http://www.nber.org/papers/w13824> (arguing that households enter into risky financial contracts due to lack of financial education). See generally Howard Lax et al., "Subprime Lending: An Investigation of Economic Efficiency", *Housing Pol'y Debate*, 15 (2004), 533, 544–6 (noting that subprime borrowers tend to be less educated and less sophisticated about the mortgage market).
94. See James M. Lacko and Janis K. Pappalardo, Fed. Trade Comm'n, "Improving Consumer Mortgage Disclosures: An Empirical Assessment of Current and Prototype Disclosure Forms" (2007) at ES-6 (demonstrating the limits of mortgage disclosures and noting that many borrowers "did not understand important costs and terms of their own recently obtained mortgages. Many had loans that were significantly more costly than they believed, or contained significant restrictions, such as prepayment penalties, of which they were unaware."); James M. Lacko and Janis K. Pappalardo, Fed. Trade Comm'n, "The Effect of Mortgage Broker Compensation Disclosures on Consumers and Competition: A Controlled Experiment" (2004) at ES-7 (identifying framing effects).
95. Annamaria Lusardi, "Americans, Financial Capability" (2011) *NBER Working Paper 17103*. See also Brian Bucks and Karen Pence, "Do Borrowers Know their Mortgage Terms?" (2008) 64 *J. Urban Econ.*, 64 (2008), 218 (finding that comprehension of mortgage terms is low among borrowers who are exposed to potentially large changes in their mortgage payments).

Other studies have documented specific mistakes that borrowers consistently make. A recent study by Sumit Agarwal, John Driscoll, Xavier Gabaix, and David Laibson identified persistent mistakes in loan applications that increased borrowers' APRs by an average of 125 basis points. Another study, by Susan Woodward, identified systemic mistakes leading to excessive broker fees of up to $1,500. In addition, numerous studies have documented borrowers' failure to make optimal refinancing decisions. For example, many consumers fail to exercise refinancing options, thereby ending up with rates that are significantly higher than the market rate. Other consumers refinance too early, failing to account for the possibility that interest rates will continue to decline. According to one estimate, these refinancing mistakes can cost borrowers tens of thousands of dollars or up to 25 percent of the loan's value.[96]

Evidence of rapid defaults—those that occur within six to twelve months of origination—provides additional support to the behavioral-economics theory. One explanation for borrowers' inability to afford the monthly payments almost from the moment of origination is that they did not fully understand the extent of the obligations that they were undertaking. Evidence that loan prices are affected by factors unrelated to the risk of non-payment provides indirect evidence of borrower mistakes. Both data and testimony by loan officers suggest that many borrowers who might qualify for prime loans ended up with higher-priced subprime mortgages—an indication of systematic mistakes. Evidence that borrowers who consider two or more price dimensions when shopping for a loan end up paying more for the loan than borrowers who consider only a single price dimension provides further support for the behavioral explanation.[97]

96. See Sumit Agarwal et al., "The Age of Reason: Financial Decisions over the Lifecycle" (October 21, 2008) 9–11, available at <http://ssrn.com/abstract=973790> (mistakes in loan applications); Susan E. Woodward, "Consumer Confusion in the Mortgage Market" (2003), available at <http://www.sandhillecon.com/pdf/consumer_confusion.pdf> (mistakes leading to excessive broker fees). On refinancing mistakes—see John Y. Campbell, "Household Finance", J. Fin., 61 (2006), 1553, 1579, 1581, 1590; LaCour-Little and Holmes, above note 52, at 644 (describing the "apparent irrationality on the part of mortgage borrowers, who fail to default to the extent predicted when house prices fall and fail to prepay to the extent predicted when interest rates fall"); Agarwal et al., above note 63, at 3 (surveying evidence that borrowers fail to make optimal refinancing decisions); Agarwal et al., above note 63, at 25, 28 tbl. 5 (many borrowers followed the NPV rule, instead of the optimal-refinancing rule, leading to substantial expected losses: $26,479 on a $100,000 mortgage, $49,066 on a $250,000 mortgage, $86,955 on a $500,000 mortgage, $163,235 on a $1,000,000 mortgage).
97. On rapid defaults—see Mayer et al., above note 23, at 16 (noting that "2 percent of outstanding loans in the 2007 vintage were in default within six months of origination, and 8 percent were in default after 12 months"). On prime borrowers who ended up with subprime loans—see

A study by Daniel Bergstresser and John Beshears directly links the limited sophistication of borrowers to product choice in the mortgage market. Specifically, Bergstresser and Beshears estimated the relationship between the ability of respondents to comprehend the financial questions in the Survey of Consumer Finances (the comprehension rating) and the mortgages chosen by these respondents. They found that "during 2004 and 2007, a change in the comprehension rating from 'Excellent' to 'Poor' was associated with a 6.6 percentage point increase in the probability that a homeowner with a mortgage had an ARM." Similarly, a study by Morgan Rose found that non-banks originate disproportionately more loans with prepayment penalties in locales with less financially sophisticated borrowers.[98]

Industry sources lend further support to the behavioral account. The National Association of Realtors, in a guide to ARMs and FRMs, writes: "ARMs are difficult to understand. Lenders have much more flexibility when determining margins, caps, adjustment indexes, and other things, so unsophisticated borrowers can easily get confused or trapped by shady mortgage companies."[99]

It seems that few people dispute the fact that at least some borrowers did not enter into their subprime mortgage contracts with a full understanding of the costs and benefits associated with these contracts. The FRB, in justifying its new mortgage regulations, referred to borrowers who "unwittingly

Freddie Mac, *Automated Underwriting: Making Mortgage Lending Simpler and Fairer for America's Families* (1996) ch. 5, available at <http://www.freddiemac.com/corporate/reports/moseley/chap5.htm> (reporting that 10 to 35 percent of subprime borrowers would qualify for lower-cost conventional loans); Freddie Mac, "Half of Subprime Loans Categorized as 'A' Quality," Inside B&C Lending, June 10, 1996 (describing a poll of fifty subprime lenders who estimated that half of subprime borrowers could have qualified for prime loans); "Fannie Mae Has Played Critical Role in Expansion of Minority Homeownership over Past Decade; Raines Pledges to Lead Market for African American Mortgage Lending," *Bus. Wire*, March 2, 2000, LexisNexis Academic (noting that up to half of subprime borrowers would qualify for lower-cost conventional loans); Lew Sichelman, "Community Group Claims CitiFinancial Still Predatory," *Origination News*, January 2002, at 25 (reporting that, in 2002, researchers at Citibank concluded that at least 40 percent of those who were sold high interest rate, subprime mortgages would have qualified for prime-rate loans); see also Willis, above note 29, at 730; Morgenson, above note 51, at 9 (recounting that in December 2006, in an agreement with the New York State Attorney General, Countrywide agreed "to compensate black and Latino borrowers to whom it had improperly given high-cost loans in 2004"). On paying more for a loan when considering more price dimensions—see Woodward, above note 96, at 2.

98. See Daniel Bergstresser and John Beshears, "Who Selected Adjustable-Rate Mortgages?: Evidence from the 1989–2007 Surveys of Consumer Finances" (2010) *HBS Working Paper* 10-083, 4; Morgan J. Rose, "Origination Channel, Prepayment Penalties, and Default", forthcoming in *Real Estate Economics*, available at <http://ssrn.com/abstract=1908375> (using education level, income, and age to proxy for financial sophistication).

99. See Bergstresser and Beshears, above note 98, at 3.

accept[ed] loans" with terms that they did not fully understand. Likewise, the CBO noted that "[t]he rise in defaults of subprime mortgages may also reflect the fact that some borrowers lacked a complete understanding of the complex terms of their mortgages and assumed mortgages that they would have trouble repaying." And HUD's Report to Congress on the Root Causes of the Foreclosure Crisis concludes: "Existing evidence suggests that some borrowers did not understand the true costs and risks of [riskier] loans."[100]

D. Market Correction

Individuals are imperfectly informed and imperfectly rational. Yet most markets work reasonably well despite these imperfections. Several market-correction mechanisms operate to minimize the effects of imperfect information and imperfect rationality. These correction forces were present in the subprime and Alt-A mortgage markets. As we'll see in the section that follows, however, these corrective forces were weak in these markets. For this reason, borrower mistakes persisted for a prolonged period of time. Changes in lending practices began only after the subprime market collapsed and legal reforms were implemented.

1. On the Demand Side: Learning by Borrowers

Individuals make mistakes. Most individuals also learn from their mistakes and learn not to repeat these mistakes. While learning is not absent from the mortgage market, it is slower. This is because the number of mortgage contracts that individuals sign during the course of a lifetime is small. Interpersonal learning (learning from others' mistakes) can compensate for limited intrapersonal learning (learning from one's own mistakes), as borrowers share mortgage-related experiences. Interpersonal learning, however, is not always common enough and detailed enough to eliminate mistakes. More generally, the evidence shows that learning about financial decisions is, at best, incomplete.[101]

100. Truth in Lending, 73 Fed. Reg. 44,522, 44,525–26 (July 30, 2008) (codified at 12 C.F.R. pt. 226) (FRB); Hearing, above note 1, at 13 (CBO); HUD Report, above note 10, at viii, 22, 52 (HUD).
101. On limited learning when decisions are infrequent—see Truth in Lending, 73 Fed. Reg. 1672, 1676 (January 9, 2008) (codified at 12 C.F.R. pt. 226) ("Disclosures, themselves, likely cannot provide this minimum understanding for transactions that are complex and that consumers engage in infrequently."); Shlomo Benartzi and Richard H. Thaler, "Heuristics and Biases in Retirement Savings Behavior" J. Econ. Persp., Summer (2007) 81. On limited learning, and persistent biases, in relatively abstract domains like math and finance—

In many markets, effective learning occurs when individuals, aware of their limitations, seek expert advice. This mechanism also works imperfectly in the mortgage market. Borrowers commonly seek the advice of mortgage brokers. These brokers face an incentive structure that prevents them from being loyal agents of the borrower. (Section 1403 of the Dodd–Frank Act addresses this concern.) Moreover, the complexity of the subprime mortgage contract is such that even so-called experts often get it wrong. For example, a recent study by Sumit Agarwal, John C. Driscoll, and David Laibson has shown that available expert advice on refinancing ignores the option value of postponing the prepayment decision—an omission that can cost borrowers up to 25 percent of the loan value.[102]

2. On the Supply Side: Mistake Correction by Sellers and Reputation Effects

Competing sellers will often have an incentive to correct consumer mistakes. This can be done, for example, through advertising. While the incentives to correct consumer mistakes are not always strong in competitive markets, they are even weaker in imperfectly competitive markets. As explained earlier, ineffective shopping by borrowers inhibited competition in the subprime mortgage market. In many markets, a seller's reputation provides a powerful deterrent to the abuse of consumers. But, again, reputational forces were weaker in the subprime mortgage market for several reasons. First, there is little repeat business, as a single borrower takes few mortgage loans and a relatively long time passes between loans. Second, many lender organizations were relatively short-lived. A downside of the securitization innovation was the opening of the market to fly-by-night originators with little reputation to lose and insufficient incentives to build a reputation.[103]

see Thomas Gilovich et al. (eds.), *Heuristics and Biases: The Psychology of Intuitive Judgment* (Cambridge University Press, 2002); Keith E. Stanovich, "The Fundamental Computational Biases of Human Cognition: Heuristics that (Sometimes) Impair Decision Making and Problem Solving," in Janet E. Davidson and Robert J. Steinberg (eds.), *The Psychology of Problem Solving* (Cambridge University Press, 2003) 291. And real-world evidence of persistent mistakes in the mortgage market confirms that learning was limited. See above Sec. IV.C.

102. See Agarwal et al., above note 63, at 24–5.
103. See Engel and McCoy, above note 27, at 2041. The proliferation of small, short-lived sellers is evidenced by the number of loan originators that have gone out of business during the recent crisis. See Worth Civils and Mark Gongloff, "Subprime Shakeout: Lenders that Have Closed Shop, Been Acquired or Stopped Loans," *Wall St. J. Online*, <http://online.wsj.com/public/resources/documents/info-subprimeloans0706-sort.html> (listing eighty loan originators that closed or filed for bankruptcy between November 2006 and September 2007).

V. Welfare Implications

What are the costs of the identified contractual designs, especially when understood as a response to borrowers' imperfect rationality? In this Part, we'll look at four potentially substantial costs:

- First, complex, multidimensional contracts hinder competition in the subprime mortgage market.

- Second, complex and deferred-cost contracts distort the remaining, weakened forces of competition, leading to excessively high prices on more salient price dimensions and excessively low prices on less salient price dimensions.

- Third, these contractual design features increase the likelihood of default and foreclosure, with all the ensuing costs—to borrowers, lenders, communities, and the economy at large.

- Fourth, the identified contractual designs raise distributional concerns, as they impose disproportionate burdens on weaker—often minority—borrowers.

A. Hindered Competition

Perhaps the costliest result of excessively complex contracts is the inhibited competition that they foster. As described above, complexity prevents the effective comparison-shopping that is necessary for vigorous competition. The market power gained by lenders clearly helps lenders at the expense of borrowers. But the limited competition also imposes a welfare cost in the form of inefficient allocation: Borrowers are not matched with the most efficient lender.

The limits of competition in the subprime mortgage market were reflected in above-cost pricing. Borrowers were paying origination fees exceeding the actual costs that these fees allegedly cover by hundreds or even thousands of dollars. Borrowers were also paying interest rates higher than what the borrower's risk profile justified. The most extreme case was that of borrowers who would have qualified for lower-cost conventional loans but were nonetheless obtaining high-cost subprime mortgages. The higher profit margin in the subprime market induced lenders to steer borrowers into subprime loans.[104] This problem was explicitly recognized by the FRB: "[A]n atmosphere of relaxed standards may increase the incidence of abusive lending practices by attracting less scrupulous originators into the market, while at the same time bringing more vulnerable borrowers into the market. These abuses can lead consumers to pay more for their loans than their risk profiles warrant."[105]

B. Distorted Competition

Limited competition allows lenders to set above-cost prices and reap supra-competitive profits. But even if borrowers engaged in vigorous shopping, eliminating all supra-competitive profits, there would still be a welfare cost, because the borrowers' shopping, while vigorous, would be misguided. Consider again the stylized example of a mortgage contract with a two-dimensional price, a short-term introductory rate, P_{ST}, and a long-term rate, P_{LT}. The two prices affect the two decisions a borrower must make—whether to get out of the loan at the end of the introductory period, and whether to take the loan in the first place. An optimal contract will set the two prices to induce efficient decisions. If borrowers are rational, competition will produce the optimal contract. This is not the case if borrowers are imperfectly rational. If borrowers underestimate the costs associated with the long-term rate, P_{LT}, competition will focus on the short-term rate, P_{ST}, resulting in an inefficient contract with an excessively low P_{ST} and an excessively high P_{LT}.[106]

There are two adverse welfare implications. First, the excessively high P_{LT} will lead some borrowers to exit, inefficiently, at the end of the introductory period. Second, and more importantly, the initial decision to take a loan will

---

104. On excess fees—see Susan E. Woodward, U.S. Dep't of Hous. and Urban Dev., *A Study of Closing Costs for FHA Mortgages* (2008). The Woodward study found that complexity and multidimensionality of origination fees prevent effective shopping, hinder competition, and lead to inflated prices. *Id.* According to HUD, borrowers are paying excess fees averaging around $700 per mortgage, and these excess fees can be eliminated by improved disclosure that would enhance competition. See News Release, U.S. Dep't of Hous. and Urban Dev., above note 61. On excess interest—see Engel and McCoy, above note 27, at 2058; Howard Lax et al., "Subprime Lending: An Investigation of Economic Efficiency", *Housing Pol'y Debate*, 15 (2004), 533 (arguing that subprime interest rates cannot be justified by risk alone); Stein, above note 51 (valuing the cost to borrowers of excess interest at $2.9 billion). On prime borrowers who ended up with subprime loans—see above note 97; Morgenson, above note 51 (describing the steering of prime borrowers into subprime loans at Countrywide).
105. Truth in Lending, 73 Fed. Reg. 1672, 1675 (January 9, 2008) (codified at 12 C.F.R. pt. 226).
106. See above Part IV.A.

be distorted. While the actual total payments, $P_{ST} + P_{LT}$, will go up to cover the increased cost generated by the inefficient contractual design, the total payments as perceived by the borrower will go down. The result is excessive borrowing.[107]

This analysis applies to all the examples of cost deferral discussed earlier; small down payments, high LTVs, escalating payments, and prepayment penalties. The analysis also applies to the complexity examples, where less-salient or indirectly specified price dimensions are ignored or underestimated. (P_{LT} corresponds to the less salient, underestimated price dimensions, and P_{ST} corresponds to the more salient price dimensions.) In all of these cases, imperfect rationality results in price distortions. These distortions increase total costs and total payments and skew both long-term and short-term decisions. Most importantly, these distortions increase the actual cost while reducing the perceived cost of the loan, which leads to an artificially inflated demand for mortgage financing.

Given the link between the demand for mortgage financing and the demand for real estate, the identified pricing distortions also contributed to the housing bubble. HUD, in its Report to Congress on the Root Cause of the Foreclosure Crisis, observed that nontraditional mortgages (where cost deferral was most pronounced) enabled buyers to bid on expensive houses, thus contributing to the housing bubble. The behavioral-market failure in the mortgage market can therefore be considered an indirect cause of the financial crisis.[108]

C. Delinquency and Foreclosure

There is evidence that the identified contractual design features increase delinquency and foreclosure rates. Deferred-cost contracts are associated with higher rates of delinquency and foreclosure. These increased delinquency

---

107. Excessive borrowing would result even absent a contractual-design response—that is, even under the optimal contract. The contractual design response exacerbates the welfare cost.

108. See HUD Report, above note 10, at 24 (referencing studies by Mian and Sufi (2008), Pavlov and Wachter (2008), and Shiller (2007)). See also Andrey Pavlov and Susan Wachter, "Subprime Lending and Real Estate Prices", *Real Estate Econ.*, 39 (2011), 1. Cf. Atif R. Mian and Amir Sufi, "Household Leverage and the Recession of 2007–09", *IMF Econ. Rev.*, 58 (2010), 74–117 (showing that "household leverage growth and dependence on credit card borrowing as of 2006 explain a large fraction of the overall consumer default, house price, unemployment, residential investment, and durable consumption patterns during the recession").

and foreclosure rates have been linked to high LTVs, escalating payments, and prepayment penalties. The FRB, in advocating its new mortgage regulations, acknowledged that "several riskier loan attributes," including "high loan-to-value ratio[s]" and "payment shock on adjustable-rate mortgages," "increased the risk of serious delinquency and foreclosure for subprime loans originated in 2005 through early 2007." HUD in its Report to Congress on the Root Cause of the Foreclosure Crisis concluded: "The sharp rise in mortgage delinquencies and foreclosures is fundamentally the result of rapid growth in loans with a high risk of default—due both to the terms of these loans and to loosening underwriting controls and standards."[109]

The welfare costs associated with foreclosure are substantial. FRB Chairman Ben Bernanke estimated that, on average, total losses from foreclosure "exceeded 50 percent of the principal balance, with legal, sales, and maintenance expenses alone amounting to more than 10 percent of principal." An

---

109. On the effect of contract design on delinquency and foreclosure—see generally Edward M. Gramlich, "*Subprime Mortgages: America's Latest Boom and Bust*" (Urban Institute Press, 2007) 66–7 (arguing that mortgage contract design is linked to borrower distress); Gene Amromin, Jennifer Chunyan Huang, Clemens Sialm, and Edward Zhong, "Complex Mortgages" (2010) FRB of Chicago Working Paper No. 2010-17 (finding that "[b]orrowers with complex mortgages experience substantially higher ex post default rates than borrowers with traditional mortgages with similar characteristics."). For assessments by the FRB and HUD on the relationship between contract design and adverse outcomes in the mortgage market—see Truth in Lending, 73 Fed. Reg. 1672, 1674 (January 9, 2008) (codified at 12 C.F.R. pt. 226) (FRB assessment); HUD Report, above note 10, at 29 (HUD assessment). On the effect of high LTVs—see Gerardi et al., above note 21, at 4; Sewin Chan, Michael Gedal, Vicki Been, and Andrew Haughwout, "The Role of Neighborhood Characteristics in Mortgage Default Risk: Evidence from New York City" (2011) *NYU Working Paper*, 12 and tbls. 3, 5. On the effect of escalating payments, there is evidence that ARMs and Hybrids, which featured escalating payments, experienced substantially higher rates of delinquency and foreclosure, as compared to FRMs. See Bernanke, March 2008 Speech, above note 38; Mayer et al., above note 23, at 8. See also Chan et al, *id.*, 12, 26 and tbl. 3. The effect of interest-rate resets was more limited than it could have been thanks to the low LIBOR rate at the time, which kept the reset magnitudes in check. On the effect of prepayment penalties—see Demyanyk and Van Hemert, above note 1, at 1862 (tbl. 3) (finding positive correlation coefficients on Prepayment Penalty in regressions that try to explain default and foreclosure rates); Roberto G. Quercia, Michael A. Stegman, and Walter R. Davis, "The Impact of Predatory Loan Terms on Subprime Foreclosures: The Special Case of Prepayment Penalties and Balloon Payments", *Housing Pol'y Debate*, 18 (2007), 311, 337 (finding, based on LP data, that "lengthy"—that is, 3 years or more—prepayment penalties increase foreclosure risk by about 20 percent). The higher default rates of mortgages with escalating payments (ARMs as compared to FRMs) and with prepayment penalties were partly due to inherent risk associated with these deferred-cost features and partly due to poor underwriting standards, which were also associated with the loan's deferred-cost features (escalating-payment mortgages enabled lenders to qualify borrowers based on the low, initial rate; similarly, according to some accounts, prepayment penalties enabled the lower initial interest rates that qualify riskier borrowers).

industry study that assumes foreclosure losses equal to 37.5 percent of a loan's value estimates total subprime foreclosure losses on loans originated between 2004 and 2006 at nearly $29 billion. Substituting Bernanke's 50 percent figure for the 37.5 percent assumption, the estimate of foreclosure losses increases to $38.7 billion. Of this $38.7 billion, the 10 percent (or $7.7 billion) in transaction costs—the "legal, sales, and maintenance expenses" that Bernanke referred to—are clearly welfare costs. The remainder is partly a welfare cost and partly a welfare-neutral transfer. The transfer component is the "foreclosure discount," the difference between the market price and the price received for a foreclosed property. This price discount, while a loss to the lender and borrower, is a benefit to the buyer of the foreclosed property. The welfare-cost component is the social loss incurred when a property is left vacant—until the foreclosure sale and often even after the foreclosure sale. In a declining real estate market, these vacancy periods are quite long.[110]

Another category of welfare costs, not included in the preceding estimates, is composed of the negative externalities that foreclosures impose on neighborhoods and cities. The FRB noted that "[w]hen foreclosures are clustered, they can injure entire communities by reducing property values in surrounding areas."[111] Finally, to the extent that foreclosures contributed

110. For the Bernanke estimate—see Bernanke, March 2008 Speech, above note 38. For the industry study estimates—see Cagan, above note 20, at 69–71. See also Paul S. Calem and Michael LaCour-Little, "Risk-Based Capital Requirements for Mortgage Loans" (2001) 12 (*Bd. of Governors of the Fed. Reserve Sys., Fin. and Econ. Discussion Series Paper* No. 2001–60) (assuming it costs 10 percent of the unpaid balance to dispose of the foreclosed property and that foreclosure transaction costs amount to 5 percent of unpaid balance). On the foreclosure discount—see Cagan, above note 20, at 70 (arguing that foreclosed properties sell at a discount of up to 30 percent).

111. Truth in Lending, 73 Fed. Reg. 44,522, 44,524 (July 30, 2008) (codified at 12 C.F.R. pt. 226). See also Vicki Been, Dir., Furman Ctr. for Real Estate and Urban Policy, Testimony before Committee on Oversight and Government Reform Subcommittee on Domestic Policy, "External Effects of Concentrated Mortgage Foreclosures: Evidence from New York City" (May 21, 2008) 4–5 (reporting that, in New York, properties adjacent to recent foreclosure filings sell at a 1.8 percent to 3.7 percent discount); see also William C. Apgar and Mark Duda, Homeownership Pres. Found., "Collateral Damage: The Municipal Impact of Today's Mortgage Foreclosure Boom" (2005), available at <http://www.995hope.org/content/pdf/Apgar_Duda_Study_Short_Version.pdf>; Ctr. for Responsible Lending, "Subprime Spillover: Foreclosures Cost Neighbors $202 Billion: 40.6 Million Homes Lose $5,000 on Average" (2008), available at <http://www.responsiblelending.org/issues/mortgage/research/subprime-spillover.html>; U.S. Dep't of Hous. and Urban Dev. and U.S. Dep't of the Treasury, "Curbing Predatory Home Mortgage Lending" (2000) 25 (detailing externalities such as declines in neighboring property values and increased crime rates); Family Hous. Fund, "Cost Effectiveness of Mortgage Foreclosure Prevention: Summary of Findings" (1998) 5 (noting foreclosure costs of around $7,000 for borrowers, $2,000 for lenders, and additional costs of $15,000 to $60,000 on third parties); Dan Immergluck and Geoff Smith, "The Impact of Single-Family Mortgage Foreclosures on Neighborhood Crime", *Housing Stud.*, 21 (2006), 851; Engel and McCoy, above note 27, at 2042 n. 12.

to the real-estate slump and to the credit crunch, staggering macroeco-
nomic costs should also be considered.

For borrowers, delinquency and foreclosure entail substantial hardship. Borrowers will face higher rates for other credit transactions and
reduced access to credit. They will also lose some or all of their accumulated home equity if the lender forecloses. In addition, the borrower will
have to bear the transaction costs of relocating to another house or
apartment.[112]

Delinquency and foreclosure also impose costs on lenders. If the net
proceeds from the foreclosure sale are smaller than the outstanding loan balance, the lender will suffer a loss. Lenders partially compensated for this risk
by increasing the interest rate.[113] During the subprime crisis, however, much
of this risk was not priced. The sheer magnitude of the ex post losses—as
reflected in the hundreds of billions of dollars in subprime-related write-
offs by financial institutions—suggests that the risks were not fully accounted
for ex ante. Moreover, SEC investigations, following the collapse of the
subprime market, revealed that at least some lenders had a very poor understanding of the risks that they were undertaking.[114]

In measuring the social cost of foreclosure, it is important to distinguish
between costs borne by borrowers and lenders on the one hand and costs
borne by third parties—neighbors, neighborhoods, and cities—on the other.
For borrowers and lenders, to the extent that the transacting parties were
rational, the ex post cost of foreclosure represents a sour realization of a
mutually beneficial ex ante gamble. Accordingly, we need to worry only
about the imperfectly rational parties who did not secure a positive ex ante
value. Now consider the costs borne by third parties. These costs—negative
externalities imposed by the loan contract—translate into a social cost, even
when both contracting parties are fully rational.

---

112. Truth in Lending, 73 Fed. Reg. 44,522, 44,524 (July 30, 2008) (codified at 12 C.F.R. pt. 226)
    ("The consequences of default are severe for homeowners, who face the possibility of fore-
    closure, the loss of accumulated home equity, higher rates for other credit transactions, and
    reduced access to credit.").
113. See Demyanyk and Van Hemert, above note 1, at 1871–3 (finding that high loan-to-value
    borrowers increasingly became high-risk borrowers over the past five years, in terms of ele-
    vated delinquency and foreclosure rates, and that lenders were aware of this and adjusted
    mortgage rates accordingly over time).
114. On the subprime-related write-offs—see above note 12. On the findings from the SEC
    investigations—see above note 13.

D. Distributional Concerns

Contractual design can also have distributional effects. While wealthy borrowers were not generally part of the subprime and Alt-A markets, there was still substantial heterogeneity in the wealth levels of subprime and Alt-A borrowers. Given the complexity of these contracts, wealthier borrowers who could afford to seek out expert advice were likely to do better than borrowers who could not afford such advice. The inverse correlation between borrower wealth and contractual complexity—wealthier borrowers generally got less complicated prime loans and poorer borrowers generally got more complicated subprime or Alt-A loans—raises another distributional concern.

Evidence that "subprime mortgages [were] concentrated in locations with high proportions of black and Hispanic residents, even controlling for the income and credit scores of these Zip codes"[115] also raises distributional concerns. Disparities in financial sophistication and in the ability to effectively comparison-shop led to substantial price variations, even if only because minority borrowers had fewer options to compare. A study, by Susan Woodward, found that African-American borrowers paid an additional $415 in fees and Latino borrowers paid an additional $365 in fees. Other price terms likewise reflected variations. Specifically, "black homeowners [were] significantly more likely to have prepayment penalties or balloon payments attached to their mortgages than non-black homeowners, even after controlling for age, income, gender, and creditworthiness."[116]

Gender disparities have also been identified: There is some evidence that women, as a group, received inferior mortgage products.[117] Socio-economic

115. Mayer and Pence, above note 83, at 2.
116. On the concentration of subprime loans in minority neighborhoods—see Mayer and Pence, above note 83, at 2. On the limited shopping by minority borrowers—see Michael S. Barr, Sendhil Mullainathan, and Eldar Shafir, "Behaviorally Informed Home Mortgage Credit Regulation," in Eric S. Belsky and Nicolas P. Retsinas (eds.), *Understanding Consumer Credit* (Brooking Press, 2009) ("[L]ow-income and minority buyers are the least likely to shop for alternate financing arrangements...."); Jinkook Lee and Jeanne M. Hogarth, "Consumer Information Search for Home Mortgages: Who, What, How Much, and What Else?", *Fin. Services Rev.* 9 (2000), 277, 283; Zywicki and Adamson, above note 55, at 55–6. On the higher fees paid by minority borrowers—see Woodward, above note 104, at ix. On race-based variations in other price terms—see Michael S. Barr, Jane K. Dokko, and Benjamin J. Keys, "Who Gets Lost in the Subprime Mortgage Fallout?: Homeowners in Low- and Moderate-Income Neighborhoods" (April 2008) 2–3, available at <http://ssrn.com/abstract=1121215>; Ruben Hernandez-Murillo, Andra C. Ghent, and Michael Owyang, "Race, Redlining, and Subprime Loan Pricing" (2011), available at <http://ssrn.com/abstract=1881894>.
117. See John Leland, "Baltimore Finds Subprime Crisis Snags Women," *New York Times*, January 15, 2008, at A1; see also Allen J. Fishbein and Patrick Woodall, Consumer Fed. of Am., "Women

status also played a role. Borrowers with less income and education were less likely to know their mortgage terms, implying greater underestimation of deferred or hidden costs and a diminished ability to effectively shop for better terms. Indeed, there is evidence that better-educated borrowers received better terms on their loans.[118]

The evidence of bias, however, is not conclusive. In a sample of more than 75,000 adjustable-rate mortgages, Andrew Haughwout, Christopher Mayer, and Joseph Tracy found no evidence of adverse pricing by race, ethnicity, or gender in either the initial rate or the reset margin. But as the authors acknowledge, their analysis focuses on interest rates, leaving open the possibility that bias affects points and fees at loan origination. In addition,

Are Prime Targets for Subprime Lending: Women Are Disproportionately Represented in High-Cost Mortgage Market" (2006) 1, available at <http://www.consumerfed.org/pdfs/WomenPrimeTargetsStudy120606.pdf> (finding that women are more likely to receive subprime mortgages than men and that disparity between men and women increases as income rises); Nat'l Cmty. Reinvestment Coal., "Homeownership and Wealth Building Impeded: Continuing Lending Disparities for Minorities and Emerging Obstacles for Middle-Income and Female Borrowers of All Races" (2006) 12–14, available at <http://www.ncrc.org/index.php?option=com_contentandtask=viewandid=344andItemid=76> (finding that women received 37 percent of high-cost home loans in 2005, compared with just 28 percent of prime loans); Prudential Ins. Co. of Am., *Financial Experience and Behaviors among Women* (2006) 7, available at <http://www.prudential.com/media/managed/2006WomenBrochure_FINAL.pdf> (finding that "a majority of financial and investment products are unfamiliar to almost half of all women"); Annamaria Lusardi and Olivia S. Mitchell, "Planning and Financial Literacy: How Do Women Fare?" (2008) (*Nat'l Bureau of Econ. Research Working Paper No. 13750*), available at <http://ssrn.com/abstract=1087003> (finding that older women display much lower levels of financial literacy than the older population as a whole); Women in the Subprime Market, Consumers Union, October 2002, <http://www.consumersunion.org/finance/women-rpt1002.htm> (attributing some of the disparity both to the instability in women's credit status that results from divorce or family medical emergency and to the fact that women have less wealth than men).

118. On the effects of income and education on knowledge of mortgage terms—see Bucks and Pence, above note 95, at 3, 20–1, 26. On the effects of education on loan terms—see Woodward, above note 104 (finding that offers made by brokers to borrowers without a college education are $1,100 higher on average); Thomas P. Boehm and Alan Schlottmann, "Mortgage Pricing Differentials across Hispanic, African-American, and White Households: Evidence from the American Housing Survey", *Cityscape: J. Pol'y Dev. and Res.*, No. 2, (2007), 9, 93, and 105 (finding a negative correlation between education and interest rates); J. Michael Collins, "Education Levels and Mortgage Application Outcomes: Evidence of Financial Literacy" (2009) *Institute for Research on Poverty Discussion Paper No. 1369–09*, available at SSRN: <http://ssrn.com/abstract=1507276> (finding, based on 2005 Home Mortgage Disclosure Act data aggregated by Census tract, that tracts with higher rates of college completion pay lower mean interest rates as reported by lenders for high cost loans); Annamaria Lusardi, "Financial Literacy: An Essential Tool for Informed Consumer Choice?" (2008) 10 (*Nat'l Bureau of Econ. Research, Working Paper No. 14084*), available at <http://ssrn.com/abstract=1149331> (citing a 2003 study by Danna Moore showing that low-literacy borrowers are more likely to purchase high-cost mortgages). Individuals with little education, women, African-Americans, and Hispanics display particularly low levels of literacy. *Id.* at 1.

the analysis does not rule out the possibility that borrowers were selectively steered into subprime mortgage products.[119]

VI. Policy Implications

As we have seen, borrowers' imperfect rationality explains several contractual design features in the subprime mortgage market. The imperfect rationality of borrowers, especially when coupled with contracts designed in response to such imperfect rationality, produced substantial welfare costs. Since market forces have proven to be too slow to respond to these problems, legal intervention should be considered to prevent a recurrence of these problems. Disclosure regulation is the right place to start. Optimally designed disclosure, while not a perfect fix, can make a significant difference. It can help less sophisticated borrowers without significantly restricting the choices available to more sophisticated borrowers.

A. Disclosing the Total Cost of Credit: The Great Promise of the APR Disclosure

Perhaps the most important reason to focus on disclosure regulation is because a disclosure mandate that already exists seems to provide, at least in theory, an effective response to the behavioral-market failure in the subprime and Alt-A mortgage markets; the APR disclosure, which lenders must provide under the TILA. The APR is a normalized measure of the total cost of credit. A lender is required to add up all the different prices and fees that the borrower is required to pay under the loan contract into a single aggregate amount, the "finance charge," and disclose this dollar amount. Then, to facilitate comparison-shopping, the lender is required to translate the finance charge, from a dollar amount into an APR, and disclose this figure as well.[120]

---

119. Andrew Haughwout, Christopher Mayer, and Joseph Tracy, "Subprime Mortgage Pricing: The Impact of Race, Ethnicity, and Gender on the Cost of Borrowing" (2009) FRB of New York Staff Report No. 368.

120. See Truth in Lending Act, Pub. L. No. 90–321, § 107, 82 Stat. 146, 149 (1968) (codified as amended at 15 U.S.C. § 1606 (2006)) (defining the APR); Truth in Lending Act §§ 121–31, 82 Stat. at 152–57 (codified as amended at 15 U.S.C. §§ 1631–49 (2006)) (requiring disclosure of the APR). See also Renuart and Thompson, above note 19, at 217 ("Congress designed the APR to be the single number that consumers should focus upon when shopping for credit.").

The importance of total cost disclosures, and of the APR specifically, has been reaffirmed by the Mortgage Reform and Anti-Predatory Lending Act, enacted as Title XIV of the Dodd–Frank Act of 2010. Section 1419 of the Dodd–Frank Act requires several quasi-total-cost disclosures: Creditors must disclose the total amount of interest the consumer will pay over the life of the loan, the aggregate amount of fees paid to the mortgage originator in connection with the loan, and the amount paid for settlement services. These are called "quasi-total-cost disclosures" because they aggregate costs in categories (interest, fees, and settlement costs) instead of disclosing a single, real total-cost figure.

The new disclosure forms being developed by the Consumer Financial Protection Bureau (CFPB) to comply with a direct Congressional mandate in the Dodd–Frank Act secure an important place for the APR, which is theoretically a real total-cost disclosure. The forms being tested by the CFPB retain the APR as a key total-cost disclosure, and include a "Comparisons" section, featuring the APR, together with Estimated Closing Costs. They even feature this notice: "Use this information to compare this loan with others."[121]

Real total-cost disclosures, and specifically the APR, should serve as a powerful antidote to the effects of imperfect rationality for two reasons. First, the APR would seem to offer an effective response to the complexity and multidimensionality of the subprime mortgage contract. Lenders are required to calculate and disclose the total loan cost to the borrower. With this standard metric at hand, borrowers should be able to compare the total cost of two different, complex loan contracts. Collecting all the rates and fees and folding them into a single aggregate price, the APR renders the borrowers' cognitive deficiencies—limited attention, memory, and processing ability—irrelevant. Second, the APR should provide an effective remedy to the myopia and optimism that give rise to deferred-cost contracts. Since the APR is a composite of short-term and long-term interest rates, capturing both long-term costs and short-term benefits, it should reveal the false allure of deferred-cost contracts.[122]

By overcoming, or bypassing, the imperfect rationality of borrowers, the APR disclosure should also discourage many of the contractual design

121. See Dodd–Frank Act, Sec. 1032(f) (directing the CFPB to develop a new disclosure form); CFPB, Know Before You Owe Initiative <http://www.consumerfinance.gov/knowbeforeyouowe/>.

122. On the APR as an antidote to complexity—see Renuart and Thompson, above note 19, at 214 (arguing that a comprehensive, fee-inclusive APR will help imperfectly rational consumers who cannot aggregate the multiple fees on their own). On the APR as a composite of short-term and long-term interest rates—see 12 C.F.R. § 226.17 (2008); Official Staff Commentary § 226.17(c)(1)–(10) (2008).

features we've already explored. Consider complexity and specifically the proliferation of "junk" fees. Adding non-salient fees was beneficial to the lender because imperfectly rational borrowers ignored them. But if these fees are included in the APR and borrowers shop for low APRs, then the incentive to pile up more fees disappears.[123] Similarly, cost deferral was an attractive strategy for lenders because myopic and optimistic borrowers placed insufficient weight on the long-term costs. If borrowers look to the APR for guidance, and the APR calculation affords appropriate weight to both short-term and long-term costs, lenders will have no incentive to defer costs.

There is already evidence that the APR disclosure can work. Many borrowers know to look for the APR and comparison-shop based on that disclosure. This has led to enhanced competition and reduced rates.[124] There is even evidence that the APR succeeded in fighting imperfect rationality. Specifically, Victor Stango and Jonathan Zinman show that the most biased consumers—consumers who substantially underestimate the APR corresponding to a given payment stream—do not overpay for credit when borrowing in markets where TILA disclosures are consistently made, while these same types of consumers pay 300 –400 basis points more in interest than less-biased consumers do in markets where TILA disclosures are not made consistently.[125]

123. See Bd. of Governors of the Fed. Reserve Sys. and U.S. Dep't of Hous. and Urban Dev., *Joint Report to the Congress Concerning Reform to the Truth and Lending Act and the Real Estate Settlement Procedures Act* (1998) 9, available at <http://www.federalreserve.gov/boarddocs/press/general/1998/19980717/default.htm> ("[T]he APR concept deters hidden or 'junk' fees to the extent that the fees must be included in the APR calculation.").

124. On consumers' use of the APR—see Lee and Hogarth, above note 116, at 286 (finding that 78 percent of homeowners who refinanced their homes report comparison shopping on the basis of the APR); Jinkook Lee and Jeanne M. Hogarth, "The Price of Money: Consumers' Understanding of APRs and Contract Interest Rates", *J. Pub. Pol'y and Marketing*, 19 (1999), 66, 74 (reporting that more than 70 percent of the population reports using the APR to shop for closed-end credit); Renuart and Thompson, above note 19, at 189 ("TILA disclosures have been remarkably effective in educating consumers to pay attention to the APR as a key measure of the cost of credit."). On the competition-enhancing role of the APR—see Rep. No. 96-368, at 16 (1979), reprinted in 1980 U.S.C.C.A.N. 236, 252 (crediting TILA with increasing consumer awareness of annual percentage rates and with a substantial reduction of the market share of creditors charging the highest rates); Randall S. Kroszner, Governor, Bd. of Governors of the Fed. Reserve Sys., Speech at the George Washington University School of Business Financial Services Research Program Policy Forum: "Creating More Effective Consumer Disclosures" (May 23, 2007), available at <http://www.federalreserve.gov/newsevents/speech/Kroszner20070523a.htm> (stating that TILA disclosure requirements and specifically the APR disclosure "are generally believed to have improved competition and helped individual consumers" (citing Bd. of Governors of the Fed. Reserve Sys., Annual Percentage Rate Demonstration Project (1987))).

125. Victor Stango and Jonathan Zinman, "Fuzzy Math, Disclosure Regulation and Credit Market Outcomes" (2007) *Tuck Sch. of Bus. Working Paper No. 2008-42*, available at <http://ssrn.com/abstract=1081635>.

B. The Failure of the APR Disclosure

Despite the achievements of the APR disclosure, there is broad consensus that the APR has not lived up to its great potential and that the current disclosure regime has failed to protect borrowers and ensure an efficient market—especially in the subprime and Alt-A markets.[126] Why? The answer lies in several defects that prevented the APR from living up to its great promise.

First, the APR was often disclosed too late. Lenders were not required to disclose a binding APR—that is, an APR that they cannot change after the disclosure—until consummation of the loan transaction (closing). In purchase loans, lenders were required to disclose a good-faith estimate of the APR three days after receiving a loan application. But lenders were not bound by this estimate. Thus, borrowers could not rely on it when shopping for loans. In addition, the estimated APR was sometimes provided only after a substantial application fee was paid. Borrowers who were understandably reluctant to pay numerous application fees could not use the estimated APR for comparison shopping. The situation was even worse with refinance loans, where lenders were not required to provide any disclosure before closing. Disclosing a binding APR only at closing discourages APR-based comparison shopping. Few borrowers who reached the closing stage would then, after finally learning the APR, refuse to sign the loan documents and start shopping again. (Note that to compare the APR on one loan with the APR on a competing loan, the borrower would have to reach the closing stage with the second loan as well.)[127]

The second reason the APR failed to live up to its potential is that while purporting to provide a total-cost-of-credit measure, the APR actually excludes numerous price dimensions, such as title insurance fees, title examination fees, property survey fees, appraisal fees, credit report fees, document

---

126. The evidence showing the success of the APR is limited to the prime market. See above notes 124–25; see also Patricia A. McCoy, "Rethinking Disclosure in a World of Risk-Based Pricing", *Harv. J. on Legis.*, 44 (2007), 123, 126, 138–9 (noting robust competition in the prime market and that TILA disclosures effectively facilitate this competition). On the general failure of the TILA disclosure regime in the nonprime segments—see, for example, GAO AMP Report, above note 26, at 21 (noting that current disclosure requirements "are not designed to address more complex products such as [Alternative Mortgage Products]"); Edward L. Rubin, "Legislative Methodology: Some Lessons from the Truth-in-Lending Act", *Geo. L.J.*, 80 (1991), 233, 236 (noting that shopping for credit is limited to "upscale consumers who would manage perfectly well without [the] benefit of [the TILA disclosures]").

127. See McCoy, above note 126, 137–43. See also Willis, above note 29, at 749–50. FTC Comment, above note 31, at 11–12. The exception was HOEPA loans, where binding early disclosures were required. See McCoy, above note 126, at 141.

preparation fees, notary fees, flood and pest inspection fees, seller's points, prepayment penalties, and late fees. By excluding these price dimensions, the APR underestimates the total cost of the loan. Moreover, this exclusion invites strategic pricing by lenders. When certain price dimensions are excluded from the APR, lenders will benefit from shifting costs to these excluded dimensions.[128] These problems undermine the effectiveness of the APR. Because the APR does not measure the total cost of credit, borrowers are less likely to focus on the APR. Borrowers who nevertheless use the APR for comparing loans may well end up with a product that, while boasting a lower APR, costs more overall.

The third defect is that the APR disclosure fails to account for the prepayment option—an option that has dramatically affected the values of subprime and Alt-A loans in the recent mortgage-lending expansion. The prepayment option can have a significant effect on a loan's value, even for traditional, prime loans.[129] The effect on subprime and Alt-A loans that were taken with intent to prepay before the end of the low-rate introductory period can be much greater. Consider a 2–28 hybrid for $150,000 with a monthly payment of $1,000 for the first two years and a monthly payment of $1,500 for the remaining 28 years. The APR on this loan, ignoring the prepayment option, is 10.74 percent. Assuming that before the 2–28 mortgage resets, the borrower can refinance into a 30-year FRM with a $1,000 monthly payment, the effective APR is 7.19 percent.[130] The effect of an attractive prepayment option is significant.

128. For price dimensions excluded from the APR—see Comptroller of the Currency, *Truth in Lending: Comptroller's Handbook* (2006) 98, available at <http://www.occ.treas.gov/handbook/til.pdf> (showing that the APR does not include late fees, title insurance fees, title examination fees, property survey fees, appraisal fees, credit report fees, document preparation fees, notary fees, flood and pest inspection fees, and seller's points); Willis, above note 29, at 744, 747, 750 (noting APR includes origination fees and points, but not interest rate escalations, prepayment penalties, late fees, title insurance, and application, appraisal, and document preparation fees) . On the resulting strategic pricing—see Renuart and Thompson, above note 19, at 185, 221; Zywicki and Adamson, above note 55, at 71.

129. On the exclusion of the prepayment option—see HUD-Treasury Report, above note 19, at 66 (noting that "the APR does not account for an early payoff"). This problem persists in the new disclosure forms that are being considered by the CFPB. The APR disclosure, in these forms, is even followed by an express statement: "This rate expresses your costs over 30 years." See CFPB, Know Before You Owe Initiative, <http://www.consumerfinance.gov/knowbeforeyouowe/>. On the effect of the prepayment option on loan value—see Agarwal et al., above note 63, at 28 (calculating a 26.8 percent impact on a $100,000 mortgage for using the wrong rule to make prepayment decisions; the impact of ignoring the prepayment option altogether may well be larger).

130. The actual (no prepayment) and effective (with prepayment) APRs were calculated using APRWIN (Ver. 6.1.0).

Moreover, since the prepayment option affects different contractual designs differently, an APR that ignores the prepayment option can skew the comparison among different loan products. The prepayment option might render the APR disclosure misleading even with simple loan contracts. Comparing two loans, Loan A and Loan B, the APR on Loan A can be lower, reflecting a lower total cost of credit absent prepayment. But with prepayment, the total cost of Loan B may well be lower.[131] This problem is exacerbated when complex contracts include a set of varying terms that interact differently with the prepayment option.

The term that most obviously affects the value of the prepayment option is the prepayment penalty. Many have expressed concerns about prepayment penalties, and their use has been substantially curtailed by the Dodd–Frank Act.[132] The fear is that since prepayment penalties are not incorporated into the APR, borrowers will underestimate their effect on the total cost of the loan.[133] These concerns are valid but address only one aspect of the problem. Those critical of prepayment penalties focus on the penalties that borrowers actually pay and on borrowers' underestimation of these payments. They ignore the effects of prepayment penalties on the value of the prepayment option. Moreover, prepayment penalties reduce the ex ante value of the prepayment option even when they are not paid ex post.

An APR that ignores the prepayment option will play a reduced role in the shopping decisions of perfectly rational borrowers. It will play an even less significant role in the shopping decisions of imperfectly rational borrowers who overestimate the value of the prepayment option. Unfortunately, this prepayment flaw in the APR calculation enabled even honest brokers and loan officers to deflect borrowers' attention from the APR disclosure. For example, the APR on a deferred-cost loan could be much higher than the initial teaser rate. Loan originators wanted borrowers to

131. In particular, by ignoring the prepayment option, the APR underestimates the importance of origination fees (those that are included in the APR calculation) that accrue at closing. See Renuart and Thompson, above note 19, at 231. This may provide another explanation for the proliferation of origination fees.

132. Pub. L. 111–203, Sec. 1414. See also Truth in Lending, 73 Fed. Reg. 44,522, 44,551 (July 30, 2008) (codified at 12 C.F.R. pt. 226).

133. See Truth in Lending, 73 Fed. Reg. 44,522, 44,525 (July 30, 2008) (codified at 12 C.F.R. pt. 226) ("Subprime loans are also far more likely to have prepayment penalties. Because the annual percentage rate (APR) does not reflect the price of the penalty, the consumer must both calculate the size of the penalty from a formula and assess the likelihood of moving or refinancing during the penalty period. In these and other ways, subprime products tend to be complex for consumers.").

focus on the low teaser rate and not on the high APR. These brokers and loan officers could truthfully tell borrowers that they are likely to prepay and exit long before the nominal thirty-year loan period ends and that they should therefore pay little attention to an APR that assumes thirty years of loan payments.

The APR disclosure has failed. It was often disclosed too late to help borrowers choose between different loan products. By excluding numerous price dimensions and by ignoring the prepayment option, the APR has failed to live up to its declared purpose of providing an accurate total-cost-of-credit measure. As a result, borrowers abandoned the APR, and it ceased to be the focal point of comparison-shopping in the subprime mortgage market. The resulting cost to borrowers and to society more generally was substantial.

As mentioned earlier, the APR has the potential to ameliorate the effects of imperfect rationality, but it can effectively respond to the imperfect rationality of borrowers only if imperfectly rational borrowers rely on the APR. Many borrowers, however, did not.

C. Fixing the APR Disclosure

Given the potential of the APR disclosure to compensate for the imperfect rationality of borrowers, it should be a priority for policymakers to fix the APR's problems. In fact, the timing problem has already been addressed—and partially solved—by recent legal reforms. Specifically, new FRB regulations require lenders to disclose an APR within three days after the loan application has been submitted and before any fees are charged, for both purchase and refinance loans. Further, the Housing and Economic Recovery Act requires lenders to disclose an updated APR three days before consummation of the loan transaction, in case the previously disclosed APR "is no longer accurate."[134]

These recent statutory and regulatory responses reduce but don't solve the timing-of-disclosure problem. Two issues remain: First, lenders can still disclose a low APR after receiving an application, and then disclose a higher APR later on. Borrowers will be wary of using the application-stage APR for comparison-shopping, since this APR can change. Three days before

---

134. See Truth in Lending, 73 Fed. Reg. 44,522, 44,590–92 (July 30, 2008) (codified at 12 C.F.R. pt. 226); Housing and Economic Recovery Act of 2008, Pub. L. No. 110–289, § 2502(a), 122 Stat. 2654, 2855–57 (codified at 15 U.S.C. § 1638(b)(2)).

closing, the time when an updated APR is provided, may already be too late for effective comparison-shopping. Second, the enforcement of these improved timing-of-disclosure rules is imperfect. Specifically, several appellate courts have interpreted TILA's civil liability section as precluding statutory damages for timing-of-disclosure violations. The borrower would thus have to claim actual damages and prove detrimental reliance—a substantial barrier to recovery.[135] While Congress and the FRB should be commended for reducing the timing-of-disclosure problem, still more can and should be done. Disclosure of a binding APR should be required at an earlier time,[136] and the civil liability provisions of TILA should be strengthened.

The second major APR problem, under-inclusiveness, has not been addressed. The purpose of the APR was to provide a uniform total-cost-of-credit measure. The current APR excludes numerous price dimensions and thus fails to present the total cost of credit. The analysis in this chapter lends further support to proposals, most recently by Elizabeth Renuart and Diane Thompson, to create a more inclusive APR.[137] Several price dimensions currently excluded from the APR definition can be easily added; others can only be added at a cost. For example, adding the price of truly optional services to the APR would generate several APRs for a single mortgage, potentially confusing rather than assisting borrowers. Adding contingent

135. On the concern that lenders will set a low APR and then increase it three days before closing—see Kathleen C. Engel and Patricia A. McCoy, "A Tale of Three Markets: The Law and Economics of Predatory Lending", *Tex. L. Rev.*, 80 (2002), 1255, 1269 (noting that lenders face no liability for errors in the Good Faith Estimate (GFE), including the GFE of the APR). Moreover, it is not clear from the language of the statute that lenders cannot change the APR again between the time of the updated disclosure (three days before closing) and consummation. On the narrow interpretation of TILA's civil liability section—15 U.S.C. § 1640 (2006)—see, e.g., *Dykstra v. Wayland Ford, Inc.*, 134 F. App'x 911 (6th Cir. 2005); *Baker v. Sunny Chevrolet, Inc.*, 349 F.3d 862 (6th Cir. 2003); *Brown v. Payday Check Advance, Inc.*, 202 F.3d 987 (7th Cir. 2000); *In re Ferrell*, 358 B.R. 777 (B.A.P. 9th Cir. 2006). Other courts have adopted a more expansive interpretation of TILA's civil liability provisions. See, e.g., *Bragg v. Bill Heard Chevrolet, Inc.*, 374 F.3d 1060 (11th Cir. 2004).
136. See HUD-Treasury Report, above note 19, at 67 (proposing that originators be required to provide an accurate, within a prescribed tolerance, Good Faith Estimate of, among other things, the APR). It should be recognized, however, that locking in an APR at an earlier time would place greater interest rate risk on the lender and that this added risk would be, at least partially, passed on to borrowers. Borrowers who need the APR as a focal point for comparison-shopping should be willing to accept these consequences. Cf. McCoy, above note 126, at 138 (arguing that similar rate lock-ins are common in the prime market even though lenders are not required to disclose a binding APR).
137. Renuart and Thompson, above note 19; see also HUD-Treasury Report, above note 19, at 69 (proposing that the law be amended "to require that the full cost of credit be included in the APR"); Eskridge, above note 19 (proposing a more inclusive APR more than twenty years ago).

prices, such as late fees and prepayment penalties, imposes a different cost. These prices can only be incorporated into the APR by estimating the average probability that the fee-triggering contingency will materialize. An APR based on this estimated average would be inaccurate for many borrowers. Of course, the current APR is similarly inaccurate for many borrowers, since it, in effect, assumes a zero probability of triggering these contingent fees. While a more inclusive APR is warranted, for some price dimensions the inclusion decision requires a careful cost-benefit analysis.

The third APR problem is the ignored prepayment option. This also has not been addressed by policymakers and has even escaped the attention of commentators. When borrowers expect, rationally or irrationally, to avoid high long-term costs by refinancing their mortgage, they will ignore an APR that does not include the prepayment option. It is, therefore, useful to consider incorporating the prepayment option into the APR calculation. To be sure, accounting for the possibility of prepayment is not an easy exercise. The likelihood and timing of prepayment would have to be estimated, as would the expected terms of the refinance loan. These estimates would need to be based on projections of future house prices (for each Metropolitan Statistical Area) and interest rates. These future market conditions would then need to be combined with estimated borrower and loan characteristics, such as future FICO score, future income, and future LTV, to estimate the refinancing options that would be available to the specific borrower.[138]

These estimates and projections would necessarily be based on a series of assumptions. While the use of assumptions is not new to disclosure regulation, it should be recognized that some degree of arbitrariness in the choice of assumptions is inevitable and that the chosen assumptions will not perfectly reflect every borrower's situation. The difficulties of generating accurate projections should not be exaggerated. The mortgage industry already employs sophisticated valuation algorithms to arrive at projections tailored to specific home and loan characteristics.[139] An APR disclosure that uses

138. Estimating the future LTV is particularly complicated. This estimate would be based on the current LTV, the contractually specified payment stream, the prepayment penalty—which would need to be financed by the new loan—and the projected future house value.

139. Projections and forecasts are commonly used in the industry. See, e.g., Cagan, above note 20; Sherlund, above note 125, at 11 ("I draw house price, interest rate, and unemployment rate forecasts from Fannie Mae's and Freddie Mac's June 2008 monthly economic outlooks...."); cf. W. Miles, "Boom-Bust Cycles and the Forecasting Performance of Linear and Non-Linear Models of House Prices", *J. Real Est. Fin. and Econ.*, 36 (2008), 249 (comparing the power of competing models to predict house prices). Futures markets can be used to help predict price trajectories. And sophisticated valuation algorithms can be used to more closely tailor predic-

these projections to account for the prepayment option will thus reduce the information asymmetry between lenders and borrowers. More importantly, this disclosure could restore borrower confidence in the APR, thus harnessing the potential of the APR to counteract the effects of imperfect rationality.[140]

It is worth reminding ourselves that even an optimally designed APR will not be perfect. It is impossible to fully capture the multidimensionality of a mortgage loan in a one-dimensional metric. This inevitable limitation, however, does not detract from the social value of the APR disclosure. Sophisticated borrowers who can deal with the complexity and multi-dimensionality will not rely solely on the APR. Those who rely solely, or mainly, on the APR will be the less sophisticated borrowers who, absent the APR disclosure, would rely on an even less accurate proxy.[141]

Conclusion

During the subprime boom years, subprime and Alt-A mortgage contracts were complex, multidimensional contracts that often deferred costs into the future. This contractual design can be explained as a market response to the imperfect rationality of borrowers. The welfare costs of this market failure were substantial: Competition was both hindered and distorted, resulting in an inefficient allocation of resources. Default and foreclosure rates increased,

tions to specific homes and specific loans. See Cagan, above note 20, at 5 (describing the valuation algorithms). See also Philip Bond, David K. Musto, and Bilge Yilmaz, "Predatory Mortgage Lending," (2008) *FRB of Philadelphia Working Paper* No. 08-24, available at SSRN: <http://ssrn.com/abstract=1288094> (describing the large amounts of information that lenders have, including information on the performance of specific mortgage types when taken by borrowers with specific characteristics).

140. The proposed disclosure would also assist rational borrowers. Currently, these borrowers must calculate the value of the prepayment option (or the probability of facing an attractive prepayment option) on their own. This is a costly exercise. And some borrowers may decide to forgo the exercise. The proposed disclosure would save the calculation costs or, for those borrowers who would forgo the exercise, reduce uncertainty about the prepayment option.

141. The limits of the APR, even when optimally designed, warrant consideration of supplementary approaches. For example, the CFPB could sponsor a web-based mortgage search tool. This tool would ask the borrower for information relevant to loan underwriting and then provide a list of best options (from the best lenders), where the best options, or at least some of them, would not necessarily be picked solely by the APR. Cf. John Lynch, *Consumer Information Processing and Mortgage Disclosures* (2008), available at <http://www.ftc.gov/be/workshops/mortgage/presentations/Lynch_John.pdf> (proposing a "personalized screening agent website for best alternatives in region").

imposing costs on borrowers, lenders, neighborhoods, cities, and the economy at large. Distributional problems also surfaced.

In this chapter, we explored how the outcome in the subprime and Alt-A markets can be improved by revitalizing the APR disclosure. The APR, by providing a common total-cost-of-credit measure, can serve as an effective antidote to imperfect rationality. The APR can only do so, however, if borrowers focus on the APR when choosing among different mortgage products. In the subprime and Alt-A markets, borrowers largely abandoned the APR. This can change. Borrowers will again rely on the APR if it is disclosed early enough and if it is redesigned to provide a comprehensive total-cost-of-credit measure. To this end, Congress and the CFPB should minimize the number of price dimensions that are excluded from the APR definition and consider incorporating the prepayment option into the APR calculation. These proposals, if successful in restoring borrower confidence in the APR, will allow the subprime and Alt-A markets to benefit from the APR's unique ability to combat imperfect rationality.

It should be noted that the Dodd–Frank Act, in addition to taking important steps towards improving the mortgage disclosure regime, also moves beyond disclosure. In particular, the Act targets some of the cost-deferral features identified above: The Act requires lenders to verify a borrower's ability-to-repay (Sec. 1411) and sets a safe harbor for the ability-to-repay requirement—the qualified mortgage, which cannot include certain deferred-cost features (Sec. 1412). Furthermore, the Act severely restricts the use of prepayment penalties (Sec. 1414). These reforms reflect Congress's recognition that imperfectly rational borrowers might underestimate the importance of deferred costs.

4

Cell Phones

Introduction

The cellular service market is an economically significant market that has substantially enhanced consumer welfare. From 1990 to 2009, the U.S. market grew from 5 million subscribers to 291 million subscribers. At the time of this writing, 93 percent of Americans have a cell phone, and an increasing number of households have given up their landlines and rely entirely on wireless communications. Annual revenues of the four national carriers—AT&T, Verizon, Sprint, and T-Mobile—total over $180 billion.

While acknowledging these successes and welfare benefits, the focus of this chapter is on the failures of this market. We'll see how carriers design their contracts in response to the systemic mistakes and misperceptions of their customers. In doing so, they impose welfare costs on consumers, reducing the net benefit that consumers derive from wireless service. We'll focus on three design features common to most cellular service contracts:

- three-part tariffs;
- lock-in clauses; and
- sheer complexity.

As you have no doubt noticed, a major theme of this book is that the interaction between consumer psychology and market forces results in contracts that feature complexity and deferred costs. Lock-in clauses and three-part tariffs together generate cost deferral. Lock-in clauses enable bundling of handsets and cellular service. This bundling allows carriers to offer free or subsidized phones—an upfront benefit—recouping costs at the back end through the price of cellular service. This cost deferral is motivated by consumers' demand for short-term perks and their relative inattentiveness to long-term costs. The underestimation of long-term costs is amplified by the three-part tariff, which responds to and exacerbates the effect of misperceptions that lead consumers to underestimate the cost of cellular service. Sheer complexity is the third of the three design features that contribute to market failure.

A. Three Design Features

The basic pricing scheme of the common cellular service contract is a three-part tariff comprising (1) a monthly charge, (2) a number of voice minutes that the monthly charge pays for, and (3) a per-minute price for minutes beyond the plan limit. The three-part tariff is a rational response by sophisticated carriers to consumers' misperceptions about their cell phone usage. Consumers choose calling plans based on a forecast of future use patterns. The problem is that many consumers do not have a very good sense of these use patterns—some underestimate whereas others overestimate their future usage. The three-part tariff is advantageous to carriers because it exacerbates the effects of consumer misperception, leading consumers to underestimate the cost of cellular service.

The overage-fee component of the three-part tariff targets the underestimators. These consumers underestimate the probability of exceeding the plan limit and incurring an overage fee. As a result, they underestimate the total cost of the cellular service. The other components of the three-part tariff, the monthly charge and the fixed number of minutes that come with it, target the over-estimators. These consumers think that they will use most or all of their allotted minutes. They therefore expect to pay a per-minute price equal to the monthly charge divided by the number of allotted minutes. In fact, the over-estimators use far fewer minutes and end up paying a much higher per-minute price. In this way, then, over-estimators also underestimate the cost of cellular service.

Carriers seem to be aware of these misperceptions. As a pricing manager a top U.S. cellular phone carrier explained, "people absolutely think they know how much they will use and it's pretty surprising how wrong they are."[1] The prevalence of consumer misperception can be empirically confirmed by using a unique dataset of subscriber-level monthly billing and usage information for 3,730 subscribers at a single wireless provider. These

---

1. Michael Grubb, "Selling to Overconfident Consumers", *Amer. Econ. Rev.*, 99 (2009), 1770, 1771 (note 2).

data enable calculation of not only the total cost of wireless service under each consumer's chosen plan, but also the total amount that the consumer would have paid had he chosen other available plans. Thus, one can determine the plan that best fits actual cell phone usage. The data show that over 65 percent of consumers chose the wrong plan. Some chose plans with an insufficient number of allotted minutes, whereas others chose plans with an excessive number of allotted minutes. Subscribers exceeded their minute allowance 17 percent of the time by an average of 33 percent, suggesting underestimation of use. And, during the 81 percent of the time when the allowance was not exceeded, subscribers used only 47 percent of their minute allowance on average, suggesting overestimation.

In addition to the three-part tariff pricing structure, most calling plans come with a free or substantially discounted phone and a long-term contract with an early termination fee (ETF) that effectively locks the consumer in for a substantial time period—typically two years. These lock-in clauses and the accompanying ETFs can also be explained as a market response to the imperfect rationality of consumers. Imperfectly rational consumers underestimate the cost of lock-in, since they underestimate the likelihood that switching providers will be beneficial down the road. Switching providers may be beneficial, for example, if current service is not as good as promised, monthly charges are higher than expected (due to the misperception of use levels discussed above), or another carrier is offering a better deal.

The lock-in that is enforced by the ETF also facilitates the common practice of bundling phones and service. The long-term revenue stream that lock-in guarantees enables carriers to offer free or subsidized phones. Rational consumers, knowing that they will pay for this "free" phone in the long term, would not be enticed by a free-phone offer. Imperfectly rational consumers, on the other hand, discount the long-term cost and seek out "free" phone offers.

Finally, the third design feature that contributes to the behavioral market failure is the sheer complexity of the cell phone contracts. Cellular service contracts are complex and multidimensional. Choosing among numerous contracts can be a daunting task. The three-part tariff itself is complex. Lock-in clauses and ETFs add further complexity. In addition, the true cost of a calling plan depends on numerous other features. For example, most plans offer unlimited night and weekend calling, but carriers offer different definitions of "night" and "weekend." Also, consumers must choose between unlimited in-network calling, unlimited calling to five numbers, unlimited Walkie-Talkie, rollover minutes, and more. Finally, different carriers offer different ranges of handsets, handset subsidies vary, and so on. Complexity is further increased when family plans are added to the mix, data services are added to voice services, prepaid plans are considered in addition to postpaid plans, and so forth. According to one industry estimate, the cellular service market boasts over 10 million plan and add-on combinations.

This level of complexity can itself be viewed as a contractual design feature that responds to the imperfect rationality of consumers. Complexity allows providers to hide the true cost of the contract. Imperfectly rational consumers do not effectively aggregate the costs associated with the different options and prices in a cell phone contract. Inevitably, consumers will focus on a subset of salient features and prices, and ignore or underestimate the importance of the remaining non-salient features and prices. In response, providers will increase prices or reduce the quality of the non-salient features. This, in turn, will generate or free up resources for intensified competition on the salient features. Competition forces providers to make the salient features attractive and the salient prices low. This can be achieved by adding revenue-generating, non-salient features and prices. The result is an endogenously derived high level of complexity and multidimensionality. Interestingly, consumer learning can exacerbate the problem. When consumers learn the importance of a previously non-salient feature, carriers have a strong incentive to come up with a new one, further increasing the level of complexity.

B. Rational-Choice Explanations?

Before we can draw normative and prescriptive implications from these behavioral theories, we must consider whether the more traditional rational-choice model can explain the same design features. If the rational-choice model comes up short, then we have good reason to appeal to behavioral economics to assess the appropriate policy response.

The leading rational-choice explanation for three-part tariffs views these tariffs as mechanisms for price discrimination or market screening among rational consumers with different ex ante demand characteristics. The price-discrimination argument rests on specific assumptions about the distribution of consumer types—assumptions that are not borne out in the cell phone market. With the distribution of types that we actually observe, providers selling to rational consumers would not offer three-part tariffs.

Lock-in clauses can arise when consumers are rational. This happens when sellers incur substantial per-consumer fixed costs and liquidity-constrained consumers cannot afford to pay upfront fees equal to these fixed costs. However, in the cell phone market, while fixed costs are high, they are also endogenous. Carriers invest up to $400 in acquiring each new customer, but much of these customer-acquisition costs are attributed to the free or subsidized phones that carriers offer. This raises a series of questions. Why do carriers offer free phones and lock-in contracts? Why not charge customers the full price of the phone to avoid the lock-in? How many consumers cannot afford to pay for a phone up-front? For how many of these liquidity-constrained consumers is the carrier the most efficient source of credit? The rational-choice model can explain the presence of lock-in clauses, but only in a subset of contracts.

The rational-choice explanation for complexity is straightforward: Consumers have heterogeneous preferences, and the complexity and multi-dimensionality of the cellular service offerings cater to these heterogeneous preferences. But while this heterogeneity likely explains some of the observed complexity in the cell phone market, it cannot fully account for the staggering level of complexity exhibited by the long menus of multi-dimensional contracts available to consumers. Even for the rational consumer, acquiring and comparing information on the range of complex products is a time-consuming and costly undertaking. At some point, the costs exceed the benefit of finding the perfect plan. Comparison-shopping is deterred, and the benefits of the variety and multidimensionality are left unrealized. It seems that in the cell phone market, the optimal level of complexity has been exceeded.

C. Welfare Costs

The design of cellular service contracts is best explained as a rational response to the imperfect rationality of consumers. Consumer mistakes and providers' responses to these mistakes hurt consumers and generate welfare costs. For example, consumers who misperceive their future use patterns choose the wrong three-part tariff; that is, they do not choose the plan that would minimize their total costs. Extrapolating from the sample of 3,730 subscribers described above, the total annual reduction in consumer surplus from the three-part tariff structure exceeds $13.35 billion. Moreover, while the average annual harm per consumer, $47.68, is small, this average masks potentially important distributional implications. The $13.35 billion harm is not evenly divided among the 250 million U.S. cell phone owners. Many of these subscribers choose the right plan. Even among those who choose the wrong plan, there is substantial heterogeneity in the magnitude of their mistakes. Each year, 42.5 million consumers make mistakes that cost them at least 20 percent of their total yearly wireless bill, or $146 per consumer annually. The distribution of mistakes implies a potentially troubling form of regressive redistribution, since revenues from consumers who make mistakes keep prices low for consumers who do not make mistakes.

Other welfare costs are a consequence of lock-in. Lock-in prevents efficient switching and thus hurts consumers. Switching is efficient when a different carrier or plan provides a better fit for the consumer. One survey found that while 47 percent of subscribers would like to switch plans, only 3 percent do so. The rest are deterred by the ETFs. Lock-in can also slow the beneficial effects of consumer learning and prolong the costs of consumer mistakes, since even consumers who learn from experience cannot benefit from their new-found knowledge by immediately switching to another carrier's plan. (Insofar as carriers allow consumers to switch among their own monthly plans, consumers can benefit from learning.) In addition to these direct costs, lock-in may inhibit competition, adding a potentially large indirect welfare cost. Since lock-in may prevent a more efficient carrier from attracting consumers who are locked into a contract with a less efficient carrier, it can deter new carriers from entering the market.[2]

Complexity is another detriment to welfare. The high level of complexity of cell phone contracts can reduce welfare in two ways. First, consumers tend to make more mistakes in plan choice when the menus are complex, and these mistakes reduce consumer welfare. Second, complexity inhibits competition by discouraging comparison-shopping. By raising the cost of comparison-shopping, complex contracts reduce the likelihood that a consumer will find it beneficial to carefully consider all available options. Without the discipline that comparison-shopping enforces, cellular service

---

2. A carrier's relative efficiency depends on its costs of providing service and the quality of service that it offers. Thus, a carrier that provides the same quality of service at lower cost than another or a higher quality service at the same cost as another is a more efficient carrier.

providers can behave like quasi-monopolists, raising prices and reducing consumer surplus.

D. Market Solutions and Their Limits

Do these behavioral market failures result from imperfect competition in the cell phone market? The simple answer is "no." In fact, enhanced competition would likely make the identified design features more pervasive and the resulting welfare costs higher. If consumers misperceive their future use levels, competition will force carriers to offer three-part tariffs. If consumers are myopic, competition will force carriers to offer free phones and cover the cost of the subsidy with lock-in contracts. Finally, if consumers ignore less salient price dimensions of complex, multidimensional contracts, competition will force carriers to shift costs to these less salient price dimensions. When demand for cellular service is driven by imperfect rationality, competitors must respond to this biased demand; otherwise, they will lose business and be forced out the market. Accordingly, given consumers' imperfect rationality, ensuring robust competition in the cellular service market would not in itself solve the problem.

But it is a mistake to take the level of imperfect rationality as given. As we have seen in previous chapters, competition, coupled with consumer learning, can reduce levels of bias and misperception and thus trigger a shift to more efficient contractual design. In fact, the cellular service market has exhibited numerous examples of such market correction in recent years and now boasts a large set of products and contracts that cater to more sophisticated consumers.

At the same time, however, the evolution of the market demonstrates limits on the power of consumer learning to correct behavioral market failures. For example, the market has responded to greater consumer awareness of the costs of underestimated use among consumers who have experienced the sting of large overage charges. Since 2008, the major carriers have been offering unlimited calling plans that arguably respond to demand generated by this heightened consumer awareness. Yet, while overage fees make it easy to learn the cost of underestimated use, the costs of overestimated use are more difficult to learn since they are not so obviously penalized. The result of this uneven learning is unlimited plans rather than the optimal two-part tariff pricing scheme comprised of a fixed monthly fee and a constant per-minute charge.

Another example: The shift from a time-invariant ETF to a time-variant, graduated ETF structure responds to consumers' increased awareness and sensitivity to ETFs. This shift is not a pure market solution. Rather, it is an example of how consumer learning and legal intervention can work in tandem to change business practices. The change in ETF structure likely began with a small number of consumers who learned to appreciate the cost of ETFs and initiated litigation against the carriers. The threat of liability and greater consumer awareness of ETFs then pushed carriers to adjust their ETF structures.

Innovations like these suggest that the market has an impressive capacity to correct for consumer misperceptions. Yet, market solutions are imperfect. Not all biases are easily purged by learning. Not all consumers learn equally fast, as evidenced by the limited adoption of many design innovations. The speed of consumer learning and the market's response matter, since welfare costs are incurred in the interim period. Moreover, when consumers learn to overcome one mistake, or when a previously hidden term becomes salient, carriers have an incentive to trigger a new kind of mistake or to add a new non-salient term. Even if consumers always catch up eventually, this cat-and-mouse game imposes welfare costs on consumers.

E. Policy Implications

While market solutions are imperfect and welfare costs remain, the potential for self-correction in the cellular service market merits a regulatory stance that facilitates rather than impedes market forces; disclosure regulation. The proposal we'll explore deviates from existing disclosure regulation and from most other proposals for heightened disclosure regulation. Current disclosure regulation and other proposals focus on the disclosure of product-attribute information; namely, information on the different features and price dimensions of cellular service. The proposal we'll explore, by contrast, emphasizes the disclosure of use-pattern information, which as you'll recall from earlier chapters is information on how the consumer will use the product. To fully appreciate the benefits and costs of a cellular service contract, consumers must combine product-attribute information with use-pattern information. For example, to assess the costs of overage fees, it is not enough to know the per-minute charges for minutes not included in the plan, as proposed in the Cell Phone User Bill of Rights. Consumers must also know the probability that they will exceed the plan limit and by how much. Use-pattern information can be as important as product-attribute information. The disclosure regime should be redesigned to ensure that consumers have access to both.

There are two possible approaches to disclosure regulation, approaches that are not mutually exclusive. The first approach focuses on designing simple disclosures that can be easily understood and utilized by imperfectly rational consumers. In particular, carriers should provide total-cost-of-ownership (TCO) information, which is the total amount paid by the consumer, given the consumer's specific use patterns. This information should be provided as an annual disclosure, such as on the year-end summary, to account for month-to-month variations in use. The TCO disclosure combines product-attribute information (pricing information) with information on the specific consumer's use patterns. This disclosure could be further supplemented by information on alternative service plans that would reduce the total price paid by consumers given their current use patterns.

The second approach to disclosure regulation re-conceptualizes disclosure, targeting the disclosed information not directly at consumers but rather at sophisticated intermediaries. Under this approach, carriers would provide comprehensive, individualized use information in electronic, database form. Imperfectly rational consumers will not try to analyze this information on their own. Instead, they will forward the information to sophisticated intermediaries. By combining the use information with the attribute information they collect on product offerings across the cell phone market, the intermediaries would be able to help each consumer find the plan that best suits his or her specific use patterns.

The remainder of this chapter is organized as follows:

- Part I provides background information on the cell phone and the cellular service market.
- Part II describes the key features of common cellular service contracts.
- Part III develops the behavioral-economics theory that explains these contractual design features, after concluding that rational-choice explanations fall short.
- Part IV discusses welfare implications.
- Part V considers the efficacy of market solutions.
- Part VI turns to policy, offering guidelines for enhanced disclosure regulation.

I. The Cell Phone and the Cellular Service Market

A. The Rise of the Cell Phone

1. Technology

The key technological innovation that underpins cellular communications is the cellular concept itself. A cellular system divides each geographic market into numerous small cells, each of which is served by a single, low-powered transmitter. This allows the system to reuse the same channel or frequency in non-adjacent cells in order to avoid interference. Thus, multiple users can simultaneously make use of the same frequency. Sophisticated technology locates subscribers and sends incoming calls to the appropriate cell sites, while complex handoff technologies allow mobile consumers to move seamlessly between cells.[3]

High demand for cellular service has prompted the development of digital technology, which generates enhanced capacity without degrading service quality. Two kinds of capacity-increasing technological solutions have emerged. The first employs time-slicing technology; signals associated with several different calls are aggregated within the same frequency by assigning to each user a cyclically repeating time slot in which only that user is allowed to transmit or receive. Time-slicing techniques include Bell Labs' time division multiple access (TDMA) and Global System for Mobile (GSM), which are used by AT&T and T-Mobile, and Integrated Digital Enhanced Network (iDEN), which is used by Nextel. Spread spectrum techniques, by contrast, spread many calls over many different frequencies while using highly sophisticated devices to identify which signals belong to which calls and decode them for end users. The family of digital

---

3. The information presented here, and below, on cellular technology and on the history of the cellphone market is based, in large part, on: FCC, FCC 06–142, "Annual Report and Analysis of Competitive Market Conditions with Respect to Commercial Mobile Services, Eleventh Report" (2006) 21 F.C.C.R. 10947, 62 (hereinafter "FCC Eleventh Report"); Jonathan E. Nuechterlein and Philip J. Weiser, *Digital Crossroads* (MIT Press, 2005); Mischa Schwartz, *Mobile Wireless Communications* (Cambridge University Press, 2005); William Stallings, *Wireless Communications and Networking* (Prentice Hall, 2002); SRI International, "The Role of NSF's Support of Engineering in Enabling Technological Innovation, Final Report Phase II 94–97" (1998), <http://www.sri.com/policy/csted/reports/sandt/techin2/contents.html> (hereinafter "SRI-NSF Report"); Theodore Rappaport, *Wireless Communications* (Prentice Hall, 1996).

standards employing spread spectrum technology is known as Code Division Multiple Access (CDMA). CDMA standards are used by Verizon and Sprint. The introduction of these digital cellular technologies, starting in the early 1990s, marked the advance from first-generation (1G) systems to second-generation (2G) systems. Third-generation (3G) systems, which began to operate in the U.S. in 2002, incorporate more advanced technologies that provide the increased speed and capacity necessary for multimedia, data, and video transmission, in addition to voice communications. And now fourth-generation (4G) systems are being deployed.

2. History

Although the key concepts essential to modern cellular systems were conceived in 1947, the Federal Communications Commission's (FCC) refusal to allocate substantial frequencies to mobile radio service meant that significant development of cellular telephone services was delayed for several decades. It was not until the early 1980s that the FCC allocated 50 MHz of spectrum in the 800 MHz band to cellular telephone service. The FCC rules created a duopoly of two competing cellular systems in each of 734 "cellular market areas"—one owned by a non-wireline company and one owned by the local wireline monopolist in the area. Each carrier received 25 MHz of spectrum. The first set of cellular licenses, which pertained to the thirty largest urban markets (the Metropolitan Service Areas or MSAs) were allocated by comparative hearings. However, the FCC was so overwhelmed by the number of applicants that in 1984 Congress authorized the use of a lottery system to allocate spectrum in the remaining markets. By 1986, all the MSA licenses had been allocated, and by 1991 licenses had been allocated in all markets. As demand for cellular service rapidly increased over subsequent years, the FCC allocated more spectrum to wireless communications. New spectrum has been allocated by auction rather than lottery ever since Congress gave the FCC authority to issue licenses through auctions in the 1993 Budget Act, a move designed to raise revenues and cut down on delays associated with the lottery system.[4]

The more recent history of the cellular service market in the U.S. is one of consolidation. As noted above, the industry began with the local structural duopolies that were created by the FCC's lottery mechanism.

---

4. See Omnibus Budget Reconciliation Act of 1993, Pub. L. No. 103-66, Title VI, § 6002(a), 6002(b)(2), 197 Stat. 312, 387–93 (1993) (codified as 47 U.S.C. § 309(j) (2006)).

With different firms operating in different geographical markets, the national market initially included a large number of players. The number of firms increased further as the FCC auctioned off more and more radio spectrum for cell phone use. But this high level of market dispersion did not last long. The FCC placed few restrictions on the ability of firms to merge across markets, and a long history of voluntary merger and acquisition activity followed. Soon a handful of firms—AT&T Wireless, Cingular, Nextel, Sprint, T-Mobile, and Verizon Wireless—gained a dominant position as nationwide carriers. Consolidation activity increased in 1999, as national carriers sought to fill in gaps in their coverage areas and increase the capacity of their networks while regional carriers sought to enhance their ability to compete with the nationwide operators. Consolidation was further facilitated by the FCC's 2003 decision to abolish the regulatory spectrum cap that had limited the amount of spectrum that a company could own in any one geographical market, since this opened the door to mergers by companies with overlapping coverage areas. Most significantly, in October 2004, Cingular and AT&T Wireless merged to become AT&T Wireless, while in December 2004 Sprint and Nextel merged to become Sprint Nextel.[5]

3. Economic Significance

The FCC estimates that at the end of 2009, there were 291 million cellular service subscribers in the U.S., which corresponds to a nationwide penetration rate of 93 percent. The market has been growing rapidly, albeit with signs that the market is approaching saturation. Cellular service providers added 11.1 million new subscribers in 2009, 16.6 million in 2008, 21.2 million in 2007, 28.8 million in 2006, 28.3 million in 2005, 24.1 million in 2004, and 18.8 million in 2003. An historical perspective underscores the stellar growth of the market; 286 million subscribers were added between June 1990 and the end of 2009. While cell phones complement landline phones for most users, a significant and increasing number of users view the cell phone as a partial or even complete replacement for the traditional, landline phone. In the first half of 2010, an estimated 26.6 percent

5. FCC, FCC 05–173, "Annual Report and Analysis of Competitive Market Conditions with Respect to Commercial Mobile Services, Tenth Report" (2005) 20 F.C.C.R. 15908, 15930 ¶ 58 (2005); Jeremy T. Fox, "Consolidation in the Wireless Phone Industry" (2005) 3, 7, 9 (*Net Inst. Working Paper No. 05-13*), available at <http://www.netinst.org/Fox2005.pdf>.

of households used only wireless phones, up from 4.2 percent at the end of 2003.[6]

The high revenues enjoyed by carriers provide an indication of the magnitude of the cellular service market. In the second quarter of 2011, Verizon posted wireless revenues of $17.3 billion, AT&T $15.6 billion, Sprint $7.5 billion, and T-Mobile $5.1 billion.[7] Total quarterly wireless revenues for the four national carriers were $45.5 billion, which potentially translates into total annual wireless revenues of $182 billion, ignoring seasonal variations. Wireless telecommunications have become the largest source of profit for nearly all major telecommunication providers. For example, Verizon's wireless services are about twice as profitable as its wireline offerings.[8] Looking at revenues from spectrum auctions is also instructive. In 2006, the FCC's Auction No. 66 raised a total of $13.7 billion in net bids from wireless providers for 1,087 spectrum licenses in the 1710–1755 MHz and 2110–2155 MHz bands.[9] In 2008, the FCC's Auction No. 73 raised a total of $19.0 billion in net bids from wireless providers for 1,099 licenses in the 698–806 MHz band (known as the "700 MHz Band").[10]

Investment in telecommunications infrastructure in general—and one could argue cellular technology in particular—promotes economic growth

---

6. FCC, FCC 11–103, "Annual Report and Analysis of Competitive Market Conditions with Respect to Commercial Mobile Services, Fifteenth Report" (2001) 8, 9, 207, available at <http://wireless.fcc.gov/index.htm?job=cmrs_reports> (hereinafter "FCC Fifteenth Report"; FCC, DA 09-54, "Annual Report and Analysis of Competitive Market Conditions with Respect to Commercial Mobile Services, Thirteenth Report" (2009) 24 F.C.C.R. 6185, at 6279–80 ¶ 197, 6301 ¶ 230 (hereinafter "FCC Thirteenth Report"); SRI-NSF Report, above note 3, at 94.

7. Verizon, "Verizon Wireless—Selected Financial Results" (July 22, 2011), <http://www22 .verizon.com/idc/groups/public/documents/adacct/2011_2q_fs_pdf.pdf>; AT&T, "Investor Briefing 2nd Quarter 2011," at 4 (July 21, 2011), <http://www.att.com/Investor/Financial/ Earning_Info/docs/2Q_11_IB_FINAL.pdf>; News Release, "Sprint, Sprint Nextel Reports Second Quarter 2011 Results" (July 28, 2011), <http://newsroom.sprint.com/article_display .cfm?article_id=1990>; Financial Release, "T-Mobile USA," T-Mobile USA Reports Second Quarter 2011 Results" Bibliog cites July 28, 2011, <http://www.t-mobile.com/company/ InvestorRelations.aspx?tp=Abt_Tab_InvestorRelationsandViewArchive=Yes> (follow "T-Mobile USA Reports Second Quarter 2011 Results" hyperlink).

8. George Gilder, "The Wireless Wars," *Wall Street Journal*, April 13, 2007, at A13 (stating that Verizon's mobile phones generated $804 million in profits, whereas its wired phones generated $393 million in profits).

9. "Auction of Advanced Wireless Services Licenses Closes: Winning Bidders Announced for Auction No. 66" (2006) 21 F.C.C.R. 10521.

10. "Auction of 700 MHz Band Licenses Closes: Winning Bidders Announced for Auction 73" (2008) 23 F.C.C.R. 4572.

by reducing the costs of interaction, expanding market boundaries, and enhancing information flow. Specifically, cellular technology can create value by facilitating communication between individuals who are on the move, thus helping individuals to better coordinate their activities and respond to unforeseen contingencies. Wireless services also boost growth by expanding telephone networks to include previously disenfranchised consumers through prepaid service that is unavailable for fixed lines. Analysts estimate that the decades-long delay in the development of cellular networks after the discovery of the cellular concept cost the U.S. economy around $86 billion (measured in 1990 dollars).[11]

B. The Cellular Service Market

1. Structure

The U.S. cellular service industry is dominated by four "nationwide" facilities-based carriers: AT&T Wireless, Verizon Wireless, Sprint Nextel, and T-Mobile. At the end of 2010, each had networks covering at least 250 million people. AT&T had 95.5 million subscribers, Verizon 94.1 million, Sprint Nextel 49.9 million, and T-Mobile 33.7 million.[12]

In addition to the national carriers, there are a number of regional carriers, including Leap, U.S. Cellular, and MetroPCS. There is also a growing resale sector, consisting of providers who purchase airtime from facilities-based carriers and resell service to the public, typically in the form of prepaid plans rather than standard monthly tariffs.

11. See Robert Jensen, "The Digital Provide: Information (Technology), Market Performance, and Welfare in the South Indian Fisheries Sector", *Q.J. Econ.*, 122 (2007), 879, 881–3 (describing how the introduction of cell phones revolutionized the fishing industry in Kerala, leading to dramatic reductions in price dispersion, the complete elimination of waste (previously 5–8 percent of the daily catch), an 8 percent average increase in fishermen's profits, a 4 percent decline in consumer prices, and a 6 percent increase in consumer surplus); Leonard Waverman, Meloria Meschi, and Melvyn Fuss, "The Impact of Telecoms on Economic Growth in Developing Countries," in *The Vodafone Policy Paper Series no. 3, Africa: The Impact of Mobile Phones* (2005), <http://www.vodafone.com/etc/medialib/attachments/cr_downloads.Par.78351.File.tmp/GPP_SIM_paper_3.pdf> ("We find that mobile telephony has a positive and significant impact on economic growth, and this impact may be twice as large in developing countries as compared to developed countries."); Nuechterlein and Weiser, above note 3, at 268.

12. Information presented here, and below, on the cellular service market is based, in large part, on FCC Fifteenth Report, above note 6.

2. Competition

The overlapping geographic coverage of the national and regional providers gives rise to competition between cellular service providers. The FCC estimates that 97.2 percent of people have three or more different operators offering cell phone services in the census blocks where they live, 94.3 percent live in census blocks with four or more operators, 89.6 percent live in census blocks with five or more operators, 76.4 percent live in census blocks with six or more operators, and 27.1 percent live in census blocks with seven or more operators. The FCC measures market concentration by computing the average Herfindahl-Hirschman Index (HHI) across 172 Economic Areas (EAs)—aggregations of counties that have been designed to capture the "area in which the average person shops for and purchases a mobile phone, most of the time." The HHI is a measure of market concentration that ranges from a value of 10,000 in a monopolistic market to zero in a perfectly competitive market.[13] In mid-2010, the average HHI, weighted by EA population, was equal to 2,848. An industry with an HHI above 2,500 is considered highly concentrated by the antitrust authorities. And these figures might well underestimate market concentration, since the FCC's methodology gives equal weight to a mobile carrier assigning cell phone numbers in one county as it does to a carrier that assigns numbers in multiple counties in a given EA.[14] Indeed, one analyst calculated an average HHI value exceeding 6,000 with 2005 data, using the amount of spectrum controlled by a carrier in a market as a proxy for market share.[15]

The relatively high level of concentration in the cell phone market is the product of an ongoing consolidation process. This consolidation is at least partly motivated by a desire to realize economies of scale and enlarge geographic scope. Broad coverage can be provided at lower cost by a single nationwide carrier than by regional carriers through roaming agreements with carriers operating in different geographic areas. In addition, extending

---

13. Formally, the HHI is given by $HHI = \sum_{i=1}^{I}(100 s_i)^2$, where s_i is the fractional market share of firm i, and I is the number of firms in the market. Thus a monopolistic market has an HHI of 10,000, a market that is equally divided between two firms has an HHI of 5,000, a market that is equally divided between three firms has an HHI of 3,333.33, a market that is equally divided between four firms has an HHI of 2,500, etc.

14. FCC Thirteenth Report, above note 6, at 6212 ¶ 45 n. 87.

15. Fox, above note 5, at 15–17. Moreover, this figure excludes data on Nextel, and so the Sprint Nextel merger does not contribute to the high HHI, suggesting that this figure may underestimate the true concentration. *Id.* at 16 n. 11.

the national network spreads fixed costs, such as marketing expenditures and investments in developing new technology, over a wider base of customers. Economies of geographic scope arising from complementarities between markets may also provide an efficiency reason for consolidation.[16] However, even if consolidation reduces certain costs, other costs may increase. Consolidation tends to reduce competition and facilitate collusion as the number of multi-market contacts between the dominant national carriers increases.[17]

The magnitude of entry barriers provides another important measure of competitiveness. If entry barriers are low, even a market with a small number of firms will behave competitively. Government control of spectrum—limiting the amount of spectrum allocated to wireless communications and requiring carriers to obtain a government-issued license—has the potential to create significant barriers to entry. However, the FCC has alleviated many of these concerns recently by increasing the amount of spectrum available for cellular communication services and allowing market forces to determine market structure through elimination of the old structural duopolies and abolition of the spectrum cap. Moreover, the Telecommunications Act and FCC regulations reduce entry barriers by imposing interconnection and roaming obligations. The ability to purchase spectrum on the secondary market further reduces entry barriers.[18] Meanwhile, advertising expenditures—amounting to billions of dollars annually[19]—and the economies of scale and scope described above continue to impose substantial entry barriers.

16. See Patrick Bajari, Jeremy T. Fox, and Stephen Ryan, "Evaluating Wireless Carrier Consolidation Using Semiparametric Demand Estimation" (2006) 5 (*Nat'l Bureau of Econ. Research, Working Paper No. 12425*), available at <http://www.nber.org/papers/w12425>; Fox, above note 5, at 10.

17. Fox, above note 5, at 12. Multi-market contact was an important factor in explaining above-competitive prices in the early mobile telecommunications industry. See Philip M. Parker and Lars-Hendrik Röller, "Collusive Conduct in Duopolies: Multi-Market Contact and Cross-Ownership in the Mobile Telephone Industry", *Rand J. Econ.*, 29 (1997), 304, 320. There were also significant cross-ownership effects, i.e., if operators co-own an operating license elsewhere, they tend to collude more. *Id.*

18. On the FCC actions—making more spectrum available, eliminating the structural duopolies and abolishing the spectrum cap—see FCC Thirteenth Report, above note 6, at 6220 ¶¶ 65–6. On interconnection and roaming obligations—see 47 U.S.C. § 251(a)(1) (2006); "Reexamination of Roaming Obligations of Commercial Mobile Radio Service Providers, Final Rule" (2007) 72 Fed. Reg. 50064, 50064–65 (hereinafter "Reexamination of Roaming Obligations"). On the role of the secondary market—see FCC Thirteenth Report, above note 6, at 6220 ¶ 67.

19. Estimated advertising spending for wireless telephone services totaled between $4.1 billion and approximately $5.1 billion in 2007, $3.7 billion in 2008, and $3.4 billion in 2009. See FCC Thirteenth Report, above note 6, at 6261 ¶ 158 (for the 2007 estimates); FCC Fifteenth Report, above note 6, at 50 (for the 2008 and 2009 estimates).

Switching costs also affect the level of competition. Switching costs in
the cellular service market are substantial, although recent developments are
reducing these costs. Until recently, most consumers signed long-term contracts with fixed ETFs of approximately $200. But now major carriers are
offering contracts with graduated ETFs that decline over the life of the
contract. Likewise, historically carriers have allowed only certain approved
phones to be used by their subscribers on their network and "locked" the
phones they sold to render them incapable of being used on other networks.[20] The recent trend, however, is toward open access, which allows
more phones onto the network, and recent regulatory action by the Copy-
right Office clarified that phones can be unlocked.[21] Being forced to change
phone numbers was also a potentially significant switching cost until it was
eliminated by the regulatory requirement that carriers provide local number
portability.[22] The high churn rates in the cell phone market—between 1.5
percent and 3.3 percent per month in 2009[23]—suggest that switching costs,
while potentially substantial, are not prohibitive for many consumers.

To sum up, while there is reason to believe that the cellular service market is less than perfectly competitive, cellular service providers are actively
competing to attract consumers. Declining prices, albeit with a leveling off
in recent years, are evidence of such active competition.[24] Competition is

20. Tim Wu, "Wireless Net Neutrality: Cellular Carterfone and Consumer Choice in Mobile Broadband" (2007) 1 *New Am. Found. Wireless Future Program Working Paper No. 17*, available at <http://
www.newamerica.net/files/WorkingPaper17_WirelessNetNeutrality_Wu.pdf>; see also Spencer
E. Ante, "Verizon Embraces Google's Android", *Business Week*, December 3, 2007, <http://www.
businessweek.com/technology/content/dec2007/tc2007123_429930.htm?campaign_id=yhoo>
("Verizon Wireless has created the most profitable U.S. cellular business by tightly restricting the
devices and applications allowed to run on its network.").
21. See 37 C.F.R. § 201.40(b)(5) (2008). Carriers are embracing the new open-access business
model. See Ante, above note 20. ("But over the past year, [Verizon's] leadership came to conclude that it was time for a radical shift. Such a move, they reckoned, might help Verizon
Wireless keep growing while holding down costs.") Sprint Nextel and T-Mobile also support
the shift to an open-handset environment, as members of the Google-led "Open Handset
Alliance." *Id.*; see also Amol Sharma and Dionne Searcey, "Verizon to Open Cell Network to
Others' Phones," *Wall Street Journal*, November 28, 2007, at B1.
22. FCC Eleventh Report, above note 13, at 11012 ¶ 146. Wireless local number portability began
on November 24, 2003. *In re Telephone Number Portability*, 19 F.C.C.R. 875, 876 (2) (order). The
FCC reports that from December 2003 to December 2007, 49.93 million consumers took
advantage of the right to retain their phone number while switching from one wireless carrier
to another. FCC Thirteenth Report, above note 6, at 6272 ¶ 183.
23. FCC Fifteenth Report, above note 6, at 154–5. A "churn rate" is the rate at which users cancel
their cellular service in a given period of time.
24. FCC Fifteenth Report, above note 6, at 12–13. On the other hand, there is substantial similar-
ity between the pricing schemes offered by the major carriers. See below Part II. This price
matching may reflect tacit collusion among the major carriers. Cf. Meghan R. Busse, "Multi-
market Contact and Price Coordination in the Cellular Telephone Industry" (2008–9) 9
J. Econ. and Mgmt. Strategy, 9 (2008–9) 287, 313–16.

also observed on non-price dimensions. Competition to attract and retain customers appears to be driving carriers to improve service quality. Carriers pursue a variety of strategies to improve service quality, including network investment to improve coverage and quality and acquisition of additional spectrum.[25] While an economic conclusion reached by politically appointed regulators should be taken with a grain of salt, it is noteworthy that the FCC described the cellular service market as one characterized by healthy competition with carriers engaging in "independent pricing behavior, in the form of continued experimentation with varying pricing levels and structures, for varying service packages, with various handsets and policies on handset pricing."[26]

3. Related Markets

The cellular service market interacts with other markets, specifically with the market for phones/handsets and with the market for cell phone applications.

a. The Handset Market

The market for handsets is controlled by five firms: Samsung, LG Electronics, Motorola, Apple, and RIM. In the U.S., Samsung enjoys the largest market share, controlling 25.5 percent of the handset market in the second quarter of 2011. LG placed second with 20.9 percent of the market, and Motorola followed with 14.1 percent. Apple and RIM, the maker of Black-Berry, lag behind considerably with 9.5 percent and 7.6 percent of the market, respectively.[27]

In the U.S., the major cellular service providers exert significant control over the handset market. Internationally, about half of handsets are

---

25. FCC Thirteenth Report, above note 6, at 6262–3. Carriers' marketing campaigns emphasize their "superior network coverage, reliability, and voice quality." *Id.*
26. FCC Eleventh Report, above note 3, at 10987 ¶ 90. Yet, since this is an industry characterized by high network costs, this phase of apparently intense competition may be nothing more than a price war designed to squeeze out smaller carriers that will ultimately result in an increase in the market power of the remaining large carriers and an attendant rise in prices.
27. Press Release, comScore, "comScore Reports July 2011 U.S. Mobile Subscriber Market Share" (August 30, 2011), <http://www.comscore.com/Press_Events/Press_Releases/2011/8/comScore_Reports_July_2011_U.S._Mobile_Subscriber_Market_Share>. The market shares of the leading handset firms are quite different outside the United States. Nokia is the global market leader, with 33.3 percent of the global market in 2010, followed by Samsung with 20.6 percent, LG with 8.6 percent, RIM with 3.6 percent, and Apple with 3.5 percent. Press Release, "Strategy Analytics, Global Handset Shipments Reach 400 Million Units in Q4 2010" (January 28, 2011), <http://www.strategyanalytics.com/default.aspx?mod=pressrelease viewerandao=5001>.

purchased through carriers and about half are sold directly to consumers through other channels. In the U.S., the vast majority of cell phones—nine out of every ten phones according to one estimate—are sold through a service provider.[28] The practice of subsidizing handset prices for consumers who sign long-term service contracts is at least partially responsible for the competitive disadvantage suffered by handset makers looking to sell directly to consumers.

Carriers in the U.S. determine which devices consumers can operate on their networks. The result of this control by service providers is that only a fraction of any given manufacturer's total line of products is offered. For example, in 2006, of the fifty new products Nokia introduced into the market, U.S. cellular service providers offered a scant few. By allowing only certain approved phones on their networks, carriers influence the design of handsets. Moreover, as a condition of network access, carriers require that developers disable certain services or features that might be useful to consumers, such as call-timers, photo sharing, Bluetooth capabilities, and Wi-Fi capabilities.[29]

But the balance of power is shifting. Handset brands and models are an increasingly important determinant of a consumer's choice of service provider. Apple's launch of the iPhone is a significant example of a handset manufacturer successfully overcoming carrier pressure. More generally, the rapid expansion of the "smartphone" market is enhancing the power of handset makers and companies who provide software for these handsets. An example is the Android operating system, developed by Google.[30]

In addition, the open-access trend is starting to limit carriers' control over the handset market.[31] Regulation is also playing an important role:

28. Marguerite Reardon, "Unlocking the Unlocked Cell Phone Market," *CNET News*, July 2, 2009, <http://news.cnet.com/8301-1035_3-10277723-94.html>.

29. See Wu, above note 20, at 10–13; Reardon, above note 28; Ante, above note 20 ("Verizon Wireless has created the most profitable U.S. cellular business by tightly restricting the devices and applications allowed to run on its network.").

30. On the increasing power of handset manufacturers—see Rita Chang, "Proof That Handset Brands Help Sell Wireless Plans," *RCR Wireless*, October 28, 2008, <http://www.rcrwireless .com/article/20081028/WIRELESS/810289995/1081/proof-that-handset-brands-help-sell -wireless-plans#>; Press Release, Nielsen, "In US, Smartphones Now Majority of New Cell-phone Purchases" (June 30, 2011), <http://blog.nielsen.com/nielsenwire/?p=28237>. On power struggles between carriers and handset manufacturers, as well as with application developers—see generally Jessica E. Vascellaro, "Air War: A Fight over What You Can Do on a Cellphone," *Wall Street Journal*, June 14, 2007, at A1; see also Miguel Helft and Stephen Labaton, "Google Pushes for Rules to Aid Wireless Plans," *New York Times*, July 21, 2007, at A1.

31. See George S. Ford, Thomas M. Koutsky, and Lawrence J. Spiwak, "Wireless Net Neutrality: From Carterfone to Cable Boxes", *Phoenix Ctr. Pol'y Bull.* 17, (April 2, 2007), at 2, <http:// phoenix-center.org/PolicyBulletin/PCPB21Final.pdf>.

One-third of the recently auctioned spectrum comes with a requirement that "cellular networks allow customers to use any phone they want on whatever network they prefer, and be able to run on it any software they want."[32] And, perhaps sensing the inevitable, carriers are beginning to embrace the new open-access business model, reasoning that they can cut costs by eliminating handset subsidies and letting handset manufacturers bear most of the development and customer service costs.[33]

b. The Applications Market

The major cellular service providers and other mobile data providers have progressively introduced a wide variety of mobile data services and applications, including text and multimedia messaging, ringtones, GPS navigation, and entertainment applications from games to TV and music players.[34] Data revenues have been growing—in absolute numbers and as a share of total revenues. In 2009, $42 billion or 27 percent of total wireless service revenues were from data revenues.[35]

The major carriers exert substantial control over the applications market. Many applications—popularly known as "apps"—are often sold by the carriers as part of the service package. Although some application developers sell their applications directly to consumers, carriers exert considerable influence over the design, content, and pricing of cell phone applications. For example, carriers impose limits on "unlimited use" pricing plans for 3G broadband data services by restricting bandwidth and designating certain applications as "forbidden" in consumer contracts. Carriers also create obstacles for application developers by restricting access to many phone capabilities, imposing extensive qualification and approval requirements before allowing them to develop applications for their cell phone platforms, and by failing to develop uniform standards.[36]

As sophisticated new applications for cell phones have proliferated, however, handset manufacturers have started to put pressure on carriers to loosen their grip on the applications market. For example, the immense popularity

---

32. Editorial, "A Half-Win for Cellphone Users," *New York Times*, August 6, 2007, at A18; *In re Service Rules for the 698–746, 747–762, and 777–792 MHz Bands*, 22 F.C.C.R. 15289, 15367, 15370–71 (2007) (second report and order) (hereinafter "Service Rules Second Report and Order").

33. See Ante, above note 20; see also Sharma and Searcy, above note 21.

34. FCC Eleventh Report, above note 3, at 11007 ¶ 136–37.

35. FCC Fifteenth Report, above note 6, at 13–14.

36. Wu, above note 20, at 13–14, 22–5.

of the iPod music player allowed Apple to persuade AT&T to sell the iPhone to its customers without also offering AT&T's own line of applications.[37]

II. The Cellular Service Contract

Cellular service contracts are complex multidimensional contracts. This chapter does not attempt a comprehensive analysis of these contracts.[38] Rather, the focus will be on the three design features mentioned earlier: (1) the three-part tariff structure, (2) the lock-in clause, and (3) the high level of complexity itself.[39]

A. Three-Part Tariffs

As noted earlier, cellular service contracts are complex and multidimensional. To begin with, most postpaid plans, which constitute the majority of plans, price their basic voice-calling service using a three-part tariff structure. This structure is a three-dimensional pricing scheme that includes a monthly charge, a number of included voice minutes, and a per-minute price for minutes beyond the plan limit ("overage"). Higher-priced plans with a higher monthly charge come with more allotted minutes and lower overages for minutes exceeding the plan limit. For example, as of this writing, AT&T, Sprint, and Verizon offer a $39.99 plan with 450 minutes and

---

37. Vascellaro, above note 30.
38. One feature that we will not address is the definition of call types for which the subscriber is charged (or that count toward the plan limit). Specifically, while in most countries subscribers are charged only for outgoing calls, in the U.S. subscribers are also charged for incoming calls. This feature of the U.S. cellular service market seems to fit nicely within the general behavioral theory, as subscribers probably find it even more difficult to accurately estimate the number/length of incoming calls along with outgoing calls than outgoing calls alone.
39. The description of products and prices provided in Part II, and in other Parts, is largely based on information available through carriers' websites focusing on services available in the New York area. See AT&T, "Cell Phones, Cell Phone Plans, and Wireless Accessories—from AT&T", <http://www.att.com/shop/wireless/#fbid=n6la6zd-YLG> (last visited September 29, 2011); Sprint, "Cell Phones, Mobile Phones, and Wireless Calling Plans from Sprint," <http://www.sprint.com> (last visited September 29, 2011); T-Mobile, "Cell Phones | 4G Cell Phone Plans | Android Tablet PCs | T-Mobile," <http://www.t-mobile.com/> (last visited September 29, 2011); Verizon Wireless, "Cell Phones—Smartphones: Cell Phone Service, Accessories—Verizon Wireless," <http://www.verizonwireless.com/b2c/index.html> (last visited September 29, 2011). It should be noted that some variation exists between online and offline (retail store) offerings and between different geographical markets across the U.S. This variation is mentioned explicitly only when it is relevant to the analysis.

$0.45 per-minute overage, a $59.99 plan with 900 minutes and $0.40 per-minute overage, and a $79.99 plan with 1350 minutes and $0.35 per-minute overage.

The three-part tariff was introduced in the U.S. in 1998. Before then, all wireless plans involved roaming and long-distance charges.[40] In 1998, AT&T began offering a plan that allowed customers to pay a fixed monthly fee for a set number of minutes that could be used for both local and long-distance calls. As a result, AT&T gained 850,000 customers in its first year, perhaps more customers than it could serve.[41] AT&T's competitors soon followed with similar pricing plans. Much of the rising usage of cellular service was attributed to this pricing structure.[42]

Industry accounts of the reason for the switch to bundle pricing vary. Some argue that bundle pricing responds to consumer demand for simplicity.[43] Others, including AT&T's CEO at the time, Mike Armstrong, suggest that the move to bundle pricing was motivated by a desire to attract heavy users. Armstrong's account is consistent with two key facts: (1) the smallest fixed fee offered was $90 per month, and (2) after the introduction of its One Rate plan, the average AT&T subscriber bill increased, raising the company's profitability.[44]

B. Lock-In Clauses

In addition to the three-part tariff pricing structure, most postpaid calling plans share the following two features; a free or substantially discounted phone and long-term contracts with ETFs. At the time of this writing, AT&T gave customers the option to buy the LG Phoenix for $379.99 without a contract. With the signing of a two-year data contract, however, AT&T charged $0.01 for the same phone. T-Mobile customers

---

40. See Elizabeth Douglass, "The Cutting Edge Special Report: Wireless Communications; 'Prepaid' Idea is Catching On in U.S. Market," *L.A. Times*, March 15, 1999, at C1 (discussing trend away from long-distance and roaming charges).
41. Roger O. Crockett, "The Last Monopolist," *Business Week*, April 12, 1999, at 55; Dan Meyer, "Coverage Problems Trigger Headaches for Carriers," *RCR Wireless News*, July 9, 2001, at 16.
42. Andrew M. Odlyzko, "The Many Paradoxes of Broadband" *First Monday*, September 1, 2003, <http://firstmonday.org/htbin/cgiwrap/bin/ojs/index.php/fm/article/view/1072/992>.
43. See Rebecca Blumenstein, "The Business-Package Plan: AT&T Sees Wireless as the Key to its Broader Strategy of Bundling Its Services," *Wall Street Journal*, September 20, 1999 at R26; see also Peter Elstrom, "Wireless with All the Trimmings," *Business Week*, November 16, 1998.
44. Peter Elstrom, "Mike Armstrong's Strong Showing," *Business Week*, January 25, 1999, at 94; Elstrom, "Wireless with All the Trimmings," above note 43.

who signed a new contract had the opportunity to receive, for free, a number of phones with suggested retail values of over $200, including the LG Optimus, the HTC Wildfire, and the Samsung Gravity. Similarly, AT&T and Apple heavily subsidized the iPhone, sacrificing short-term revenues, and Sprint sold Samsung's music phones far below cost at only $149.[45] The free or heavily subsidized phone strategy pervades the U.S. cell phone market. A 2011 survey by J.D. Power found that 42 percent of customers receive a free cell phone when subscribing to a wireless service.[46]

Of course, free phones are not really free. Carriers recoup the costs of the phones through subscription fees. To make sure that they collect enough subscription fees to cover the cost of the phone, carriers lock consumers into long-term contracts.[47] Such lock-in is secured by substantial ETFs. For example, in June 2007, T-Mobile charged a fixed termination fee of $200, AT&T charged $175, and Sprint charged up to $200, depending on the service selected. Historically, the same termination fees were charged regardless of when the agreement was broken, meaning that a consumer would have paid a $200 termination fee for ending a two-year contract just one month early. In the wake of a number of class action lawsuits challenging the legality of these fees, providers have begun to offer contracts with termination fees that decline over the life of the contract. Verizon led this transition when, in June 2007, it started charging customers a termination fee of $175, less $5 for each full month that the customer remains on the initial contract. By the end of 2008, all the major carriers were offering similar graduated ETFs.[48]

45. See Amol Sharma and Roger Cheng, "iPhone Costs Prove a Drag for AT&T," *Wall Street Journal*, October 23, 2008, at B4 ("The company said $900 million in customer-acquisition costs related to the iPhone shaved 10 cents off its earnings," but "AT&T executives said the investment will pay off because iPhone users are lucrative in the long-term, spending about $95 a month on average, or about 1.6 times the amount other customers do."); Cliff Edwards and Roger O. Crockett, "New Music Phones—Without the i," *Business Week*, April 16, 2007, at 39.

46. Press Release, J.D. Power and Associates, "The Right Blend of Design and Technology is Critical to Creating an Exceptional User Experience with Smartphones and Traditional Mobile Devices" 2 (September 8, 2011), <http://businesscenter.jdpower.com/JDPAContent/CorpComm/News/content/Releases/pdf/2011146-whs2.pdf>.

47. When no-contract plans are offered, phone subsidies disappear. For example, a customer with no contract would be required to pay an additional $400 beyond the contract price for the same iPhone. "AT&T Plans to Offer No-Contract iPhone," Wall St. J., July 2, 2008, at B5.

48. See Verizon Wireless, Customer Agreement, <http://www.verizonwireless.com/b2c/index.html> (follow "Customer Agreement" hyperlink at the bottom of the page); AT&T, Plan Terms, <http://www.wireless.att.com/cell-phone-service/legal/plan-terms.jsp#gsm>; Press Release, Sprint Nextel Corp., "Sprint Launches One of the Industry's Most Customer-Friendly

C. Complexity

The complexity and multidimensionality of cellular service contracts can be viewed as a contractual design feature. Most cellular service contracts are highly complex in and of themselves. This high level of complexity increases substantially when the perspective shifts from a single-contract to the many different multidimensional contracts being offered. According to one industry estimate, the cellular service market boasts "more than 10 million different plans and add-on combinations."[49]

1. Postpaid Plans—The Basics

Even the basic components of the common postpaid calling plan are complex. As described above, the basic pricing scheme is three-dimensional. Each dimension of the basic pricing scheme is one of the tariffs that make up the three-part tariff. Moreover, each provider offers a long menu of different three-part tariffs. To make things even more complicated, the menus of three-part tariffs vary among providers.[50] Further complexity is introduced by the diversity of additional service features covered by the fixed monthly fee. Some of these features are offered by all carriers in the exact same way. Others are offered by some carriers but not others or are offered in varying formats by the different carriers.

For example, all four major carriers offer unlimited calls during off-peak times, usually nights and weekends. There is, however, some potentially significant variation. Nights are defined differently by different carriers. For AT&T and Verizon, the night begins at 9 p.m. and ends at 6 a.m. For T-Mobile, the night begins at 9 p.m. and ends at 7 a.m. For Sprint, the night begins at 7 p.m. and ends at 7 a.m., except for its more basic plans, where the night begins at 9 p.m. and ends at 7 a.m. By varying the definition of "night," providers can offer up to three extra hours of unlimited calling.

Policies on Pro-Rated Early Termination Fees" (October 31, 2008), <http://newsroom.sprint .com/article_display.cfm?article_id=771>; T-Mobile, T-Mobile Terms and Conditions, <http://www.t-mobile.com/templates/popup.aspx?passet=ftr_ftr_termsandconditions>.

49. See BillShrink.com, Cell Phone Plans, Compare Best Cellular Service Carrier Deals on BillShrink, <http://www.billshrink.com/cell-phones/plans.html> (last visited September 29, 2011).

50. We briefly mention two additional dimensions: (1) The directionality of the calls that consume allotted minutes, and (2) the one-time activation charge. Along dimension (1), allotted minutes are typically used up on both outgoing calls and incoming calls. As for (2), AT&T and Sprint charge a $36 activation fee while Verizon and T-Mobile charge $35.

These three extra hours represent an additional 33.3 percent of unlimited calling time. But since most consumers probably talk more during the three hours between 7 and 9 p.m. and between 6 and 7 a.m. than they do during the three hours between, say 1 and 4 a.m., these extra three hours of unlimited calling probably represent much more than a 33.3 percent increase in value.

To take another example, consumers might also consider whether to select Verizon's Friends and Family program, offering unlimited calls to five (or ten) phone numbers selected by the user. Sprint, T-Mobile, and AT&T offered similar programs, but as of this writing their plans were no longer available to new users.

2. Family Plans

We have thus far focused on individual calling plans. The four major carriers also offer family plans, adding another layer of complexity. The identifying feature of a family plan is the ability to share the allotted minutes between up to five users, each operating on a different line. For example, Verizon offers family plans with monthly charges ranging from $69.98 to $119.98, allotted minutes ranging from 700 to unlimited, and overages ranging from $0.45 to $0.35. These monthly prices include two phone lines, and families can add up to three more lines for an additional $9.99 per month per line (or $49.99 under the unlimited plan).

3. Add-Ons

Cell phones can be used for much more than voice communication. Carriers offer advanced communication services, including text messaging, multimedia messaging, and Internet and email data services. Carriers also offer applications, such as ringtones and games, as well as monthly mobile Internet access packages. These services and applications are marketed to consumers primarily as add-ons to their voice services.

Pricing of these services adds additional complexity. Providers offer advanced communication services to consumers in one of three modes:

(1) Pay-as-you-go, applied mainly to text and multimedia messaging, where the consumer pays per message sent or received

(2) Fixed-quantity monthly packages, where the consumer pays a monthly fee for a fixed number of allotted messages or megabytes of data

(3) Unlimited-quantity monthly packages, where the consumer pays a monthly fee for unlimited messaging or data transmission.[51]

Entertainment applications, specifically ringtones and games, can be purchased for a one-time download rate. Advanced applications, such as GPS location services and music and TV applications, are now also available from some providers—usually for an additional monthly or daily fee.

4. Phones and Lock-In Clauses

Free or discounted phones that come with most postpaid plans add another dimension of complexity to the cellular product. Different carriers offer different phones with varying discounts. The carrier's choice between an outright discount and a rebate adds another twist. The flipside of the free or discounted phone is the lock-in clause that ties the consumer to the specific carrier. Lock-in clauses vary in duration and in the magnitude of the ETF. The common lock-in period is two years, but one- and three-year periods are also offered. The termination fees vary between $175 and $200 for standard phones and often reach $350 for "advanced devices," such as smartphones. The recent move to graduated ETFs introduced additional variation as different carriers adopted different formulas to govern the gradual reduction in ETFs over the life of the contract.

5. Prepaid Plans

Not only is it difficult to choose among the many different postpaid plans, the consumer must make a preliminary choice between postpaid and prepaid plans. The prepaid plan is another option offered by the cellular service market that features a substantially different contractual design than postpaid plans.

---

51. For an example of pay-as-you-go pricing—see Verizon Wireless, "Cell Phones—Smartphones: Cell Phone Service, Accessories—Verizon Wireless," above note 39 (as of September 29, 2011, Verizon charged $0.20 per text message and $0.25 per multimedia message). Verizon also offers fixed-quantity monthly packages (as of September 29, 2011, Verizon charged $5.00 per month for 250 text or multimedia messages and $10.00 for 500 messages). For an example of unlimited-quantity monthly packages—see AT&T, "Cell Phones, Cell Phone Plans, and Wireless Accessories—from AT&T," above note 39 (AT&T charged $20.00 per month for unlimited messaging as of September 29, 2011.) Unlimited messaging and even data are covered by the monthly fee component of the basic three-part tariff in some premium plans. *Id.*

Prepaid offerings fall into two categories: the monthly prepaid category, in which customers pay a monthly fee for a fixed number of minutes, and the pay-as-you-go category, in which customers buy credit to pay for minutes on a minute-by-minute basis.

The monthly prepaid category more closely resembles the postpaid calling plans. The three main differences are that, unlike postpaid plans, with prepaid plans:

- The fixed monthly fee is paid in advance.
- There is no commitment. The subscriber can leave the carrier at any time without incurring an ETF.
- The allotted number of minutes cannot be exceeded, not even for a high overage charge.

In addition, per-minute prices (the monthly charge divided by the allotted number of minutes) are generally higher in prepaid plans, perhaps to make up for the loss of revenue from precluding overage minutes and charges. For example, for a $25 monthly charge, AT&T's prepaid GoPhone plan offers 250 minutes ($0.10 per minute), as compared to the 450 minutes for $39.99 offered under AT&T's postpaid plan ($.09 per minute). Prepaid plans also offer fewer additional features. For example, night and weekend minutes are not always unlimited, and roaming charges are levied.[52]

The second category of prepaid plans offers pay-as-you-go service. Consumers purchase calling cards that hold varying numbers of minutes. For example, Verizon's pay-as-you-go service offers prepaid cards with a minimum purchase of $15. These card values translate into calling minutes at a $0.25 per minute rate. Pay-as-you-go calling cards come with expiration dates. At Verizon, cards with values of $15 to $29.99 expire in 30 days, cards with values of $30 to $74.99 expire in 90 days, cards with values of $75 to $99.99 expire in 180 days, and cards with values of at least $100 expire in 365 days. Verizon's pay-as-you-go consumers can also pay a fixed fee of $2 to use the phone for an unlimited number of minutes in a particular day, or use the phone for a day at a rate of $0.10 per minute. Like the monthly prepaid plans, pay-as-you-go services typically offer higher per-minute prices and fewer additional features, as compared to the postpaid plans. Prepaid and pay-as-you-go plans are not available for smartphone users with any of the four national carriers.

52. None of the four major operators charges for roaming in its postpaid pricing plans.

III. Explaining the Cellular Service Contract

What explains the contractual design features described in Part II? Why does the common cellular service contract look the way it does? In this Part, we'll explore possible rational-choice, efficiency-based theories for each of the three design features: three-part tariffs, lock-in clauses, and complexity. But as we'll see, these theories provide only a partial account of the contractual outcomes in the cellular service market. We'll fill the explanatory gap by developing a behavioral-economics theory that explains contractual design in the cellular service market as a market response to consumer mistakes.[53]

A. Three-Part Tariffs

1. Rational-Choice Theories and Their Limits

The leading rational-choice explanation for three-part tariffs views these pricing schemes as a mechanism for price discrimination or market screening of rational consumers with different ex ante demand characteristics. For expositional purposes, let's focus on two dimensions of demand heterogeneity: average (or mean) monthly minutes of use and variance of minutes used.

Suppose that consumers vary only on the first dimension, average monthly minutes used. Here, the rational model cannot explain three-part tariffs. To discriminate between heavy users with high average usage and light users with low average usage, carriers would use a menu of two-part, not three-part, tariffs. A two-part tariff includes a fixed monthly fee and a constant per-minute charge. Carriers can discriminate between heavy users and light users by offering an "H" tariff with a higher monthly fee and a lower per-minute charge and an "L" tariff with a lower monthly fee and a higher per-minute charge. The heavy users care more about the per-minute charge, and will thus prefer the H tariff. The light users care more about the monthly fee, and will thus prefer the L tariff.

While two-part tariffs provide a mechanism for discriminating between consumers based on their mean usage, three-part tariffs can provide a mech-

---

53. The analysis of the three-part tariff, in Section A, relies heavily on Grubb, above note 1. The behavioral explanation described in Section A is also closely related to the one developed in K. Eliaz and R. Spiegler, "Contracting with Diversely Naive Agents", *Rev. Econ. Stud.*, 73 (2006), 689; K. Eliaz and R. Spiegler, "Consumer Optimism and Price Discrimination", *Theor. Econ.*, 3 (2008), 459.

anism for discriminating between consumers based on variance of use. Assume that there are two types of consumers: one type with highly variable—or High-Variation (HV)—demand, and another type with more predictable, Low-Variation (LV) demand.[54] Specifically, suppose that the HV type's demand will either be $H + h$ or $H − h$ with equal probability, while the LV type's demand will be either $L + l$ or $L − l$ with equal probability, where $h > l$ and $H + h > L + l > L − l > H − h$. A monopolistic carrier can discriminate between the HV types and the LV types using a menu of three-part tariffs. This is because HV types are more concerned than LV types about: (i) using a very large number of minutes, which makes them more inclined to choose a tariff with a larger allocation of minutes to reduce the risk of paying substantial overage fees; and (ii) using only a very small number of minutes, since then, for any given fixed monthly fee, they end up paying a higher per-minute price.

The monopolist can exploit this difference by designing a three-part tariff for LV types with steep overages above $L + l$, LV's highest possible demand, and offering HV types a tariff with at least $H + h$ free minutes for a higher monthly price. LV types like the LV tariff more than the HV types since: (i) they are indifferent to the possibility of overages as they never consume minutes above $L + l$, while the HV types will end up paying overages half of the time if they choose the LV tariff, and (ii) the zero marginal price on allotted minutes within their plan is worth relatively more to LV types, since, unlike the HV types, they always consume at least $L − l$ of those minutes, whereas HV types still end up paying a high average price per minute in the event that their demand is low.

While a three-part tariff pricing structure can facilitate price discrimination, the assumptions required for this rational-choice explanation are often unrealistic. In the price-discrimination model, the HV type chooses a plan with a high number of allotted minutes and the LV type chooses a plan with a low number of allotted minutes. Moreover, their highly variable use levels imply that HVs are more likely than LVs to use a very low number of minutes. Using the data described in subsection 2 below, Figure 4.1 shows the cumulative distribution functions of usage for consumers choosing different three-part tariff plans: Plan 1 with 200 included minutes, Plan 2 with 300 included minutes, Plan 3 with 400 included minutes, and Plan 4 with 500 included minutes.

54. Formally, the cumulative distribution function ("c.d.f.") describing the priors over the demand parameter of the predictable type must cross that of the variable type once from below. Grubb, above note 1.

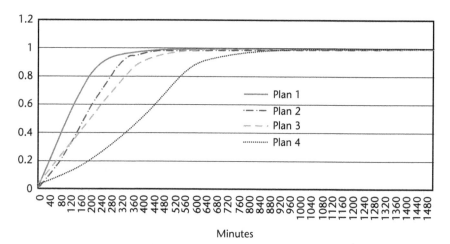

Figure 4.1. Cumulative distribution functions of cell phone usage

Figure 4.1 confirms that the cumulative distribution function corresponding to a plan with a higher number of allocated minutes first-order stochastically dominates the cumulative distribution function corresponding to a plan with a lower number of allocated minutes.[55] In other words, consumers who choose plans with a higher number of allotted minutes are less likely to end up using a very low number of minutes. These findings are inconsistent with the price-discrimination theory.[56]

An alternative rational-choice explanation is based on risk aversion. In theory, the use patterns revealed in the data (see subsection 2 below) are consistent with the behavior of perfectly rational but risk-averse subscribers. Such subscribers would choose plans with more allotted minutes than they expect to use to reduce the risk of paying substantial overage fees. As a result, most of these subscribers will end up using much less than their allotted minutes. This explanation fails for three reasons. First, given the sums of money involved, the observed plan choices are not consistent with risk aversion under the rational-choice Expected Utility Theory.[57] Second, as demonstrated below, subscribers often

55. The data aren't completely consistent with a strict FOSD ranking, however, since Plan 2's cumulative distribution function crosses Plan 3's towards the bottom of the graph. But it is likely that the Plan 2 data are less reliable.
56. Grubb's analysis of a different dataset yields the same conclusion. Grubb, above note 1.
57. See Matthew Rabin, "Note, Risk Aversion and Expected-Utility Theory: A Calibration Theorem", *Econometrica*, 68 (2000), 1281. However, they may be consistent with certain behavioral accounts of risk aversion. See *id.*, at 1282 n. 3.

choose the wrong plan. And, importantly, these mistakes in plan choice are not only ex post mistakes as the risk-aversion explanation would imply; many of them are ex ante mistakes. Finally, while risk aversion may explain the observed usage patterns, it cannot explain the emergence of the three-part tariff as the equilibrium pricing structure. With rational, risk-averse subscribers, we should expect to see two-part tariffs.

2. A Behavioral-Economics Theory
a. Theory

Basic voice services are commonly priced using three-part tariffs. To choose the optimal three-part tariff from the menu of tariffs offered by the carriers, consumers must accurately anticipate their future cell phone usage. But many consumers, when asked to choose a calling plan, are not armed with accurate estimates of how they will use their cell phones. According to a pricing manager at a top U.S. cell phone service provider, "people absolutely think they know how much they will use and it's pretty surprising how wrong they are."[58] The three-part tariff responds to consumers' misperceptions about their future use.

Consumers both overestimate and underestimate their use levels. A carrier who is aware that consumers suffer from such misperceptions can make its service plan appear more attractive to consumers than it really is by using a three-part tariff that charges a low (zero) per-minute price for minutes up to the plan limit and a high per-minute price thereafter. Consumers who overestimate their usage overestimate the value of the low prices because they overestimate the probability that they will use most of these free minutes. Conversely, consumers who underestimate their usage pay insufficient attention to the high overage fees because they underestimate the probability of exceeding the plan limit. For a monopolistic carrier, the three-part tariff creates opportunities for increased profits, while carriers operating in a competitive market will adopt the three-part tariff because it maximizes perceived consumer surplus.[59]

These ideas can be illustrated using a simple numeric example. Assume that several carriers are operating in a highly competitive market. All carriers

---

58. Grubb, above note 1.
59. Three-part tariffs can arise also when consumers are overconfident about their ability to predict their future use. Namely, when the same consumers exhibit a tendency to both over- and underestimate future use. See Grubb, above note 1.

face the same cost structure: a $10 per-consumer fixed cost and a $0.10 per-minute variable cost. Consumers have the following preferences: they value each minute of airtime at $0.40 per minute up to a certain saturation point, *s*, while minutes beyond the saturation point are worth zero to the consumer. There are two types of consumers: heavy users and light users. Fifty percent are heavy users with a saturation point of 300 minutes, and 50 percent are light users with a saturation point of 100 minutes. If consumers are rational and accurately predict their saturation points, then the carriers will set a two-part tariff with a fixed monthly fee of $10 and a constant, per-minute marginal price of $0.10. Heavy users will pay $10 + 300 \cdot 0.1 = 40$, light users will pay $10 + 100 \cdot 0.1 = 20$, and the carriers will just cover their costs, as expected in a perfectly competitive market. Under this two-part tariff, heavy users enjoy a surplus of $300 \cdot (0.4-0.1) -10 = 80$ and light users enjoy a surplus of $100 \cdot (0.4-0.1) -10 = 20.$[60]

Let's introduce consumer misperceptions into the mix. We assume that light users overestimate their saturation point, mistakenly perceiving a saturation point of 200 minutes instead of the actual 100 minutes. And heavy users underestimate their saturation point, mistakenly perceiving a saturation point of 200 minutes instead of the actual 300 minutes. With such misperceptions, a three-part tariff becomes more appealing than the two-part tariff.

Consider the following three-part tariff: a fixed $10 monthly fee, 200 allotted minutes (at a marginal price of zero), and an overage charge of $0.40 per minute beyond the 200-minute allocation. The 200-minute allocation tracks the common perceived saturation point, the $0.40 overage is the maximal marginal price that would not deter usage beyond the plan limit, and the $10 fixed fee is calculated to exactly cover the carrier's expected costs: $10 + \left(\dfrac{1}{2} \cdot 100 + \dfrac{1}{2} \cdot 300\right) \cdot 0.1 - \dfrac{1}{2} \cdot (300 - 200) \cdot 0.4 = 10.$[61] Under this tar-

---

60. Price calculations add the fixed monthly fee to the number of minutes multiplied by the per-minute price. Surplus calculations take the number of minutes multiplied by the difference between the per-minute benefit and the per-minute price and subtract the fixed monthly fee.

61. The carrier's costs include a fixed cost of $10 and an expected variable cost of $0.1 per minute multiplied by the expected number of minutes—100 minutes for light users (50 percent of users) and 300 minutes for heavy users (50 percent of users). The total cost is $30. The carrier gets $20 from overage charges that the heavy users pay on their last 100 minutes. The remaining $10 is collected as a fixed monthly fee.

iff, heavy users will pay 10+(300−200). 0.4=50. They will enjoy a surplus of 300 0 .04−(300−200). 0.4-10=70, less than the surplus of 80 under the two-part tariff. But since they underestimate their use, they misperceive the surplus. The perceived surplus under the three-part tariff is 200 0 .04−10=70, greater than the perceived surplus of 200. (0.4−01)−10=50 under the two-part tariff. Light users will pay $10 under the three-part tariff. They will enjoy a surplus of 100 0 .04−10=30, more than the surplus of 20 under the two-part tariff. More importantly, the perceived surplus under the three-part tariff is 200 0 .04−10=70, greater than the perceived surplus of 200. (0.4−0.1)−10=50 under the two-part tariff.

The three-part tariff extracts payments in the form of overage fees that are invisible to consumers,[62] while reducing or eliminating payments that are visible to consumers—specifically, fixed fees and charges for minutes within the plan limit. Notice that the heavy users, who underestimate their usage levels and end up paying overage fees, are subsidizing the light users. But since the heavy users do not anticipate paying the overage fees, a competitor cannot lure them away ex ante by, for example, offering a different tariff with lower overage fees. The three-part tariff maximizes the perceived consumer surplus for both types of consumers, and thus will be selected as the equilibrium tariff in a competitive market.

b. Data

A unique dataset of subscriber-level monthly billing and usage information for 3,730 subscribers at a single wireless provider was used to test the misperception theory. These data provide information on which calling plan (of four) subscribers chose, as well as monthly consumption of peak minutes for the period of September 2001 to May 2003. Each of the four calling plans offered a standard three-part tariff with a fixed allocation of peak minutes and steep overages for additional peak minutes consumed, as described in Table 4.1 below.[63]

---

62. In a more general model, overage charges would be underestimated, but not completely invisible.
63. The database was provided by the Center for Customer Relationship Management at Duke University. The description of the data in the text is based on the description provided by the Center. See The Center for Customer Relationship Management, *Telecom Dataset*, available at <http://www.fuqua-europe.duke.edu/centers/ccrm/index.html#data>; see also Raghuram

Table 4.1. Menu of Three-Part Tariffs

	Plan 1	Plan 2	Plan 3	Plan 4
Market share (%)	22.15	2.00	73.28	2.57
Monthly fixed charge ($)	30	35	40	50
Number of included minutes	200	300	400	500
Overage rate ($)	0.40	0.40	0.40	0.40

The data reveal substantial variance in usage. Summary statistics are provided in Tables 4.2a–e below. For plans 1, 2, 3, and 4, Tables 4.2a–d present the overall mean and standard deviation of minutes used. To gain an initial sense of usage underestimation versus overestimation of usage, average figures for under-usage (unused minutes per month) and over-usage (minutes over the plan allocation) are also presented. This information is aggregated across all plans in Table 4.2e.

In aggregate, subscribers exceeded their minute allowance 11.4 percent of the time by an average of 34.3 percent. In the 88.4 percent of the time when the allowance was not exceeded, subscribers used, on average, only 45.4 percent of their minute allowance. Notice that "underages" and overages do not, in and of themselves, imply overestimation and underestimation of use. A perfectly rational consumer with variable use will experience both underages and overages.

Let's now look at consumers who arguably chose the wrong plan, and the cost of the mistake to those consumers. A plan choice is a mistake when, given the consumers' usage, the selected plan is different from another available plan that would have cost less. The unit of analysis is the consumer's tenure with a plan, and only the 3,456 consumers who stayed with a plan for at least ten months are considered. Given the variance in usage from month to month, identifying mistakes over shorter time horizons is less reliable. For each of the 3,456 consumers, the total cost of

Iyengar, Asim Ansari, and Sunil Gupta, "A Model of Consumer Learning of Consumer Service Quality and Usage", *J. Mktg. Res.*, 44 (2007), 529, 535–7. It is not entirely clear from the data that all four plans were offered at all dates in all markets. We acknowledge this limitation of the data and qualify our results accordingly. Our empirical strategy builds on Grubb, above note 1, who tested a related behavioral explanation, the overconfidence theory, using a different dataset.

Table 4.2a. Summary Statistics—Plan 1

| | Share | Usage/Allowance | |
		Mean	Std. Dev.
Under allowance	0.819	0.45	0.294
Over allowance	0.179	1.46	0.624
All consumers	1	0.633	0.538

Table 4.2b. Summary Statistics—Plan 2

| | Share | Usage /Allowance | |
		Mean	Std. Dev.
Under allowance	0.872	0.51	0.274
Over allowance	0.126	1.25	0.279
All consumers	1	0.607	0.368

Table 4.2c. Summary Statistics—Plan 3

| | Share | Usage/Allowance | |
		Mean	Std. Dev.
Under allowance	0.911	0.45	0.287
Over allowance	0.089	1.284	0.324
All consumers	1	0.524	0.375

Table 4.2d. Summary Statistics—Plan 4

| | Share | Usage/Allowance | |
		Mean	Std. Dev.
Under allowance	0.718	0.573	0.296
Over allowance	0.279	1.259	0.29
All consumers	1	0.766	0.425

Table 4.2e. Summary Statistics—Aggregate

| | All Plans Share | Usage/Allowance | |
		Mean	Std. Dev.
Under allowance	0.884	0.454	0.289
Over allowance	0.114	1.343	0.457
All consumers	1	0.557	0.422

wireless service under the consumer's chosen plan was compared to the
total amount that this consumer would have paid had each of the other
three plans been chosen. The magnitude of the mistakes is measured by
the difference (in both percentages and dollars) between the consumer's
actual wireless costs and the lowest possible cost—the cost that the consumer would have paid if the consumer could have predicted usage with
certainty.[64]

The results are summarized in Tables 4.3a and 4.3b. In these tables, each
row represents the group of subscribers who chose a certain plan. (Note
that there is no row for Plan 2, since no Plan 2 subscriber remained with the
plan for more than 10 months.) This group is then divided into four subgroups according to the plan that these subscribers *should* have chosen. For
instance, the cell located at the intersection of the Plan 3 row and the Plan
1 column represents the subgroup of subscribers who chose Plan 3 but
should have chosen Plan 1. Table 4.3a presents the size, in percentage terms,
of these subgroups. Table 4.3b presents the magnitude of the mistakes or
cost-savings, both in percentage terms and in annual dollar terms, for each
subgroup.[65]

The results for one group of subscribers, those who chose Plan 3, are
presented in Figure 4.2. This group of subscribers is noteworthy for its significant numbers of both under-estimators, who should have chosen Plan 4,
and over-estimators, who should have chosen either Plan 2 or Plan 1. Figure
4.2 displays the share of Plan 3 consumers who should have chosen each of
the four plans (the dark gray bars). For those who should not have chosen

Table 4.3a. The likelihood of mistakes

		Optimal Plan			
		Plan 1	Plan 2	Plan 3	Plan 4
Chosen plan	Plan 1	74.09%	21.79%	1.49%	2.49%
	Plan 3	27.20%	35.61%	21.19%	16%
	Plan 4	9.00%	10.66%	8.00%	73.33%

64. This analysis assumes risk neutrality. The sums involved are small enough that this assumption
seems reasonable.

65. The magnitude of the mistake (or cost saving) is calculated as follows (this calculation is performed for each cell in Table 4.3b): We calculate the actual total price paid by a consumer
under her chosen plan over the period that she stayed with the plan. We then calculate the
hypothetical total price that this consumer would have paid had she chosen the best plan
given her actual usage. The difference between these actual and hypothetical total prices is the

Table 4.3b. The magnitude of mistakes

		Optimal Plan			
		Plan 1	**Plan 2**	**Plan 3**	**Plan 4**
Chosen	Plan 1	0%	9.56%	26.97%	28.22%
plan		$0	$54.16	$203.58	$341.71
	Plan 3	21.09%	6.55%	0%	11.34%
		$101.58	$32.59	$0	$102.98
	Plan 4	36.71%	12.38%	7.00%	0%
		$220.27	$75.31	$39.90	$0

Plan 3, Figure 4.2 shows the amount of money they would have saved, both in percentage terms (the light gray bars) and in dollar figures.

These figures underestimate the number and cost of mistakes, especially for plans with a lower allocation of minutes. For example, for subscribers who chose Plan 1, the data only reveal mistakes arising from underestimation of use (selection of Plan 1) when the subscriber should have chosen Plan 2, Plan 3, or Plan 4. But it is likely that many Plan 1 subscribers who overestimated their use could have done better by choosing a prepaid plan that is not included in the dataset. A conservative estimate of the number and magnitude of the cost of such overestimation can be generated by adding a hypothetical prepaid plan with a high per-minute charge of $0.40 (equal to the overage charges in our data). An estimated 24.4 percent of Plan 1 subscribers would have saved $149 annually on average had they chosen the prepaid plan.[66]

The mistakes in plan choice that we have discussed are ex post mistakes. Since consumers face ex ante uncertainty about their future use, even consumers who forecast their use ex ante in a rational manner will make predictions that turn out to be incorrect ex post. To assess the extent of ex ante mistakes in our data and again focusing on subscribers who stayed with the same plan for at least 10 months, each subscriber's tenure with the plan was divided into two: the first-half and the second-half periods.

---

magnitude of the mistake and, when reporting dollar values, we transform this number into annual figures (by dividing the difference by the actual number of months under the plan and then multiplying by 12 months). The mistakes thus calculated are then averaged out across all consumers in the specific Table 4.3b cell, e.g., across all consumers who chose Plan 3 but should have chosen Plan 1.

66. These conclusions are tentative, since prepaid plans may differ from postpaid plans on other dimensions. In particular, while the service quality offered by prepaid plans is improving, in the period when the data were collected there was still a non-negligible difference in quality between prepaid and postpaid plans.

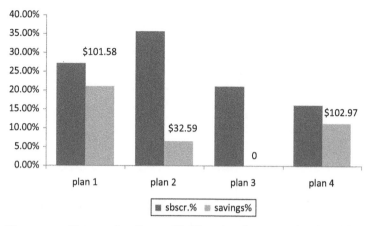

Figure 4.2. Plan 3 subscribers—likelihood and magnitude of mistakes

Consider a subscriber who, given her usage in the first-half period, should have chosen Plan 1 but chose Plan 3 instead. This subscriber, who could have easily switched to Plan 1 at the end of the first-half period (subscribers were not locked in to a plan), stayed with Plan 3 in the second-half period even though Plan 1 remained the optimal plan based on the second-half period usage. Since the same plan was optimal in both half periods, her usage must have remained roughly the same during the two half periods, which means that her first-half period usage provided her with a basis to update her predictions about her usage in the second-half period. Since subscribers were free to switch plans and their switching costs were likely to be low, we can surmise that the subscriber's decision to choose Plan 3 was probably an ex ante mistake—at least for the second-half period. The data reveal that a substantial percentage of subscribers who chose the wrong plan in the first-half period also chose the wrong plan in the second-half period.[67]

67. This analysis is performed in Oren Bar-Gill and Rebecca Stone, "Pricing Misperceptions: Explaining Pricing Structure in the Cell Phone Service Market" forthcoming in *J. Empirical Legal Stud.*, Vol. 9. Evidence of "bill shock"—a sudden increase in the monthly bill that is not caused by a change in service plan—also suggests that many consumers are making ex ante mistakes. A 2010 FCC survey study found that one in six mobile users have experienced "bill shock," and that for a sizeable proportion of users the magnitude of the "shock" was substantial—more than a third reported an increase of at least $50, and 23 percent reported an increase of $100 or more. See FCC, News Release: "FCC Survey Confirms Consumers Experience Mobile Bill Shock and Confusion about Early Termination Fees," May 26, 2010, available at <http://www.fcc.gov/document/fcc-survey-confirms-consumers-experience-mobile-bill-shock-and-confusion-about-early-termin>; last visited November 17, 2011.

To sum up: Many consumers fail to accurately anticipate their use patterns, and the three-part tariff design is a market response to such misperceptions.

Consistent with this story, providers do not seem to be troubled by consumers' use-pattern mistakes. In fact, until recently they actively foster these mistakes by requiring, as a condition for network access, that handset manufacturers disable the call-timer feature that would make it easier for consumers to monitor their usage.[68] However, consumers are becoming more aware of their use-pattern mistakes and more frustrated with carriers who take advantage of them. As elaborated in Part V below, the market is responding to the demand generated by these more sophisticated consumers.

B. Lock-In Clauses

1. Rational-Choice Theories and Their Limits

Lock-in clauses can arise in a rational-choice framework. When the seller incurs substantial per-consumer fixed costs and the liquidity-constrained consumer cannot afford to pay an upfront fee equal to these fixed costs, the optimal solution may be a lock-in contract. In the cell phone market, fixed costs are high but, more importantly, they are endogenous. Carriers invest up to $400 in acquiring each new customer.[69] Many of these customer-acquisition costs, however, are attributed to the free or subsidized phones that carriers offer.[70] This raises several questions. Why do carriers offer free phones and lock-in contracts? Why not charge customers the full price of the phone and avoid lock-in? Many cell phone consumers can afford to purchase the phone up-front. Moreover, it is unlikely that the carrier is the most efficient source of credit available to all of those consumers who are in fact liquidity-constrained. Thus, the rational-choice

68. Wu, above note 20, at 9. For an example of the carrier-imposed difficulty customers face in determining their unused plan-minute allowances—see Sherrie Nachman, "Cranky Consumer: How to Check Up on Your Cell Phone Minutes," *Wall Street Journal*, June 18, 2002, at D2.

69. Lauren Tara Lacapra, "Breaking Free of a Cellular Contract—New Web Sites Help Customers Swap or Resell Phone Service; Avoiding $175 Termination Fee," *Wall Street Journal*, November 30, 2006, at D1 ("It costs a cell phone company approximately $350 to $400 to acquire a new customer, according to Phil Doriot, a partner in the consulting firm CFI Group, who has studied company performance and customer satisfaction for major cellular service providers."); Jane Spencer, "What Part of 'Cancel' Don't You Understand?—Regulators Crack Down on Internet Providers, Phone Companies That Make It Hard to Quit," *Wall Street Journal*, November 12, 2003, at D1 (noting that customer acquisition costs are approximately "$339 per new customer, according to Yankee Group, a technology research firm").

70. Jared Sandberg, "A Piece of the Business," *Wall Street Journal*, September 11, 1997, at R22.

model can explain the presence of these design features in only a subset of contracts.[71]

An alternative argument views lock-in clauses as instrumental in stabilizing demand and helping providers match capacity to demand (especially in peak hours), thus reducing costs and benefiting consumers. While lock-in clauses may reduce churn and thus variation in demand, there are still significant variations in the use patterns of the locked-in consumers, as shown above. More importantly, it is not clear that providers need lock-in clauses to match capacity to demand. Providers have good information about their customers' use patterns, including how long they will stay with a specific provider. A related argument is that ETF-enforced lock-in generates a more predictable stream of revenues, which is necessary for carriers to recoup their large capital investments.[72] Again, while lock-in reduces uncertainty for the carriers, these carriers could generate reasonably accurate revenue estimates without it. Though reduced risk is desirable, the presence of manageable risk should not prevent investment.

2. A Behavioral-Economics Theory

The lock-in clauses that are common in postpaid plans and the termination fees that enforce them can be explained as a market response to the imperfect rationality of consumers. Consumers often underestimate the likelihood that switching carriers will be beneficial down the road, because the service provided by the current carrier is not as good as promised, monthly charges are higher than expected, or another carrier is offering a better deal. Since they underestimate the likelihood of eventually wanting to switch carriers, consumers underestimate the long-term cost of the lock-in clause. When consumers underestimate the likelihood that they will want to switch providers before their contract expires, they will be

---

71. The fact that termination fees were initially structured such that consumers paid the same fee regardless of when they terminated the contract raises doubts about the argument that ETFs were necessary to cover the cost of the free or subsidized phones, either by inducing consumers to stay on and pay the monthly subscription fees or by replacing the subscription fees of consumers who leave.

72. See Thomas J. Tauke, Executive Vice President, Verizon, "Testimony at FCC Early Termination Hearing" 2 (June, 12, 2008) (hereinafter Verizon Testimony), available at <http://www.fcc.gov/realaudio/presentations/2008/061208/tauke.pdf>; see also CTIA, "Early Termination Fees Equal Lower Consumer Rates", *CITA.org*, April 2006, <http://files.ctia.org/pdf/PositionPaper_CTIA_ETF_04_06.pdf>.

relatively insensitive to the ETF. Increasing the size of the ETF thus becomes an appealing pricing strategy for carriers. Moreover, the ETF-enforced lock-in facilitates the common practice of bundling phones and service. Termination fees guarantee a long-term revenue stream, as subscribers must either refrain from switching carriers and pay for service for the duration of their contracts or switch and pay the termination fee.[73] This guaranteed revenue enables carriers to offer free or subsidized phones to attract consumers.

But the story is more complicated. To subsidize the cost of phones, carriers must charge an above-cost price for service. This pricing strategy is attractive only if the price of service is underestimated. As we have seen in Part III.A, such underestimation is common. Consumers underestimate the price that they will pay in overage fees when they underestimate usage. When they overestimate usage, they underestimate the per-minute price that they will pay under the plan. Of course, a single month's worth of underestimated service prices cannot cover the large phone subsidies. Consequently, lock-in is crucial. Lock-in ensures that the carrier will benefit from (typically) two years' worth of above-cost and underestimated service charges or, if lock-in fails, from the underestimated termination fee. These compounded above-cost service charges can then pay for the free or subsidized phones. Lock-in and bundling also play into consumers' myopia, further compounding the problem. The immediate cost of the phone looms larger in the decision calculus than the costs of the service contract, which are spread over time.

Carriers are quite explicit about their strategy of offering free or subsidized phones and recouping their costs through long-term contracts with ETFs. According to the vice president of marketing for Cingular Wireless (now AT&T), the penalties are the price that consumers must pay for the inexpensive or free phones customers get when they sign up for service: "We subsidize the handset; in exchange we want a commitment from the

---

73. The ETF effectively deters switching. See Lacapra, above note 69 (according to a July 2005 survey by the U.S. PIRG Education Fund, "[r]oughly 47 percent of cell customers would switch or consider switching cellphone companies if early-termination fees were abolished," but "because of the fee, only 3 percent of customers go ahead with terminating the contract").

customer."[74] Similarly, at the FCC hearing on ETFs, an Executive Vice President of Verizon argued:

> Term contracts allow the consumer to take advantage of bundled services at competitive prices and the latest devices they choose in exchange for a commitment to keep the service for usually one or two years. In return, service providers have some measure of assurance over a fixed period of time that they may recover their investment, including equipment subsidies, costs of acquiring and retaining customers, and anticipated revenue for providing wireless services.[75]

The pricing of the iPhone is a good example of this strategy in action. In June 2008, Apple made a big splash when it announced that the new iPhone model would sell for $200 less than its predecessor ($199 versus $399). However, at the same time, Apple and its partner AT&T raised the iPhone's minimum monthly service subscription from $60 to $70, adding $240 to the total cost of the two-year contract.[76] AT&T and Apple executives were very clear about the short-term versus long-term trade-off. They were willing to lose money on the front end, but only because they were counting on making even more money off the back end, due to the two-year lock-in contract. Not surprisingly, when the same iPhone was later offered in unbundled form, without a two-year service plan, it was priced at $599, which is $400 above the subsidized price (with a service plan).[77]

The practice of offering free or subsidized phones with lock-in contracts provides strong evidence of consumer bias. Carriers seem to understand that consumers are attracted by the short-term benefit (the free phone) even when this benefit is completely offset or even outweighed by increased long-term costs. While bundling of phones and service is still the norm in the U.S. cellular service market, this practice seems to be in decline. Consumers are more aware of ETFs and carriers are reducing ETFs in

74. Caroline E. Mayer, "Griping about Cellular Bills; Differences from 'Regular' Phones Take New Users by Surprise," *Washington Post*, February 28, 2001, at G17; see also Fawn Johnson, "FCC Head Seeks Rules on Cell-Termination Fees," *Wall Street Journal*, June 13, 2008, at B7 ("Wireless carriers argue that the termination fees are used to subsidize the cost of cellphones to customers. People who sign up for one- or two-year contracts receive discounts on phones and their monthly wireless rates."); CTIA, above note 72, at 1 (arguing that prohibiting carriers from charging ETFs will cause prices for wireless services to increase).
75. See Verizon Testimony, above note 72, at 1.
76. See Paul Wagenseil, "That 'Cheaper' iPhone Will Cost You More," *FoxNews.com*, June 11, 2008, <http://www.foxnews.com/story/0,2933,365347,00.html>.
77. AT&T Plans to Offer No-Contract iPhone, above note 47.

response—changes that can be attributed, at least in part, to the ETF litigation. With lower ETFs and thus weaker lock-in, phone subsidies become more difficult to sustain. The drive towards open access also threatens the future of the bundling strategy. After initially resisting open access, carriers are beginning to realize the benefits of shifting development and customer service costs to handset manufacturers. Finally, it is interesting to note that the practice of bundling phones and service has always been less common outside the U.S.[78]

C. Complexity

1. Rational-Choice Theories and Their Limits

The rational-choice explanation for complexity is straightforward. Consumers have heterogeneous preferences. Different consumers want different kinds of cellular services, so the complexity and multidimensionality of the cellular service offerings cater to the heterogeneous preferences of cell phone users. This surely explains some of the observed complexity in the cell phone market. But it doesn't fully explain the staggering level of complexity exhibited by the long menus of cell phone contracts. Even for the rational consumer, acquiring information on the range of complex products is costly. Comparing different plans with different multidimensional features is costly, even for this rational consumer. At some point, these costs exceed the benefits of finding the perfect plan. When complexity deters comparison-shopping, the benefits of the variety and multidimensionality are left unrealized. The rational-choice account must balance the costs and benefits of complexity. It seems that in the cell phone market the level of complexity has reached a point beyond what we should expect if it was simply a response to rational consumer demand.[79]

---

78. See Ante, above note 20.
79. A market for "comparison shopping services" is emerging, with vendors such as BillShrink and Validas offering to find the best product/plan for any consumer who is willing to pay a fee. See below note 102 and accompanying text. The availability of comparison-shopping services reduces the cost of comparison-shopping and increases the optimal level of complexity in a rational-choice model. However, it seems that most cell phone users do not avail themselves of the services offered by BillShrink and Validas. The emergence of a market for "comparison shopping services" suggests that complexity makes it difficult for consumers to comparison-shop by themselves. But since the majority of consumers do not seek help from professional comparison-shoppers and thus do not benefit from the high level of complexity, the rational choice explanation for complexity is less convincing.

2. A Behavioral-Economics Theory

The complexity and multidimensionality of the cell phone contract can be explained as a market response to the imperfect rationality of consumers. Consider four basic plans offered by the four major carriers:

(1) AT&T's $39.99 plan with 450 minutes, $0.45 per minute overage, unlimited night (9:00 p.m. to 6:00 a.m.) and weekend minutes (which are, in fact, limited to 5,000 minutes), unlimited calling to AT&T customers, and rollover minutes.

(2) Verizon's $39.99 plan with 450 minutes, $0.45 overage, unlimited night (9:01 p.m. to 5:59 a.m.) and weekend minutes, unlimited calling to Verizon customers, and unlimited calling to five "Friends & Family" numbers.

(3) Sprint's $39.99 plan with 450 minutes, $0.45 overage, unlimited nights (7:00 p.m. to 7:00 a.m.) and weekends.

(4) T-Mobile's $39.99 plan with 500 minutes, $0.45 overage, unlimited calls to customers on the T-Mobile network, and unlimited nights (9:00 p.m. to 6:59 a.m.) and weekends.

To choose among these products, the consumer must answer a series of difficult questions. How important to the consumer is unlimited calling within the network? If unlimited calling within the network is important, on which network are most of the consumer's friends located? How valuable is unlimited calling during weekends? How valuable is unlimited calling at night? What are the cost implications of unlimited calling at night when "night" is between 7:00 p.m. and 7:00 a.m. as compared to a shorter "night" between 9:00 p.m. and 6:00 a.m.? How valuable is the rollover feature?

There is considerable complexity even when the comparison is between Plans 1, 2, and 3, which offer consumers the same monthly charge, number of allotted minutes, and overage charge. But, of course, the different dimensions of the three-part tariff also change from one carrier to the next and from one plan to the next in a single carrier's menu of offerings. Consumers must choose the combination of monthly charge, allotted minutes, and overages they prefer. This choice requires accurate estimates of the distribution of their future usage.

A perfectly informed and perfectly rational consumer could navigate this maze and find the optimal plan. But the amount of information required to do so is substantial, since it includes information about both available plans and the consumer's own use patterns. The cost of collecting and processing all this information may well outweigh the corresponding benefit. Thus, even a rational consumer will generally be imperfectly informed. For the imperfectly rational consumer, this imperfect information will also lead to bias and to systematic underestimation of the total cost of cellular service.

Complexity allows providers to hide the true cost of the contract. Imperfectly rational consumers cannot effectively aggregate the costs associated with the different options and prices in a single cell phone contract. Inevitably, consumers will focus on a subset of salient features and prices and ignore or underestimate the importance of the remaining, non-salient features and prices. In response, carriers will increase prices or reduce the quality of the non-salient features, which in turn will generate or free up resources for intensified competition on the salient features. Competition forces providers to make the salient features attractive and salient prices low. This can be achieved by adding revenue-generating, non-salient features and prices. The result is an endogenously derived high level of complexity and multidimensionality.

Complexity as a response to imperfect rationality is a dynamic process. Consumer learning implies that a feature or a price that was not salient last month may become salient next month. ETFs provide such an example. When one price dimension becomes salient, competition focuses on this dimension and carriers shift to a new, less salient price dimension. According to some accounts, carriers facing increased competition on fixed monthly fees and allocations of included minutes are now relying more heavily on revenues from charges for data services.[80] The proposed account of complexity not only allows for consumer learning, but also uses consumer learning to explain the increasing level of complexity of the cellular service contract: When consumers learn the importance of a previously non-salient price dimension, carriers have a strong incentive to create a new price dimension that will be, at least initially, non-salient.

IV. Welfare Implications

We have seen how the design of cell phone contracts can be explained as a response to the imperfect rationality of consumers. In this Part, we'll assess the extent to which the mistakes that consumers make—and

80. Andrea Petersen and Nicole Harris, "Hard Cell: Chaos, Confusion and Perks Bedevil Wireless Users," *Wall Street Journal*, April 17, 2002, at A1.

providers' responses to these mistakes—harm consumers and generate welfare costs.

A. Three-Part Tariffs

As we have seen, misperceptions of use levels lead many consumers to
choose the wrong plan; more specifically, the wrong three-part tariff.
The average consumer in our data made a mistake that cost 8 percent of the
total wireless bill, or $47.68 annually. Extrapolating from our data
onto the entire U.S. population of cell phone users, which is approximately
280 million, we obtain a $13.35 billion annual reduction in consumer
surplus.

While the $13.35 billion figure is substantial, the average per-consumer
harm, $47.68, seems small. But these averages hide potentially important
distributional implications. The $13.35 billion is not evenly divided among
the 280 million U.S. subscribers. In our data, 35 percent of subscribers
chose the right plan. Even among subscribers who chose the wrong plan,
the magnitude of the mistake—that is, the extra payment as compared to
the right plan—varies substantially. In our data, 34 percent of consumers
made mistakes that cost them at least 10 percent of their total wireless bill,
or $113 annually, and 17 percent of consumers made mistakes that cost
them at least 20 percent of their total wireless bill, or $146 annually. (10
percent of consumers made mistakes that cost them at least 25 percent of
their total wireless bill, or $60 annually; this implies that the really large
mistakes, in percentage terms, had smaller stakes in dollar terms.)

It should be emphasized that a reduction in the consumer surplus is not
a welfare cost in and of itself. Yet the identified consumer mistakes do generate welfare costs for two reasons. First, consumer mistakes imply inefficient allocation, since they cause consumers to buy the wrong products.
Second, social welfare is reduced by regressive redistribution. Such redistribution occurs when carriers profit from consumer mistakes (assuming that
carriers' shareholders tend to be richer than their customers). But regressive
redistribution may occur even if these excess profits are reduced through
competition. The distribution of mistakes implies that revenues from consumers who make mistakes keep prices low for consumers who do not
make mistakes. If the former tend to be poorer than the latter, then wealth
is redistributed in the wrong direction.

B. Lock-In Clauses

Lock-in prevents efficient switching and thus hurts consumers. A 2005 survey by the U.S. PIRG Education Fund found that 47 percent of subscribers would like to switch plans, but only 3 percent do so—the rest are deterred by the ETF.[81] While more recent changes in the structure and magnitude of ETFs likely resulted in increased switching, current ETFs are still substantial and still deter switching.

Switching is efficient when a different carrier or plan provides a better fit for the consumer. In light of the rapid advances in handset technology, a two-year lock-in is a relatively long period of time. Beyond these efficiency costs, consumers lose from lock-in when it prevents them from accepting a better deal offered by a competing carrier. Lock-in can also slow down the beneficial effects of consumer learning. Consumers gradually learn to avoid misperception and form more accurate estimates of their future use. If lock-in prevents these consumers from switching to a plan that better fits their actual use patterns, it prolongs the welfare costs identified in Part IV.A. Similarly, consumers will gradually learn the implications of their complex cell phone contract. For example, they may learn that they do not use their phone very often between 6 a.m, and 7 a.m., and thus conclude that they are not benefiting from the longer definition of "night" in Sprint's unlimited night calling. If lock-in prevents these consumers from switching to a different carrier, it prolongs the welfare costs of complexity.

In addition to these direct costs, lock-in may inhibit competition, adding a potentially large indirect welfare cost. We have already mentioned that lock-in may prevent a more efficient carrier from attracting consumers who are locked into a contract with a less efficient carrier. Since lock-in makes large-scale entry into the market more difficult, incumbents may have a greater incentive to seek monopolization through predation or merger than in markets where easy entry limits incumbents' market power.[82]

---

81. Lacapra, above note 69.
82. Joseph Farrell and Paul Klemperer, "Coordination and Lock-In: Competition with Switching Costs and Network Effects" in Armstong, M. and Porter, R. (eds.), *Handbook of Industrial Organization*, Vol. 3, pp. 1967, 2005 (North-Holland, 2007).

C. Complexity

The high level of complexity of cellular service contracts can reduce welfare in two ways. First, consumers will tend to make more mistakes when the choices are complex. Second, complexity inhibits competition by raising the cost of comparison-shopping (which discourages comparison-shopping). This is true for the perfectly rational consumer; imperfect rationality only exacerbates the problem. Without the discipline that comparison-shopping enforces, cell phone service providers can behave like quasi-monopolists, raising prices and reducing consumer surplus.

D. Countervailing Benefits?

Three-part tariffs, lock-in clauses, and complexity harm consumers and increase carriers' profits. Competition among carriers, even if imperfect, forces carriers to give back to consumers some of these profits. Carriers will respond to competition by lowering prices that are salient to consumers. Handset subsidies are the primary way in which benefits flow back to consumers.

However, these countervailing benefits do not eliminate the identified welfare costs. Even if all excess profits are returned to consumers, there will still be an efficiency cost. Consumer mistakes and the contractual design features that respond to these mistakes lead consumers to misperceive the relative costs and benefits of different products. As a result, consumers often choose the wrong products and use these products less optimally than they otherwise might.

Moreover, even if all excess profits are returned to consumers as a group, there is no reason to believe that the benefit received by a consumer will precisely offset the harm to that same consumer. In fact, it is likely that consumers who are more prone to mistakes will be cross-subsidizing consumers who are less prone to mistakes. The resulting redistribution can reduce social welfare.

Finally, one important effect of lock-in and complexity is to reduce the level of competition in the cellular services market. Reduced competition means that less of the excess profits will find their way back into the hands of consumers.

V. Market Solutions

Consumers make mistakes and carriers respond to these mistakes. However, consumers also learn from their mistakes, and carriers respond to demand generated by the growing number of increasingly sophisticated consumers. Indeed, in a competitive market carriers may have an incentive to correct consumer mistakes—at least when these mistakes prevent consumers from fully appreciating the benefits of the correcting carrier's product.

We'll begin by describing a number of products and contracts that, arguably, respond to demand by more sophisticated consumers. Then, in Section B, we'll examine whether these market solutions in fact solve the behavioral market failures identified in this chapter.

A. Catering to Sophisticated Consumers

The cellular service market boasts a large set of products and contracts that arguably cater to more sophisticated consumers.

1. Unlimited Calling Plans

In February 2008, Verizon broke with industry pricing norms by offering a $99 unlimited calling plan. Soon after, AT&T followed suit. T-Mobile went even further by including unlimited text messaging with unlimited voice in its unlimited plan. Sprint then unveiled a $99 plan that featured "unlimited voice, text messages, email, web surfing, video, and other premium services."[83] Unlimited calling plans arguably respond to consumer complaints about overage fees. Most likely, a sufficiently large subset of disgruntled consumers, experiencing the sting of large overage charges, generated demand for plans without overage fees.

The rise of unlimited plans demonstrates both the power and potential unevenness of consumer learning. We have presented the three-part tariff as a response to consumer misperception about future use. Of the different components of the three-part tariff, the overage fee is likely to be the one that consumers learn to appreciate most quickly. When consumers exceed

---

83. Roger Cheng, "Business Technology: Virgin Mobile to Join Flat Rate Phones Frenzy," *Wall Street Journal*, June 24, 2008, at B4.

the plan limit, they receive direct and painful feedback (an overage fee) that helps them learn. But as argued earlier, the underestimation of use that triggers overage charges is just half of the problem. The other half—overestimation of use—is more difficult to learn. For a consumer using 50 percent of the allotted minutes, implying a much higher per-minute rate than initially expected, there is no direct feedback because the consumer still pays the same monthly fixed fee. It's doubtful that many consumers divide this fee by the number of minutes actually used to derive the real per-minute price. The result of this uneven learning is unlimited plans, rather than the optimal two-part tariff pricing scheme.

The currently available unlimited plans are attractive only to a relatively small fraction of heavy users. With their high monthly fees, the unlimited plans are less attractive than the standard three-part tariff plans for most users.[84] Therefore, the unlimited plans are, at best, a limited market solution targeted at a small segment of cell phone users. These heavy users may learn more quickly and demand products that cater to their needs. A more general market solution to consumer learning about underestimation and overage costs, such as a two-part tariff, is still absent, as is a market solution to the overestimation problem.

Bundling voice, messaging, and data services in a single "unlimited" plan with a single monthly fixed fee may be a response to learning of a different kind. Consumers are confused by complex, multidimensional contracts and are demanding greater "simplicity." While a single-price, "unlimited everything" plan is simpler, its simplicity can be exaggerated. In measuring simplicity, it is not enough to consider the price and other product attributes of only a single plan. The level of complexity is a result of the interaction between product attributes and consumer usage patterns across a carrier's entire menu of plans. For example, in order to choose between a $99 unlimited plan and a limited plan with a lower monthly fee (plus possibly separate charges for text messaging and data services), consumers must still form accurate estimates of their future use and calculate the expected total price of both plans—no easy task.

2. Rollover Minutes

Consumer use varies from month to month. A consumer may talk 350 minutes one month and 550 minutes the next. With a standard 450-minute plan, this consumer will waste 100 minutes in the first month and pay overage

---

84. See Jeff Blyskal, "Mostly Talk: New Unlimited Cell Plans Won't Pay for Most," *Consumer-Reports.org*, February 26, 2008, <http://blogs.consumerreports.org/electronics/2008/02/mostly-talk-new.html>.

charges for 100 minutes in the second. With AT&T's 450-minute plan, which includes the rollover minutes feature, the 100 spare minutes in the first month are not wasted. Rather they are "rolled over"—added to the available minutes for the second month.[85] This means that in the second month, the consumer has 550 minutes instead of 450 minutes and thus will not pay any overage.[86] The rollover feature, which predates the unlimited calling plans described above, can also be seen as a response to consumer learning about the costs of underestimated use and overage charges. But unlike unlimited plans that directly respond to underestimation of use, the rollover feature seems to respond to a different bias—overconfidence about use levels, which implies underestimation of use in some months and overestimation of use in others. By enabling the consumer to smooth uneven use over time, the rollover feature mitigates the costs of overconfidence.

3. Prepaid Plans

Prepaid, no-contract plans are the natural choice for a sophisticated consumer who wants flexibility and has learned the costs of lock-in. This flexibility, however, comes at a cost. Not only do prepaid, no-contract subscribers forgo the phone subsidies offered to postpaid, locked-in subscribers, but they also pay higher per-minute charges (at least as compared to postpaid subscribers who use all the allotted minutes under their plans). As a result, even sophisticated consumers would be reluctant to choose a prepaid plan. In fact, prepaid, no-contract plans, with their lower profitability, were designed for distinct segments of consumers—specifically younger and poorer consumers who have low credit scores and do not qualify for a postpaid plan.[87] The numbers confirm this: In 2008, only 16 percent of U.S. cell phone users had prepaid plans; among households with incomes above $75,000, only 6 percent of cell phone users had prepaid plans.[88]

This is starting to change. With the growth of unlimited prepaid offerings and the reduction in per-minute rates, prepaid plans are now attracting

85. Unused minutes do not roll over forever. They expire after a year.
86. In this example, the rational non-AT&T customer will switch to a 900-minute plan and pay an additional $20 per month because this charge is smaller than the average overage paid in the seemingly cheaper plan: $45/2 months = $22.50.
87. FCC, FCC 08–28, "Annual Report and Analysis of Competitive Market Conditions with Respect to Commercial Mobile Services, Twelfth Report" 2297–98 ¶¶ 116–18 (2008), available at <http://wireless.fcc.gov/index.htm?job=cmrs_reports>.
88. Opinion Research Corporation, "Prepaid Phones in the U.S.: Myths, Lack of Consumer Knowledge Blocking Wider Use" 4, 10 (2008), <http://www.newmillenniumresearch.org/archive/120408_prepaid_myths_survey_report.pdf>.

consumers from segments of the market previously controlled by postpaid plans. Prepaid is becoming a real alternative to postpaid.[89]

While having a prepaid alternative is valuable, prepaid plans are not a panacea. While solving the lock-in problem and avoiding underestimation of lock-in costs, prepaid plans trigger other consumer mistakes. Misperceptions about future use may still lead consumers to choose the wrong monthly prepaid or pay-as-you-go plan. In fact, expiration dates on minutes purchased under pay-as-you-go plans—important design features of such plans—may be a response to consumers' overestimation of use.

4. Graduated ETFs

As described in Part II.B, carriers have been moving from a time-invariant ETF to a time-variant, graduated ETF structure. This shift is a response to consumers' increased awareness and sensitivity to ETFs. The change in the design of ETF provisions is not a pure market solution. Rather, it is an example of how consumer learning and legal intervention can work in tandem to change business practices. The ETF story likely began with a small number of consumers who learned to appreciate the cost of ETFs and initiated litigation against the carriers. The threat of liability probably pushed carriers to adjust their ETF structure. But the litigation also facilitated greater awareness and sensitivity to ETFs among consumers. This adjusted demand was something that carriers could not ignore.

5. Open Access

The open-access movement in wireless telecommunications is a market-driven development that could reduce the costs of lock-in and handset-service bundling. While carriers are still the leading handset retailers, recent developments are diminishing their power such that it is likely that handset manufacturers will increasingly sell their products directly to consumers, who can use the phone on any network. Open access is not a response to consumer learning about biases and the cost of lock-in. Nevertheless, it is an important development that can reduce the costs of consumer biases.

89. FCC Fifteenth Report, above note 6, at 67; Jenna Wortham, "Cellphones Without Strings," *New York Times*, February 20, 2009, at B1 (describing the growing attraction of prepaid plans and citing Pali Research, an investment advisory firm, reporting that, in 2008, sales of prepaid plans grew 13 percent in North America, nearly three times faster than traditional postpaid plans).

B. Market Solutions and Consumer Welfare

The cellular service market seems quite responsive to demand generated by increasingly sophisticated consumers who learn from their mistakes. From a policy perspective, the question is to what extent market solutions mitigate the welfare costs identified in Part IV. As we have seen, the market promptly responds when consumers quickly learn about the implications of their mistakes, as they do when underestimated use leads to overage charges. But we have also seen that the market responds more sluggishly when learning is slower because the feedback mechanisms are weaker, as is the case with overestimated use.

While the market solutions described above have the potential to minimize the welfare costs of the identified behavioral market failure, in practice their impact is more limited. The reason is that many consumers do not take advantage of these market solutions. For example, unlimited plans with their high monthly fees are attractive only to a small fraction of heavy users. Prepaid plans are chosen by a minority of consumers. If consumers are not aware of their mistakes, they will not search for products that reduce the likelihood and consequences of those mistakes.

It is evident, then, that consumers learn and that the market responds to the demand generated by these more sophisticated consumers. But welfare costs are incurred during the interim period. To assess the magnitude of welfare costs, we need to ascertain the speed of consumer learning and of the market response to changing demand. Moreover, when consumers learn to overcome one mistake or when one hidden term becomes salient, carriers have an incentive to add a new non-salient term and to trigger a new kind of mistake. Even if consumers always catch up eventually, this cat-and-mouse game imposes welfare costs. Wireless operators are among the leading generators of consumer complaints.[90] Market solutions, while important, are clearly imperfect.

---

90. See Spencer E. Ante, "The Call for a Wireless Bill of Rights," *Business Week*, March 20, 2008, at 80, available at <http://www.businessweek.com/magazine/content/08_13/b4077080431634 .htm?campaign_id=rss_tech> (noting that, according to the Better Business Bureau, for each of the past three years, the wireless sector has received more complaints than any other industry). In the fourth quarter of 2011, the FCC received 21,076 complaints about wireless telecommunications. FCC, Quarterly Report on Informal Consumer Inquiries and Complaints for Fourth Quarter of Calendar Year 2010 August 15, 2011, available at <http://transition.fcc .gov/Daily_Releases/Daily_Business/2011/db0815/DOC-309057A1.pdf>.

VI. Policy Implications

The identified behavioral market failure imposes substantial welfare costs. Consumer learning coupled with market forces works to reduce these welfare costs but do not eliminate them. Can legal intervention help?

In this Part, we'll focus on disclosure mandates which, we believe, can help. We'll start with a brief survey of existing rules and regulations. We'll then outline several potential reforms.

A. Existing Regulations

Regulation of the consumer–carrier relationship is largely limited to the information that the provider must disclose to its consumers.[91] The FCC exercised its powers under the Communications Act by promulgating rules intended to prevent fraudulent behavior by telecommunications providers and by increasing the transparency of providers' billing practices. Providers must clearly identify the name of the service provider associated with each billed charge and prominently display a toll-free telephone number that customers can call to inquire about or dispute any charges.[92] Most importantly, since 2005, charges must "be accompanied by a brief, clear, non-misleading, plain-language description of the service or services rendered" that is "sufficiently clear in presentation and specific enough in content so that customers can accurately assess that the services for which they are billed correspond to those that they have requested and received, and that the costs assessed for those services conform to their understanding of the price charged."[93] The underlying rationale is "to allow consumers to better understand their telephone bills, compare service offerings, and thereby promote a more efficient competitive marketplace."[94] Further disclosure

---

91. Prohibitions against unfair or deceptive advertising should also be mentioned. On one important dimension, early termination fees, the law has moved beyond the regulation of information provided by carriers. See Oren Bar-Gill and Rebecca Stone, "Mobile Misperceptions" *Harv. J.L. & Tech.* 23 (2009) 49.
92. 47 C.F.R. § 64.2401(a)(1), (d) (2008).
93. 47 C.F.R. § 64.2401(b) (2008).
94. *In re Truth-in-Billing and Billing Format, Second Report and Order, Declaratory Ruling, and Second Further Notice of Proposed Rulemaking*, FCC CC Docket No. 98–170, 20 F.C.C.R. 6448, 6450 (2005) (hereinafter Truth-in-Billing 2005).

requirements are imposed at the state level. In particular, state laws regulate wireless line item charges—discrete charges that are separately identified on a consumer's bill.[95]

There have been calls for more stringent disclosure requirements. For instance, in 2003, Senator Charles Schumer introduced a bill—The Cell Phone User Bill of Rights—designed to improve disclosure and make it easier for consumers to choose among providers and plans. The bill sought to ensure that marketing materials and contracts clearly spell out the terms and conditions of service plans by requiring that all wireless contracts and marketing materials display a box containing standardized information on a number of key price dimensions, including the monthly fixed charge, per-minute charges for minutes not included in the plan, and the method for calculating minutes charged. Information on included weekday and day-time minutes and nights and weekend minutes, long-distance charges, roaming charges, incoming call charges, and charges for directory assistance would also have to be displayed. Termination and start-up fees and trial periods would have to be outlined as would any taxes and surcharges. In addition, the bill would authorize the FCC to monitor service quality industry-wide and make the resulting data publicly available to enable consumers to make informed choices among providers.[96] The bill has not been enacted into law.

In 2004, the California Public Utility Commission (CPUC) promulgated a similar set of rules. These regulations required wireless providers and other telecommunications operators to (1) ensure that subscribers receive clear and complete information about rates, terms, and conditions when customers sign up for the service; (2) produce clearly organized bills that only contain charges that the subscriber has authorized; and (3) list all federal, state, and local taxes, surcharges, and fees separately.[97] The regulations were suspended by the CPUC less than a year after their

95. *Id.*, at 6462.
96. Cell Phone User Bill of Rights, S. 1216, 108th Cong. (2003). A similar bill, the Wireless Consumer Protection and Community Broadband Empowerment Act, was proposed more recently by Representative Edward Markey. See Press Release, Office of Rep. Edward Markey, "Markey Holds Hearings on Draft Bill to Address Wireless Customer Protections," February 27, 2008, <http://markey.house.gov/index.php?option=com_contentandtask=viewandid=3 281andItemid=241>.
97. See Press Release, California Public Utilities Commission, PUC Sets Protection Rules for Consumers through Telecommunications Bill of Rights, May 27, 2, <http://docs.cpuc.ca .gov/published/NEWS_RELEASE/36910.htm>; Robert W. Hahn et al., "The Economics of 'Wireless Net Neutrality'" *J. Competition L. and Econ.* 3 (2007), 399, 413.

adoption, after the terms of two commissioners who supported the rules expired.[98] The drive for improved disclosure, however, is continuing: Twenty-two states have introduced some form of a Cell Phone User Bill of Rights.[99]

B. Rethinking Disclosure

1. From Product Attributes to Use Patterns

Consumers in the cellular service market learn, often quite effectively, to appreciate the implications of their biases and mistakes. Carriers respond with products that reduce resulting costs to consumers. While these market solutions are imperfect, the market's responsiveness suggests that the regulation best suited for the cellular service market would facilitate rather than inhibit market forces. It is, therefore, not surprising that many of the existing and proposed laws and regulations focus on the provision of information. We too focus on rules governing information provision; specifically, on disclosure regulation.

Our proposals, however, deviate from existing disclosure regulation and from other proposals for heightened disclosure regulation in an important way. Current disclosure regulation focuses on the disclosure of product-attribute information; in other words, information on the different features and price dimensions of cellular service. Our proposal emphasizes the disclosure of use pattern information—information on how the consumer will use the product.

The proposed Cell Phone User Bill of Rights illustrates the current exclusive focus on product-attribute information. It requires comprehensive disclosure of fees and charges. However, a truly informed choice cannot be based on product attributes alone. To fully appreciate the benefits and costs of a cellular service contract, consumers must combine product-attribute information with use-pattern information. To assess the costs of overage fees, it is not enough to know the per-minute charges for minutes not included in the plan (as proposed in the bill); consumers must also know the probability that they will exceed the plan limit and by how much. Likewise, to assess the benefit of unlimited night and weekend calling, consum-

---

98. "California Suspends Wireless Bill of Rights," *ConsumerAffairs.com*, January 28, 2005, <http://www.consumeraffairs.com/news04/2005/cpuc_wireless.html>.
99. See Ante, above note 20.

ers must also know how many "night" and "weekend" minutes they will use as well as the precise contractual definition of "night" and "weekend." Use-pattern information can be as important as product-attribute information. The disclosure regime should be redesigned to ensure that consumers have both categories of information.

2. Disclosing Use-Pattern Information

Conventional wisdom assumes that sellers have better information on product attributes while buyers have better information about use patterns. If a buyer has better information about how she will use the product, then it makes no sense to require sellers to disclose use-pattern information. The best that sellers can do is to provide general statistical information on product use. The buyer, on the other hand, has specific information on how *he or she*, not the average consumer, will use the product—or so the conventional account goes.

While the conventional wisdom is correct in many markets, it is not correct in the cellular service market. Carriers have valuable statistical use-pattern information that is not available to subscribers. More importantly, they have individualized use-pattern data, collected over the course of their relationships with subscribers. As suggested below, disclosing this information can empower consumers and facilitate the efficient functioning of the cellular service market.

a. Average-Use Disclosures

Carriers collect and analyze enormous amounts of use-pattern information. They know how the average subscriber will use his or her cell phone. This statistical use information is not limited to averages taken across the entire subscriber population. Carriers have, and can be required to disclose, average-use information for subgroups of consumers who are similar (in terms of demographic characteristics, product choices made, and so forth) to the consumer receiving the use-pattern disclosure. As the subgroup over which the averaging takes place becomes smaller, intra-group heterogeneity decreases, and the value of the average-use information to the individual consumer increases. However, excessively small subgroups may also be undesirable. Averaging over large numbers has the benefit of reducing randomness. Reducing the size of the subgroup reduces this benefit. The optimal size of a subgroup is the product of a tradeoff between the benefit of reducing heterogeneity and the benefit of reducing randomness.

One potentially beneficial average-use disclosure would target the misperception of use levels that underlies three-part tariffs by requiring carriers to disclose the average overage charges that consumers pay. Carriers could also be required to disclose the percentage of consumers who use, for example, 50 percent or less of their allotted minutes, or the percentage of consumers who would save money if they switched to a lower fixed-fee, lower-limit plan. Consumers' underestimation of the cost of lock-in could be addressed by requiring carriers to provide information about the percentage of consumers who stop using their phones before the end of the lock-in period but continue paying for them. Carriers could also be required to disclose the percentage of consumers who broke the contract and paid the exit penalty.[100]

b. Individual-Use Disclosures

Despite their potential benefits, average-use disclosures suffer from important shortcomings. Even when averaging across smaller subgroups of consumers, substantial heterogeneity remains. Heterogeneity limits the value of average-use information to any individual consumer. Moreover, heterogeneity allows optimistic consumers to further discount the value of average-use information. Most people think that their driving skills are above average, even though most people cannot be better than average (given a symmetrical distribution of ability about the mean). Similarly, optimistic consumers might all think that they will never exceed the plan limit, even when provided with information that the average consumer pays $50 a month in overage fees.

Fortunately, use-pattern disclosure in the cellular service market need not be limited to average-use information. The long-term relationship between carriers and consumers allows for the provision of individualized use-pattern information.[101]

Individual-use disclosure can reduce consumers' misperception of use levels. Carriers already provide consumers with individualized information on overage charges. Arguably, this disclosure reduced consumers' underestimation of use and contributed to the demand to eliminate overage fees—a

---

100. Both of these disclosures are incomplete measures of the cost of lock-in since they do not capture consumers who continue using their phones only because they are locked in.
101. Of course, consumers have access to the same use-pattern information. But while providers save the information and analyze it, consumers tend not to notice it and even if they do notice it, they tend to forget it.

demand satisfied by unlimited calling plans. A parallel disclosure would help reduce the costs consumers incur due to overestimation of use. Carriers should be required to disclose the number of minutes used and the effective per-minute price, calculated as the monthly fixed fee divided by the number of minutes used.

Individual-use disclosure can also help consumers evaluate the costs and benefits of other plan features. Carriers could be required to disclose the number of night and weekend minutes used and the costs saved by the unlimited nights and weekends feature. They could also be required to disclose the number of minutes used in in-network calling and the associated savings. Similarly, Verizon, which offers unlimited calls to five numbers, could be required to disclose the number of minutes used calling these five numbers, along with the costs saved by this feature.

The proposed individual-use disclosures should be provided on the monthly bill and in aggregate form on a year-end summary to account for month-to-month variations. Lawmakers should also revisit another key feature of the proposed Cell Phone User Bill of Rights. This bill focuses on disclosures provided at the time of contracting, which makes perfect sense when carriers are disclosing product-attribute information. Individual-use information, on the other hand, is not available to carriers when a new subscriber signs up for service. Continuous disclosures throughout the life of the contract are equally important.

3. Combining Use-Pattern Information with Product-Attribute Information

We have focused on the disclosure of use-pattern information as opposed to product-attribute disclosures. But the more appealing proposals argue for total cost disclosures, which combine both. For example, the disclosure of effective per-minute prices combines product-attribute information (the monthly fixed fee) and use-pattern information (the number of minutes used).

Taking total cost disclosure one step further, carriers could be required to disclose a comprehensive TCO figure for their calling plans—the total amount paid, or to be paid, by a consumer, including overage charges, on a yearly basis or over the duration of a plan. For new subscribers, this TCO figure can be based on average-use information. For existing subscribers, who are considering whether to renew or switch plans or even switch carriers, the TCO figure can be based on individual-use information.

TCO information for a single plan, specifically for the subscriber's current plan, may be insufficient. To effectively compare different plans, the subscriber needs TCO information on all plans. Carriers could be required to provide TCO information for their entire menu of plans or, at least, for several main offerings. Perhaps a better solution would be to require carriers to disclose only the plan with the lowest TCO for the prospective subscriber and for the existing subscriber whose use patterns have changed. For example, the monthly bill or yearly summary can include a notice if an alternative plan would have a lower TCO than the subscriber's current plan.[102]

TCO disclosures are simple and thus useful even to the imperfectly rational consumer. An alternative paradigm focuses on more complex and comprehensive disclosures for sophisticated intermediaries, and carriers rather than consumers. Specifically, carriers could be required to provide comprehensive use-pattern information in electronic form. Consumers would not use this information themselves. Rather, they would forward it to intermediaries that provide comparison-shopping services. Such intermediaries already exist. Companies like BillShrink and Validas promise to find the right plan for each consumer.[103] But they currently do this based on minimal, usually self-reported, use-pattern information, which, as we have seen, is often inaccurate. If carriers were required to provide comprehensive use-pattern information in electronic form, intermediaries such as BillShrink or Validas could combine this information with the product-attribute information that they already have and find the carrier and plan with the lowest TCO for each individual consumer.

Comprehensive use-pattern information disclosed in electronic form can be helpful even without the intervention of intermediaries. The consumer could provide the information to competing carriers, soliciting individualized TCO figures from each. Consumers could then choose the carrier and plan with the lowest TCO, given their individual use patterns.

102. Utility companies in Germany have voluntarily adopted an even more pro-consumer policy. At the end of the year they retroactively match each consumer to the service plan under which the consumer pays the lowest total price given her use over the past year. See Ian Ayres and Barry Nalebuff, "In Praise of Honest Pricing", *M.I.T. Sloan Mgmt. Rev.* 45 (2003), 24, 27. A similar idea is already being applied by cell phone companies in other countries. See, e.g., Orange.fr, "Forfait Ajustable Pro," <http://sites.orange.fr/boutique/files/html/pe_packpro_forfait_ajustable.html> (Orange in France offers to charge the subscriber at the end of the month according to the plan that best fits the subscriber's usage during that month).

103. "What is BillShrink?," <http://www.billshrink.com/about/> (last visited September 20, 2011); "About Validas," <http://www.validas.com/about.aspx> (last visited September 20, 2011).

To sum up, consumer choice should be guided by information about the total cost of the product. Conventional wisdom assumes that consumers have better information about their own use patterns and thus need only product-attribute disclosures to calculate total cost. We have seen that carriers may well have better use-pattern information, as well as better product-attribute information. Carriers can more easily combine the two categories of information into a total cost disclosure. Alternatively, carriers can provide comprehensive use-pattern information in electronic form, so that intermediaries, or competing sellers, can use it to calculate TCO figures.

4. Real-Time Disclosure

In addition to disclosures made at the time of purchase and after-the-fact disclosures in the monthly bill and/or in a year-end summary, individual-use information can and should be provided in real time. The challenge of keeping track of cumulative use has increased with the invention of multiple-limit plans. For example, plans with different limits for peak and off-peak minutes (as well as limits for messaging and data services) have increased the chance that consumers inadvertently exceed their plan limits. To help consumers avoid this, carriers should be required to notify their subscribers when they are about to exceed the plan limit. A consumer receiving such notification may well decide to cut the conversation short, switch to a land line, or postpone the conversation until off-peak hours.

In late 2010, the FCC proposed new regulations that mandated such real-time disclosures. Concerned about what it terms "bill shock"—unexpected increases in the monthly bill that come from high roaming fees or exceeding a monthly allotment of voice minutes, texts, or data consumption—the FCC, in its proposed rules, would require carriers to provide usage alerts in real time.[104] The proposed regulations were put on hold when the carriers, through their trade group CTIA, agreed to voluntarily implement the real-time disclosures.[105]

---

104. See FCC, News Release: "FCC Proposes Rules to Help Mobile Phone Users Avoid 'Bill Shock'," October 14, 2010, available at <http://www.fcc.gov/rulemaking/10-207>; (last visited: September 21, 2011). Similar rules already exist in Europe. While some U.S. carriers voluntarily provide certain usage alerts, the FCC found that "[t]he tools in place to eliminate bill shock vary widely between service providers and type of service, and can be difficult to find. Most of the alerts that are offered do not cover all services or are not sent before the overage charges are incurred." *Id.*

105. See FCC Chairman Julius Genachowski, Remarks at Bill Shock Event, Brookings Institution, Washington, DC, October 17, 2011, available at <http://www.fcc.gov/document/chairman-genachowski-remarks-bill-shock-event>; (last visited): November 17, 2011).

5. Mobile Disclosure

Traditional disclosure mandates require sellers to provide information printed on a piece of paper. Mobile technology opens the door to a variety of additional, more innovative disclosure methods. For example, carriers can provide information via voice messages, text messages, and even multimedia messages. These modes of disclosure may be more effective than the traditional paper disclosure.

6. Enhanced Disclosure in Action

Some carriers are already providing product-use information. "Usage analysis" functions are beginning to appear on some carriers' secured websites. AT&T's capped data plans offer usage tracking and alert options. And there are other examples.[106] Certain carriers even provide information that combines product-use and product-attribute information. For instance, AT&T offers Personal Plan Review, which lets you know if your plan fits your usage or if you should switch to a different AT&T plan. Moreover, there are smartphone applications that can track usage. Smartphones can even serve as virtual intermediaries, providing a recommendation on the best available plan in the market by combining the subscriber's individual use information with rate information available online. These developments should be applauded. They provide further evidence that market forces can work to the benefit of consumers. Still, as the FCC observed in the "bill shock" context, these voluntarily provided, enhanced disclosures vary widely between service providers and types of service and, in many cases, are insufficient. A regulatory nudge is probably required.[107]

Conclusion

The cellular service market, boasting annual revenues exceeding $180 billion, is one of the largest and most important consumer markets in the United States. While cell phones provide obvious benefits to consumers, cellular service contracts, designed in response to consumer biases, hurt

---

106. See Amy Schatz and Sara Silver, "A Plan to Ease the Shock of Cellphone Bills," *Wall Street Journal*, May 12, 2010; David Pogue, "AT&T's Capped Data Plan Could Save You Money," *New York Times*, June 3, 2010.

107. Indeed, in the "bill shock" context, such a regulatory nudge, or the threat of a regulatory nudge, spurred the industry into action. See above Sec.VI.B.4.

consumers and reduce social welfare. Mistakes in plan choice, triggered by a key contractual design feature—the three-part tariff—cost consumers over $13 billion annually. Consumer welfare and market efficiency are further reduced by the ETF-enforced lock-in feature and by the sheer complexity of the cell phone contract, which also respond to the imperfect rationality of consumers. Since consumer mistakes often result from consumers' misperceptions about their own future use patterns, disclosure mandates should require carriers to provide consumers with use-pattern information. This information should be combined with product-attribute information in TCO or total-annual-cost disclosures and made available in electronic, database form to facilitate the work of intermediaries.

Conclusion

We are all consumers. The contracts discussed in this book are part of our everyday experience. We enjoy the benefits from the products and services that these contracts make possible. And we bear the costs created by these contracts, when they are designed to exploit our cognitive biases. Legal policy should strive to minimize the costs, while preserving the benefits. This book has set out to further our understanding of consumer contracts and to provide guidance for optimal regulation of these contracts.

I conclude by noting three directions for future research and study:

(1) more contracts;
(2) more countries; and
(3) more regulatory strategies.

After developing, in Chapter 1, a general framework for the study of consumer contracts and their regulation, I proceeded to apply this framework in three consumer markets—credit cards (in Chapter 2), mortgages (in Chapter 3), and cell phones (in Chapter 4). The case-study chapters served a dual purpose: First, they presented a detailed analysis of three important consumer markets, discussing specific legal policy solutions in each market. Second, they demonstrated how the general theoretical framework (of Chapter 1) can be fruitfully applied to important real-world problems.

The second purpose is of particular importance for future research. One book cannot provide a comprehensive analysis of all consumer contracts. But it can lay out a general theoretical approach and show how the theory applies to an important subset of contracts. Future research can then focus on other consumer markets and contracts. Among the leading candidates for such future research are insurance contracts and contracts for transportation services.

The domain of analysis can also be expanded geographically. The in-depth analysis in the case-study chapters focused on the United States. While some results from the analysis of the U.S. cell phone market, for example, are relevant to cell phone markets in other countries, other results are not. As emphasized at the outset, to fully understand the dynamics of contract design and the potential role of legal intervention, a market-specific analysis is required. This is true for the different consumer markets in the U.S. It is similarly true when moving from, say, the U.S. cell phone market to the cell phone market in the U.K. (or in the EU). The general framework developed in this book applies wherever sophisticated sellers design con-tracts for less sophisticated consumers. But a market-specific analysis is needed to derive operational results from the general framework.

Finally, future research should explore the range of legal policy strategies that can be used to correct the behavioral market failure—the distortions created when sellers design their contracts in response to the imperfect rationality of their customers. This book focused on one regulatory strategy: disclosure mandates. In many markets, disclosure is probably the right place to start. But policymakers concerned about market failure should consider the full range of available regulatory strategies. Consumer education can supplement disclosure mandates. Other soft-paternalism strategies include setting optimally designed default rules and safe harbors. And, in certain cases, stronger interventions, such as banning of abusive contracts and prac-tices, may be justified.

Consumer contracts are ubiquitous. They produce substantial benefits, but can also cause substantial harm. A better understanding of consumer contracts, and how they can be improved, should be of interest to policy-makers, as well as to us consumers. This book is an attempt to advance our understanding of consumer contracts.

Bibliography

Agarwal, S., Amromin, G., Ben-David, I., Chomsisengphet, S., and Evanoff, D. "Can Mandated Financial Counseling Improve Mortgage Decision-Making? Evidence from a Natural Experiment." (2009) *Fisher Coll. of Bus. Working Paper No. 2008-03-019.*

—— —— "Learning to Cope: Voluntary Financial Education Programs and Loan Performance During a Housing Crisis." (2009) *Charles A. Dice Center Working Paper No. 2009-23.*

Agarwal, S., Driscoll, J., Gabaix, X., and Laibson, D. "Learning in the Credit Card Market." February 8, 2008.

—— —— "The Age of Reason: Financial Decisions over the Life-Cycle and Implications for Regulation." (2009) *Brookings Papers on Economic Activity.* Issue 2.

Driscoll, J., and Laibson, D. "Optimal Mortgage Refinancing: A Closed Form Solution." (2007) *NBER Working Paper No. 13487.*

Ainslie, G. "Derivation of 'Rational' Economic Behavior from Hyperbolic Discount Curves." *Am. Econ. Rev,* 81(1991). 334.

Amromin, G., Chunyan Huang, J., Sialm, C., and Zhong, E. "Complex Mortgages." (2010) *FRB of Chicago Working Paper No. 2010-17.*

Andrews, E.L. "Fed and Regulators Shrugged as the Subprime Crisis Spread: Analysis Finds Trail of Warnings on Loans." *New York Times,* December 18, 2007.

Angeletos, G.-M., et al. "The Hyperbolic Consumption Model: Calibration, Simulation, and Empirical Evaluation." *J. Econ. Perspect,* 15 (2001). 47.

Ante, S.E. "The Call for a Wireless Bill of Rights." *Business Week,* March 20, 2008.

—— "Verizon Embraces Google's Android." *Business Week,*. December 3, 2007.

Apgar, W.C., and Duda, M. Homeownership Pres. Found. "Collateral Damage: The Municipal Impact of Today's Mortgage Foreclosure Boom." (2005).

—— and Herbert, C.E., U.S. Dep't of Hous. and Urban Dev. "Subprime Lending and Alternative Financial Service Providers: A Literature Review and Empirical Analysis." (2006).

Appelbaum, B., and Nakashima, E. "Banking Regulator Played Advocate over Enforcer: Agency Let Lenders Grow out of Control, Then Fail." *Wash. Post.,* November 23, 2008.

Armstrong, M. "Interactions between Competition and Consumer Policy." *Competition Policy International.* 4 (2008). 97.

AT&T. *Cell Phones, Cell Phone Plans, and Wireless Accessories—from AT&T.*

—— *Plan Terms.*

Ausubel, L.M. *Adverse Selection in the Credit Card Market.* (1999) 20 (unpublished manuscript).

—— "Credit Card Defaults, Credit Card Profits, and Bankruptcy." *Am. Bankr. L.J.,* 71 (1997). 249.

—— "The Credit Card Industry: A History, by Lewis Mandell." *J. Econ. Lit.,* 30 (1992). 1517.

—— "The Failure of Competition in the Credit Card Market." *Am. Econ. Rev.,* 81 (1991). 50.

Avery, R.B., Brevoort, K.P., and Canner, G.B. "Opportunities and Issues in Using HMDA Data." *J. Real Est. Res.,* 29 (2007). 351.

Ayres, I., and Nalebuff, B. "In Praise of Honest Pricing." *M.I.T. Sloan Mgmt. Rev.,* 45 (2003). 24.

Bakos, Y., Marotta-Wurgler, F., and Trossen, D.R. "Does Anyone Read the Fine Print? Testing a Law and Economics Approach to Standard Form Contracts." (2009) *NYU Law and Economics Research Paper No. 09-40.*

Bar-Gill, O. "Bundling and Consumer Misperception." *U. Chi. L. Rev.,* 73 (2006). 33.

—— and Board, O. "Product Use Information and the Limits of Voluntary Disclosure." *American Law and Economics Review.,* 14 (2012). 235.

—— and Bubb, R. "Credit Card Pricing: The CARD Act and Beyond." forthcoming in *Cornell L. Rev.*

—— and Ferrari, F. "Informing Consumers About Themselves." *Erasmus Law Review.,* 3 (2010). 93.

—— and Stone, R. "Pricing Misperceptions: Explaining Pricing Structure in the Cell Phone Service Market." forthcoming in *J. Empirical Legal Stud.,* Vol 9.

—— and Warren, E. "Making Credit Safer." *U. Pa. L. Rev.,* 157 (2008). 1.

Barr, M.S., Mullainathan, S., and Shafir, E. *Behaviorally Informed Financial Services Regulation.* New America Foundation, 2008.

——————— "Behaviorally Informed Home Mortgage Credit Regulation." in Belsky, E.S., and Retsinas, N.P. (eds.). *Understanding Consumer Credit.* Brooking Press, 2009.

Barr, M.S., Dokko, J.K., and Keys, B.J. "Who Gets Lost in the Subprime Mortgage Fallout: Homeowners in Low-and Moderate-Income Neighborhoods." (April 2008).

Beales, H., Craswell, R., and Salop, S. "The Efficient Regulation of Consumer Information." *J. L. & Econ.,* 24 (1981). 491.

Been, V. Testimony Before Committee on Oversight and Government Reform Subcommittee on Domestic Policy. "External Effects of Concentrated Mortgage Foreclosures: Evidence from New York City." (May 21, 2008).

Belsky, E.S., and Retsinas, N.P. (eds.). *Understanding Consumer Credit.* Brooking Press, 2009.

Ben-Shahar, O., and Schneider, C.E. *More Than You Wanted To Know: The Failure of Mandated Disclosure.* Princeton University Press, forthcoming.

Benartzi, S., and Thaler, R.H. "Heuristics and Biases in Retirement Savings Behavior." *J. Econ. Persp.*, 21 (2007) 81.

Bergstresser, D., and Beshears, J. "Who Selected Adjustable-Rate Mortgages: Evidence from the 1989–2007 Surveys of Consumer Finances." (2010) *HBS Working Paper 10-083*.

Bernanke, B.S. Speech at the Independent Community Bankers of America Annual Convention, Orlando, Florida: "Reducing Preventable Mortgage Foreclosures." (March 4, 2008).

—— Speech at the Women in Housing and Finance and Exchequer Club Joint Luncheon, Washington, D.C.: "Financial Markets, the Economic Outlook, and Monetary Policy." (January 10, 2008).

—— Testimony Before the Committee on the Budget, U.S. House of Representatives: The Economic Outlook. (January 17, 2008).

Bethel, J.E., Ferrell, A., and Hu, G. "Legal and Economic Issues in Litigation Arising from the 2007–2008 Credit Crisis." (2008) *Harvard Law and Econ. Discussion Paper No. 212*.

BillShrink.com. *Cell Phone Plans, Compare Best Cellular Service Carrier Deals on BillShrink*.

Blumenstein, R. "The Business-Package Plan: AT&T Sees Wireless as the Key to its Broader Strategy of Bundling Its Services." *Wall Street Journal*, September 20, 1999.

Blyskal, J. "Mostly Talk: New Unlimited Cell Plans Won't Pay for Most." *Consumer-Reports.org.*, February 26, 2008.

Boehm, T.P., and Schlottmann, A. "Mortgage Pricing Differentials Across Hispanic, African-American, and White Households: Evidence from the American Housing Survey." *Cityscape: J. Pol'y Dev. and Res.*, No. 2 (2007). 9.

Bond, P., Musto, D.K., and Yilmaz, B. "Predatory Mortgage Lending." (2008) *FRB of Philadelphia Working Paper No. 08-24*. 183.

Bostic, R.W., et al. "State and Local Anti-Predatory Lending Laws: The Effect of Legal Enforcement Mechanisms." *J. Econ. and Bus.*, 60 (2008). 47.

Brevoort, K.P., and Cooper, C.R. "Foreclosure's Wake: The Credit Experiences of Individuals Following Foreclosure." (October 12, 2010).

Brito, D.L., and Hartley, P.R. "Consumer Rationality and Credit Cards." *J. Pol. Econ'y*, 103 (1995). 400.

Bubb, R., and Kaufman, A. "Consumer Biases and Firm Ownership." (2009) Working Paper.

Bucks, B., and Pence, K. "Do Borrowers Know their Mortgage Terms?" *J. Urban Econ.*, 64 (2008). 218.

—— et al. "Changes in U.S. Family Finances from 2004 to 2007: Evidence from the Survey of Consumer Finances." *Fed. Reserve Bull.*, vol. 95 (February 2009).

Bureau of the Census. *Statistical Abstract of the United States*: 2011.

Busse, M.R. "Multi-market Contact and Price Coordination in the Cellular Telephone Industry." *J. Econ. and Mgmt. Strategy*, 9 (2008–9) 287.

Cagan, C.L., First Am. CoreLogic, Inc. *Mortgage Payment Reset: The Issue and the Impact*. (2007).

Calem, P.S., and LaCour-Little, M. "Risk-Based Capital Requirements for Mortgage Loans." (2001). *Bd. of Governors of the Fed. Reserve Sys. Fin. and Econ. Discussion Series Paper No. 2001-60.*

——et al. "Switching Costs and Adverse Selection in the Market for Credit Cards:
New Evidence." *J. Banking and Fin.,* 30 (2006). 1653.

Camerer, C., et al. "Regulation for Conservatives: Behavioral Economics and the
Case for 'Asymmetric Paternalism' " *U. Penn. L. Rev.,* 151 (2003). 1211.

Campbell, J.Y. "Household Finance." *J. Fin,.* 61 (2006). 1553.

CardFlash.

——"BofA Basic." September 17, 2009.

——"BofA Changes." August 18, 2009.

——"BofA Clarity." November 30, 2009.

——"CARD Act Impact." November 10, 2009.

——"Chase Pricing." November 20, 2007.

——"Citi Offers Credit with Single APR and No Late Fees." July 26, 2011.

——"Consumer Reports." October 20, 2010.

——"Debit Cards." August 18, 2008.

——"Debit Overdraft." July 12, 2007.

——"Debit Rewards." August 28, 2009.

——"Dec Card Offers." December 23, 2008.

——"Fee Factor 08." January 14, 2009.–3, 95–6.

——"Fee Income." January 11, 2010.–4.

——"Fees and Recession." December 19, 2008.

——"Merchant Fees." January 13, 2009.

——"Minimum Payments." December 17, 2008.

——"Monthly Payment Rates Edge Up Slightly." March 18, 2009.

——"Payment Rates Hit a Four-Year Low in July." August 27, 2008.

——"Reward Card Analysis." June 2, 2008.

——"Reward Card Review." June 2, 2008.

——"Straight Talk." February 23, 2010.

——"Visa Debit." May 5, 2009.

Case, K.E., and Shiller, R.J. "Home Buyer Survey Results 1988–2006." unpublished
paper, Yale University, 2006.

————"Is There a Bubble in the Housing Market?" (2003) *Brookings Papers on
Econ. Activity.* No. 2.

————"The Behavior of Home Buyers in Boom and Post-Boom Markets."
New. Eng. Econ. Rev., (November–December 1988) 28.

Center for Am. Progress, et al. Frequency Questionnaire. (2006).

Center for Customer Relationship Management. *Telecom Dataset.*

Center for Responsible Lending. "A Snapshot of the Subprime Market."

——"Mortgage Lending Overview."

——"Priceless or Just Expensive? The Use of Penalty Rates in the Credit Card
Industry." (2008).

——"Subprime Spillover: Foreclosures Cost Neighbors $202 Billion: 40.6 Million Homes Lose $5,000 on Average." (2008).

——"What's Draining Your Wallet? The Real Cost of Credit Card Cash Advances." (2008).

Chakravorti, S., and Emmons, W.R. "Who Pays for Credit Cards?" (2001) *Fed. Reserve Bank of Chi. Emerging Payments Occasional Paper Series.* No. 1.

Chan, S., Gedal, M., Been, V., and Haughwout, A. "The Role of Neighborhood Characteristics in Mortgage Default Risk: Evidence from New York City." (2011) *NYU Working Paper.*

Chang, R. "Proof that Handset Brands Help Sell Wireless Plans." *RCR Wireless.* October 28, 2008.

Cheng, R. "Business Technology: Virgin Mobile to Join Flat Rate Phones Frenzy." *Wall Street Journal.* June 24, 2008.

Ching, A., and Hayashi, F. "Payment Card Rewards Programs and Consumer Payment Choice." (2008).

Civils, W., and Gongloff, M. "Subprime Shakeout: Lenders that Have Closed Shop, Been Acquired or Stopped Loans." *Wall Street Journal Online.*

Collins, J.M. "Education Levels and Mortgage Application Outcomes: Evidence of Financial Literacy." (2009) *Institute for Research on Poverty Discussion Paper No. 1369-09.*

Comptroller of the Currency. "Advisory Letter: Credit Card Practices." (September 14, 2004).

——"Guidance on Unfair or Deceptive Acts or Practices." *Advisory Letter No. AL 2002-3* (March 22, 2002).

——*Truth in Lending: Comptroller's Handbook.* (2006).

Congressional Budget Office. *The Budget and Economic Outlook: Fiscal Years 2008 to 2018.* (2008).

ConsumerAffairs.com. "California Suspends Wireless Bill of Rights." January 28, 2005.

Consumers Union. *Women in the Subprime Market.* October 2002.

Courchane, M.J., Surette, B.J., and Zorn, P.M. "Subprime Borrowers: Mortgage Transitions and Outcomes." *J. Real Est. Fin. and Econ.,* 29 (2004). 365.

Craswell, R. "Taking Information Seriously: Misrepresentation and Nondisclosure in Contract Law and Elsewhere." *Va. L. Rev.,* 92 (2006). 565.

Credit Suisse, *Mortgage Liquidity du Jour: Underestimated No More.* (2007).

Crockett, R.O. "The Last Monopolist." *Business Week,* April 12, 1999.

CTIA. "Early Termination Fees Equal Lower Consumer Rates." *CITA.org.* April 2006.

De Long, J.B., et al. "Noise Trader Risk in Financial Markets." *J. Pol. Econ'y,* 98 (1990). 703.

————"Positive Feedback Investment Strategies and Destabilizing Rational Speculation." *J. Fin.,* 45 (1990). 379.

DellaVigna, S., and Malmendier, U. "Contract Design and Self-Control: Theory and Evidence." *Quar. J. Econ.,* 119 (2004). 353.

————— "Paying Not to Go to the Gym." *Amer. Econ. Rev.,* 96 (2006). 694.

Dēmos, "The Plastic Safety Net: The Reality Behind Debt In America." (2005).

Demyanyk, Y., and Van Hemert, O. "Understanding the Subprime Mortgage Crisis." *Rev. Fin. Stud.,* 24 (2011). 1848.

Department of Business Innovation and Skills and Cabinet Office Behavioural Insights Team. *Better Choices: Better Deals.,* April 13, 2011.

Douglass, E. "The Cutting Edge Special Report: Wireless Communications; "Pre-paid." Idea is Catching On in U.S. Market." *L.A. Times,* March 15, 1999.

Draut, T., and Silva, J. *Borrowing to Make Ends Meet: The Growth of Credit Card Debt in the '90s.* Dēmos, 2003.

Duhigg, C. "What Does Your Credit-Card Company Know About You?" *New York Times,* May 17, 2009.

Durkin, T.A. "Consumers and Credit Disclosures: Credit Cards and Credit Insurance." *Fed. Reserve Bull.,* (April 2002).

————— "Credit Cards: Use and Consumer Attitudes, 1970-2000." *Fed. Reserve Bull.,* vol. 98 (September 2000).

Edwards, C., and Crockett, R.O. "New Music Phones—Without the i." *Business Week.,* April 16, 2007.

Eggert, K. "Limiting Abuse and Opportunism by Mortgage Servicers." *Housing Pol'y Debate,* 15 (2007). 753.

Eliaz, K., and Spiegler, R. "Consumer Optimism and Price Discrimination." *Theoretical Economics,* 3 (2008). 459.

————— "Contracting with Diversely Naïve Agents." *Rev. Econ. Stud.,* 73 (2006). 689.

Elliehausen, G., Staten, M.E., and Steinbuks, J. "The Effect of Prepayment Penalties on the Pricing of Subprime Mortgages." *J. Econ. and Bus.,* 60 (2008). 33.

Ellis, D. "The Effect of Consume Interest Rate Deregulation on Credit Card Volumes, Charge-Offs and the Personal Bankruptcy Rate." (1998) 98-05 *Bank Trends.*

Ellison, G. "A Model of Add-On Pricing." *Q.J. Econ.,* 120 (2005). 585.

————— "Bounded Rationality in Industrial Organization." in R. Blundell, W. K. Newey and T. Persson (eds.). *Advances in Economics and Econometrics: Theory and Applications, Ninth World Congress.* Vol. II, ch. 5 (2006).

————— and Ellison, S.F. "Search, Obfuscation, and Price Elasticities on the Internet." *Econometrica,* 77 (2009). 427.

Elstrom, P. "Mike Armstrong's Strong Showing." *Business Week,* January 25, 1999.

————— "Wireless With All The Trimmings." *Business Week,* November 16, 1998.

Engel, K.C., and McCoy, P.A. "A Tale of Three Markets: The Law and Economics of Predatory Lending." *Tex. L. Rev.,* 80 (2002). 1255.

————— "Turning a Blind Eye: Wall Street Finance of Predatory Lending." *Fordham L. Rev.,* 75 (2007). 2039.

Epstein, R.A. "Second-Order Rationality." in E. J. McCaffery and J. Slemrod (eds). *Behavioral Public Finance,* (2006) 355.

Eskridge, W.N., Jr. "One Hundred Years of Ineptitude: The Need for Mortgage Rules Consonant with the Economic and Psychological Dynamics of the Home Sale and Loan Transaction." *Va. L. Rev.,* 70 (1984). 1083.

Evans, D.S., and Schmalensee, R. *Paying with Plastic.* MIT Press, 1999. 211.

Family Hous. Fund. "Cost Effectiveness of Mortgage Foreclosure Prevention: Summary of Findings." (1998).

Farrell, J., and Klemperer, P. "Coordination and Lock-In: Competition with Switching Costs and Network Effects." (2007) in Armstrong, M., and Porter, R. (eds.). *Handbook of Industrial Organization.* Vol. 3 (2007).

FCC. "Annual Report and Analysis of Competitive Market Conditions With Respect to Commercial Mobile Services, Fifteenth Report." (2011) FCC 11-103.

—— "Annual Report and Analysis of Competitive Market Conditions With Respect to Commercial Mobile Services, Thirteenth Report." (2009) 24 F.C.C.R. 6185.

—— "Annual Report and Analysis of Competitive Market Conditions With Respect to Commercial Mobile Services, Twelfth Report." (2008) FCC 08-28.

—— "Annual Report and Analysis of Competitive Market Conditions With Respect to Commercial Mobile Services, Eleventh Report." (2006) 21 F.C.C.R. 10947.

—— "Annual Report and Analysis of Competitive Market Conditions With Respect to Commercial Mobile Services, Tenth Report." (2005) 20 F.C.C.R. 15908.

—— News Release: "FCC Proposes Rules to Help Mobile Phone Users Avoid 'Bill Shock'." October 14, 2010.

—— "Notice of Inquiry: Consumer Information and Disclosure." CG Docket No. 09-158, released August 28, 2009.

—— "Quarterly Report on Informal Consumer Inquiries and Complaints for Fourth Quarter of Calendar Year 2010." August 15, 2011.

Federal Reserve Bank of Boston. "Consumer Behavior and Payment Choice: 2006 Conference Summary." (2007) *Public Policy Discussion Paper 07-4.*

Federal Reserve Board. "Credit Card Lending: Account Management and Loss Allowance Guidance." SR Letter 03-1. January 8, 2003.

—— "Credit Cards—Fees."

—— "Credit Cards—Interest Rates."

—— "Profitability of Credit Card Operations of Depository Institutions."

—— "Report to the Congress on Practices of the Consumer Credit Industry in Soliciting and Extending Credit and their Effects on Consumer Debt and Insolvency." June 2006. 108.

—— "Report to the Congress on the Profitability of Credit Card Operations of Depository Institutions." June 2009.

—— "What You Need to Know: New Credit Card Rules Effective February 22."

—— "What You Need to Know: New Overdraft Rules for Debit and ATM Cards."

—— and U.S. Dep't of Hous. and Urban Dev. *Joint Report to the Congress Concerning Reform to the Truth and Lending Act and the Real Estate Settlement Procedures Act.* (1998).

——et al. *Interest-Only Mortgage Payments and Payment-Option ARMs—Are They for You?* (2006).

Feinberg, R.A. "Credit Cards as Spending Facilitating Stimuli: A Conditioning Interpretation." *J. Consumer Res.,* 12 (1986). 384.

Fishbein, A.J., and Woodall, P. "Women Are Prime Targets for Subprime Lending: Women Are Disproportionately Represented in High-Cost Mortgage Market." (2006).

Ford, G.S., Koutsky, T.M., and Spiwak, L.J. "Wireless Net Neutrality: From Carterfone to Cable Boxes." *Phoenix Ctr. Pol'y Bull.,* 17 (April 2007). 2.

Forrester, J.P. "Still Mortgaging the American Dream: Predatory Lending, Preemption, and Federally Supported Lenders." *U. Cin. L. Rev.,* 74 (2006). 1303.

Fox, J.T. "Consolidation in the Wireless Phone Industry." (2005) *Net Inst. Working Paper No. 05-13.*

Frank, J.M. "Dodging Reform: As Some Credit Card Abuses Are Outlawed, New Ones Proliferate." Center for Responsible Lending, 2009.

Fratantoni, M., et al. Mortgage Bankers Ass'n. *The Residential Mortgage Market and Its Economic Context in 2007.* MBA Research Monograph Series, 2007.

Freddie Mac. *Automated Underwriting: Making Mortgage Lending Simpler and Fairer for America's Families.* (1996).

——"Half of Subprime Loans Categorized as 'A' Quality." *Inside B&C Lending.* June 10, 1996.

Frederick, S., et al. "Time Discounting and Time Preference: A Critical Review." *J. Econ. Lit.,* 40 (2002). 351.

Frontline. "The Credit Card Game." November 24, 2009.

Furletti, M. "Credit Card Pricing Developments and Their Disclosure." (2003) *Fed. Res. Bank of Philadelphia Payment Cards Center Discussion Paper.*

Gabaix, X., and Laibson, D. "Shrouded Attributes, Consumer Myopia, and Information Suppression in Competitive Markets." *Q.J. Econ.,* 121 (2006). 505.

Genachowski, J. Remarks at Bill Shock Event, Brookings Institution, Washington, DC. October 17, 2011.

General Accounting Office, Report to the Chairman and Ranking Minority Member, Special Committee on Aging, U.S. Senate. "Consumer Protection: Federal and State Agencies Face Challenges in Combating Predatory Lending." Gao-04-280 (2004).

Gerardi, K., et al. "Making Sense of the Subprime Crisis." Fed. Reserve Bank of Boston. (2008) *Public Policy Discussion Paper No. 09-1.*

———"Subprime Outcomes: Risky Mortgages, Homeownership Experiences, and Foreclosures." (2007) *Fed. Reserve Bank of Boston Working Paper No. 07-15.*

Gilder, G. "The Wireless Wars." *Wall Street Journal,* April 13, 2007.

Gilo, D., and Porat, A. "The Hidden Roles of Boilerplate and Standard-Form Contracts: Strategic Imposition of Transaction Costs, Segmentation of Consumers, and Anticompetitive Effects." *Michigan Law Review,* 104 (2006). 983.

Gilovich, T., et al. (eds.). *Heuristics and Biases: The Psychology of Intuitive Judgment.* Cambridge University Press, 2002.

Glaeser, E.L. "Psychology and the Market." *Amer. Econ. Rev. Papers & Proceedings*, 94 (2004) 408.

Government Accountability Office. *Credit Cards: Increased Complexity in Rates and Fees Heightens Need for More Effective Disclosures to Consumers.* (2006).

——Report to the Committee on Financial Services, House of Representatives. "Real Estate Brokerage: Factors That May Affect Price Competition." GAO-05-947 (2005).

Gramlich, E.M., *Subprime Mortgages: America's Latest Boom and Bust.* Urban Institute Press, 2007.

Green, R.K., and Wachter, S.M. "The American Mortgage in Historical and International Context." *J. Econ. Persp.*, 19 (2005). 93.

Grubb, M.D. "Selling to Overconfident Consumers." *Amer. Econ. Rev.*, 99 (2009). 1770.

Gruber, J., and Koszegi, B. "Is Addiction 'Rational'? Theory and Evidence." (2000) *NBER Working Paper No. 7507.*

Guiso, L., Sapienza, P., and Zingales, L. "Moral and Social Constraints to Strategic Default on Mortgages." (2009) *NBER Working Paper No. 15145.*

Hahn, R.W., et al. "The Economics of 'Wireless Net Neutrality'." *J. Competition L. and Econ.*, 3 (2007). 399.

Haughwout, A., Mayer, C., and Tracy, J. "Subprime Mortgage Pricing: The Impact of Race, Ethnicity, and Gender on the Cost of Borrowing." (2009) *FRB of New York Staff Report No. 368.*

Heidhues, P., and Koszegi, B. "Exploiting Naiveté about Self-Control in the Credit Market." *Amer. Econ. Rev.*, 100 (2010). 2279.

Helft, M., and Labaton, S. "Google Pushes for Rules to Aid Wireless Plans." *New York Times*, July 21, 2007.

Hernandez-Murillo, R., Ghent, A.C., and Owyang, M. "Race, Redlining, and Subprime Loan Pricing" (2011).

Hirschman, E.C. "Differences in Consumer Purchase Behavior by Credit Card Payment System." *J. Consumer Res.*, 6 (1979). 58.

Hoak, A.," 100 Percent More Difficult: First-Time Home Buyers Struggle to Find Down-Payment Money." *MarketWatch*, March 9, 2008.

Immergluck, D., and Smith, G. "The Impact of Single-Family Mortgage Foreclosures on Neighborhood Crime." *Housing Stud.*, 21 (2006). 851.

Iyengar, R., Ansari, A., and Gupta, S. "A Model of Consumer Learning of Consumer Service Quality and Usage." *J. Mktg. Res.*, 44 (2007). 529.

Jackson, T.H. *The Logic and Limits of Bankruptcy Law.* Harvard University Press, 1986.

Jensen, R. "The Digital Provide: Information (Technology). Market Performance, and Welfare in the South Indian Fisheries Sector." *Q.J. Econ,.* 122 (2007). 879.

Johnson, F. "FCC Head Seeks Rules on Cell-Termination Fees." *Wall Street Journal*, June 13, 2008.

Jolls, C., et al. "A Behavioral Approach to Law and Economics." *Stan. L. Rev.*, 50 (1998). 1471.

Kahneman, D., Slovic, P., Tversky, A., (eds.) *Judgment under Uncertainty: Heuristics and Biases.* Cambridge University Press, 1982.

Kjos, A. "Proposed Changes to Regulation Z: Highlighting Behaviors that Affect Credit Costs." (2008) *FRB of Philadelphia Payment Cards Center Discussion Paper No. 08-02.*

Klein, L. *It's In The Cards: Consumer Credit and the American Experience.* Praeger, 1999.

Koopmans, T.C. "Stationary Ordinal Utility and Impatience." *Econometrica,* 28 (1960). 287.

Korobkin, R. "Bounded Rationality, Standard Form Contracts, and Unconscionability." *U. Chi. L. Rev.,* 70 (2003) 1203.

Kronman, A.T. "Mistake, Disclosure, Information, and the Law of Contracts." *J. Legal Stud.,* 7 (1987). 1.

Kroszner, R.S. Speech at the George Washington University School of Business Financial Services Research Program Policy Forum: "Creating More Effective Consumer Disclosures" (May 23, 2007).

Lacapra, L.T. "Breaking Free of a Cellular Contract—New Web Sites Help Customers Swap or Resell Phone Service; Avoiding $175 Termination Fee." *Wall Street Journal,* November 30, 2006.

Lacko, J.M., and Pappalardo, J.K. Fed. Trade Comm'n. "Improving Consumer Mortgage Disclosures: An Empirical Assessment of Current and Prototype Disclosure Forms." (2007).

————— "The Effect of Mortgage Broker Compensation Disclosures on Consumers and Competition: A Controlled Experiment." (2004).

LaCour-Little, M. "Economic Factors Affecting Home Mortgage Disclosure Act Reporting." *J. Real Est. Res.,* 29 (2007). 479.

————— and Holmes, C. "Prepayment Penalties in Residential Mortgage Contracts: A Cost-Benefit Analysis." *Housing Pol'y Debate.,* 19 (2008). 631.

Laibson, D., et al. "Self-Control and Saving for Retirement." *Brookings Papers Econ. Activity,* 1 (1998). 91.

Larson, M.D. "Mortgage Lenders Want a Commitment—and They're Willing to Pay You for It." *Bankrate.com,* August 26, 1999.

Lax, H., et al. "Subprime Lending: An Investigation of Economic Efficiency." *Housing Pol'y Debate,* 15 (2004). 533.

Lazich, R.S. (ed.). *Market Share Reporter: An Annual Compilation of Reported Market Share Data on Companies, Products, and Services: 2008* (2008).

Lee, J., and Hogarth, J.M. "Consumer Information Search for Home Mortgages: Who, What, How Much, and What Else?" *Fin. Services Rev.,* 9 (2000). 277.

————— "The Price of Money: Consumers' Understanding of APRs and Contract Interest Rates." *J. Pub. Pol'y and Marketing,* 18 (1999). 66.

Leland, J. "Baltimore Finds Subprime Crisis Snags Women." *New York Times,* January 15, 2008.

Liebowitz, S.J. "Anatomy of a Train Wreck: Causes of the Mortgage Meltdown." in Holcombe, R.G., and Powell, B. (eds.). *Housing America: Building Out of a Crisis.* The Independent Institute, 2009.

Loewenstein, G.F., and O'Donoghue, E. "Animal Spirits: Affective and Deliberative Processes in Economic Behavior." (2004).

Lusardi, A. "Americans' Financial Capability." (2011). *NBER Working Paper 17103.*

—— "Financial Literacy: An Essential Tool for Informed Consumer Choice?" (2008) *Nat'l Bureau of Econ. Research Working Paper No. 14084.*

—— "Household Saving Behavior: The Role of Financial Literacy, Information, and Financial Education Programs." (2008) *Nat'l Bureau of Econ. Research Working Paper No. 13824.*

—— and Mitchell, O.S. "Planning and Financial Literacy: How Do Women Fare." (2008) *Nat'l Bureau of Econ. Research Working Paper No. 13750.*

McCoy, P.A. "Rethinking Disclosure in a World of Risk-Based Pricing." *Harv. J. on Legis.,* 44 (2007). 123.

MacDonald, D.A. "Viewpoint: Card Industry Questions Congress Needs to Ask." *American Banker,* March 23, 2007.

McGeehan, P. "Soaring Interest Compounds Credit Card Pain for Millions." *New York Times,* November 21, 2004.

Macro International. "Design and Testing of Effective Truth in Lending Disclosures." (2007).

Madison, M.T., Dwyer, J.R., and Bender, S.W. *The Law of Real Estate Financing.* Thomson Reuters/West, rev. ed. 2008.

Madrian, B.C., and Shea, D. "The Power of Suggestion: Inertia in 401(k) Participation and Savings Behavior." *Quart. J. Econ.,* 116 (2001). 1149.

Mandell, L. *The Credit Card Industry: A History.* Twayne Publishers, 1990.

Mann, R.J. "Adopting, Using, and Discarding Paper and Electronic Payment Instruments: Variation by Age and Race." (May 1, 2011).

—— "Bankruptcy Reform and the 'Sweat Box' of Credit Card Debt." *U. Ill. L. Rev.,* (2007). 375.

—— *Charging Ahead: The Growth and Regulation of Payment Card Markets Around the World.* Cambridge University Press, 2006.

—— " 'Contracting' For Credit." *Mich. L. Rev.,* 104 (2006). 899.

Martin, A. "Credit Card Industry Aims to Profit From Sterling Payers." *New York Times,* May 19, 2009.

Massey, C., and Thaler, R.H. "The Loser's Curse: Overconfidence vs. Market Efficiency in the National Football League Draft." (2010).

Massoud, N.Z., Saunders, A., and Scholnick, B. "The Cost of Being Late: The Case of Credit Card Penalty Fees." (2006) *AFA 2007 Chicago Meetings Paper.*

Mayer, C.E. "Griping About Cellular Bills; Differences From 'Regular' Phones Take New Users by Surprise." *Washington Post,* February 28, 2001.

Mayer, C.J., and Pence, K.M. "Subprime Mortgages: What, Where, and to Whom?" (2008) *Nat'l Bureau of Econ. Research Working Paper No. 14083.*

Mayer, C.J., Pence, K.M., and Sherlund, S. "The Rise in Mortgage Defaults." (2008) *Bd. of Governors of the Fed. Reserve Sys. Fin. and Econ. Discussion Series Paper No. 2008-59.*

——and Sinai, T. "Housing and Behavioral Finance" (2007) (unpublished manuscript).

——Piskorski, T., and Tchistyi, A. "The Inefficiency of Refinancing: Why Prepayment Penalties Are Good for Risky Borrowers." (2011) *Columbia Business School Working Paper.*

Medoff, J., and Harless, A. *The Indebted Society: Anatomy of An Ongoing Disaster.* Little Brown & Co., 1996.

Meier, S., and Sprenger. C. "Present-Biased Preferences and Credit Card Borrowing." *Amer. Econ. J.,* 2 (2010). 193.

Mester, L.J. "Why Are Credit Card Rates Sticky?" *Econ. Th.,* 4 (1994). 505.

Meyer, D. "Coverage Problems Trigger Headaches for Carriers." *RCR Wireless News,* July 9, 2001.

Mian, A.R., and Sufi, A. "Household Leverage and the Recession of 2007-09." *IMF Econ. Rev.,* 58 (2010). 74.

Miles, D. "The U.K. Mortgage Market: Taking a Longer-Term View, Interim Report: Information, Incentives and Pricing." (2003).

Miles, W. "Boom-Bust Cycles and the Forecasting Performance of Linear and Non-Linear Models of House Prices." *J. Real Est. Fin. and Econ.,* 36 (2008). 249.

Morgenson, G. "Inside the Countrywide Lending Spree." *New York Times,* August 26, 2007.

——"Countrywide Subpoenaed by Illinois." *New York Times,* December 13, 2007.

——"Clicking the Way to Mortgage Savings." *New York Times,* December 23, 2007.

——"Given a Shovel, Digging Deeper Into Debt." *New York Times,* July 20, 2008.

——"S.E.C. Accuses Countrywide's Ex-Chief of Fraud." *New York Times,* June 4, 2009.

Nachman, S. "Cranky Consumer: How to Check Up on Your Cell Phone Minutes." *Wall Street Journal,* June 18, 2002.

Nalebuff, B., and Ayres, I. *Why Not?* Harvard Business School Press, 2003.

National Consumer Law Center. *Report, Fee-Harvesters: Low-Credit, High-Cost Cards Bleed Consumers.* (2007).

——*Truth in Lending.* 27 (2002 Cumulative Supplement).

Nat'l Cmty. Reinvestment Coal. "Homeownership and Wealth Building Impeded: Continuing Lending Disparities for Minorities and Emerging Obstacles for Middle-Income and Female Borrowers of All Races." (2006).

Nuechterlein, J.E., and Weiser, P.J. *Digital Crossroads.* MIT Press, 2005.

Odlyzko, A.M. "The Many Paradoxes of Broadband." *First Monday.* September 1, 2003.

O'Donoghue, E., and Rabin, M. "Doing It Now or Later." *Amer. Econ. Rev.,* 89 (1999). 103.

————"Procrastination in Preparing for Retirement." in Aaron, H. (ed.). *Behavioral Dimensions of Retirement Economics.* Brookings Institution Press, 1999.

Opinion Research Corporation. "Prepaid Phones in the U.S.: Myths, Lack of Consumer Knowledge Blocking Wider Use." (2008).

Parker, P.M., and Röller, L.H. "Collusive Conduct in Duopolies: Multi-Market Contact and Cross-Ownership in the Mobile Telephone Industry." *Rand J. Econ.*, 28 (1997). 304.

Paulson, H.M., Jr., U.S. Sec'y of the Treasury. "Remarks on Current Housing and Mortgage Market Developments at the Georgetown University Law Center." (October 16, 2007).

Pavlov, A. and Wachter, S. "Sub-prime Lending and Real Estate Prices." *Real Estate Econ.* 39 (2011). 1.

Peek, J. "A Call to ARMs: Adjustable Rate Mortgages in the 1980s." *New Eng. Econ. Rev.* March-April (1990) 53.

Pennington-Cross, A., and Ho, G. "The Termination of Subprime Hybrid and Fixed Rate Mortgages." (2006) *Fed. Reserve Bank of St. Louis, Research Div. Working Paper No. 2006-042A.*

Petersen, A., and Harris, N. "Hard Cell: Chaos, Confusion and Perks Bedevil Wireless Users." *Wall Street Journal,* April 17, 2002.

Peterson, C.L. "Preemption, Agency Cost Theory, and Predatory Lending by Banking Agents: Are Federal Regulators Biting Off More Than They Can Chew?" *Am. U. L. Rev.,* 56 (2007). 515.

PEW Charitable Trusts. "Safe Credit Card Standards." (2009).

——— "Safe Credit Cards Project: Curing Credit Card Penalties." (2009).

Pogue, D. "AT&T's Capped Data Plan Could Save You Money." *New York Times,* June 3, 2010.

Prelec, D., and Simester, D. "Always Leave Home Without It: A Further Investigation of the Credit-Card Effect on Willingness to Pay." *Marketing Letters,* 12 (2001). 5.

Privacy Rights Clearinghouse/UCAN. "Paper or Plastic? What Have You Got to Lose." (2011).

Prudential Ins. Co. of Am. *Financial Experience and Behaviors Among Women.* (2006).

Quercia, R.G., Stegman, M.A., and Davis, W.R. "The Impact of Predatory Loan Terms on Subprime Foreclosures: The Special Case of Prepayment Penalties and Balloon Payments." *Housing Pol'y Debate,* 18 (2007). 311.

Rabin, M. "Risk Aversion and Expected-Utility Theory: A Calibration Theorem." *Econometrica,* 68 (2000). 1281.

Rappaport, T. *Wireless Communications.* Prentice Hall, 1996.

Reardon, M. "Unlocking the Unlocked Cell Phone Market." *CNET News,.* July 2, 2009.

Renuart, E. "An Overview of the Predatory Mortgage Lending Process." *Housing Pol'y Debate,* 15 (2004). 467.

——— and Thompson, D.E. "The Truth, The Whole Truth, and Nothing but the Truth: Fulfilling the Promise of Truth in Lending." *Yale J. on Reg,.* 25 (2008). 181, 188.

Rose, M.J. "Origination Channel, Prepayment Penalties, and Default." forthcoming in *Real Estate Economics.*

Rotemberg, J. *Subprime Meltdown: American Housing and Global Financial Turmoil.* Harvard Business School, 2008.

Rubin, E.L. "Legislative Methodology: Some Lessons from the Truth-in-Lending Act." *Geo. L.J.,* 80 (1991). 233.

Samuelson, P. "A Note on Measurement of Utility." *Rev. Econ. Stud.,* 4 (1937). 155.

Sandberg, J. "A Piece of the Business." *Wall Street Journal,* September 11, 1997.

Schatz, A., and Silver, S. "A Plan to Ease the Shock of Cellphone Bills." *Wall Street Journal,* May 12, 2010.

Schuh, S.D., and Stavins, J. "Summary of the Workshop on Consumer Behavior and Payment Choice." (2008) *FRB of Boston Public Policy Discussion Paper No. 08-5.*

Schwartz, A. "Who Takes Out Adjustable Rate Mortgages?" (2009) *Harvard University Working Paper.*

Schwartz, A. and Wilde, L.L. "Imperfect Information in Markets for Contract Terms: The Examples of Warranties and Security Interests." *Va. L. Rev.,* 69 (1983). 1387.

———— "Product Quality and Imperfect Information." *Rev. Econ. Stud.,* 52 (1985). 251.

Schwartz, M., *Mobile Wireless Communications.* Cambridge University Press, 2005.

Semeraro, S. "The Reverse-Robin-Hood-Cross-Subsidy Hypothesis: Do Credit Card Systems Effectively Tax the Poor and Reward the Rich?" *Rutgers L. J.,* 40 (2009). 419.

Shah Goda, G., Flaherty Manchester, C., and Sojourner, A.J. "What's My Account Really Worth? The Effect of Lifetime Income Disclosure on Retirement Savings." (2011) *RAND Working Paper No. WR-873.*

Sharma, A., and Cheng, R. "iPhone Costs Prove a Drag for AT&T." *Wall Street Journal,* October 23, 2008.

——and Searcey, D. "Verizon to Open Cell Network to Others' Phones." *Wall Street Journal,* November 28, 2007.

Sherlund, S.M. "The Past, Present, and Future of Subprime Mortgages." (2008) *Bd. of Governors of the Fed. Reserve Sys. Fin. and Econ. Discussion Series Paper No. 2008-63.*

Shiller, R.J. *Irrational Exuberance.* Princeton University Press, 2000.

—— "Speculative Prices and Popular Models." *J. Econ. Persp.,* Spring (1990). 58.

—— "Understanding Recent Trends in House Prices and Home Ownership." (2007) *Yale Univ. Econ. Dep't Working Paper No. 28.*

Shleifer, A., and Summers, L.H. "The Noise Trader Approach to Finance." *J. Econ. Persp.,* 4 (1990). 19.

Shroder, M.D. "The Value of the Sunshine Cure: The Efficacy of the Real Estate Settlement Procedures Act Disclosure Strategy." *Cityscape: J. Pol'y Dev., and Res.* No. 1(2007). 73.

Shui, H., and Ausubel, L.M. "Time Inconsistency in the Credit Card Market." (2004) *Working Paper.*

Sichelman, L. "Community Group Claims CitiFinancial Still Predatory." *Origination News,* January 2002.

Souleles, N.S. "Do Liquidity Constraints and Interest Rates Matter for Consumer Behavior? Evidence from Credit Card Data." *Quar. J. Econ.*, 117 (2002). 149.

Spencer, J. "What Part of 'Cancel' Don't You Understand?—Regulators Crack Down on Internet Providers, Phone Companies That Make It Hard to Quit." *Wall Street Journal,* November 12, 2003.

Spiegler, R. *Bounded Rationality and Industrial Organization.* Oxford University Press, 2011.

—— "Competition over Agents with Boundedly Rational Expectations." *Theoretical Econ.,* 1 (2006). 207.

Sprint. "Cell Phones, Mobile Phones, and Wireless Calling Plans from Sprint."

SRI International. "The Role of NSF's Support of Engineering in Enabling Technological Innovation, Final Report Phase II 94-97." (1998).

Stallings, W. *Wireless Communications and Networking.* Prentice Hall, 2002.

Stango, V. "Pricing with Consumer Switching Costs: Evidence from the Credit Card Market." *J. Indus. Econ.,* 50 (2002). 475.

—— and Zinman, J. "Fuzzy Math, Disclosure Regulation and Credit Market Outcomes." (2007) *Tuck Sch. of Bus. Working Paper No. 2008-42.*

—— —— "What Do Consumers Really Pay on Their Checking and Credit Card Accounts? Explicit, Implicit, and Avoidable Costs." *Amer. Econ. Rev.,* 99 (2009). 424.

Stanovich, K.E. "The Fundamental Computational Biases of Human Cognition: Heuristics that (Sometimes) Impair Decision Making and Problem Solving." in Davidson, J.E., and Steinberg, R.J. (eds.). *The Psychology of Problem Solving.* Cambridge University Press, 2003.

Stein, E. Coal. for Responsible Lending. "Quantifying the Economic Costs of Predatory Lending." (2001).

Sullivan, T.A., Warren, E., and Westbrook, J.L. *As We Forgive Our Debtors: Bankruptcy and Consumer Credit in America.* Oxford University Press, 1989.

—— —— *The Fragile Middle Class: Americans in Debt.* Yale University Press, 2000.

Sunstein, C.R. "Disclosure and Simplification as Regulatory Tools." Memorandum for the Heads of Executive Departments and Agencies (2010).

—— "Informing Consumers through Smart Disclosure." Memorandum for the Heads of Executive Departments and Agencies (2011).

—— and Thaler, R.H. "Libertarian Paternalism is not an Oxymoron." *U. Chi. L. Rev.,* 70 (2003). 1159.

Svenson, O. "Are We All Less Risky and More Skillful than Our Fellow Drivers?" *Acta Psychologica,* 47 (1981). 143.

T-Mobile, Financial Release. "T-Mobile USA Reports Second Quarter 2011 Results." July 28, 2011.

—— "Cell Phones / 4G Cell Phone Plans / Android Tablet PCs / T-Mobile."

—— "T-Mobile Terms and Conditions"

Tauke, T.J., Executive Vice President, Verizon. Testimony at FCC Early Termination Hearing (June, 12, 2008).

Thaler, R.H. "Mental Accounting Matters." *J. Behav. Decision Making.*, 12 (1999). 183.

—— "Some Empirical Evidence on Dynamic Inconsistency." *Econ. Letters.*, 8 (1981). 201.

—— *The Winner's Curse: Paradoxes and Anomalies of Economic Life.* Princeton University Press, 1992.

——and Sunstein, C.R. *Nudge: Improving Decisions about Health, Wealth and Happiness.* Yale University Press, 2008.

Tversky, A., and Kahneman, D. "Rational Choice and the Framing of Decisions." in R. M. Hogarth and M. W. Reder (eds). *Rational Choice: The Contrast Between Economics and Psychology.* University of Chicago Press, 1987.

U.S. Dep't of Hous. and Urban Dev. *Report to Congress on the Root Causes of the Foreclosure Crisis.* (2010).

—— "HUD Proposes Mortgage Reform to Help Consumers Better Understand Their Loan, Shop for Lower Costs." (March 14, 2008).

——and U.S. Dep't of the Treasury. "Curbing Predatory Home Mortgage Lending." (2000).

U.S. Dep't of Justice and Fed. Trade Comm'n. "Competition in the Real Estate Brokerage Industry: A Report by the Federal Trade Commission and the U.S. Department of Justice." (2007).

Vascellaro, J.E. "Air War: A Fight Over What You Can Do on a Cell-phone." *Wall Street Journal.*, June 14, 2007.

Verizon Wireless. "Cell Phones—Smartphones: Cell Phone Service, Accessories—Verizon Wireless."

—— "Customer Agreement."

—— "Verizon Wireless—4Selected Financial Results." (July 22, 2011).

Wagenseil, P. "That 'Cheaper' iPhone Will Cost You More." *FoxNews.com*, June 11, 2008.

Waverman, L., Meschi, M., and Fuss, M. "The Impact of Telecoms on Economic Growth in Developing Countries." in *The Vodafone Policy Paper Series no. 3, Africa: The Impact of Mobile Phones.* (2005).

Weeks, W. "An Analysis and Critique of Retroactive Penalty Interest in the Credit Card Market." (2007).

Weinstein, N.D. "Unrealistic Optimism About Future Life Events." *J. Personality & Soc. Psychol.*, 39 (1980). 806.

White, M.J. "Bankruptcy Reform and Credit Cards." *J. Econ. Persp.*, 21 (2007). 175.

Willis, L.E. "Decisionmaking and the Limits of Disclosure: The Problem of Predatory Lending: Price." *Md. L. Rev.*, 65 (2006). 707.

Woodward, S.E. "Consumer Confusion in the Mortgage Market." (2003).

——U.S. Dep't of Hous. and Urban Dev. *A Study of Closing Costs for FHA Mortgages.* (2008).

Wu, T. "Wireless Net Neutrality: Cellular Carterfone and Consumer Choice in Mobile Broadband." (2007). *New Am. Found. Wireless Future Program Working Paper No. 17.*

Zinman, J. "Debit or Credit?" (2006) *Dartmouth College Economics Department Working Paper.*

Zywicki, T.J. "The Economics of Credit Cards." *Chap. L. Rev.*, 3 (2003). 79.

——and Adamson, J.D. "The Law and Economics of Subprime Lending." *U. Colo. L. Rev.,* 80 (2009). 1.

Index